The Precarious Balance

State and Society in Africa

African Modernization
and Development Series

Paul Lovejoy, Series Editor

About the Book and Editors

Since independence, the political institutions of many African states have undergone a process of consolidation and subsequent deterioration. Constrained by external economic dependency and an acute scarcity of economic and technical resources, state officials have demonstrated a diminished capacity to regulate their societies. Public policies are agreed upon but ineffectively implemented by the weak institutions of the state. Although scholars have analyzed the various facets of state-building in detail, little systematic attention has been given to the issue of the decline of the state and mechanisms to cope with state ineffectiveness in Africa.

This book focuses especially on the character of the postcolonial state in Africa, the nature of and reasons for state deterioration, and the mechanisms and policies for coping with state malfunction. Scholars from Africa, the United States, Europe, and the Middle East combine a broad understanding of African political processes with expertise on specific regions. Their analytic and comparative perspective provides a comprehensive and timely treatment of this vital and heretofore neglected theme in African politics.

Donald Rothchild is professor of political science at the University of California, Davis. He is the author of *Racial Bargaining in Independent Kenya* and coeditor of *State Versus Ethnic Claims: African Policy Dilemmas* (Westview, 1982). **Naomi Chazan** is senior lecturer in political science and African studies at the Hebrew University of Jerusalem. She is the author of *An Anatomy of Ghanaian Politics: Managing Political Recession, 1969–1982* (Westview, 1983) and coauthor of *Ghana: Coping with Uncertainty* (Westview, 1986).

The Precarious Balance

State and Society in Africa

edited by
Donald Rothchild
and Naomi Chazan

Westview Press / Boulder and London

African Modernization and Development Series

Copyright © 1988 by Westview Press, Inc.

Published in 1988 in the United States of America by Westview Press, Inc.; Frederick A. Praeger, Publisher; 5500 Central Avenue, Boulder, Colorado 80301

Library of Congress Cataloging-in-Publication Data
The Precarious balance: state and society in Africa/edited by
   Donald Rothchild, and Naomi Chazan.
      p.   cm.—(African modernization and development)
   Includes index.
   ISBN 0-86531-738-0
   1. Africa—Politics and government—1960-   2. Africa—Economic
conditions—1960-   3. Africa—Social conditions—1960-
I. Rothchild, Donald S.   II. Chazan, Naomi, 1946-   . III. Series.
JQ1872.P74 1988
960′.32—dc19
                                                                87-27302
                                                                CIP

Printed and bound in the United States of America

The paper used in this publication meets the requirements of the American National Standard for Permanence of Paper for Printed Library Materials Z39.48-1984.

10   9   8   7   6   5   4

Contents

PART FOUR
The Changing State in Africa: Government
and International Perspectives

PART FIVE
Conclusion

     Naomi Chazan   325

     About the Contributors   343
     Index   347

Preface

Contemporary research on state-society relations in Africa has been almost as elusive as its subject matter. Much of the literature on African politics, reflecting a concern with stability and economic development, focuses extensively upon aspects of state consolidation. After independence, African leaders concentrated upon securing, extending, and transforming the institutions of rule they had inherited. Hence they impeded certain institutions that placed checks on their power while facilitating others that they thought would increase their control. Some leaders (Jomo Kenyatta in Kenya, Robert Mugabe in Zimbabwe, Felix Houphouet-Boigny in the Ivory Coast) have proved reasonably successful in building a coherent framework. In other countries, however, the results have been disappointing. Very different regimes were unable to stop the gradual erosion of state capabilities and a concomitant loss of legitimacy, authority, and power. As specific groups came to question the validity and viability of state institutions and organizing rules, state structures were undermined.

Those focusing on the twin processes of state consolidation or deterioration, whether approaching the subject from a modernization, Marxist, or neo-Marxist conceptual framework, have tended to make some similar assumptions: that political, social, and economic development are valued preferences in and of themselves and that participation at the political center is desirable because the state constitutes a superior mechanism for the fulfillment of economic and social aspirations. However, in recent years doubts have been cast on these assumptions. Many processes, such as the expansion of nonformal socioeconomic and political activities, could not be understood easily within the consolidation paradigm. Moreover, the premise of the centrality of the state could no longer be glibly corroborated in practice.

Consequently, a new research focus centering on the dynamic processes of interaction between state and society is now emerging and gaining scholarly attention. Remaining attentive to the operations of public institutions and official agencies while highlighting coping mechanisms in the informal sector, this approach attempts to uncover where and why transactions occur and to pinpoint areas and spheres of separation. The message emanating from Africa today is one of straddling—of constant movement between the official and unofficial, the private and the public, the rural and the urban. The result is a precarious balance between state and society. This book explores the rhythm of this changing relationship. In this respect, it seeks to gain an understanding of the historical context, the current manifestations, and some of the possible socioeconomic and political ramifications of these interactions. It is a study of shifting power relations and the complex exchanges that are essential to a more comprehensive understanding of the contemporary African scene.

This book took shape in the course of an international workshop on "The Reordering of the State in Africa" that was held July 1-8, 1985, at the Harry S. Truman Research Institute for the Advancement of Peace of the Hebrew University of Jerusalem. It brought together a diverse group of scholars from Africa, Europe, North America, and the Middle East who spent the week engaging in a lively interchange on the issues at hand.

We wish to express our very great appreciation to the Truman Institute for making the conference possible. Its administrative staff—especially Dr. Edy Kaufman, Dahlia Shemer, and the library staff (Cecile Panzer, Katya Azoulay, Eti Yakobovich-Abu, Becky Rowe, and Drora Shihuda)—gave indispensable assistance in preparing and organizing the conference. Professor Zvi Schiffrin, the institute's academic chairman, backed this undertaking throughout. Professors Nehemia Levtzion, Michael Wade, John Voll, Dov Ronen, Michel Abitbol, and Galia Golan and Drs. Steve Kaplan, Yekutiel Gershoni, and Mordechai Tamarkin joined in the discussions and thereby contributed significantly to the molding of this work. We also wish to express our appreciation to Professor Paul Lovejoy for his careful analysis of the entire manuscript and to Professor Cynthia L. Brantley for her helpful suggestions on revising the chapters.

Preparation of this book for publication was overseen by Norma Schneider, director of publications at the Truman Institute. We would like to express our sincere appreciation to Siva Azulay for her careful editing of the entire manuscript and to the University of California, Davis (particularly Caroline Hartzell and Eunice Carlson), for providing assistance and facilities that made work on this volume possible.

Donald Rothchild
Naomi Chazan

PART ONE

Introduction

1

Reordering
State-Society Relations:
Incorporation and Disengagement

Victor Azarya

State Centrism in Current Research

The declining performance of the postcolonial state has been a recurrent theme in the social sciences literature on Africa in recent years. After focusing for a decade or more on the capabilities of the state in its incessant efforts to mold society in its image, scholarly debate has shifted to the state's *incapabilities*, its functional decline, instability and inability to bring about intended changes in society. The state has been variously characterized as "soft," "weak" or "overdeveloped" by scholars seeking to explain its apparent failure to meet the aspirations not only of the civil society at large but even of those occupying central political positions.[1] The postcolonial history of African states has been marked by conflict, turmoil and stagnation. State leaders have been unable to extricate themselves from powerful domestic and international interest groups. State control over the society has diminished despite increasing repressive and extractive tendencies. Corrupt and inefficient administrations have led to great waste. Compliance with the law has declined and state institutions have lost legitimacy in the eyes of large segments of their population.

Jackson and Rosberg doubt that many African states can meet an empirical definition of the state based on its ability to exercise control (i.e. to articulate, implement and enforce commands, laws, policies and regulations)[2] over the people in the territory under its jurisdiction. What has maintained them as states, they claim, is a more juridical definition which identifies them as the recognized territorial unit of the international community.[3] Thus, such states have been more relevant in the international arena than within their own territorial borders. Jackson and Rosberg are concerned with instances in which states have lost effective political control over substantial segments of the population, such as coups d'état, internal wars and regional separatism. They have found that even in cases where political control has not been

3

lost and states have maintained a monopoly over organized means of coercion, they have been unable to solve basic economic problems or prevent the emergence of alternative systems which flout their laws and principles and circumvent their inefficient channels.

Observers have looked for reasons beyond specific government policies, personal failures of leaders and ideological considerations for the equivocal performance of certain African states. They have attempted to discover inherent structural weaknesses of the state, ingrained in the very process of postcolonial political development in Africa. Some attribute the present weakness to the legacy of the colonial state which, despite its very authoritarian nature, touched only intermittently the lives of the people within its boundaries.[4] Others relate it to international dependency or see it as an outgrowth of the class structure and internal conflicts.[5] Whatever the preferred explanation, emphasis on such general underlying causes has tended to represent the state's weakness as a universal African phenomenon. While the more historical or structural roots of the problem cannot be disregarded, we should also note that some African states clearly exhibit greater weaknesses than others, even though they all share common underlying factors such as dependence on the global system or a similar colonial legacy. The turnabout in the fortunes of the states may also stem from specific current difficulties that are partially the result of policy decisions made by contemporary rulers. Hence the decline of and differences between African states cannot be ascribed only to long-range historical factors.

The increasing preoccupation with the decline of the state in Africa marks a sharp departure from the earlier scholarly interest in state consolidation, which emanated from the underlying assumption that the state is a major means of bringing about societal change and fulfilling economic and social aspirations. At first, in the heyday of the modernization studies (in the 1960s), this assumption had a strong integrative and developmental connotation. Observers traced the process of "nation building" which was expected to follow decolonization. They were concerned with analyzing the mechanisms by which viable political entities responsive to their social and economic environment were formed on broader bases of solidarity and collective action. Scholarly emphasis was placed on the formation of central institutions (the term "state" was not yet fashionable) and their ability to transform civil society.[6] Later, as the initial enthusiasm of decolonization waned and the postcolonial political crises and instability became more visible, the state came to be seen as an arena of struggle between different groups vying for control over its resources. The integrative connotation of earlier studies was replaced by a conflict connotation. Pluralists drew attention to pressures rooted mostly in ethno-cultural primordial sources, whereas Marxists sought to identify the contending parties in terms of class differences and to show how the new state apparatus became a major vehicle for new class formation. State positions, however, were still regarded as the main channels of resource control. Furthermore, since the state was assumed to expand its control over the entire society, the stakes of the political struggle were much higher. The state apparatus was expected to enable the control over peripheral resources as well as central ones. By the same token, a failure to share power in the center could also endanger a given group's grip over its own peripheral resources.[7] In Geertz's words, "it is the very process of the formation of a sovereign civil state that, among other things, stimulates sentiments of parochialism, communalism, racialism and so on because it introduces into society a valuable new prize over which to fight and a frightening new force with which to contend."[8] When it appeared that the shape of the polity was being settled rapidly, perhaps once and for all, a multitude of groups began to stake their claims for the protection of their way of life and for a more satisfactory distribution of benefits.[9]

The shift in emphasis from state consolidation to decline also hints that perhaps the state has played a lesser role in African social life than was previously assumed. Suddenly, the state did not seem such a formidable force in determining economic and social well-being. On the contrary, in many cases the vulnerability attendant upon exposure to pressure and insecurity (physical as well as economic) outweighed the spoils of association with the state. It was belatedly realized that influence and authority were not the exclusive domain of the state and that the earlier studies of state consolidation often mistook for fact the aspirations of the political elite. However, despite the acknowledgement of the state's more limited social role, scholarly interest still focused on the state itself; it tried to explain what went wrong with the state and the reasons for its weakness. When the society was brought into the analysis, it was usually in order to explain why the state did not function properly. The focus has thus remained state-centric. With some notable exceptions, such as Goran Hyden's work on peasant responses to state policies and some recent studies on the parallel economy, relatively little attention has been paid to how societies cope with the state, rather than how the state acts upon the society.[10]

It is also interesting to note that the earlier image of a strong political center being the motor force behind the society's rapid transformation was espoused by the very scholars who avoided the use of the term "state" (perhaps they took it for granted). They used instead such terms as "central institutions," the "rulers" and the "elite." Just as the focus shifted to the weakness and decline of the state, the term "state" paradoxically started to come into vogue and scholars increasingly referred to the state's autonomous actions.[11] The very concepts of state consolidation and state decline indicate, of course, that the phenomenon studied is the state, not the society. However, by thinking in terms of incorporation into or disengagement from the state, greater attention may be drawn to what happens to various groups and sectors in the civil society as they respond to whatever the state is able or unable to achieve. An examination of incorporation and disengagement can thus lead us to the long-neglected society end of state-society relations in contemporary Africa.

Incorporation and Disengagement

Incorporation and disengagement denote societal responses to state actions (or anticipated state actions) which lead to a perceived change in the field of opportunities of given groups or individuals. They are the counterparts of state consolidation and decline when the focus is shifted from the state to the society. Incorporation is the process whereby large segments of the population associate with the state and take part in its activities in order to share its resources. It follows a perception of an expanded field of opportunities linked with the state.[12] Such incorporation might be initiated by the individuals or groups in question or might be solicited by the state itself as a means of expanding its penetration into the periphery. Indeed, I use the term "incorporation" rather than "engagement" or "participation" because it seems more neutral regarding initiation of the association. In any event, the result is the same: the state is a magnet; substantial segments of the population find it desirable, for whatever reason, to have close ties with the state.

Incorporation may manifest itself in population migration from rural to urban areas and from remote regions to economic and communication centers. It may include greater receptivity to mass media and an influx of immigrants from neighboring countries. In more specifically economic fields we are likely to find an increase in the production of goods and services, a larger wage-labor force, greater commercialization of agricultural products and the emergence of new forms of entrepreneurship encouraged and subsidized by the state.[13] Farmers move from subsistence to cash and export crops and increasingly become state-supported entrepreneurs whose wealth depends on certain state-determined price arrangements which yield them high returns for their crops. Their surplus is invested partly in acquiring more land, expanding their agriculture and hiring more manpower, and partly in commerce, transportation, construction and other business activities, probably again entailing an arrangement with some state agency and the receipt of some kind of state subsidy. Some farmers might move to the city, invest part of their capital in urban businesses or accede to government positions and gradually become absentee landlords. Many urban dwellers, on their part, take advantage of state loans and investment incentives to buy land and enter the agro-business. Urban-rural differences are thus mitigated at the highest income levels though not at the lower levels.

Government employment is highly valued, and many people seek public administrative positions as a further means of accumulating resources. The central administrative machinery penetrates the local community and is welcome there since it is regarded as an important distributive agent. Traditional structures and authorities are incorporated into the state; traditional chiefs and leaders become state agents and their status is preserved and even enhanced by being made part of the state symbol. Local elites or strongmen increasingly depend on a share of state resources to distribute them further to their segment of the population in order to maintain their allegiance; they are thus bound to state resources and personnel in order to maintain their local control.[14] Even self-help schemes, which in theory are supposed to be autonomous, vie for association with the state, under the assumption that that would ensure higher quality performance (e.g. better teachers), greater resource allocation and greater respectability.[15]

Common to all these activities is a perception of the state as a center of attraction and superior means of resource distribution, which also includes the more symbolic resources of identity and legitimacy. In stressing economic resources I do not mean to uphold a narrow utilitarian view of state-society relations. As Rothchild and Foley have rightly pointed out, some other issues, such as group status, identity and preservation of culture, may form the basis for rather inelastic and nonnegotiable communal claims.[16] In these respects, too, incorporation will occur if the state, because of its efforts to represent and balance such claims, is considered by the parties involved to be an appropriate channel to promote these more symbolic and ascriptive objectives and perhaps to amalgamate communal identities into broader bases of solidarity.

Great differences may obviously exist in the extent to which various groups are incorporated and accede to state resources. Incorporation is likely to be accompanied by greater inequality. A landowning capitalist class may emerge above the rest of the peasantry. The income gap is likely to widen in both urban and rural areas. Regional inequalities may be exacerbated and foreign immigrants who perform the most menial tasks and lack the basic protection provided by citizenship might form a new underclass. Incorporation does not necessarily create a better social environment and is not free of intergroup tensions or social unrest. Incorporation may also be higher in, for example, economic spheres than political and cultural ones. It is not necessarily accompanied by greater political participation. People may wish to be associated with the state as "consumers," because of the state's distributive capacities or because they identify with the ruler, even if they are allowed only a minor share in state decision making. It is not clear, however, how long such a passive consumer attitude can be sustained, and the more educated segments of the population would probably be less content with it.

Disengagement, in contrast, is the tendency to withdraw from the state and keep at a distance from its channels as a hedge against its instability and dwindling resource base.[17] As skepticism rises concerning the effectiveness and legitimacy of state actions, they are undermined by subtle means of popular evasion and dissimulation. Typical forms of disengagement include moving away from the state-cash nexus to a subsistence economy or to alternate channels such as black markets and smuggling. Economic activities turn to outlets less easily regulated by the state. Production either falls or is diverted away from state control. State enacted laws and ordinances and the judiciary system lose their credibility and noncompliance with laws become commonplace. Cynicism, satire, ridicule of both the state and the difficulties of everyday life, and a whole array of popular art forms that develops around them provide an important psychological outlet for the population, especially for those unable to disengage in other forms. As people increasingly dissociate themselves from values attributed to the state, authority and prestige are differentiated from political power and lead to greater status incongruence. Traditional structures and authority regain force as familiar bases in which people seek protection from the instability and arbitrariness of state channels. Narrower bases of communal solidarity (village, family, ethnic, religious or other) are reinforced and lead to greater fragmentation of subsectors. People also tend to move from public to private employment, especially from highly visible administrative positions to less conspicuous professional and technical jobs in the nonformal sector. These are all responses to the economic and social vulnerabilities which arise from the declining capabilities of the state. People are constantly preoccupied with devising ways to shield themselves from the state's harmful consequences or to somehow "manage" if they cannot extricate themselves from them. We should also note that some forms of disengagement, such as parallel markets, depend partly on diverted state channels and would be hard to sustain without some sort of official collusion.

In more extreme cases of disengagement, people may leave the country altogether in search of better economic opportunities or to escape state oppression and restrictions on personal freedoms. However, disengagement does not include active opposition to the regime if the objective is to replace the rulers and/or change government policies. Military coups d'état or other attempts to overthrow the regime, strikes, demonstrations and assassination attempts do not represent disengagement, insofar as they try to control the state and modify its actions according to one's values and interests, rather than by keeping distance from it. On the other hand, some other violent forms of opposition, such as secession, civil war and regional separatism, may be part of disengagement if the objective is an effective detachment from the state, rather than an attempt to capture its center. Attempted secessions and civil wars challenge the state's monopoly of power over sections of the population and territory on which it claims juridical rule, whereas the more moderate forms of disengagement, such as retreat to private occupations, a subsistence economy and parallel markets, acknowledge the continuing state monopoly over organized means of coercion but devise ways to circumvent it. In the case of emigration, the actor involved acquiesces to the state's monopoly of power within its juridical territory but removes himself from it by vacating the territory.

Incorporation and disengagement can obviously occur in the same country in various combinations at different times and have different effects on various groups and social spheres. For example, withdrawal from state-regulated commodity markets because of low producer prices may be accompanied by continued attraction to state educational or social services. The extent and type of incorporation and disengagement vary greatly according to the region, ethnicity, education or occupation of the people involved, the degree of their initial closeness to the state channels, whether they are salaried or self-employed, whether the activity takes place in an urban or rural setting, etc. Some activities are usually combined, such as hoarding and black marketeering. Smuggling may coincide with illegal migration and perhaps highway banditry. It would be quite interesting to examine empirically what kinds of activities tend to seek each other out and what parameters of group affiliation (e.g. class, ethnicity, education, rural/urban, age, gender) are more conducive to a given type of incorporation and disengagement. However, besides occurring simultaneously in the same country, processes of incorporation and disengagement may also be more predominant in certain societies or certain periods than in others. Looking at the contemporary African scene, disengagement is clearly more prevalent in Tanzania, Ghana and Guinea than in the Ivory Coast and Kenya. In Ethiopia, Chad and Sudan it has also taken a more extreme and violent form through continued civil war. Thus, incorporation and disengagement can help us compare African states as well as different sectors or time periods within a given state. The interstate as well as intrastate comparative aspects should not be lost in studying the various facets of state-society relations in postcolonial Africa.

Some Conceptual Difficulties

It may be argued that disengagement misrepresents the real issue of the *continuing gap* between state and society in Africa, which stems from technological and infrastructure limitations and may also be a legacy of the alien nature of the colonial rule. The term "disengagement" assumes the existence of a prior engagement; it indicates a reverse trend, a shift in direction which may never have happened in many parts of Africa (e.g. Chad, Niger, Burkina Faso, parts of Zaire or Sudan). However, other areas (e.g. Ghana, Guinea, Tanzania) did experience considerable grass roots mobilization and popular participation, at least in the few years preceding independence. Hence, at least in these areas a reversal of early processes of engagement and participation can definitely be detected.

We may also question whether or not the state is the critical referent of the various forms of incorporation and disengagement discussed here. In some instances, such as emigration, the disengagement is from the country as a whole; in others, such as reduced production, it may be a response to changing economic conditions. Why, then, refer to these as disengagement from or incorporation in the *state*? The view taken here is that in most cases these activities are construed by the actors as responses to government policies, and not to general economic, social or metaphysical forces. Their critical referent is the central public domain, identified as the state, which manifests itself in a network of public officials, rules, regulations and sanctions.[18] Sometimes the reference is to a certain government and its policy; however, since changing governments and their policies do not seem to make much difference, the response is generalized to the entire public authority beyond a specific government. Thus, we are dealing here with responses to more than the government, though admittedly it is not always clear how much beyond the government they go and we might, at times, deal with disengagement from the regime rather than the state. In any event, the term "state" is not used here in Jackson and Rosberg's juridical sense, i.e. as a unit identifying an entire country or society in the international arena.[19] Whatever its other advantages, such a definition, by equating the state with society, precludes a discussion of state-society relations. "State," as used here, refers to an organization *within* the society where it coexists and interacts with other formal and informal organizations, from families to economic enterprises or religious organizations. It is, however, distinguished from the myriad of other organizations in seeking predominance over them and in aiming to institute binding rules regarding the other organizations' activities, or at least to authorize (i.e. to delegate power to) the other organizations to make such rules for themselves.[20]

It should be pointed out that the very notion of state-society relations which presupposes the state to be different from society is a Western liberal idea. It was stressed very strongly by MacIver, who saw in the state-society distinction the essence of democracy in which the state is controlled by and serves the society (or as he called it, the community).[21] Hegel would probably not have accepted such a notion of the state; nor would Fascist ideology, which considers the state to be the organized expression of the entire society. Marxists, on the other hand, would agree with the notion of the state being a product of society, eventually to be dissolved, though in practice some totalitarian states which claim to be Marxist may have gone a long way to fuse the state and the society into one.

The state is thus active within the society, and different segments of the society react to its activities. They may wish to be more closely associated with them or may try to withdraw from that problematic plane. Skocpol, Nordlinger and Rothchild have rightly pointed out that the state is not merely an arena where different sectors of the society interact, cooperate or compete in a quest for influence over public policymaking. The state can also be an autonomous actor in the social arena, facing society, regulating its actions, competing with other political, economic and social organizations for scarce resources, as well as setting the rules by which societal conflicts are played out.[22] The state can have distinctive interests and self-generated preferences, but by the same token, various segments of the civil society will react to it as a separate actor and will use it as a specific referent in their attempts at incorporation or disengagement. I do not share Skocpol's conclusion that the state has to be "brought back in" to the social science literature.[23] While in the 1960s the term "state" may have been shunned by social scientists, it has now returned with a vengeance into social science discourse, perhaps exaggeratedly so. Rather than continuing to mull over state actions, it might be more fruitful to examine how various segments of the civil society respond to those actions.

A vexing problem faced in dealing with incorporation and disengagement is that their specific manifestations are not always easily differentiated. Under different circumstances similar phenomena occur in connection with contrary trends, creating a methodological quandary and frustrating attempts to draw clear categories of activities related to either incorporation or disengagement. Parallel markets and the informal sector, for example, are as widespread in a context of incorporation as they are in disengagement, but they occur for very different reasons. In a country where processes of incorporation in the state are predominant, the informal sector will flourish at the margin of the state system because of the state's inability or unwillingness to accommodate all those who wish to be part of its system. Too many people might migrate to the cities in hopes of obtaining government employment or taking part in state-subsidized business. The state cannot absorb all of them or perhaps is unwilling to share with all the spoils of incorporation. Severe shortages are likely to develop in housing, formal employment and government salaries. An informal sector will emerge, including makeshift housing (shantytowns), temporary and often illegal employment, subcontracting of official jobs and street vending of various commodities, some of them stolen or contraband, all in order to survive at the margin of the state sector while waiting for the opportunity to be incorporated into it. In disengagement similar activities are undertaken not because the state cannot absorb all those "knocking at the door" but because they are *preferable* to the state-controlled ones. More commodities are found in the black market than in the government stores and higher prices are obtained by the producers or the sellers. In the context of disengagement the informal sector emerges as an alternative to the declining state system; it enables people to withdraw from the state and still meet their basic needs.

Similarly, ethnicity may be as strong in processes of incorporation as in those of disengagement, but again for different reasons. In disengagement it is a protected base of narrower solidarity to which one would retract, whereas in incorporation it is a vehicle through which one attempts to accede to more central state positions at the expense of other contenders. Corruption and disregard for the law may also be as prevalent under conditions of incorporation as under those of disengagement. Despite the outward similarity between these phenomena, in disengagement they stem from a more general contraction in the flow of communication and resources between the state and society and among different segments of the society. In incorporation, by contrast, they derive from a rapid and at times uncontrolled expansion in the flow of resources. Furthermore, the rush for incorporation is likely to leave some groups with a sense of being cheated, abused or neglected. They might turn against what they perceive as the accompanying evils of corruption, injustice and rapid change of values. Religious cults, messianic movements and popular antiestablishment art and literature feed upon the uncertainties and frustrations attendant upon rapid and unequal incorporation as much as they do upon disillusionment leading to disengagement.

In contrast to similar phenomena appearing in both incorporation and disengagement, some other manifestations, such as immigration versus emigration or increasing versus declining cash crop production, are more clearly indicative of either incorporation or disengagement. As for smuggling, it is quite widespread in both cases; but in incorporation most of the smuggling is directed *into* the country, whereas in disengagement most of it goes *out* of the country. These last phenomena are thus more sensitive indices of incorporation versus disengagement than are parallel markets, corruption, disregard for the law, ethnic strife or the emergence of religious cults.

Exit and Voice

The concept of "disengagement" is similar to the idea of "exit" proposed by Hirschman as a possible response to declining performance in various formal organizations.[24] Exit indicates a withdrawal from the organization (i.e. leaving the organization or ceasing to use its goods and services) in response to its unsatisfactory performance. It contrasts with "voice," whereby dissatisfaction is vocally expressed in an effort to modify the organization's performance. Exit, according to Hirschman, is the more economic response, since it relies on market mechanisms: it reduces demand for the deteriorating product. Voice is the more political response insofar as it entails some kind of confrontation with the organization, trying to induce it to alter its performance. Because of the conflict implied in voice, Hirschman regards it as a more "messy" response; it exposes the actor and involves him or her in the imponderables of relative success and failure. Exit is the "neater" response; it is impersonal and carried out in the anonymity of the market.[25]

The exit option presupposes the existence of a market situation, i.e. the availability of alternative products or organizations to which the withdrawing actor could turn in order to satisfy his or her needs. It also assumes that the actor and the society have not developed strong loyalty to the organization in question and would not be concerned by its loss and eventual demise, as its share is being taken over by market competitors. This may not be a realistic proposition when dealing with organizations such as the family, church or state. Alternatives to the malfunctioning organization may be less available or desirable. The well-being of the organization may still matter to the withdrawing actor. In such cases Hirschman expects voice to be preferred to exit. In his own words, "the voice option is the only way in which dissatisfied customers or members can react whenever the exit option is unavailable. This is very nearly the situation in such basic organization as the family, the state or the church."[26] However, disengagement from the state implies that in some cases the situation may be reversed: exit is the residual option when voice is unavailable (not tolerated and punished by the state) or ineffective (disregarded by the state). In later essays Hirschman does realize the importance of exit from the state, for he discusses attempted secession, emigration and the outflow of capital as responses to the state.[27] However, his examples deal more with exit from the country as a whole than with exit from the state without physical withdrawal from the country.

He also continues to claim that "exit has *not* often been used to provide an avenue of self defense for the voiceless."[28] It should be stressed that our concept of disengagement from the state suggests that the exit option is far more common (and takes various forms) even in the relation to an organization like the state which has a monopoly of power and that the only major reactions are not opposition or submission.

The exit-voice dichotomy should draw our attention to another dimension of societal response to state action: the degree of activism versus the degree of passivity of the response. Coupled with favorable versus unfavorable attitudes, the degree of activism of the response creates a two-dimensional scheme which breaks the unilinearity of incorporation versus disengagement.[29] A favorable attitude toward the state may lead to active cooperation or more passive support. It may also be reflected more indirectly in increased production or greater participation in voluntary work projects. The degree of favorable or unfavorable attitude shown to the state is not necessarily correlated with the degree of activism of the response. One may be so actively opposed to the regime as to risk one's life trying to overthrow it, while another person no less opposed to it may opt for the more passive response of emigration and exile.[30]

Figure 1 represents a selected number of societal responses distributed according to their estimated degree of activism toward the ruling authority and the intensity of their favorable or unfavorable attitude to it. The curve represents the possible relationship between the degree of activism and the intensity of one's attitude toward the ruling authority. Responses located closer to the curve indicate a stronger relationship. Most of the responses illustrated here are indeed located on or near the curve. In contrast, political emigration or exile shows the discrepancy between the intensity of the opposition and the relative passivity of the response. Exile is also differentiated from other types of emigration which do not derive from strong opposition to the regime. With regard to the activities of the informal sector, they are located in two different points on the diagram and illustrate again the difficulty mentioned earlier of having similar manifestations which occur for different reasons under different circumstances. In what I call informal sector "a" those engaged in these activities are basically favorable to the state and wait for their opportunity to be incorporated in it. In informal sector "b", in contrast, a similar activity is undertaken out of dissatisfaction with the state and as a means of retreat from its deteriorating channels. Generally speaking, responses related to incorporation are found on the right ("pro") side of the graph but vary in the extent of activism. Responses related to disengagement are on the left ("anti") side, but, with the notable exception of secession, are concentrated at the lower, i.e. more passive, levels. Strong opposition coupled with great activism is generally characteristic of those who still feel closely related to the political center, have a stake in it and have not lost hope of altering its policies and personnel. Those actively opposed to the state, except for the separatists, are still strongly engaged in the state. Their response is one of voice, rather than exit.

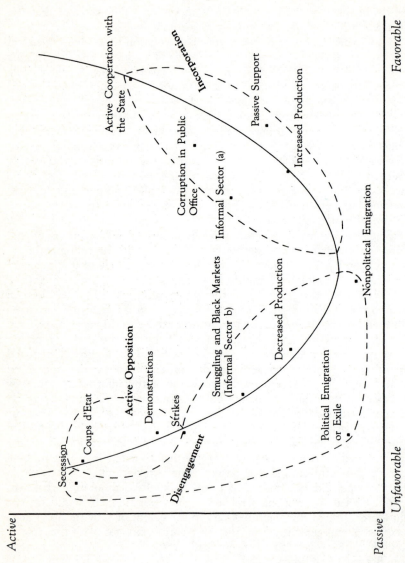

Figure 1 Societal Responses by Degree of Activism and Intensity of Attitude.

State Reactions to Incorporation
and Disengagement

State reactions to incorporation and disengagement vary widely, ranging from encouragement to policy adjustments, repression and even reconciliation to a palpable decline in state control over the society. They also affect the future response of the society. For example, state clamping down on black markets in an attempt to forestall such disengagement may lead to increased smuggling out of the country or reduced production altogether. If the state imposes production quotas and punishes producers for reducing their marketed produce, it might force them to emigrate. State-society relations are thus interlinked in a dynamic network of action and reaction which, in some instances, exacerbates existing tendencies and pushes them into more radical forms.

It is generally assumed that states encourage incorporation and try to obstruct disengagement, since the former strengthens the state's control over the society, whereas the latter further weakens its authority and depletes its resources. The state may obviously foster incorporation and use it to penetrate further into the periphery, for incorporation entails a certain loss of autonomy on the part of the incorporated body. However, the state may also prefer to limit the extent of incorporation if it cannot absorb all those who wish to be incorporated or is concerned with some undesirable side effects, such as growing inequality, intergroup conflict or rapid dislocation of traditions. Greater incorporation increases the burden on the state and may cause an overextension of its capabilities, insofar as the input of the incorporated groups does not always match (at least in the short run) the resources allocated to them. The state may also discriminate against certain groups on an ethnic, religious, class or political basis and deny them incorporation in order to minimize their share of its rewards. Under certain circumstances the state may prefer to keep certain groups in marginal positions where their net input is expected to be higher than if they were more closely incorporated into the state. A clear case in point is the attitude of many African states toward foreign migrant workers. However, such marginal positions may also breed frustration, communal tension and social unrest.

Regarding disengagement, as it further undermines the state's ability to control resources and to exert authority, we generally expect states to combat such tendencies and try to cut off outlets of retreat, if necessary by coercive means. The state may attempt to extend its grass roots control; it may regulate more aspects of the citizen's life, outlaw many of the disengagement devices and impose stiff punishments on transgressors. Complex networks of customs agents, currency checks and economic policies may be established to track down and punish hoarders, black marketeers and smugglers. In reaction to declining agriculture, production brigades may be formed to till the fields, with the symbolic appearance of government ministers in their ranks. Local officials may be threatened with dire sanctions if their area fails to meet the production targets. Education abroad may be curtailed to prevent a brain drain. Folk festivals and sports activities may be orchestrated to counteract the attraction of foreign or antiestablishment mass culture and entertainment.[31]

These mobilization attempts do not reduce disengagement so much as push it to more extreme forms. If withdrawal is impossible legally, it is undertaken by defying or bypassing the law; and if that course of action is too risky, it may lead to physical escape from the country or to collective revolt in the form of regional separatism and civil war. The coercive reaction to disengagement is also very costly and depletes the state's already meager resources. The administrative overhead of maintaining a large machinery of coercive mobilization may be beyond the means of most African states (though it is not quite clear why North Korea or Vietnam can achieve what Ethiopia or Mozambique cannot). As with other "campaigns," such mobilizatory attempts cannot be sustained for long. After a while the state lowers its vigilance and reaches some sort of accommodation with the recalcitrant population, in order to ensure that some modicum of order is maintained and the most essential societal functions are performed. The periodic fluctuations in government vigilance further erode the credibility of state-issued orders and laws.

States do not always fight disengagement. They may also reconcile themselves to reduced control over a withdrawn periphery. Those in ruling positions may even reap some profit from such a situation. Some state officials have a stake in the perpetration of the underground economy and are privileged partners of its principal entrepreneurs. In addition to the corrupt practices of public officials, disengagement also reduces the number of contenders for state-controlled resources. A small ruling group, gradually retracting around the person of the head of state may reduce its expectations from other citizens but also closes itself to their participation and reduces the services offered to them.[32] In addition, as the ruling elite shrinks and its interests narrow, its total needs diminish (even if they rise per capita), as do the resources that have to be extracted from the society. The periphery acknowledges the central authority and transfers to it some resources but otherwise preserves its internal autonomy. The state is authoritarian, arbitrary and extractive, but its control is limited.

The obvious difficulty of such mutual closure of state and society is that the more detached rulers are from other sectors of the society, and the narrower their basis of support, the more vulnerable they become to forces of opposition. By closing itself off to the civil society, the state also loses political information.[33] The rulers try to counteract this danger by building a strong coercive apparatus, which may itself become a threat. Since few resources are redistributed to the civil society, more can be spared to beef up the coercive machinery (police, military, spy rings, etc.). The coercive apparatus may also be used to engage in periodic crackdowns and disrupt outlets of disengagement when they become too threatening to the state. Thus, periods of coercive mobilization can intercede with periods of mutual withdrawal between the state and the civil society.

The state's reconciliation to reduced control over the civil society would be greatly helped if foreign enterprises, such as mineral or oil companies, tapping the country's natural resources would provide a substitute for the resources that cease to come from the disengaged periphery. The income received from the foreign companies as a share of their profits would enable the government to fill the personal needs of the ruling elite, to strengthen its coercive forces and to distribute just sufficient resources to maintain the population above the survival level and prevent an explosion of unrest. Typically, such foreign enterprises would form enclaves having little contact with the rest of the society and enjoying special conditions of work and life-style. Their boundaries would be well guarded by the state in order to minimize their influence on the rest of the society. It should be noted, however, that foreign connections may also flourish under conditions of incorporation and may provide the state with the extra resources needed to maintain its distributive attractiveness in the eyes of the citizens. In the latter case foreign activities would probably be more pervasive in the country and less enclosed in enclaves.

The reconciliation reaction to disengagement mechanisms, much like its coercive mobilizatory counterpart, evinces a lack of concern for the reasons for state decline. But unlike the upholders of the mobilization strategy, proponents of this approach do not attempt to thwart these practices. Instead, they adjust to them with the aim of reducing state responsibility without relinquishing the benefits of state power. At the core of this response is the assumption that disengagement can be sanctioned without upsetting existing distribution arrangements.

State reaction to both incorporation and disengagement can thus go in opposite directions. Incorporation is generally encouraged, but the state might also seek to restrict it if its participatory pressures become too demanding. Similarly, states usually oppose disengagement but sometimes reconcile themselves to its mechanisms. These contradictory patterns of reaction are not mutually exclusive. They can be adopted by the same state at different times or with regard to different groups or spheres of activity. There might also be a discrepancy between the state's intentions and its means of implementation, which give opposite results. Again, as with the different forms of incorporation and disengagement, the analysis of state reaction is conducive to both intrastate and interstate comparisons: it enables us to distinguish between different measures adopted by the same state as well as between states in which different types of reaction are more predominant.

There may also be a third possible state reaction to disengagement, and *prima facie* the most constructive one: the state may attempt to introduce reforms that would increase its efficiency, enhance its penetrative capacity and re-create the attractiveness of its channels. In practice, however, reformist efforts have been far from gratifying and have developed into one of the other two reactions discussed above, most commonly the coercive mobilization type. Implicit in the reform strategy is the desire to create conditions that would make existing forms of disengagement unnecessary and obsolete. But the opposite result is obtained when the government, in order to implement its reform program, makes increasing use of force and lets the coercive aspects of reform implementation overshadow the reform per se. Reform programs often ignore and compete with ongoing survival strategies, and the state is mostly occupied with imposing restrictions, breaking opposition and punishing transgressors who stand in the way of its reforms. A curious paradox thus occurs: on the one hand, the reforms try to resuscitate state-society collaboration, while on the other, daily activities focus on quashing strikes, repressing opposition, promoting signs of allegiance and trying to counteract self-enclosure tendencies. By overlooking actual survival strategies in the society, the reform programs have generally shown an ironic detachment on the part of the state itself. They have shown little understanding of ongoing processes and hence have had a very poor record of success.

Conclusion

In conclusion, I have tried to present here some ideas on how state-society relations in contemporary Africa can be studied with greater emphasis on societal responses. This is not a methodological point; nor is it simply a plea for a new research agenda. It raises some substantive questions about the relevance of the state to African social life, which make it imperative to know how the society behaves *irrespective of* or *despite* certain state actions. The working assumption behind the focus on incorporation and disengagement is that the state is not always the most desirable magnet for social action and that it constitutes one of many possible poles for social and economic exchange.

This does not mean, of course, a total collapse of the state; it only asks that its relevance to various aspects of social life be empirically weighed rather than taken for granted. The African state's resilience is remarkable, and its relative influence on society is still greater than that of any other organization. The state continues to be the major instrument for solving social and economic problems, and its special claims for the monopoly of power set it apart from other organizations affecting social life. The state is the repository of tremendous resources obtained from international sources in the form of foreign aid, investment of foreign capital, international loans and political military support. Internally, it has a substantial ability to extract resources and regulate specific sectors, regions or policy areas. However, various segments of the society manage to maintain patterns of behavior which are at variance with state codes. They hold on to their ways of life with great tenacity or devise new forms in response to, though not necessarily in accordance with, state actions. They are quite successful in circumventing the greater power and determination of state leaders.[34]

By focusing on the society's responses to state action, we have, paradoxically, reasserted the importance of the state in understanding social processes in present day Africa: we have seen the state to be as much a cause as a consequence of socioeconomic occurrences. We cannot say that the state's influence necessarily declines. It does wane in some cases when processes of disengagement are predominant, but not in others when incorporation is more prevalent. However, even in incorporation the state's capabilities are limited. It cannot, or will not, accommodate all those seeking a closer association with it and indirectly causes parallel systems to emerge at its margin. Some groups or individuals may also regret the turmoil, tensions and loss of traditional values or privileges that may accompany incorporation. Hence the desirability of incorporation for both citizens and the state should not be taken for granted. We should pay more attention to how a given society lives beyond the scope of state capabilities in urban as well as rural areas, among educated as well as less educated people, among women and men, young and old, in cultural and religious as well as economic activities, and in such fields as sports, entertainment, the use of time and space and the structure of residential communities and formal organizations. These are exciting challenges to scholarly work, as society's response to the state assumes a long deserved movement to the center of the stage.

Notes

I would like to thank Eti Yakobovich-Abu and Drora Shihuda for their research assistance and Naomi Chazan and Erik Cohen for their invaluable comments at various stages. The Harry S. Truman Research Institute of the Hebrew University of Jerusalem provided the financial support and facilities for the research which led to this paper. The paper was written while I was a North Carolina–Israel Exchange Visitor at the Department of Sociology, The University of North Carolina at Chapel Hill.

1. See for example Robert H. Jackson and Carl G. Rosberg, "Why Africa's Weak States Persist: The Empirical and the Juridical in Statehood," *World Politics,* 27 (October 1982): 1–24; and Colin Leys, "The 'Overdeveloped' Post-Colonial State: A Re-evaluation," *Review of African Political Economy,* No. 5 (January-April 1976): 39–48.

2. Jackson and Rosberg, "Africa's Weak States," p. 6.

3. Ibid., pp. 1–4.

4. On the alien nature of the colonial state and its problematic relations with the civil society see Victor Azarya, *Aristocrats Facing Change: The Fulbe in Guinea, Nigeria and Cameroon* (Chicago: University of Chicago Press, 1978), pp. 59–64. See also Crawford Young's paper in this volume.

5. Claude Ake, *A Political Economy of Africa* (London: Longman, 1981); Samir Amin, *Neo-Colonialism in West Africa* (Harmondsworth: Penguin, 1976); John Saul, *The State and Revolution in Eastern Africa* (New York: Monthly Review Press, 1979); Richard L. Sklar, "The Nature of Class Domination in Africa," *Journal of Modern African Studies,* 17, 4 (1979): 531–552.

6. Joel S. Migdal, "Studying the Politics of Development and Change: The State of the Art" (Paper delivered at the 1982 Annual Meeting of the American Political Science Association, Denver, 1982), p. 3. For an early critique of the integration-modernization approach see Jonathan Barker, "Local-Central Relations: A Perspective on the Politics of Development in Africa," *Canadian Journal of African Studies,* 4, 1 (1970): 3–16.

7. This was the main thrust of some of my own earlier works. See Azarya, *Aristocrats Facing Change;* and idem, *Dominance and Change in North Cameroon* (Beverly Hills: Sage, 1976).

8. Clifford Geertz, "The Integrative Revolution," in Clifford Geertz, ed., *Old Societies and New States* (New York: Free Press, 1963), p. 120.

9. Aristide R. Zolberg, "The Structure of Political Conflict in the New States of Tropical Africa," *American Political Science Review,* 62, 1 (March 1968): 74.

10. Goran Hyden, *Beyond Ujamaa in Tanzania: Underdevelopment and an Uncaptured Peasantry* (London: Heinemann, 1980). See also Martin A. Klein, ed., *Peasants in Africa: Historical and Comparative Perspectives* (Beverly Hills: Sage, 1980); and Victor Azarya and Naomi Chazan, "Disengagement from the State in Africa: Reflections on the Experience of Ghana and Guinea," *Comparative Studies in Society and History,* 29, 1 (January 1987): 107–131. For an interesting discussion on the parallel economy see Janet MacGaffey's chapter in this volume.

11. Joel S. Migdal, "Struggle and Accommodation Between States and Societies in the Third World," unpublished paper, 1984, p. 2.

12. Erik Cohen rightly points out that incorporation may also lead to a contracting field of opportunities, as among groups who feel that incorporation has whittled away some of their traditional privileges and prerogatives. However, such groups with contracting fields of opportunities are not likely to respond by continuing to seek incorporation, unless they see it as a lesser evil (i.e. better opportunities than the alternative option). My focus in this article is *not* on the effect of incorporation on the perceived field of opportunities but rather on the opposite, i.e on the effect of changes in the field of opportunities on incorporation or disengagement. See Erik Cohen, "Recent Anthropological Studies of Middle Eastern Communities and Ethnic Groups," *Annual Review of Anthropology,* 6 (1977): 326.

13. Ibid., pp. 324–325.

14. Migdal, "Struggle and Accommodation," pp. 55–56.

15. See Edmond J. Keller, "Harambee, Educational Policy, Inequality and the Political Economy of Rural Community Self-Help in Kenya," *Journal of African Studies,* 4, 1 (Spring 1977): 86–106.

16. See Donald Rothchild and Michael Foley's paper in this volume.

17. For a detailed discussion of the different forms of disengagement see Azarya and Chazan, "Disengagement from the State."

18. The approach taken here resembles Nordlinger's view of the state as "public officials taken together" or, in a more elaborate definition, "all the individuals who occupy offices that authorize them and them alone to make and apply decisions that are binding upon any and all segments of society." See Eric Nordlinger, *On the Autonomy of the Democratic State* (Cambridge, Mass.: Harvard University Press, 1981), pp. 3, 11. In a similar vein, but stressing the organizations rather than the individuals, Ralph Miliband refers to the state as being constituted of the government, the administration, the military and police, the judicial branch, subcentral government and parliamentary assemblies. See Ralph Miliband, *The State in Capitalist Society* (London: Quadrant, 1970), p. 50. In his essay in this volume Crawford Young attempts to come to grips with the elusive concept of the state by enumerating its various defining characteristics.

19. Jackson and Rosberg, "Africa's Weak States," pp. 12–18.

20. Migdal, "Struggle and Accommodation," p. 10.

21. Robert M. MacIver, "The Community and the State," in idem, *The Web of Government* (New York: Macmillan, 1948), pp. 192–208.

22. Nordlinger, *Autonomy of the State*, p. 25; Theda Skocpol, "Bringing the State Back In," *Items*, 36, 1–2 (June 1982): 2. Rothchild provides a more balanced view of the state, stressing its dual role as an autonomous actor and an organizing principle for the society's conflicts. See Donald Rothchild, "Social Incoherence and the Mediatory Role of the State," in Bruce E. Arlinghaus, ed., *African Security Issues: Sovereignty, Stability and Solidarity* (Boulder: Westview, 1984), pp. 102–108.

23. Skocpol, "Bringing the State Back In."

24. Albert O. Hirschman, *Exit, Voice and Loyalty: Responses to Decline in Firms, Organizations and States* (Cambridge, Mass.: Harvard University Press, 1970).

25. Ibid., pp. 4, 15–17. Boycott is a borderline case between exit and voice. It is a withdrawal, albeit an open and publicized one. It uses withdrawal as another vocal way of raising opposition to the organization's performance. See ibid, p. 86.

26. Ibid., p. 33.

27. Albert O. Hirschman, *Essays in Trespassing: Economics to Politics and Beyond* (New York: Cambridge University Press, 1980) pp. 211–265.

28. Ibid., p. 243 (italics are mine).

29. I owe this idea to a conversation with Erik Cohen in Jerusalem, 1984.

30. We are interested here with activism toward the state. Emigration is an activist response for an actor's own life; this response is less activist vis-à-vis the state.

31. For some examples of such phenomena in Guinea under Sékou Touré's regime see R. W. Johnson, "Guinea," in John Dunn, ed., *West African States: Failure and Promise* (London: Cambridge University Press, 1978) pp. 49, 54–56.

32. On the state's withdrawing itself from responsibility for the society's well-being see the papers by Kwame Ninsin and Victor Olorunsola in this volume.

33. Rothchild, "Mediatory Role of the State," p. 110.

34. Migdal, "Politics of Development and Change," pp. 29–30.

PART TWO

The Changing State in Africa: Historical and State-Centric Perspectives

2

The African Colonial State and Its Political Legacy

Crawford Young

The Crisis in the Contemporary African State

Few would dispute the proposition that the African state today is beset with a profound crisis in the political, economic and social spheres. Countries that a few years ago were regarded as hopeful experiments in development are devastated. Mozambique, which grasped its independence more than a decade ago under the guidance of its remarkably effective liberation movement, the Frente de Libertaçao de Mozambique (FRELIMO), appeared poised to strike out on a new path of effective socialist construction. By 1984 it was forced to sign a humiliating nonaggression pact on terms dictated by South Africa, headlined by *Le Monde* as the "last hope of a ruined country."[1] Sudan, a decade earlier seen as the prospective "breadbasket" for the rich but arid oil states of the Middle East, has confronted bankruptcy, famine, renewal of the civil war in the south and a crisis of legitimacy at the center unresolved by the 1985 coup. Nigeria, whose innovative 1979 constitutional engineering and buoyant oil revenues rallied the hopes of many observers, by the mid-1980s evoked despair. The incorrigible venality of its ruling group, the reckless overcommitment of public resources to such projects as the new capital at Abuja and the corrosion of public institutions has transformed its political economy, concluded one of its shrewdest students, from nurture capitalism into pirate capitalism.[2] Berry brilliantly demonstrates the mechanisms by which the postcolonial state channels the energies and endeavors of civil society into "unproductive accumulation."[3]

State crisis has been even more severe in some countries. In Zaire Catholic bishops, in an angry 1981 pastoral letter, portrayed the state as nothing more than "organized pillage for the profit of the foreigner and his intermediaries."[4] Chazan, in her recent study of Ghana, concludes:

> By the early 1980s it was apparent that Ghana had forfeited its elementary ability to maintain internal or external order and to hold sway over its population. Although its existence as a *de jure* political entity on the international

scene was unquestionable, these outward manifestations did raise doubts as to its *de facto* viability. The Ghanaian state thus seemed to be on the brink of becoming less distinctive and relevant. Indeed, some kind of disengagement from the state was taking place . . . an emotional economic, social, and political detachment from the state element.[5]

Not all African states have been afflicted in equal measure. Those with small populations and high value minerals (Gabon, Libya) and with unusual stability and cautious husbanding of resources (Botswana, Burundi since 1972, Malawi, Algeria) have been in less parlous condition. But the overall prognosis has been disheartening. The 1983 *World Bank Development Report* noted the particularly discouraging development prospects in Africa, particularly in the low-income countries, where "per capita income has continued to fall, and there is now a real possibility that it will be lower by the end of the 1980's than it was in 1960."[6]

The contemporary crisis of the African state has several dimensions. In part it lies in the fraying character of state-civil society relationships. Growing disillusionment with the performance of the state and cynicism in many countries about the ruling groups lead to apathy and detachment. Suddenly the concept of the uncaptured peasantry captures the sociological imagination; whatever its accuracy, this notion did not occur to anyone two decades ago.[7] Important segments of civil society derive their livelihood from the *magendo* world, and novel social categories germinate within this occult universe.[8] Even within the public realm, it becomes more apparent that formulas of authoritarian incorporation, to bring civil society within a framework of "conforming participation," are losing their credibility; as Bayart suggests, "the projects of the power-holders have been partially undermined, if not completely ruined," by the subtle modes of popular action: evasion, dissimulation and ridicule.[9]

A second general dimension to state crisis has been the propensity to overconsumption. In 1967 the average fraction of Gross Domestic Product (GDP) consumed by the African state was less than 15 percent.[10] By 1982 in many states the figure surpassed 30 percent, and in some it was substantially higher; for example, in 1974 Zaire absorbed 59 percent of its GDP in state expenditures.[11] In Kenya public sector employment rose from 188,000 in 1965 to 390,000 in 1978; the civil service per se expanded from 14,000 in 1945 to 45,000 in 1955 and 170,000 by 1980. The Senegalese government employed 10,000 persons on the eve of independence and 61,000 in 1973.[12] In Congo-Brazzaville agricultural extension service staff expanded tenfold from 1960 to 1972, reaching a level where their salaries exceeded the total cash income of the 600,000 peasants.[13] Nigeria transformed virtually all of its oil bonanzas in 1973 and 1979 into state consumption; government expenditure increased from N. 997.4 million in 1971 to N. 17,513.1 million in 1980.[14] In some respects the nature of national income accounts may understate the magnitude of government consumption, particularly for those portions consisting of wage and salary payments and purchases of goods for immediate state use; "government" enters the national income reckoning at factor cost, irrespective of its "product."

Problems arise not only from the scale of state consumption, but from its impact. To the extent that it translates into welfare delivery and economic accumulation, there might be no special cause for concern. But there is reason to doubt whether this has been the case in many instances. The *1983 World Development Report*, in laconic official prose, concludes that "government interventions can result in large losses of efficiency and should therefore be selective." It notes with evident satisfaction that "today's widespread reexamination of the role of the state is evidence of a new realism." The World Bank choice of the state as the primary focus for this report is a measure of the growing conviction that the state itself lies at the heart of the African development impasse.[15]

Although Africa ranks well behind other world regions in military expenditures, these have been rising significantly (for the developing world as a whole, there was a 117-fold increase from 1960 to 1980).[16] Recent research by West demonstrates that since the mid-1970s real military expenditures of African states as a whole have been increasing as a fraction of government expenditure faster than in any other group of countries, substantially exceeding economic growth rates, and that currently, for small low-income countries, these expenditures constitute a higher effective burden than security costs for the major world powers.[17] An important component of state consumption has gone into theatrical self-display (e.g. monumental architecture, such as the $500 million presidential palace in Libreville; the Bokassa coronation in Central African Republic; the Organization of African Unity (OAU) conference facilities in Accra, Freetown, Monrovia, Libreville and Kinshasa). The parastatal sector in many countries expanded at a remarkable pace. But its quantitative increase was rarely matched by its qualitative performance; in the sprawling parastatal domain in Algeria in the mid-1970s only the hydrocarbon enterprise, SONATRACH, operated profitably.[18] In Ghana in the early 1980s the Cocoa Marketing Board employed 105,000 persons to handle a crop half as large as that which 50,000 employees had managed more effectively in 1965. Schatz, in reviewing the impact of the oil revenue boom in Nigeria, concludes that government utilization of these resources bred an "inert economy," with "no growth generating power of its own outside of the crude oil-producing sector."[19] Ellis marshalls eloquent evidence demonstrating the scale of income transfer from peasants to bureaucrats brought about by Tanzania's overextended and underperforming parastatal sector.[20]

The problem of state consumption leads directly to the third dimension of the crisis: the anemic rates of development. By the end of the 1970s a consensus was taking form, inside and outside of Africa, on the magnitude of the problem. A report prepared for the 1979 OAU meeting declared, "Africa . . . is unable to point to any significant growth rate or satisfactory index of general well-being."[21] In the soft-spoken words of a leading Nigerian intellectual, Jacob Ajayi, in 1982: "The optimism of development plans of the 1960's has given way to increasing frustration in the 1970's and disillusionment in the 1980's. The general lament is that this is not what was expected from independence."[22]

The crisis of the postcolonial African state has many causes. Some are attributable to inexplicably angered fates, who inflicted punishing droughts upon large stretches of the continent in the 1970s and 1980s. Some arise from inherent intractabilities of resource endowment, particularly for the poorest of the states: limitations of rainfall amount and reliability, and soil fertility, compounded by the world's highest population growth (three percent annually) and ecological degradation (particularly by deforestation). The international environment has been hostile. Aid levels have been stingy and distribution heavily influenced by the global strategic objectives of the superpowers, for whom Africa is one more arena of competitive encounter. Lenders share responsibility with the African borrowers for the excessive indebtedness of many countries. The impact of this indebtedness is today aggravated by irresponsible budgetary policies of the United States, which imposes exorbitant interest rates on African (and other) Third World debtors by its massive deficits. The poor performance of Western economies during much of the 1970s also took its toll on export-oriented African states.[23] Other causes may be found in contemporary developments in some African states: singularly inadequate rulers in some countries, such as Idi Amin in Uganda (1971-1979) or Jean-Bedel Bokassa in Central African Republic (1966-1979); exceptionally venal predators upon the public purse in others (Ignatius Acheampong in Ghana, 1971-1978, Mobuto Sese Seko in Zaire, 1965-); prolonged civil war in still others (Chad intermittently since 1965; Angola since 1975).

In addition to these factors, some illumination into the current distress, we believe, can be obtained by a retrospective examination of the colonial state in Africa. We make no claim that the political legacy of the colonial state can stand as the central source of any explanation. But we are persuaded that deeply embedded in the contemporary state are a number of characteristics and behavioral dispositions which originate in the colonial era. A step backward to review the complex phenomenon of colonial rule may thus be helpful as one part of a process of interrogation of the contemporary state in crisis.

In pursuit of our quarry, we begin by introducing the analytical weapons to be used in the hunt: our employment of the concept of state in the colonial setting. We then survey the wider landscape, to consider the ways in which colonial-state construction in Africa may have differed from patterns in other parts of the world once part of imperial domains. We next follow the development of the African colonial state through three stages: initial construction, where the basic framework was established, up to 1914; institutionalization as an enduring form of alien hegemony, in the interwar period; and transformation into a decolonizing mode, after World War II. Finally, we consider the residues of the colonial state which persisted in the postindependence era and some of the consequences of the legacy.

To presume to cover too vast a topic in so brief a compass will entail a highly compressed and excessively generalized presentation. Many statements will have exceptions; others will assert central tendencies which would require nuancing in application to individual contexts. The premise of depature is a good case in point: the crisis of the postcolonial state. Such a postulate is premature for Zimbabwe and can hardly be applied to such states as Cameroon, Rwanda, Ivory Coast, Algeria or Libya. For Ghana, Zaire or Equatorial Guinea, "crisis" is if anything an understatement. The array of problems evoked by the term "crisis" is sufficiently general for a trend to be declared. The generalizations we will advance with respect to the colonial state doubtlessly stand in similar relation to the range of actual variations around what we hope to identify as central trends.

Characteristics of the State

The colonial state is a subsidiary variety of the broader genus of "state." In contemporary understanding the term refers usually to the modern state, a particular form which originated in Europe in the fifteenth century, evolved into a nation-state by the end of the eighteenth century, and became diffused throughout the globe by imperial conquest and anticolonial revolt or defensive adaptation (Japan, China, Thailand, Ethiopia).[24] There have been various forms of states over the past 6000 years of history, from city-states to nomadic confederations. Geertz reminds us that only recently has the term "state," "master noun of political discourse," become exclusively focused upon institutions of rule; former meanings remain in such derivations as "stately," or "status."[25] The master form which imposes its imprint upon global space and dominates both discourse and politics is what we term the modern state.

Space precludes indulging ourselves here in the rejuvenated debate on this master noun.[26] We will confine ourselves to a summary statement of our usage in this analysis. The modern state may be understood in terms of several defining characteristics. In setting these forth, note will be taken of the particularities of the colonial state. The state is not simply an inert abstraction; it is, above all, a historical actor, a collective agent of macropolitical process. To grasp this dimension we will sketch the primary imperatives which govern its behavior. These elements, taken cumulatively, constitute a "reason of state" embedded in the "official mind" of the human agents who staff its institutions.

To begin with, a state has territoriality. For the modern state, this is a precisely demarcated domain, within whose boundaries the claim to exclusive ultimate authority is asserted. A prime icon of the state is invariably its national map, with borders delineated in bold lines and the territory tinted with warm and friendly colors.

Secondly, a state is invested with sovereignty. This potent jural weapon, forged by the philosophers of absolutism, equips the state with a doctrine of inherent absolute, indivisible and unlimited power and authority. Its real exercise may be limited by constraints of state capabilities and resources, or circumscribed by law or constitution. But these are restrictions of circumstance or negotiated accords with civil society; a hidden potential for expansion of hegemony remains. The doctrine of sovereignty places at the potential disposition of the state land, resources and the population of the territory.[27]

Thirdly, a state possesses nationality. This warm, vibrant concept vests the state with a moral personality. The early modern state was anthropomorphically expressed as a projection of its ruler: "for king and country." The triumph of the idea of nation after the French Revolution represented the state as a transcendent embodiment of its civil society. In this mythological reconstruction of the state as an expression of citizenry as a collective self, its sovereign hegemony acquires overpowering moral sanction.[28] However important the cultural pluralism or class cleavages which divide civil society, the doctrine of indivisibility and oneness, of membership as citizens, has commanding normative force.

Fourthly, the state is a participant in a global system of juridically equivalent units, the "anarchical society" of the international order. The absence of binding authority within this system along with the active pursuit of self-defined "national interest" in competition and potential conflict with other units by all states, defines the international system. Power is a primary currency within this realm, creating the necessity for armed defense against external threats and on occasion for enforcement of claims upon rival members of the system. The role of force in the international system has been a driving imperative in the enhancement of state power and consolidation of its internal hegemony.[29]

Fifthly, the state is a set of institutions of rule. In everyday understandings of the state, no doubt its visibility as a "government" is its most readily perceived aspect. For the contemporary state, the proliferation of its functions and expansion of its scope render these institutions complex, diverse and fragmented: bureaucracy for routine implementation of its tasks; political, legislative and executive agencies for choice and decision; police and judicial structures for enforcement of its commands and adjudication of disputes; military force, for its external defense and ultimate internal security; a host of ancillary agencies for the delivery of services, education of the young and discharge of economic functions.

Sixthly, the state is a legal system. Its commands are codified into uniform, predictable and impersonal rules. A public law defines the structure and exercise of authority; a criminal code defines impermissible behavior; civil jurisprudence regulates transactions and relationships between individuals and legal persons. In the words of legal philosopher Hans Kelsen, the modern state is a King Midas, whose touch turns everything into law.[30] The state as a legal system incorporates not only formal law, but also the informal norms and understandings included in what Rothchild terms its "organizing principles."[31]

Finally, the state is an idea, deeply implanted in the minds of its citizens and officials, as something abstract yet personal which is much more than the simple sum of its institutions of governance; hence its generally diffused icons, legitimating myths, theory of its origins, normative doctrines relating to its operation and ultimate aims. It is in this metaphysical sense that the state functions as a historical actor; history, suggests Henry Kissinger, is the collective memory of states.[32] States render their images concrete through monumental architecture;[33] they breathe life into their abstractness by self-celebratory ritual. The Geertz model of the Indic state as a majestic theater dramatizing itself as an exemplary center has some application: "The equation of the seat of rule with the dominion of rule . . . is a statement of a controlling political idea—namely, that by the mere act of providing a model, a paragon, a faultless image of civilized existence, the court (state) shapes the world around it into at least a rough approximation of its own excellence."[34]

Behavioral Determinants: Elements of Reason of State

The major imperatives which shape the behavior of the state may be condensed under five headings: hegemony, security, autonomy, legitimation and revenue. We do not wish to imply that these factors constitute some mechanical law of determination. In the final analysis, state behavior is carried out through human agents. States as abstractions cannot act; only the skilled human beings who staff its institutions can do so. As Giddens argues, "All human action is carried out by knowledgeable agents who both construct the social world through their action, but yet whose action is also conditioned or constrained by the very world of their criticism."[35] Possessed of volition, yet as state agents operating within the womb of its reason of state, human actors have some latitude in interpreting its dictates and are affected by individual idiosyncracies. To paraphrase Marx, state agents make history, but not entirely as they choose. The broad parameters governing state behavior supplied by these imperatives help give history its patterned regularities and structural forms.

States seek hegemony over territory which they rule. The modern state, Weber observes, "is a compulsory association which organizes domination."[36] States will not tolerate resistance to the supremacy of their laws, nor accept challenge to their ultimate authority over territory or populace.

States respond to perceived threats to their security, whether from the international arena or their civil society. They accumulate and store power resources, arming themselves in function of self-calculated quantums of security. Resource limitations and possibly consent of civil society constrain the response to the security imperative. States, however, have an innate tendency to err on the side of "safety," as a cursory glance at global military budgets will suggest.

States pursue the goal of maximum feasible autonomy. The doctrine of sovereignty, in its external dimension, prescribes independence as the fundamental norm of true statehood. The impossibility of total autonomy in the contemporary world state system in practice in no way diminishes the desirability of the ideal. State autonomy also has an internal dimension; states represent themselves as pursuing a "national" or "public" interest distinct from those of any segment of civil society or even the sum of its parts.

States need legitimation for the effective exercise of authority and economic accumulation of power. States, in the Weberian phrase, may be defined by the monopoly of legitimate use of coercion, but force cannot be constantly applied. Habitual acquiescence to state authority permits parsimony in employment of coercion. Rulers find their tasks simplified if volitional compliance supplants fear-driven obedience. Ideological formulas (hegemony in the Gramscian sense), engagement of civil society in consent-gathering processes of consultation and participation (even if merely ritual), constitutionalizing authority in the form of a solemn compact between state and civil society: all of these may contribute to meeting the legitimation imperative. Effective performance is also indispensable; the modern state must ground its legitimation in upholding external interests, meeting to some degree material expectations of civil society, assuring public safety within the realm and competently managing the national economy.

Perhaps most fundamental of all is the state's drive to assure its revenue base. Responding to all of the other imperatives mentioned above requires extensive revenues. From the birth of the modern state, the relentless search for money has been a constant theme of statecraft and the pivot for a ceaseless struggle with civil society, anxious to limit state extraction. The primacy of the revenue imperative is an axiom of reason of state.[37]

Special Characteristics of the Colonial State

The colonial state, as a dependent appendage of the set of European states that participated in the partition of Africa, had a number of particularities which require attention. Its territoriality was ambiguous. The introduction of sharply defined frontiers—when it was finally accomplished on the ground, two or three decades after the diplomatic settlements were reached—was a dramatic change from most precolonial arrangements. But the boundaries which assumed some degree of significance were those demarcating the domains of different colonial powers, not those separating the different territories into which an imperial state subdivided its possessions. Within contiguous zones ruled by a single power there was generally free movement of goods and persons. Pieces of territory were moved about from one administrative division to another (Eastern Province of Uganda to Kenya; Karasuk in Kenya administered by Uganda; Upper Volta incorporated into Ivory Coast in 1931, reestablished in 1947). The difference between administrative divisions and territories with a separate state personality was unclear, above all in the case of the two vast federations of Afrique Occidentale Française and Afrique Equatoriale Française. Periodic efforts were made to regroup, at least for common services, contiguous territories ruled by a given power: Ruanda-Urundi and Belgian Congo; Uganda, Kenya,

Tanganyika and Zanzibar; Northern and Southern Rhodesia, Nyasaland. In the early stages, only a handful of colonial possessions had a strong territorial identity, particularly those which had a precolonial existence (Egypt, Tunisia, Morocco, Madagascar, Swaziland, Lesotho).

Paradoxically, the territorial legacy has proved to be one of the most enduring impacts of colonial rule. As anticolonial struggle gathered momentum, it necessarily adopted as the unit of self-determination the colonial territory. As a new ruling class the nationalist leadership sought legitimation and security through sanctifying their territory as an embodying nationality. The OAU entrenched in its charter in 1963 the principle of preservation of the existing colonial partition boundaries, and this notion that territorial integrity is identified with the extant state system is a basic premise of the emerging code of African international law.

Sovereignty for the colonial state was exercised by the imperial occupant. For the most part it was held to originate in conquest, with European rule imposed upon lands lacking international standing as sovereign entities. There were, in the initial stages, many contradictions in this connection. In the northern tier of the continent, Egypt, Tunisia and Morocco (and to a lesser extent Ethiopia) were recognized as second class, but nonetheless entitled, members of the Europe-centered consort of states, if for no other reason than that they enjoyed sufficient standing to contract substantial debts, whose collection was a major pretext for occupation. In some other cases, overrule was justified *ab initio* by contractual accords entered into by rulers of existing African states; where the entirety of the colonial territory was covered by these agreements, as in the cases of Swaziland, Basutoland and to a lesser extent Bechuanaland, they were used by African ruling groups to circumscribe the scope of colonial sovereignty.[38]

For the most part, however, African colonial territories were considered to be sovereign voids. Nineteenth-century international law became tinged with social Darwinism and accentuated diplomatic distinctions between "civilized" and barbaric zones. By 1895 British law officers had ruled that "the exercise of a protectorate in an uncivilized country imported the right to assume whatever jurisdiction over all persons may be needed for its effectual exercise.[39] Paradigmatic of the concept of colonial sovereignty which dominated in most instances was Lord Lugard's celebrated statement to the Sokoto ruling class after he found an opportunity to defeat them in battle:

> The old treaties are dead, you have killed them. Now these are the words which I, the High Commissioner, have to say for the future. . . . The Fulani in old times under Dan Fodio conquered this country. They took the right to rule over it, to levy taxes, to depose kings and to create kings. They in turn have by defeat lost their rule which has come into the hands of the British. All these things which I have said the Fulani by conquest took the right to do now pass to the British. Every Sultan and Emir and the principal officers of State will be appointed by the High Commissioner throughout all this country. The High Commissioner will be guided by the usual laws of succession and the wishes of the people and chiefs, but will set them aside

if he desires for good cause to do so. The Emirs and Chiefs . . . will obey
the laws of the Governor and act in accordance with the advice of the
Resident. . . . You have always heard that British rule is just and fair, and
people under our King are satisfied.[40]

The plenitude of the sovereignty doctrine applied by colonizers to their
African domains was important in supplying ideological justification for a
number of the sweeping measures adopted. Particularly for the continental
European states, an axiomatic derivative of sovereignty is the state claim
to ultimate proprietary rights over land. On the very day of its establishment
in 1885, the Congo Free State of King Leopold issued a decree asserting
state domain proprietorship over the entire territory, recognizing only the
occupancy rights to cultivated lands in the immediate vicinity of villages.
Only the British were cautious in the application of this principle, where
they anticipated stirring up undue trouble (southern parts of Nigeria and
Gold Coast) or where they feared treaty agreements might be used as a
basis for a litigated challenge in their own courts (Swaziland, Basutoland).
All the colonial occupants had potent legal cultures at home; expediency
might suffice for a peremptory action by an agent on the spot, but general
policies required the cover of a jurisprudential doctrines.

The colonial state was conceded a derivative territorial personality, but
emphatically not a national one. The subject populations of Africa were
invited to share a subordinated affective tie to the imperial center. Until
relatively late in the colonial game, the proposition that there was a Nigerian,
Algerian or Congolese "nation" would have been treated as utterly ludicrous.
The French went furthest in constructing a colonial myth which presumed,
as the organizing officials for the 1900 Paris Universal Exposition declared,
". . . forty-five million men of all races, who have achieved the most diverse
degree of civilization, have entered the French community."[41]

The colonial myth had potent vitality until after World War II;[42] testimony
to its persistence is the classical phrase of the 1944 Brazzaville conference
of French officials to chart postwar reform in Black Africa: "The aims of
the civilizing effort accomplished by France in her colonies rules out any
idea of autonomy, any possibility of evolution outside the French bloc of
the empire; the eventual or even the ultimate institution of self-government
must be avoided."[43] The Portuguese version of the submersion of Africa in
a global lusotropical national community, which received full ideological
statement only under Salazar's *Estado Novo* in the 1930s, likewise denied
to the last the possibility of a national personality for its territories. Belgian
state doctrine insisted upon the separateness of the colony, but its very
title of "Belgian Congo" was emblematic of the suffusion of a Belgian
overlayer into its territorial identity.

In the British case, from the Durham Report and British North American
Act in 1837 and 1867, there was a presumption in the dominion model of
ultimate self-rule. Not until the 1917 pledge of dominion status to India,
however, was it evident that this was of application to non-European
holdings of the crown. No unambiguous statement that dominion self-

government implied full sovereignty was made until the 1926 Imperial Conference. Even then, the dominions remained implicitly subordinate entities incorporated within the broader frame of the British Empire, whose dissolution Sir Winston Churchill vowed to prevent. In 1928 Sir Cecil Hurst wrote: "The British Empire is a strange complex. It is a heterogeneous collection of separate entities, and yet it is a political unit."[44]

In the African case, with the exception of Egypt and the white-dominated territories of South Africa and Rhodesia, self-rule on this model prior to World War II was seen as such a distant contingency that little heed needed to be paid to the implications of a territorial personality. Ormsby-Gore, on tour for the Colonial Office in 1926, wrote, " 'Self-Government' in Nigeria, if ever it comes, will be the self-government of the country by the Native Administrations and not be any elected Council in Lagos!"[45] Early Nigerian nationalists were seen as "denationalized" Africans, disqualified for any governance role; within this logic, the central secretariat ruling Nigeria and the regional administration by definition could only be British.

The centrality of the law in metropolitan state ideologies required the creation of a legal realm in the colonial state. However, as a legal order the colonial state was a hybrid construction. The Belgians were farthest in creating a comprehensive constitution for their colony by parliamentary enactment in 1908 (the Charte Coloniale). In the French instance the ambiguous incorporation of the overseas domains into the enlarged republic produced a theoretically unified legal community but in practice a sharply divided one. The French parliament had the right to legislate for the colonies, but in practice colonial law was usually invoked by presidential decree or ordinances enacted by the governors. At the personal level this duality translated into the division between subject and citizen, between those subordinated to law-as-hegemony and those enjoying full status as members of civil society (the Muslim versus French civil status which was of particular importance in Algeria).[46]

The British had constructed out of their Western hemisphere experience the crown colony formula, by which each territory was a distinct legal domain, with law-making powers essentially vested in the governor. It was nominally exercised by a legislative council, which accommodated settler and colonial-establishment private interests, but remained under the thumb of the governor until the decolonization stage. In spite of this segmentation, important uniformities emerged from the applicability of British legal concepts and precedents in the courts and the possibility of appeal to the British judicial summit. By the time of the British imperial occupation of African territory, the dangers to colonial hegemony in indiscriminate transfer of British legal practices was well recognized. Thus, there was no question of application of the jury system in criminal law, which had so undermined the effectiveness of the law as a vehicle for colonial control in Ireland and the North American colonies.[47] Even so, the particular flavor of a legal order less tightly bound to the unitary Bonapartist framework of the continental state provided more openings for the subjugated civil societies to employ litigation as a weapon against hegemony.

The colonial state in general, while insisting upon the ascendancy of its law, did not (and could not) enforce a comprehensive legal monopoly. The colonial legal order confined its demands for exclusivity to economic and social spheres covering the activity of the external estate of Europeans and other immigrants, as well as criminal offenses which were deemed, directly or indirectly, to affect the colonial peace. Civil or criminal matters having no impact upon the colonial realm and concerning solely the subject populace could be treated in African jurisdictions according to customary law. In these fields the ultimate hegemony of the colonial state could be enforced by tutelage and monitoring of the African courts, whose verdicts were subject to review and whose personnel were subject to screening by the colonial authority.

At the time of the creation of the African colonial state, the world state system was perhaps more Europe-centered than at any point in modern history. Thus, the automatic consequence of imperial partition was the extinguishment of any semblance of international personality for the African territories. The state system, through the final paroxysm of empire building, incoporated the entire globe. Before World War I it was totally dominated by the imperial states, which had not the slightest doubt that their preeminence of power was ordained by science and providence as a natural reflection of their moral and cultural superiority.[48]

As appendages of an empire, the colonial state thus had no distinctive external interests except as accessories of the empire. The effortless presumption of African assimilation of an empire interest by grace of conquest was reflected in intriguing ways. African conscripts were freely employed in both world wars, not only to subdue German territories in Africa in World War I, but in such distant theaters as Burma, the Middle East and Europe. In the cases of France and Belgium, the African territories were used during World War II as refugees of metropolitan sovereignty placed in doubt by the German occupation of Europe. Italy used many thousands of Eritrean troops in its bitter pacification struggles in Libya in the 1920s, who were viewed as imperial auxiliaries, not mercenaries. The more integrated imperial state concepts of France and Portugal meant as a matter of course that sovereignty was indivisible and assured by the metrpolitan army, though with extensive recruitment of colonial subjects. For Britain and Belgium, which conceded more of a territorial personality to their African domains, armies were usually trans-territorial (the West African Frontier Force, the King's African Rifles, the Force Publique garrisoning both the Belgian Congo and Ruanda-Urundi).

In the formative years particularly, the *telos* of the colonial state was entirely externally directed. Characteristic of the ideological premises of the colonial state was the 1912 assertion of a liberal spokesman for the empire in France, Jules Harmand:

> That the colonies are made for the metropolis, for the many and varied advantages that the metropolis may draw from them, is evident: if colonies, the foundation of which nearly always costs the metropolis so much money

and sacrifices and which exposes them to such great risks, were not made to serve those metropoles, *they would have no raison d'être*, and one cannot see by what aberration civilized states would dispute them with so much rude jealousy.[49]

Justification of colonial rule had to be supplied to metropolitan civil society and the European concert of states. The law of force and necessity was sufficient legitimation for the subjugated African societies; one may recall the Lugard speech at Sokoto cited earlier. In European reason, those lacking in "civilization" did not possess the cultural capacity for moral evaluation of rule; conquest was thus self-explanatory. Until imperialism became fully assimilated into the metropolitan state ideology at home, officialdom and influential segments of public opinion required reassurance of the advantages to be derived from overseas estates, and guarantees that these would not be offset by inconvenient costs. Because of the competitive nature of the African partition and lingering uncertainties into the early twentieth century as to the permanence of the initial settlements, imperial purpose also had to be clothed in claims of benefits accruing to subjugated populations; abolition of slavery was particularly salient in the early arguments, with the 1890 Brussels Anti-Slavery Conference a landmark in the diplomacy of African partition. Vivifying commerce and uplifting Christian conversion opportunities were other components to initial colonial state ideology, which appealed to significant metropolitan groups interested in African expansion.

In sum, the colony as a subspecies of the state had several distinctive characteristics. It was a dependent appendage of an externally located sovereign entity. It was alien to its core; the overall ruler-subject antimony contained several nesting dualities: foreign/local; white/black; European culture/African heritage. Its inner logic was shaped by the vocation of domination. The very success of its hegemonic project constituted a civil society which over time was bound to reject its legitimacy.

The African Colonial State
in Comparative Perspective

The African colonial state may be classified in the broader category of colonial states generally in most of these respects, but there are some points of distinctiveness which deserve brief notice. Except for Indochina, the Pacific islands and Japanese imperial domains, an empire was established in Asia much earlier, in a mercantile age. For the most part, the colonial state could superpose itself upon existing state structures of substantial scope and institutions of social power long accustomed to the extraction of revenue from the land. Of the major colonial domains, only the Philippines really fell outside the Indic, Buddhist or Islamic state systems. Potent structures of intermediation and fiscal collection were in place, which with force and diplomacy might be incorporated into the colonial state. Resilient and absorptive religions and cultures in the core areas of Asian colonial states (again with the exception of the Philippines) filtered the colonial impact.

Particularly after the 1857 Sepoy Mutiny revealed the dangers of mobilization of the subject population by cultural threat, colonizers were cautious in their evangelical instincts; Christian mission action tended to be confined to peripheral communities (Karens in Burma, Minahassans and Moluccans in Indonesia, depressed classes and northeast hill groups in India). There were harsh periods (the "cultures" system in nineteenth-century Java), plundering episodes (Bengal in the late eighteenth century), and disruptive impacts (*chettyar* land foreclosures in lower Burma in the twentieth century). But the ready availability of adequate revenues, especially from land taxation and customs, viable political and social intermediary structures, and the relatively limited cultural scope of colonial teleology produced a colonial state whose imprint upon civil society was less dislocative and comprehensive than its African counterpart.[50] It was able, with a very modest infrastructure of alien force, to maintain its control and assure its security; in the interwar period the British ruled India with only 15,000 British (and over a quarter million Indian) troops and (in 1939) only 760 British officers in the elite Indian Civil Service, which was the administrative spinal column of British India.[51]

The imperial phenomenon had, in the Middle East, a decisive impact upon the state system through its influence upon boundaries, and the territorial units which came to acquire identity as sovereign units (the post–World War I partition of Ottoman domains, the British string of protectorates around the coastal fringes of the Arabian peninsula). However, the colonial state per se had either a brief and turbulent life (Iraq, Palestine, Syria, Lebanon) or a long and superficial one (Aden, the Persian Gulf protectorates). In the mandated territories there was in the circumstances prevailing after World War I no possibility of imposing the kind of comprehensive colonial state characteristic of Africa. In the Persian Gulf sheikdoms British interest, until the petroleum age, was merely preemptive, in the security interests of the empire in India. Such purposes were easily met by forming an alliance with a ruling family, whose domestic governance was of no concern unless British security interests were threatened. Access to petroleum could be had by simple arrangement with the ruling family; no overrule was required. In the Levant stratagems of managing cultural pluralism to facilitate low-cost hegemony left in their wake many postcolonial problems: the bitter legacy of the Palestinian mandate, Alawi and Druze domination of the Syrian officer corps, the fragility of confessional politics in Lebanon. But the colonial state itself had only a weak hold on its subjects. The only exceptions in this region were the Central Asian emirates conquered by imperial Russia in the late nineteenth century and eventually fully annexed and incorporated into the Soviet state.[52]

The Western hemisphere colonial states likewise diverged from the African pattern. In North America the British learned some painful lessons about the requisites of hegemony by permitting groups of settlers to constitute autonomous civil societies before much of an effort was made to superpose an apparatus of imperial control. By the eighteenth century, when consolidation of imperial machinery became a conscious concern, civil society had constructed potent doctrines and institutions of autonomy. The colonial state superstructure lacked a reliable revenue base or a standing military force (only available, in small numbers, after the 1756–1763 French war). Such agencies of social control as churches and the law enforcement system eluded its control. Only guile, diplomacy, corruption (placemen) and the ultimately fragile resource of loyalty were available to the royal governors. These kinds of rudimentary errors in colonial statecraft were not repeated.[53]

The slave plantation colonial societies of the Caribbean were based upon minimal states and ruthless private structures of social control and exploitation. The small salience of the state itself is symbolically reflected in the relative absence of the term in West Indian political discourse concerning the colonial past.[54] Slavery, and not the state, was the central fact of colonial times. Hegemony was maintained by overseers, not district commissioners. The state was present only as a guarantor of the plantation order, whose reserves of forces were insurance against much-feared servile insurrection. After abolition destroyed the initial economic base of the Caribbean states, the inertial disposition of an imperial state to retain its territorial holdings kept the islands under colonial rule. But they remained minimal states, imperial holding operations; gone were the days of the sugar fortunes, when in 1763 the British nearly opted to trade all of Canada for Guadalupe. The islands remained colonial into contemporary times in good measure because their black majorities had themselves assimilated a mystique of empire loyalty. As Gordon Lewis put it: ". . . not the least ironic aspect of the Englishness of the West Indies was the fact that West Indians for so long preserved among themselves a Victorian Anglophilism, an almost imperialist chauvinism, and an uncritical loyalty to the Crown long after those attitudes had waned in Britain itself."[55] In this environment, hegemony could rest lightly on civil society.

The Spanish empire might appear at first glance to be the closest approximation to the African colonial state. The precociously absolutist Castilian state had a precast model for incorporation of new domains, populated by culturally differentiated subjects, in the drawn-out process of *reconquista* in the centuries preceding trans-Atlantic expansion. Tested formulas of control were transferred in the erection of a remarkably thorough bureaucratic-absolutist apparatus of rule, in particular in those zones where it was fully implanted (Mexico and Peru above all, Cuba somewhat later). Indispensable to its success were the precious metals in its key centers, and later the sugar system, and dense, sedentary, politically subordinated indigenous populations which could be organized into a semiservile labor force. The vice-royalties, *audiencias,* church and *encomiendas* constituted overlapping hierarchies of imperial control, bound together by the Crown, the Council of the Indies and the Seville mercantile monopoly, monitored through institutionalized distrust among its various hierarchies. Its control over its far-flung domains was uneven; it could neither cope with horseborne nomadic groups nor prevent encroachment by its rivals in the Caribbean region. But in its 300 years of rule it created new societies more or less unified into a single sociocultural hierarchy, whose apex was Hispanic and Christian. In this attribute lies its decisive difference from the African colonial state; the civil society which eventually revolted against imperial rule was firmly creole in its elite ranks. Indian culture and society had been thoroughly subordinated and peripheralized, even in those zones of the Andes and Central America where Indians constituted a large majority of the total.[56]

In considering the African colonial state in comparison with the broader universe of imperial formations, three major specific features stand out. Firstly, the conquest of Africa was much more competitive than that in any other major region. After beating the French in the mid-eighteenth century, the British essentially had south Asia to themselves. The frontier psychosis, which torments the official mind into the belief that security lies in extending the boundaries one step further, caused the formidable expansion from the Calcutta-Delhi-Bombay-Madras core into Burma and Afghanistan, and permanent anxieties about potential Russian thrusts, but no real direct competition. Similar frontier-building reflexes explained French expansion into Cambodia and Laos or Dutch expansion into the Indonesian outer islands, but neither was an immediate encounter with other colonizers. Similarly, in the Western hemisphere there was some competition between the Portuguese, Spanish, Dutch, French and British, particularly in the Caribbean, but the process was protracted, and most of the time each power had its acknowledged zone of activity. In Africa the scramble was concentrated, intense and in many areas involved multiple competitors for given territory.

Secondly, the colonial state-building venture in Africa included in most areas a far more comprehensive cultural project than was the rule in Asia or the Middle East (although the New World was comparable). Racialist ideas were much more ideologically elaborated than they had been in earlier centuries at the time of African colonial occupation. The European ruling class had both a more pronounced conviction of its own cultural, biological and technological superiority and held a more systematically negative view of the Africans.[57] Africa was a *tabula rasa* (except for Islamic areas), a fitting field for the surge of evangelical energy welling up in the Christian churches. The disposition to remake African society was less pronounced on the part of the British than the others, but it was present in all.

Thirdly, colonial expansion in Africa occurred at a historical moment when European states were far more comprehensive and elaborated than was the case in earlier centuries. When the Dutch East Indies Company was chartered in 1602, the Netherlands as a state barely existed to invest with its sanction the cartel of merchants from its maritime ports. Sir Thomas Roe, the first British royal ambassador to visit the Mogul court in 1615 on behalf of the East India Company, was seen by the Emperor as the threadbare representative of a distant land of sheep and fishermen.[58] There was little comparison between these states and the late nineteenth-century European states, with their professionalized bureaucracies, vastly greater resources, permanent military forces equipped with imposing weapons and doctrines concerning the scope and range of state action which went well beyond those of an earlier age. There was, of course, a deepening of the colonial state in Asia in tandem with the elaboration of the state at home. But this proceeded by degrees, and lacked the intensity of first encounter which characterized colonial state building in Africa.

Phase I of the African Colonial State: Construction

We now return to the colonial state in Africa, in its three stages of construction, institutionalization and decolonization. To decode the internal logic which shaped its growth, we make use of the five components of reason of state considered earlier: hegemony, security, autonomy, legitimation and revenue. In the first two periods the autonomy goal was missing from colonial reason of state, for reasons set forth above. Hegemony and security became fused; external insecurity could be a product only of an inability to rule one's domains. Thus, hegemony was the key to security.

The hegemony imperative was given particular urgency, both by the competitive intensity of the scramble and by the specific innovation of the doctrine of effective occupation. This principle was adopted at the 1884–1885 Berlin Congress, summoned to make partition possible without triggering a European war. The concept was not entirely novel; it had been used since the sixteenth century by French, British and others to challenge the more exorbitant Spanish claims to Western hemisphere dominion. But the Berlin accord elevated this notion to new standing as international law of colonial conquest. "Effective occupation" required that, within a reasonable period of time, a colonizer had to validate his claim to an imperial title over African territory by establishing the rudimentary infrastructure of hegemonical institutions: military outposts, particularly around the periphery, and a modest network of administrative centers. The matter was urgent; boundaries were not necessarily definitive, and were in any case poorly defined on the ground. Rival predators had ample opportunity to take advantage of the slightest lethargy or procrastination in establishing effective occupation.

Military supremacy was indispensable to the achievement of hegemony. Few if any African communities would have accepted submission to European rule unless European military power was a part of the calculus of choice. Once imperial military dominance was established, a number of African groups found voluntary alliance with one or another European powers advantageous, either to protect against conquest by a more feared state (e.g. Sotho and Swazi acceptance of British rule as preferable to subjugation by the Boer republics) or to gain advantage over neighboring kingdoms (e.g. the Fanti confederacy in Ghana).

In most places the direct use of European armies for conquest was far too expensive. Algeria was an important object lesson; General Thomas

Bugeaud in pursuit of what Schumpeter termed "imperial atavism" ("the objectless disposition on the part of the state to unlimited frontier expansion") had required 100,000 troops to subdue Abd-el-Kader.[59] Altogether, the first four decades of the hegemonial drive cost 150,000 military casualties; Algerian deficits from 1830 to 1900, mainly military, were nearly five billion francs.[60] At the peak of the partition, only the Italians habitually employed large metropolitan armies in attempted conquest; the Boer War in South Africa, 1899–1902, and the Riff War in the mid-1920s in Morocco were the two main exceptions.

Indian experience in the mid-eighteenth century had taught both the British and the French that it was possible to assemble at a low cost large indigenous forces.[61] Organized into disciplined units under European officers, enjoying the superior firepower of European arsenals and the military doctrine of European armies, these units—augmented frequently by allied African forces or irregular bands—could defeat with small losses much more numerous resisting forces, above all those without access to firearms.

Rapidly changing military technology in the late nineteenth century added decisive firepower advantages to the organizational weapon of the African-manned colonial army. First-generation machine guns—the Gatling— were initially used in the Ashanti war in 1874. Much more effective was the single barrel, eleven rounds-per-second Maxim, deployed in Africa from 1889.[62] On occasion, African leaders with armed followers could make European conquest expensive (Samoury Touré), or on rare occasions defeat them (Ethiopians at Adwa in 1896, the Mahdists at Khartoum in 1885). But the military balance tilted heavily to the imperial side.

The capacity to inflict military defeats upon African rulers, however, was not enough. Effective occupation also required structures of control outward from the string of military and administrative outposts which dotted the communications routes and frontier zones. The potential cost of assuring such control through European agents was prohibitive. In some areas— French Equatorial Africa, the Belgian Congo, southern Nigeria, Rhodesia— the task was initially delegated to the private sector, employing the charter company formula which in various guises had been a primary vehicle for colonial expansion in the mercantile age of earlier centuries. These minimally capitalized groups had in mind high and swift returns on small stakes; the delegated state function of hegemony was a secondary consideration. Only the British South Africa Company succeeded as a state surrogate for three decades; the others quickly failed—and in the worst cases, in French Equatorial Africa and the Belgian Congo—degenerating into ruthless and sanguinary plundering expeditions.[63]

The solution found was the recruitment of a network of collaborating intermediaries. The British through long Indian experience had become accustomed to annexing indigenous structures to colonial state institutions, though the formula required extensive adaptation in Africa; the zamindar of Bengal land-settlement areas of north India was a delegate land-revenue collector. In Africa the intermediaries were political; around them, the administrative ideology of indirect rule, especially associated with Lugard, was developed in various forms, with particular success in areas such as Buganda or northern Nigeria, where strong structures and willing collaborators were found. Though the application of this ideology of mediated hegemony was uneven (not employed in Kenya or Southern Rhodesia, ambiguously used in southern Nigeria, largely unsuccessful in hinterland Sierra Leone), by the end of the epoch of construction of the African colonial state it was dominant British state doctrine and influential with the Belgians.[64]

The French concepts of the institutionalizing administrative hegemony emerged through a proconsular apostolic succession stretching from Marshall Bugeaud in Algeria; to Louis Faidherbe in Senegal, after service in Algeria; to Joseph Gallieni in Indochina and Madagascar, after service in Senegal; and to Marshall Hubert Lyautey in Morocco, after service in Indochina and Madagascar. The cartesian, Bonapartist, prefectoral, command doctrine of state which characterized France interpenetrated with more pragmatic concepts of empirical adaptation to local circumstance. On the one hand, a 1917 administrative circular of Joost Von Vollenhoven, Governor-General of Afrique Occidentale Française, stated unambiguously. ". . . there are not two authorities in a *cercle* [unit of local administration], French and indigenous authority; there is only one. Alone, the *cercle* commandant commands; alone he is responsible. The indigenous chief is only an instrument, an auxiliary."[65] Balancing this Bonapartist edict were such administrative slogans as the *politique des races* (adapting instrumentalities of rule to the nature of each group) and *tache d'huile* (integrated military, political and economic action to permit an oil-spot spread of influence and control), associated with Gallieni.[66] French theory of colonial state construction, in its final form, was summarized by Gallieni in 1899:

> It is the combined action of political and military which must bring as its result the pacification of the country and the primitive organization to bring to it initially. Political action and military action are the two principal agencies in the first period of an occupation or a conquest. If their combination succeeds, a second period opens at once: the period of organization, which has recourse to a third factor, economic action. As pacification becomes more thorough, cultivation is resumed, markets reopen, trade rebuilds. The role of the soldier becomes secondary; that of the administrator begins.[67]

The canton chiefs who were intermediaries in this venture were chosen with less concern for ancestral credentials and more priority to malleability.

In areas where Islam was solidly implanted, religious hierarchies were particularly important to at least neutralize. Indeed, in a number of notable instances the colonial state found ways to co-opt leaders of influential religious orders; the Mourides in Senegal were the most prominent example.[68] At the price of material advantages and cultural autonomy, many others were won over (successors to the Mahdiyya in Sudan, diverse marabouts in Morocco and Algeria). The Christianizing cultural project of the colonial state had to be set aside where Islamic structures were to mediate, with the colonizer assuming the ironical tacit role as protector of Islam.

Economic intermediaries were a requisite of the colonial state as well. These were readily available in coastal West Africa, where an Atlantic trading system, initially built on slaves, was long established.[69] In the inner West African savannah, well-established mercantile communities long engaged in long-distance trade also existed, although their activity was not oriented to supplying European mercantile houses.[70] On coastal East Africa, Zanzibari and Swahili planters filled the economic intermediary niche.[71] In many cases petty traders able to operate with low costs and small margins from Mediterranean commercial communities or the Indian subcontinent filled these interstices. Frequent friction occurred around the boundaries of this niche, between African and immigrant petty traders or between both and the large metropolitan houses such as United Africa Company or Compagnie Française d'Afrique Occidentale, which sought to monopolize the upper end of the export-import trade. All were needed in the construction of an economic order which could provide sustenance to the colonial state.[72]

Thus, militarily, politically and economically, the architects of the colonial state responded to the hegemony imperative by rapidly constructing an apparatus of domination. While this vast task could not be accomplished overnight, overall it went forward with remarkable speed—at a pace far more rapid than colonial state building in any other part of the world. By World War I the basic framework had been established. Some zones were not brought under full control until the 1920s (Kivu region of the Belgian Congo, portions of Angola, desert reaches of Libya and northern Chad, mountain zones of Morocco), but lines of communication were assured and boundaries were secured. The colonial hegemony had assumed its basic form.

As we have argued above, the legitimation imperative in this first stage had as its primary referent the European audience. In the parliaments and official circles, and in some segments of civil society, there was significant opposition to colonial conquest into the 1890s. Some feared squandering national resources and energies which should be directed to the defense of national interests on the European front. In France some argued that aggressive enforcement of French claims against Germany would become impossible if African and Indochinese adventures were pursued.[73] In Germany voices were raised to urge a priority for settlement and control of the Polish marches. The Belgian parliament adamantly refused to permit Belgian state responsibility for the Leopoldian venture, and until the monarch began to realize substantial profits from his personal empire in the first years of this century, it regarded his promise to bequeath his colony to his country as a poisoned gift.

To overcome this reticence, advocates of imperialism strenuously pointed to the flow of benefits that would ensue. The size of colonial domains was claimed to be a tangible asset in the unending and mechanistic calculations made in chanceries about the balance of power, along with other measures such as army size, capital warships, population and coal-iron-steel production. As Baumgart expressed it, "Comparing statistics in these was a common game among the great powers and served in an almost magical way to define their sense of security based on political-power potential or as a warning of the increasing strength of a neighbor."[74] Strategic requirements were an elastic, all-purpose argument, as was the claim that guaranteed access to markets for textile products required colonial control. For Italy, an outlet for surplus Italian populations which made them a national asset was invoked.[75] A field for mission endeavor, a pasture for surplus capital: all grist for the mill producing metropolitan legitimation for colonial conquest. The very nature of the debate made axiomatic the premise that African colonial states were created for the benefit of the metropolitan polity. The most careful student of the construction of the French colonial state (and supporter of its creation), Roberts, stated the settled view:

> The colony will be ruled from above and retained for the benefit accruing to the mother-country: incidentally, of course, the position of the native population will improve, by the very transformation of the conditions of material existence, but that is not an essential feature . . . the absolute subservience of the colony to the mother-country has been the very mortar giving cohesion to the whole French colonial structure.[76]

While in Africa, at bottom, the initial legitimation of the colonial state rested upon perceptions of European strength, ultimately underwritten by brute force, in Europe it was finally secured on the basis of one crucial, overriding principle: the colonial state had to be financially self-sufficient. This premise was written into the 1900 colonial reform law in France as its most basic provision. The 1908 Colonial Charter for the Belgian Congo had "separation of patrimonies" as its foundation. The British treasury always insisted on budgetary autonomy for each colonial territory and permitted only the most hopelessly impoverished (British Somaliland) to line up at its gates for tiny doles. Only Italy permitted continuing deficits on its colonial budgets. France generally covered military costs; the British and Belgians funded security outlays on local budgets.

This leads us to the revenue imperative as a determinant of colonial state construction. Hegemony had to be self-financing. The elemental challenge to statecraft was virtually to simultaneously meet the needs for a resource-consuming apparatus of domination and the generation of a revenue flow to pay for it. The newly subordinated African societies were called upon to finance their own conquest. The task was urgent and immediate.

It was also excruciatingly difficult—and for the African subjects, brutally painful. The cold fact which quickly confronted colonial state agents was the lack of an existing revenue source in many parts of the continent. Africa offered nothing comparable to the established land revenue of India, the long-standing bureaucratic machinery of a Vietnam to extract rice surpluses, the high-value export commodities of the Dutch East Indies, the sugar of the Caribbean slave plantation colonies, or the precious metals of Mexico and Peru.

Nonetheless, there were some exceptions. On coastal West Africa, trade in palm oil, textiles and some other commodities provided modest customs revenues—which explains how Britain could avoid capitation taxes in the early years in Gold Coast and southern Nigeria. Revenue issues were not central in South Africa, where particularly after diamond and gold discoveries an adequate economic base for state construction existed. Well-organized Islamic states of the West African interior, and northern Africa, have in the *zakat* and its derivatives a well-grounded fiscal ideology, religiously legitimated. In these areas the colonial state needed only to regulate its application and divert part of the flow to its own needs. The quick success of British colonial state construction in northern Nigeria is explained in good part by the immediate establishment of a secure revenue base without coercive intervention by the colonizer; the 1914 amalgamation was partly motivated by the desire to secure the parlous southern Nigerian finances by the guarantee of the buoyant northern fiscal flows.[77]

Aggravating the revenue crisis was the technological coincidence that imperial conquest coincided with a historical conjuncture when supply side reason ran rampant in railway promotion. The imaginations of many were captured by the impact of such epic lines as the Union Pacific (1872), the Canadian National (1885) and the Trans-Siberian (1891–1893). By virtue of the enthusiasm of the day, it sufficed to run iron tracks across any stretch of territory, to fructify impoverished lands and make deserts bloom. The mere existence of a railroad line, it was believed, would generate its own traffic for amortization of the capital costs. Thus were born such colossal schemes as the French trans-Saharan, and the Rhodes Cape-to-Cairo; the French parliament even voted funds in 1879 to begin the trans-Saharan, promptly used by local military commanders to finance additional unauthorized colonial conquests.

While these grandiose schemes never materialized, many lesser ones did. Supply side theories of railway fnance were not shared by private bankers and capital holders, who insisted that debts incurred to construct these lines be assumed or guaranteed by the colonial states. The result was that, in many instances, the fledgling colonial state was at once encumbered by what were, given their scale and circumstances, very onerous debts. These redoubled the urgency of generating a cash flow for the colony and also necessitated policies which could assure some traffic for the railroad lines, to minimize their operating losses.

For important parts of the continent, there was only one possible way to meet the revenue imperative: by organizing African labor. As one French administrator in the Ivory Coast put the matter in 1908: "Day by day, we come to understand better that the real treasure of which we must make use in our colonies, is neither natural riches, nor the open spaces, but the indigenous races . . . it is the population which makes the strength and the wealth of a country; the capital which we must develop is the man."[78]

The resource of African labor could be converted into the currency of state revenue in several ways. It could be taxed directly, through some form of capitation levy. It could be conscripted for labor service on European plantations or, in those few places where exploitable minerals were discovered early, into mines on whose output state rents could be collected. It could be coerced into production of such export crops as cotton, which could then be subjected to export taxation.

Thus, in its formative phases the colonial state acquired formidable responsibilities in the organization and direction of, as well as direct extraction from, African labor. It equipped itself with a legal arsenal of arbitrary regulations to carry out these responsibilities: diverse masters-and-servants ordinances, specified periods of obligatory labor service at state-defined tasks, plenary powers to local administrators to impose penalties for disobedience (the French *indigénat* code). Early administrative instructions left no doubt as to the priorities of the state; as one interpreter of the French Ecole Coloniale doctrines of the day put it:

> The European commandant is not posted in a region, is not paid to observe nature, to carry out ethnographic, botanical, geologic or linguistic studies. He has a mission of administration. This word translates into the obligation . . . to impose regulations, to limit individual liberties for the benefit of all, to collect taxes.[79]

A 1903 circular to AEF administrators was even more blunt:

> I will not conceal from you the fact that, in completing your efficiency report, I will base myself above all on the results you will have achieved in the collection of the head tax, which must be for each of you a constant preoccupation.[80]

The diverse measures imposed to satisfy state revenue needs triggered revolts in many areas, such as the Sierra Leone hut tax war in 1896 and the 1906 Maji-Maji uprising in Tanganyika, among others. These revolts in turn led to a tightening of the superstructure of hegemony. The colonial state could not back down in the face of a threat to its supremacy.

The first phase of colonial state construction closed with the settled conviction of its builders that their hegemony was secure for the indefinite future. Challenges to its legitimacy in the metropole had died down. Its proconsuls in the field were certain of the permanency of their role; not long before World War I, Lord Cromer, principal architect of British rule in Egypt, wrote:

> Egyptians are not a nation—they are a fortuitous agglomeration of a number of miscellaneous hybrid elements. . . . To suppose that the characters and intellects of even a small number of Egyptians can in a few years be trained to such an extent as to admit of their undertaking the sole direction of one of the most complicated political and administrative machines the world has

ever known, and of guiding such a machine along the path of even fairly good government, is a sheer absurdity.[81]

The daily operation of its machinery on the eve of World War I was well captured by a British administrator, Captain O.H. Stigand: "Ask any official what he is doing in his district, and he will reply that he is administering it. Ask different officials, 'what is administration?' and you will get divergent answers. The general idea will be that it is to hear cases and get revenue for the government."[82]

Phase II: Institutionalization

The second stage in the development of the African colonial state, during the interwar period, may be characterized as institutionalization. The basic foundations had been laid; the initial crises of hegemony and revenue had been overcome. Although Egypt acquired nominal sovereignty in 1922, its status was more akin to a reversion to a nineteenth-century informal empire than full independence; British influence was pervasive. Otherwise, aside from the white-ruled states of South Africa and Southern Rhodesia, a change of political status was not on the colonial agenda. The colonial state was digging itself in for the *longue durée*. On its roster of postwar objectives were such matters as perfection of its institutions, rationalization of its machinery and professionalization of its cadre of officials.[83] The most significant evolution came within its hegemonical framework and legitimating ideology; we will concentrate upon these aspects.

In this era the age of constant application of brute force was by and large over. The district officers, "kings of the bush," enjoyed an infrequently challenged ascendancy. In the words of an influential former servant of the French colonial administration who became its historian, Hubert Deschamps:

> To imagine a police state, founded on force, would be to be totally deceived. In my last district, which contained 100,000 inhabitants, dispersed in the bush, forty policemen, recruited in the same area, largely sufficed to ensure order and the observance of regulations. I always went about, from ten to fifteen days per month, without escort and unarmed, and everywhere I was well received, without servility and with dignity. . . . It is through all these "kings of the bush" . . . that the incoherent whole of the French possessions had been upheld and had been able to give the impression of a solid bloc, despite the absence of doctrine from Paris, despite its unkept promises and its horror of the future.[84]

A routinization of hegemony had thus occurred. The pattern of domination gained the tacit acceptance bred by familiarity and the absence of an apparent alternative. It was a time, as Berque expressed it for the Mahgreb, when "colonization dominated everything. Only a few bold spirits at that time defied it, only a few pioneers realized its fragility."[85]

The self-confident colonial services became much more professionalized. Belgium and France had colonial institutes for the training of their prospective civil servants. Britain had access to the cream of the Oxbridge crop, selected by the intuitional methods of Sir Ralph Furse at the Colonial Office. His targets were those energetic young men of aristocratic demeanor worthy of the colonial calling: ". . . the chance of dedicating himself to the service of his fellow men, and of responsibility at an early age on a scale which life at home could scarcely ever offer; the pride of belonging to a great service devoted to a mighty and beneficent task."[86]

The diverse assortment of military officers, adventure seekers and occasional psychopaths who mingled with the early generation of proconsuls was phased out in favor of an earnest cohort of professional functionaries schooled for their service.[87] Improved medical conditions, better communications and more attractive material circumstances made colonial careers inviting, which—particularly for the French and Belgians—they were not before 1914. Specialized technical services began to be added to the basic authority infrastructure.

The intermediary structure of rule at the chieftaincy level was rationalized. Theories of administration were elaborated in the colonial academies; Lugard published his *Administrative Memoranda* (1919) and his classic work *Dual Mandate in Tropical Africa* (1922), in which the ideology of indirect rule was given comprehensive statement. After exhaustive study the Belgians gave definitive cast to their local administrative system in the decree of December 5, 1933. The rationalizing mood is well conveyed in the accompanying legal note explicating the decree, which provided for approximately 1000 indigenous circumscriptions of roughly uniform scale: "While respecting traditional administration, the legislator wanted to establish a single administrative system: he made of the chieftaincy (or sector) the lowest echelon of the administrative organization, and the chief a functionary integrated into the system without prejudice to his traditional role."[88]

This level of administration was also subjected to the first steps toward professionalization. Literate skills and competence began to be factors in nomination, as well as ancestry, customary credentials and pliability to colonial authority. This was particularly evident in Uganda, where chieftaincy was on its way to becoming a civil service.[89]

There were also significant shifts in the nature of colonial state ideology during these years. There was no longer a need to justify preservation of colonial domains at home; they were by now safely covered by the inherent proprietary impulses of the state to preserve its territorial heritage. Now that the existence of an African empire was taken for granted, new doctrinal themes emerged concerning its purposes. Contributing to the context for these novel ingredients in colonial state ideology was a heightened awareness of the potential value of these territories. France in particular benefited militarily from its empire; 250,000 of its overseas subjects (mostly African) died under the French flag in World War I and some one million served in the armed forces. In Britain the overseas territories were viewed as "the undeveloped colonial estates," whose economic exploitation was a trump card for the empire. In the Belgian case the basic infrastructure of capital installations and supportive communication routes was in place for the swift expansion of mineral output.

The concept of "development," from these antecedents, first became a consciously articulated part of state ideology. In its French version, labelled *mise en valeur*, the doctrine received resonant statement from Albert Sarraut, colonial minister from 1920 to 1924 and a former governor-general of Indochina. Colonial development was represented as an obligation to the world at large. "No one state had a right to allow its fertile soils to lie fallow indefinitely, and a world in need of raw materials placed certain obligations on the colonial powers."[90] The 1929 British Colonial Development and Welfare Act, as a symbolic statement of the premise that development was a major aim of the colonial state, was an ideological landmark. Its metaphorical import was not matched by its practical impact, owing to the anemic funding levels of one million pounds yearly. But the idea was abroad.

Notions of "good government" likewise became more explicitly woven into the legitimating fabric of colonial state doctrine. Rational, prudent management of the colonial estates, by a professional cadre of administrators, applying increasingly scientific methods to their development, impartial adjudication of conflicts: these were the themes of self-composed encomium to colonial rule. Their credibility as a legitimating ideology was doubtlessly enhanced by the conviction they carried for the official classes themselves.[91]

A corollary theme was "trusteeship" as a vindication of hegemony. The concept intruded into international discourse in the peace treaty debates, where it was utilized as a theoretical bulwark for the mandate system. The League Covenant spoke of the "sacred trust of civilization" held by mandatory states to supply governance services for "peoples not yet able to stand by themselves under the strenuous conditions of the modern world." Perhaps the most important statement of the doctrine appeared in the 1923 Devonshire White Paper concerning Kenya, precipitated by the claims to dominance of the immigrant communities:

> Primarily Kenya is an African territory, and His Majesty's Government think it necessary definitely to record their considered opinion that the interests of the African Natives must be paramount, and that if and when those interests and the interests of the immigrant races should conflict, the former should prevail. . . . In the administration of Kenya His Majesty's Government regard themselves as exercising a trust in behalf of the African population, and they are unable to delegate or share this trust, the object of which may be defined as the protection and advancement of the Native races.[92]

This reformulated doctrine of state was still primarily directed toward the metropolitan and external audience, but no longer exclusively so. The sense of new stirrings in civil society began to percolate into the official consciousness. In Egypt the shock of the 1919 Cairo riots brought to an early end the brief period of incorporation into an empire. The first nationalist agitation in Tunisia, the 1925 uprisings in Syria, the novel mass actions in India: so many distant warning signals. There began to emerge out of colonial encounter new social categories not easily absorbed into the intermediary structures of subordination, whose idiom of proto-nationalism was jarring, even if summarily dismissed. Civil society was also knitting itself (as well as dividing itself) in new forms, as once-dispersed communities, as Low puts it, found that:

> for social, cultural, political and even economic purposes, they increasingly aggregated with their kith and kin, and with those who lived within their neighborhoods who were ready to associate with them . . . a heightened sense of community amongst peoples who previously had not often emphasized the links they possessed with those who shared their own language, and their cultural and social practices.[93]

Vague forebodings entered the official mind; in the Mahgreb retired administrators wrote novels about insurrection.[94] A distinguished Belgian colonial magistrate, Paul Salkin, penned a gloomy fantasy forecasting a century hence that the colonial edifice would crumble before the assaults of fanatical Garveyite mobs.[95] Sarraut in 1923 gave voice to these inchoate fears: "The profound shudders that are running, in swelling, unseemly waves through the immense flood of the colored races, marking the new awakening of aspirations . . . may again bring together the old fanaticisms, the nationalisms, or the mysticisms against the enlightenment that has come from the Occident."[96]

In the implementation of its new doctrines of development, good government and trusteeship, the action of the colonial state remained relatively circumscribed. Its revenue flow sufficed to finance its infrastructure of hegemony, but there was little left over for large-scale action as a welfare dispenser—and indeed welfare-state doctrine was not yet ascendant in the metropolitan states. The Gold Coast under the energetic stewardship of Sir Gordon Guggisberg was a partial exception—mainly because export taxation of cocoa provided a substantially higher revenue base than was available elsewhere. Secondary schooling for Africans was very scarce; in all of the Sub-Saharan French-ruled territories there were only four *lycées* (two in Senegal, two in Madagascar, with a majority of European pupils). A large part of the modest, mainly primary school, infrastructure owed its existence to missionary societies.

Some significant efforts did begin in the health field, again with shared responsibilities with missions and in some areas corporations. Here the revenue imperative supplied part of the energizing force. African labor was the linchpin of the system, and the belief grew that it was not only scarce but dwindling. France, according to Roberts, came to realize that "West Africa was a country without negroes," yet also became aware that labor "would to no small degree determine the extent and direction of development."[97] Worse yet, depopulation threatened, as epidemics of sleeping sickness, measles, smallpox and other maladies took a heavy toll. There was a widespread conviction among Belgians in the 1920s that the Belgian Congo's population had fallen by half since the days of Stanley's exploration. There might be no Africans left to build railways, mine copper, grow cotton—and pay taxes. Further, the colonial state as trustee recognized its own responsibility for the spread of disease; as Governor-General Gabriel Angoulvant wrote in 1917, sleeping sickness "had followed a path parallel to our colonization . . . we have been the principal agents of propagation. . . . These facts create a special obligation toward the affected population."[98]

Phase III: Decolonization

World War II was a watershed for the African colonial state. The international environment which enveloped it had decisively altered; no longer was it secure against external challenge. New relationships had to be constituted with its subjugated civil society, whose voice of protest now resonated in a receptive global arena. Older doctrines of trusteeship were now interpreted in ways which made much more insistent demands upon the colonizers.

The imperial mind did not at once consider its vocation of domination to be at an end. A ranking Colonial Office official wrote in 1942 that "we all know in our hearts that most Colonies, especially in Africa, will probably not be fit for complete independence for centuries."[99] The empire was to be recast as a partnership, but certainly not abandoned. The greatest of the Belgian proconsuls, Pierre Ryckmans, solemnly declared at the end of the war that "the days of colonialism are over," but he had in mind some new form of permanent imperial relationship. The Brazzaville 1944 conference pledged colonial reform, but rejected self-government. And the Portuguese, marching throughout this period to a different drummer, were busy constructing *Estado Novo* ideology of a far-flung, global lusotropical state.

Wartime necessities had given rise to a systematic mobilization of colonial resources, which had several consequences. Colonial policy came to be seen as a whole in a more compelling way; particularly in the British case, territorial governors from 1940 on had much less latitude to pursue territorially specific policies. Increasingly, policies of imperial reform were drafted for general application. The great postwar debate over the Fourth Republic constitution, and from 1946 on the continuous colonial war in Indochina, then Algeria, made overseas policy a central concern of the metropolitan state. Important new regulatory responsibilities were assumed by the colonial state over export commodities; much of this machinery, in particular the agricultural marketing boards, then proved permanent.

Decolonization forced itself onto the official agenda little by little and, retrospectively, came to dominate the entire period. The 1948 Gold Coast disturbances were the first jolt to the British, compelling an adjustment of timetable assumptions. But it was not until 1959 that the British official classes became persuaded that all dependent territories should move toward self-rule as expeditiously as possible. In the French case the middle 1950s was the pivotal period, at which time a critical shift in the dominant view of colonial control occurred, leading to Tunisian and Moroccan independence in 1956 and the Loi-Cadre that same year which provided for African rule in the Sub-Saharan territories. Six years of bitter war in Algeria remained before the full implications of altered imperial perspectives worked themselves out. And although the Belgians did not accept the imminence of independence until 1959, from 1952 there was recognition that some form of autonomous institutions would have to be created with African participation.

The premise of decolonization, with its gradually unfolding sense of urgency, totally altered the problematic of hegemony. The colonial state had to be made self-standing. This implied above all the preparation of personnel able to occupy its core structures; as Hailey puts it in his wartime blueprint of postwar colonial development, the key task was "to identify potential political and administrative elites who could gradually be trained to assume the enlarged responsibilities of the colonial state."[100] Hegemony required constitutionalization; organic institutional links with civil society were needed, which invested subjects with citizenship. Out of these institutions would arise the political class, whose members would succeed to power after a tutelary period, to exercise rule in collaboration with their bureaucratic colleagues, who were schooled in the arts of administration.

An intriguing paradox in the nature of this process deserves note. The model of the constitutional state utilized as the exemplary vision of the ideal polity to be replicated in the structures of decolonization was the metropolitan state. For the colonial official class, it was the only version of the political good which they knew. For the nationalists, the metropolitan constitutional order was an equally inevitable model; they had long used the contradiction between its theory and colonial practice as a polemical weapon, all the more effective because the colonial official class could not disavow the normative validity of metropolitan standards. Democracy, for nationalist forces in the era of decolonization, was a theory of challenge to the colonial order, a vehicle to contest its hegemony and accelerate its departure. Both sides, accordingly, accepted the basic framework of the metropolitan state as an authoritative blueprint for the postcolonial state.

The model was entirely at odds with the autocratic tradition of the colonial era. Profoundly embedded in the colonial state was a command relationship with civil society, reflected in its laws, its routines, its mentalities, even its imagery. The gulf between these two types of state was wider than was apparent at the time.

Other far-reaching and difficult adjustments were required in the nature of hegemony. The metamorphosis of subject into citizen had many implications in the individual interactions of state and society. At the collective level it had always been an article of faith to the official mind that there was no civil society in the organic sense; a major justification for alien rule was the impossibility of generating a general will from the disparate populations joined in subjugation. Absent the Rousseauvian Legislator, the Lugardian Trustee is indispensable. These engrained convictions now had to be set aside, to accept the nationalist theses that a nation was historically ordained and immediately forthcoming.

In the ambiguous hegemony of the power-transfer period, the colonial state and its metropolitan overlayer assumed a new pedagogical role. For the first time, priority was accorded to training high-level personnel, through not only formal degree programs but also innumerable internships and short courses. At all levels in the hierarchy a tutelary, instructional role devolved upon the official class, as the array of new institutions through which civil society was to find expression were nurtured—local governments, councils, cooperatives, unions—all bodies with little or no place in the earlier colonial order.

Permeating the reason of the metropolitan state throughout this period was the implicit assumption of continuing proprietary rights. There was an amazingly resilient myth, in the face of its empirical invalidity, that great sacrifices of blood and treasure had been made; in fact, as we have argued, the colonial state was carefully crafted to insulate the metropole precisely against such risks.[101] But the prescription of long-standing political monopoly was held to confer, by natural law, special standing to the colonizer. With the exception of decolonization by armed revolution (Algeria, Zimbabwe, the Portuguese territories), power transfer was informed by the presumption of continuing privileged relationships. Only in the French case were these comforting expectations borne out by postcolonial fact, but they played an important part in all the managed decolonizations.

These proprietary assumptions affected the emergent concerns with security. New enemies appeared on the horizon, which colonial security agencies began to track. Intrusion of foreign influences which might challenge the claims of the colonizer to preeminent postcolonial ties were unwelcome, above all those that spoke the language of anti-imperialism (the Soviet Union, China, Nasser's Egypt). Although as decolonization accelerated the European official classes found their power crumbling, they nonetheless retained significant room to maneuver and could on occasion outwit or isolate segments of the nationalist movement found particularly offensive (forces favoring unification with Egypt in Sudan, Ignatius Musazi in Uganda, I.T. Wallace-Johnson in Sierra Leone). For example, in Cameroon the French successfully excluded their most militant tormentors, the *Union des Populations Camerounaises* (UPC); as Joseph noted, ". . . the politicians in Cameroon who inherited power from the French . . . were the very ones who had played no part whatsoever in the nationalist struggle—whether as radicals or as moderates."[102]

As step by step an African political class gained access to and influence over the terminal colonial state machinery, autonomy began to enter the calculus of reason of state. African leaders desired to enhance the territorial personality of their own state and to sharpen its differentiation with contiguous territories under common colonial rule. The British projects for promoting larger units (except for Sudan and Egypt, whose separation was assiduously fostered) were suspected of being schemes for preserving settler interests. In the French administrative federations of West and Equatorial Africa the wealthier units (Ivory Coast and Gabon) were determined to prevent the redistribution of their resources to finance the impoverished, and the outlying territories suspected designs of the old federation centers to preserve their roles as subimperial centers.

More discreetly nurtured were expectations of diversifying their external linkages to avoid a merely satellite standing in the world arena. The optimistic mood of the time fostered exaggerated expectations about the benefits likely to flow from new partners. But it was in any case impolitic at the moment of seeking acceleration in the timetable of power transfer to speak of other aspirations than full membership in the Commonwealth or the French community.

Doctrines of legitimation had to be extensively revised. The claim to rule was to be grounded in representativity, not conquest. Thus, political parties had to mobilize an electoral clientele and authenticate their credentials in electoral contests subject to the supervision of the withdrawing power. The administration was not above employing its dwindling resources in the support of movements deemed least offensive to colonial interests, most flagrantly and frequently the French.

Two legitimating themes originating in the institutionalization phase achieved central importance and redefined the character of the terminal colonial state in crucial ways: development and welfare. On these points there was a convergence of interest on the part of the colonial official class and nationalist forces. For the colonial state, on the defensive both internationally and within the territory, the ability to bring rapid and tangible improvement to the well-being of its subjects became a crucial claim. In its dying gasp the colonial order in Algeria advanced the argument that what was truly significant was the welfare of each individual Algerian, and not the collective status of civil society as united by nationalism. For the nationalists, mobilization of a mass clientele depended absolutely upon the promise of a more abundant life.

By World War II the colonial state had gradually accumulated the institutional capacity to manage this process. Although in the institutionalization stage it had expanded very little, the professionalization and rationalization had gradually built the reservoir of competency necessary to contemplate such schemes. To this skeletal structure was added, from the early postwar years, a rapid enlargement of its technical and specialized services, which, as Hargreaves suggests, ". . . produced a 'second colonial occupation' in the form of a large-scale infusion of technical experts, whose activities not only increased the 'intensity' of colonial government, but seemed to imply its continuance in some form until the new policies had an opportunity to mature."[103]

The construction of a developmental, welfare state progressed with remarkable vigor. In the Belgian Congo a rudimentary prewar educational system had become by 1959 a vast network serving 70 percent of the primary school age children. Whereas in the 1920s it could be said that a medical service for Africans did not exist, by the late 1950s the Belgians could justifiably claim that their health service was "without doubt the best in the whole tropical world."[104]

The developmentalist, welfare terminal colonial state expanded its consumption in tandem with its services. In the Belgian Congo outlays increased eleven-fold between 1939 and 1950, and tripled in the final colonial decade. In the final decade of British rule in Gold Coast, state expenditures multiplied by ten; in the preceding 35 years, they had merely doubled.[105] These patterns were general.

The escalation of state consumption was facilitated by several exceptionally favorable factors on the revenue side. The long postwar commodity boom for African exports brought huge windfalls in export taxes. The major colonial powers, for the first time, were willing to make large-scale developmental public investments in their African domains, through the Colonial Development and Welfare Act and its analogues. High prices stimulated a rapid increase in planting for such crops as coffee and cocoa. Thus, the colonial state had a revenue base to sustain its formidable pace of expansion through the 1950s. The marketing board monopolies which had been created in many territories succeeded in accumulating large surpluses by holding producer prices well below world levels in the early postwar years.

In meeting its revenue imperative during these years of prosperity, there were some dangerous trends which were to return to haunt postcolonial regimes, although they were little noted at the time. An excessive share of the fiscal burden of state expansion was placed upon the rural population, through the various mechanisms of export taxation, pricing policies and other imposts. Calculations made in Uganda in the 1950s show that the effective rate of taxation of the peasant household then was well over 50 percent, while far lower fiscal levies applied to the wealthier strata in the urban sector, immigrant or African.[106]

The Colonial State Legacy and the Current Crisis

The above patterns, however, were much less apparent at the moment of power transfer than the seeming success of the colonial state, in most instances, in organizing its own metamorphosis. The extraordinary prosperity of the 1950s contributed heavily to the mood of optimism and good feeling, excepting the revolutionary liberation war situations. The metropolitan states looked forward to fruitful continuing partnerships with their erstwhile appendages and turned over the keys to the kingdom in a veritable orgy of self-celebration.

The institutional synthesis of the terminal colonial state, however, proved exceedingly short-lived; only in a tiny handful of states (Botswana, Mauritius) did it survive very long. The fragile decolonization innovations of a constitutionalized state-civil society relationship, mediated by open political competition, served as a legitimating myth for the power transfer process itself, but soon ran afoul of the autocratic and hegemonical impulses which were the more enduring legacy of the colonial state.

Two trends which became apparent almost at once after independence made evident the ephemeral nature of the graft of cuttings of parliamentary democracy upon the robust trunk of colonial autocracy. First, the more radical, mobilizational parties which had secured a dominant electoral position under terminal colonial rules (Convention People's Party in Ghana and Parti Démocratique du Guinée in Guinea, among others) became intransigent political monopolies. Those that were merely preponderant (e.g. the Union Camerounaise, Kenya African National Union) established exclusive oligarchies. Secondly, the military coup appeared as the institutionalized mechanism for succession, with precursors in Egypt in 1952 and Sudan in 1958, then in 1965–1966 a drumfire of armed interventions. Military regimes themselves, which often aspired to more than a caretaker role, created from the summit regime single parties to legitimate a permanent claim to rule.

In these developments one may perceive the interaction of hegemony and legitimation imperatives in postcolonial state construction. New rulers quickly became aware of the insecurity of their hold on power, while at the same time becoming persuaded that the implementation of their programs necessitated resumed ascendancy of the state over civil society—a dominance often shaken by the very effectiveness of the agitational campaigns of political parties as nationalist contestants of alien rule. But in reasserting the hegemony of the state, they could not fall back upon the formulas which had served so well as colonial ideology: trusteeship, good government. They were thus driven to weave together radical and populist political language and exclusionary political institutions. The single party, the argument ran, incarnated the popular will of the new nation. For this reason the party was entitled to unencumbered exercise, through its leadership, of national sovereignty. Thus, the new states were not simply bureaucratic autocracies, alien to boot, like their colonial predecessors. They were political monopolies legitimated by frequently radical nationalist ideology, ritually consecrated by periodic electoral ceremonies. There were some interesting and important experiments, pioneered by Tanzania in 1965 and widely copied since, in permitting an element of competition in the selection of parliamentarians to carry the party banner. But this *abertura* did not alter the basic fact of monopoly.

Nor was this formula of fusion of the bureaucratic core and a single party overlayer sufficient. In pursuit of hegemony there was a powerful tendency toward personalization of rule and patrimonialization of the state. Formal hierarchy, bureaucratic regulation and abstract administrative norms, which generally sufficed for the colonial state, were not alone adequate after independence. The inner core of state personnel—key political operatives, top elements in the security forces, ranking technocratic state servants—needed more incentives to perform zealously and pledge personal fidelity than could be supplied by arid jurisprudence or the public vocabulary of nationalism. Many more personal incentives and sanctions for the ruling class were required.

Thus, the award of high office became linked to personal service to the ruler. Public resources at the command of the ruler became a reservoir of benefits and prebends to assure fidelity. Dismissal from office, disgrace and, not infrequently, prosecution for malfeasance were the sanctions. Holders of high office, individually, became clients of the ruler; collectively, they were a service class.

Viewed as a system, patrimonialism is well defined as personal rule by Jackson and Rosberg: ". . . a system of relations linking rulers not with the 'public' or even with the ruled (at least not directly), but the patrons, associates, clients, supporters, and rivals, who constitute the 'system.' If personal rulers are restrained, it is by the limits of their personal authority and rivals, who constitute the 'system.' "[107] However, the system as a whole must be seen as not simply patrimonialism, but rather as an interpenetration of the inherited patterns of colonial autocracy, the nationalist political monopoly and personalized patrimonial rule.

Autonomy and security have become vital preoccupations for the post-colonial state, and the difficulties of meeting these imperatives have become more apparent over time. Even before dependency theory appeared to provide a paradigm for the weakness of most African states in the global economic arena, African states had become acutely aware of the limitations of their bargaining power in the Western-centered world trading system. Most of the states formerly under French rule simply accepted their subordinate economic role, opting for whatever advantages could be gained from membership in the franc zone and participation in an informal but nonetheless efficient French-operated security system.[108] Others struggled to sever themselves from a neocolonial subordination deemed intolerable (Nkrumah's Ghana, Touré's Guinea, Mozambique), but without signal success. As the crisis has deepened in many states, the autonomy imperative has receded into a short-term recognition of its impossibility.

The security imperative has posed agonizing choices. During colonial times, after the hegemony of the colonial state was assured, we have argued that security concerns became secondary and were met at a very low cost. The incorporation of Africa into the world system of sovereign states and the incidence upon it of global patterns of power balances and great power rivalries have introduced new elements of threat into the continent. Several crisis areas within Africa have emerged, spawning regional arms races and conflictual interstate relations (the Horn, the Middle East spillover zone, Western Sahara, Chad, southern Africa).[109] The impact of the international arena, along with access to the external supply which it offers, has also demonstrated that liberation movements resisting annexations of the power-transfer period (Eritrea, Western Sahara) and internal dissident movements (Angola, Zaire, Mozambique, southern Sudan) can sustain themselves virtually indefinitely. Colonial constabularies were only infantry battalions; postcolonial armies have not only (in most cases) expanded considerably, but have also moved upstream in the sophistication (and thus cost) of their equipment. With some exceptions (especially the set of states that, in practice, accepts security services from France), sharp increases in security outlays have been a significant factor in state overconsumption.

Beyond nationalism and single-party systems, the legitimation imperative has been met with an intensification of the terminal colonial claims to development and welfare, in a number of instances placed within a new ideological context of socialism, scientific or populist. Nationalist campaigns for political office invariably claimed that colonial management of development was too slow, cautious and tilted toward imperial interests. The first wave of development plans in the 1960s promised in confident tone rates of development exceeding the record pace of the 1950s, economic transformation through import substitution industrialization, and rapid extension of amenities throughout the countryside. These documents, icons of state ideology, carried at the time the benediction of most of the new breed of development economists, irrespective of their ideological persuasion.[110]

The provision of such basic amenities as schools, clinics, wells and roads was fundamental to the claim to legitimation. Not only were they the central plank of populist nationalism during the final colonial era, but there was in place a formidable momentum of expansion from the terminal colonial state, which could hardly be arrested despite the spiraling recurrent costs. As Ayoade points out in this volume, the profound paternalism of the colonial state imprinted on the popular mind the expectation that these services were an entitlement; yet at the same time the state was perceived as a hostile, alien intrusion.[111] Preservation of amenity expansion was also fundamental to the exclusionary mode of exercise of hegemony by the state class staffing the institutions of the postcolonial state; as Tanzanian economist Ndulu well expresses the matter, "although the bulk of the population is politically immobilized, their power is implicitly acknowledged and the regimes cater clientelistically to some of their demands (through amenity provision) while assuring that these pressures do not reach levels requiring severe structural reforms."[112]

Several factors propelled the implementation of legitimating ideology in a very statist direction. The hegemonical habits of the state legacy were an important element; paternalistic, tutelary, pedagogical dispositions by long usage were innate habits of government. In the well-chosen words of Olorunsola, "The procedures, structures, as well as the skills of civil servants trained during the colonial period were designed for custodial and punitive tasks."[113] Embedded in this disposition is a habitual, reflexive thrust by state agents toward control, regulation and sanction, however ineffectual in practice. Political doctrines also played some role; in the roughly half of African states committed to some vision of socialism, ideology prescribed state control of the commanding heights of the economy and urged state enterprise as a dike against the seepage of capitalism and the dangerous class structures it would generate. The ramifying state itself became the prime instrument of class formation, fostering the ascendancy of a political-administration class whose own interests were tied to state expansion.

By the 1980s a downward spiral of state deflation had set in. The fabric of hegemony was unraveling, as an increasingly sullen rural sector found growing opportunities for exit. Parallel economies silently expanded and, in cases such as Uganda and Ghana, appeared on the verge of swallowing up the public realm. Inflation became more difficult to contain, and a number of currencies lost their international value. The patrimonial and personalist mode of decision making exposed states to heavy risks on major development projects. The five imperatives of state reason joined hands and enclosed regimes in an ever-shrinking circle of constraint. The postcolonial state was at bay.

How can these trends be reversed? The question is asked, in anguished tones, up and down the continent. "No condition is permanent," a West African proverb tells us. Doubtless there is wisdom as well as solace in this aphorism, and possibly unseen forces of resurrection are at work. Part of the answer probably lies in a reconceptualization of the state. The nature of state-civil society linkages is ripe for reconsideration. The hegemonic impulses which we have suggested flow from the logic of the first construction of the colonial state seem impossible to sustain. Possibly out of the mood of anxiety and foreboding will emerge a formula for the decolonization of the state.

Notes

The initial draft of this essay was composed while the author was resident at the Woodrow Wilson International Center for Scholars. The support of the Wilson Center and the University of Wisconsin–Madison Graduate School Research Committee is gratefully acknowledged.

1. *Le Monde*, March 10, 1984.

2. Sayre P. Schatz, "The Inert Economy of Nigeria: From Nurture-Capitalism to Pirate Capitalism," *Journal of Modern African Studies*, 22, 1 (March 1984).

3. Sara Berry, *Fathers Work for Their Sons* (Berkeley: University of California Press, 1985).

4. *Le Monde*, July 28, 1981.

5. Naomi Chazan, *An Anatomy of Ghanaian Politics: Managing Political Recession, 1969–1982* (Boulder: Westview, 1982), pp. 334–345.

6. International Bank for Reconstruction and Development, *World Development Report 1983* (Washington, D.C., 1983), p. 2.

7. Goran Hyden, *Beyond Ujamaa in Tanzania* (Berkeley: University of California Press, 1980).

8. Vwakyanakazi Mukohya, "African Traders in Butembo, Eastern Zaire (1960–1980); A Case Study in a Cultural Context of Central Africa" (Ph.D. diss., University of Wisconsin-Madison, 1982); Nelson Kasfir, "State, Magendo, and Class Formation in Uganda," *Journal of Commonwealth and Comparative Studies*, 21, 4 (November 1983).

9. Jean-Francois Bayart, "L'hommage à la reine: les modes d'action politique en situations autoritaires" (Workshop on The Entry of Socially Subordinate Groups into the Political Arena, University of Salzburg, April 1984).

10. Alex Radian, *Resource Mobilization in Poor Countries: Implementing Tax Policies* (New Brunswick, N.J.: Transaction Books, 1980), pp. 5–11.

11. Crawford Young, "Zaire: The Unending Crisis," *Foreign Affairs*, 57, 1 (Fall 1978): 169–185.

12. David B. Abernethy, "Bureaucratic Growth and Economic Decline in Sub-Saharan Africa" (Paper presented at Annual Meetings, African Studies Association, Boston, December 1983).

13. Hugues Bertrand, Le Congo (Paris: Francois Maspero, 1975), pp. 188, 256.

14. Schatz, "The Inert Economy of Nigeria," p. 19; Pauline H. Baker, The Economics of Nigerian Federalism (Washington, D.C.: Battelle Memorial Institute, 1984); Richard A. Joseph, "Affluence and Underdevelopment: The Nigerian Experience," Journal of Modern African Studies, 16, 2 (1978): 221–240.

15. World Development Report 1983, p. 56.

16. Ruth Leger Sivard, World Military and Social Expenditures 1982 (Leesburg, Va.: World Priorities, 1982), p. 26.

17. Robert C. West, "National Security Provision in African Countries: Military Expenditures in the 1970s," unpublished paper, 1984.

18. John R. Nellis, "Socialist Management in Algeria," Journal of Modern African Studies, 20, 4 (December 1977): 534.

19. Schatz, "The Inert Economy of Nigeria," p. 1.

20. Frank Ellis, "Agriculture Price Policy in Tanzania," World Development, 10, 4 (1982): 263–283.

21. Quoted in Crawford Young, Ideology and Development in Africa (New Haven: Yale University Press, 1984), p. 6. See also Robert S. Browne and Robert J. Cummings, The Lagos Plan of Action vs. The Berg Report (Lawrenceville, Va.: Brunswock Publishing, 1984).

22. Quoted in Carl K. Eicher, "West Africa's Agrarian Crisis" (Paper presented at Fifth Bi-Annual Conference, West African Association of Agricultural Economists, Abidjan, Ivory Coast, December 1983).

23. Many would go on to assert a systematic deterioration in the terms of trade for Africa. The 1981 Berg Report for the World Bank offers refutation of the validity of this more general theory; International Bank for Reconstruction and Development, Accelerated Development in Sub-Saharan Africa (Washington, D.C., 1981), pp. 17–23.

24. Charles Tilly, ed., The Formation of National States in Western Europe (Princeton: Princeton University Press, 1973); Gianfranco Poggi, The Development of the Modern State (Stanford: Stanford University Press, 1978); Hugh Seton-Watson, Nations and States (Boulder: Westview, 1977); Perry Anderson, The Lineages of the Absolute State (London: New Left Books, 1974); J.H. Shennan, The Origins of the Modern European State 1450–1725 (London: Hutchinson University Library, 1974).

25. Clifford Geertz, Negara: The The Theatre State in Nineteenth-Century Bali (Princeton: Princeton University Press, 1980), p. 121.

26. We find especially useful Heinz Lubasz, ed., The Development of the Modern State (New York: Macmillan, 1964); Theda Skocpol, States and Social Revolutions (Cambridge: Cambridge University Press, 1979); Kenneth H.F. Dyson, The State Tradition in Western Europe (New York: Oxford University Press, 1980); Eric A. Nordlinger, On the Autonomy of the Democratic State (Cambridge, Mass.: Harvard University Press, 1981); "The State," Daedalus, 108, 4 (Fall 1979); Alexandre Passerin d'Entreves, The Notion of the State (Oxford: Clarendon Press, 1967); Robert Fossaert, Les états (Paris: Editions du Seuil, 1981); Anthony Giddens, A Contemporary Critique of Historical Materialism: Power, Property and the State (Berkeley: University of California Press, 1981); Henri Lefebvre, De l'état (Paris: Union Générale des Editions, 1976); Nico Poulantzas, State, Power, Socialism (London: New Left Books, 1978); Ralph Miliband, The State in Capitalist Society (London: Camelot Press, 1969); Bob

Jessop, The Capitalist State: Marxist Theories and Methods (New York: New York University Press, 1982).

27. The history of this crucial doctrine is traced by F.H. Hinsley, Sovereignty (London: C.A. Watts, 1966); Bertrand de Jouvenal, Sovereignty: An Industry into the Political Good (Cambridge: Cambridge University Press, 1957).

28. Lefebvre, De l'état, pp. 11–43. Classic statements include Hans Kohn, "Nationalism," International Encyclopedia of the Social Sciences (New York: Macmillan Company, 1968), Vol. 11, pp. 63–70; Rupert Emerson, From Empire to Nation (Cambridge, Mass.: Harvard University Press, 1960).

29. Michael Howard, "War and the Nation-State," Daedalus, 108, 4 (Fall 1979): 101–110; Hedley Bull, The Anarchical Society (New York: Columbia University Press, 1977).

30. Cited in Dyson, The State Tradition, p. 108.

31. Donald Rothchild, in a lucid contribution, views the state as at once "a set of organizing principles used as a general guide to public action . . . and a group of public institutions . . . that allocate values authoritatively. . . ." "Social Incoherence and the Mediatory Role of the State," in Bruce E. Arlinghaus, ed., African Security Issues: Sovereignty, Stability, and Solidarity (Boulder: Westview, 1984), p. 100.

32. Cited in Lefebvre, De l'état, p. 34.

33. Harold D. Lassell, The Signature of Power (New Brunswick, N.J.: Transaction Books, 1979).

34. Geertz, Negara, p. 13.

35. Giddens, A Critique of Historical Materialism, pp. 49–68.

36. Max Weber, "Politics as a Vocation," reprinted in H.C. Gerth and C. Wright Mills, eds., From Max Weber (New York: Oxford University Press, 1958), p. 82.

37. See the seminal study of Robert H. Bates, Markets and States: Tropical Africa (Berkeley: University of California Press, 1981).

38. For fascinating details on the inhibitions these records reported and their skillful exportation by some of the Swazi chiefs see Lord Hailey, Native Administration in the British African Territories, Vol. 5 (London: His Majesty's Stationery Office, 1953).

39. Henry S. Wilson, The Imperial Experience in Sub-saharan Africa since 1870 (Minneapolis: University of Minnesota Press, 1977), p. 84.

40. Quoted in ibid., p. 94.

41. D. Bruce Marshall, The French Colonial Myth and Constitution-Making in the Fourth Republic (New Haven: Yale University Press, 1973), 39.

42. On French state colonial ideology see also Raymond Betts, Tricouleur: The French Overseas Empire (London: Gordon & Cremonesi, 1978); Raoul Girardet, L'idée coloniale en France de 1871 à 1962 (Paris: La Table Ronde, 1972).

43. Betts, Tricouleur, 136.

44. Cecil J.B. Hurst et al., Great Britain and the Dominions (Chicago: University of Chicago Press, 1928). See also Klaus E. Knorr, British Colonial Theories 1570–1850 (Toronto: University of Toronto Press, 1944).

45. Jeremy White, Central Administration in Nigeria, 1914–1948 (Dublin: Irish University Press, 1981).

46. Stephen H. Roberts, The History of French Colonial Policy 1870–1925 (London: P.S. King, 1929).

47. Tom Garvin, The Evolution of Irish National Politics (Dublin: Gill and Macmillan, 1981) shows the problems in sustaining state controls through the established legal machinery of the British state in conditions of deepening hostility of much of the population.

48. Martin Wight, *Systems of States* (Leicester: Leicester University Press, 1977).

49. Jules Harmand, *Domination et colonisation*, cited in Roberts, *History of French Colonial Policy*, p. 29.

50. I have found particularly helpful Philip Woodruff, *The Men Who Ruled India*, 2 vols. (London: Jonathan Cape, 1953-1954); D.A. Low, *Lion Rampant. Essays in the Study of British Imperialism* (London: Frank Cass, 1973); and Amry Vandenbosch, *The Dutch East Indies* (Berkeley: University of California Press, 1942). John Phelan, *The Hispanization of the Philippines* (Madison: University of Wisconsin Press, 1959), makes clear the many respects in which Spanish rule in the Philippines had a much more comprehensive impact socially and culturally.

51. Woodruff, *The Men Who Ruled India*, Vol. II, pp. 230-231, 297.

52. Of the regions into which the Russian state expanded in its continental expansion, Turkestan most resembles the classic colonial pattern. Until World War I a system resembling indirect rule was applied to the Emirates of Bukhara, Kholkand and Khiva, and the Russian military governors ruled according to colonial metaphors. See in particular Richard A. Pierce, *Russian Central Asia 1867-1917: A Study in Colonial Rule* (Berkeley: University of California Press, 1960); Hugh-Seton-Watson, *The Russian Empire 1801-1967* (Oxford: Clarendon Press, 1967); Serge A. Zenkovsky, *Pan-Turkism and Islam in Russia* (Cambridge, Mass.: Harvard University Press, 1960).

53. Among a vast literature see in particular Bernard Bailyn, *The Ideological Origins of the American Revolution* (Cambridge: Belknap Press, 1967); Klaus Knorr, *British Colonial Theories*; James Lang, *Commerce and Conquest: Spain and England in the Americas* (New York: Academic Press, 1975); Peter Marshall and Glynn Williams, eds., *The British Atlantic Empire Before the American Revolution* (London: Frank Cass, 1980).

54. This intriguing observation was made by a West Indian scholar, Carl Campbell (personal communication, May 1984).

55. Gordon Lewis, *The Growth of the Modern West Indies* (New York: Monthly Review Press, 1968), p. 71.

56. On the Spanish colonial state see especially Claudio Veliz, *The Centralist Tradition of Latin America* (Princeton: Princeton University Press, 1980); J.H. Elliott, *The Old World and the New 1492-1650* (Cambridge: Cambridge University Press, 1970); Jacques LaFaye, *Quetzalcoatl and Guadalupe: The Formation of Mexican National Consciousness 1531-1831* (Chicago: University of Chicago Press, 1976); John Lynch, *Spanich Colonial Administration, 1782-1810: The Intendant System in the Viceroyalty of the Rio de la Plata* (New York: Greenwood Press, 1958); J.H. Parry, *The Spanish Theory of Empire in the Sixteenth Century* (Cambridge: Cambridge University Press, 1940); Magali Sarfati, *Spanish Bureaucratic-Patrimonialism in America* (Berkeley: Institute of International Studies, University of California, 1966); and Jorge Dominguez, *Insurrection or Loyalty: The Breakdown of the Spanish American Empire* (Cambridge, Mass.: Harvard University Press, 1980). The Portuguese system had a number of similarities to the Spanish (and was under Spanish rule 1580-1640) in Brazil, where, until the twentieth century, the sea-oriented Portuguese built their only land empire. Its absolutism was less thorough, and its colonial society, built on African slave labor, lacked the Indian component of Spanish America. See *inter alia* James Lang, *Portuguese Brazil: The King's Plantation* (New York; Academic Press, 1979); Fernando Uricoechea, *The Patrimonial Foundations of the Brazilian Bureaucratic State* (Berkeley: University of California Press, 1980); and David Alden, *Royal Government in Colonial Brazil* (Berkeley: University of California Press, 1968).

57. Philip D. Curtin, *The Image of Africa: British Ideas and Action* (Madison: University of Wisconsin Press, 1964); William B. Cohen, *The French Encounter with*

Africans: White Responses to Blacks, 1530–1880 (Bloomington: Indiana University Press, 1980).

58. Woodruff, *The Men Who Ruled India*, pp. 33–36.

59. Cited in D.K. Fieldhouse, *Economics and Empire 1830–1914* (London: Weidenfeld and Nicolson, 1973), p. 70.

60. Roberts, *History of French Colonial Policy*, pp. 177–187.

61. The discovery of this formula is recounted by Philip Mason, *A Matter of Honour* (New York: Holt, Rinehart, and Winston, 1974), pp. 17–39.

62. Daniel R. Headrick, *The Tools of Empire* (New York: Oxford University Press, 1981).

63. The A.E.F. concession companies are well analyzed by Samir Amin and Catherine Coquéry-Vidrovitch, *Histoire économique du Congo 1880–1968* (Paris: Editions Anthropos, 1969), pp. 40–51.

64. Exhaustive details on British administrative practices may be found in Hailey, *Native Administration*. For an excellent treatment of the contrasts between southern and northern Nigerian colonial state doctrines see White, *Central Administration in Nigeria*.

65. Quoted in Amin and Coquéry-Vidrovitch, *Histoire économique du Congo*, p. 26.

66. This argument is stressed by Betts, *Tricouleur*.

67. Joseph Gallieni, *Trois colonnes au Tonkin*, cited in Robin Bidwell, *Morocco under Colonial Rule* (London: Frank Cass, 1973), p. 12.

68. Lucy Behrman, *Muslim Brotherhoods and Politics in Senegal* (Cambridge, Mass.: Harvard University Press, 1970); Donal Cruse O'Brien, *The Mourides of Senegal* (Oxford: Clarendon Press, 1971).

69. The importance of this petty mercantile class is well documented by A.G. Hopkins, *An Economic History of West Africa* (New York: Columbia University Press, 1973).

70. For a recent interpretation see John Iliffe, *The Emergence of African Capitalism* (Minneapolis: University of Minnesota Press, 1983).

71. Frederick Cooper, *From Slaves to Squatters: Plantation Labor and Agriculture in Zanzibar and Coastal Kenya 1890–1925* (New Haven: Yale University Press, 1980).

72. The classic contribution on the intermediary concept is Ronald Robinson, "Non-European Foundations of European Imperialism," in Roger Owen and Bob Sutcliffe, eds., *Studies in the Theory of Imperialism* (London: Longman, 1972), pp. 117–142.

73. Giaradet, *L'idée coloniale in France*, pp. 51–74.

74. Winfried Baumgart, *Imperialism: The Idea and Reality of British and French Colonial Expansion, 1880–1914* (Oxford: Oxford University Press, 1982).

75. J.L. Miège, *L'impérialism colonial italien de 1870 à nos jours* (Paris: Société d'Edition d'Enseignment Superieur, 1968); Claudio G. Segre, *Fourth Shore. The Italian Colonization of Libya* (Chicago: University of Chicago Press, 1974).

76. Roberts, *History of French Colonial Policy*, pp. 34–35.

77. White, *Central Administration in Nigeria*, pp. 19–58.

78. Timothy C. Weisbrod, *French Colonial Rule and the Baoule Peoples: Resistance and Collaboration, 1880–1911* Oxford: Clarendon Press, 1980), pp. 231–244.

79. Ibid., p. 86.

80. Amin and Coquéry-Vidrovitch, *Histoire économique du Congo*, pp. 22–23.

81. Cited in Bidwell, *Morocco under French Rule*, p. 30.

82. Quoted in Wilson, *The Imperial Experience*, p. 113.

83. Particularly useful for this period are several of the contributions in Prosser Gifford and Wm. Roger Louis, eds., *France and Britain in Africa* (New Haven: Yale University Press, 1971), especially those of Hubert Deschamps, Robert Heussler and David K. Fieldhouse. See also Lewis Gann and Peter Duigan, eds., *Colonialism in Africa*, 5 vols. (Cambridge: Cambridge University Press, 1969-1973).

84. Hubert Deschamps, "French Policy in Africa between the World Wars," in Gifford and Louis, *France and Britain in Africa*, p. 569.

85. Jacques Berque, *French North Africa: the Mahgreb Between Two World Wars* (New York: Praeger, 1962).

86. Major Sir Ralph Furse, *Aucuparius: Recollections of a Recruiting Officer* (London: Oxford University Press, 1962).

87. On the character of this professionalization see William B. Cohen, *Rulers of Empire: The French Colonial Service in Africa* (Stanford: Hoover Institution Press, 1971); and Robert Heussler, *Yesterday's Rulers* (Syrcuse: Syracuse University Press, 1963).

88. Pierre Piron and Jacques Devos, *Codes et Lois du Congo Belge*, 8th ed. (Brussels: Maison Ferdinand Larcier, 1960), Vol. 2, p. 211.

89. See the data contained in Aubrey Richards, ed., *East African Chiefs* (London: Faber and Faber, 1960). With respect to Uganda, Hailey drew a sharp distinction between its system of chiefly nomination, which he regarded as no longer traditional, and that of northern Nigeria; *Native Administration*, Vol. 1, pp. 263.

90. Albert Sarraut, *Grandeur et servitude coloniales*, cited in Marshall, *The French Colonial Myth*, p. 46.

91. On this theory see J.M. Lee, *Colonial Government and Good Government* (Oxford: Clarendon Press, 1967).

92. Cited in Lord Hailey, *An African Survey*, rev. 1956 (London: Oxford University Press, 1957), p. 190.

93. Low, *Lion Rampant*, p. 203.

94. Berque, *French North Africa*, p. 70.

95. Paul Salkin, *L'Afrique Centrale dans cent ans* (Paris: Payot, 1926).

96. Cited in Marshall, *The French Colonial Myth*, p. 45.

97. Roberts, *History of French Colonial Policy*, p. 311.

98. Cited in Ralph A. Austin and Rita Hendricks, "Equatorial Africa under Colonial Rule," in David Birmingham and Phyllis M. Martin, eds., *History of Central Africa*, Vol. 2 (London: Longman, 1983), p. 64.

99. Cited in J.M. Lee and Martin Petter, *The Colonial Office, War, and Development Policy* (London: Maurice Temple Smith, 1982), pp. 115-142.

100. Cited in John D. Hargreaves, *The End of Colonial Rule in West Africa* (London: Macmillan, 1979). On the decolonization era, see especially the invaluable collection assembled by Prosser Gifford and Wm. Roger Louis, *The Transfer of Power in Africa and Decolonization, 1940-1960* (New Haven: Yale University Press, 1982).

101. The "imperial balance sheet" literature is instructive in this regard. In its prewar versions the major thrust is to deny that colonial rulers reaped great benefits, which in terms of the measures used is undoubtedly true; see Grover Clark, *The Balance Sheets of Imperialism*, (New York: Columbia University Press, 1936). More recent studies show how little in fact was paid (except for the Italians); Charles Issawi, *An Economic History of the Middle East and North Africa* (New York: Columbia University Press, 1972). Jean Stengers jolted Belgium by showing that Belgium had actually put very little into its colonies; *Le Congo: combien a-t-il couté à la Belgique?* (Brussels: Academie Royale des Sciences d'Outre-Mer, 1957).

102. Richard Joseph, *Radical Nationalism in Cameroun* (Oxford: Clarendon Press, 1977), p. 2.

103. Hargreaves, *The End of Colonial Rule*, p. 41.

104. Jean Stengers, "La Belgique et le Congo," *Histoire de le Belgique Contemporaine* (Brussels: La Renaissance du Livre, 1974).

105. Crawford Young, Neal Sherman and Tim Rose, *Cooperation and Development: Agricultural Politics in Ghana and Uganda* (Madison: University of Wisconsin Press, 1981), p. 165.

106. The calculations were made for Bwaamba, but we believe they are applicable to many, if not most, areas; E.H. Winter, *Bwaamba Economy* (Kampala: East African Institute of Social Research, 1958), pp. 34–35. Vali Jamal, "Taxation and Inequality in Uganda, 1900–1964," *Journal of Economic History*, 18, 2 (June 1978): 418–438, shows the pervasive discrimination in import and excise taxes against rural households.

107. Robert H. Jackson and Carl G. Rosberg, *Personal Rule in Black Africa* (Berkeley: University of California Press, 1982), 19.

108. These mechanisms are well described in Edward Corbett, *The French Presence in Black Africa* (Washington: Black Orpheus Press, 1972).

109. The impact of this type of conflict pattern on the states in the area is well analyzed in Bereket Haile Selessie, *Conflict and Intervention in the Horn of Africa* (New York: Monthly Review Press, 1980); and Marina Ottaway, *Soviet and American Influence in the Horn of Africa* (New York: Praeger, 1982).

110. This argument is developed in engaging style by Tony Killick, *Development Economics in Action* (London: Heinemann, 1978).

111. John A. Ayoade, "States Without Citizens: An Emerging African Phenomenon," Chapter 4 of this volume.

112. Benno J. Ndulu, "Economic Management in Sub-Saharan Africa: Putting the Farmer in Control" (Paper for Committee on African Development Strategies, April 1985).

113. Victor A. Olorunsola, remarks at the International Workshop on the Reordering of the State in Africa (The Hebrew University of Jerusalem, July 1985).

3

The State and the Development of Capitalism in Africa: Theoretical, Historical, and Comparative Reflections

Thomas M. Callaghy

. . . most significant has been the loss of the rule of law. Legitimacy is gone, citizens are alienated, the intelligentsia dream of revolution or reform, some others expect liberation or a millennium, most have sunk into a gloomy resignation. Naked power and bribes erode the law. In turn, the strongly centralized state has lost much of its effective grip, because its legal directives are ignored, except under duress or when they seem to be opportune. Lack of security does not allow anyone to plan for the longterm. If democratic rights had been upheld, the country's leaders would have been repudiated long ago. Without foreign intervention, the regime would have been overthrown, and profound changes would, perhaps, have occurred. But perhaps not. The future is uncertain, and uncertainty paralyzes.

Jan Vansina, "Mwasi's Trials"[1]

Introduction

Most of Africa is now suffering from dual crises of the state and the economy. The state is seen as being in decline, characterized variously as "overdeveloped," "underdeveloped" and "soft." Evidence abounds of diminishing control, repression and extraction, resilience of traditional authority patterns, corrupt and inefficient administration, enormous waste, poor policy performance, debt and infrastructure crises, curtailment of capacities, endemic political instability, and societal resistance and withdrawal. On the economic side, with declining or negative growth rates and stagnant or falling per capita income figures, problems concerning the balance of payments and debt service are becoming more severe, requiring the intercession of International Monetary Fund (IMF) and World Bank programs, with their attendant conditionality packages and consequences. Many commodity prices remain low, while most import prices remain high. In many countries agricultural production is falling, while aid levels continue to decline. Health and nutrition levels are dropping, while *magendo* (illegal) economies become more important as states weaken and formal markets decline. Hopes for economic growth and development have shriveled on all sides. "Socialist" states have performed poorly, while "capitalist" ones have not fared significantly better.[2]

These two crises of state and economy are clearly linked. As one analyst has asserted, "Africa's economic crisis is above all a political crisis."[3] What is the problem? We have the contrasting views of dependency theory and neoclassical development theory. One stresses largely externally based obstacles; the other, internally based ones. The IMF and the World Bank, on the one hand, and the Organization of African Unity (OAU) and the Economic Commission for Africa, on the other, have their own perspectives and proposed remedies.

This current dismal politico-economic conjuncture in Africa raises some larger questions. Is Africa capitalist now? What are the prospects for the development of modern capitalism in Africa? Is the state a hindering or facilitating factor, or both? In this regard, the following questions are crucial in the African context: how real and well developed are markets in labor and other factors of production?; where investment exists, is it for productive or nonproductive purposes? (trade alone, for example, does not equal modern capitalism); is there a socioeconomic and political environment which facilitates rational calculation, reasonable predictability and long-term investments?; how real are the capacities of the state and the legal system, and do they facilitate or inhibit capitalist activity by both domestic and foreign capitalists?

How do we get a conceptual handle on these issues? Most of the theoretical constructs and interpretations of the world historical record have either Marxian or Smithian roots. Max Weber's views have usually been seen as fully reflected in his *The Protestant Ethic and the Spirit of Capitalism* and have not been considered a third major perspective. There has recently been a dramatic increase in interest in Weber's views, inspired by a reassessment of the set of lectures that he gave just before his death in 1920 and published together in *General Economic History*. This paper will look at Weber's views on the nature and development of capitalism, contrast them with Marxian and Smithian views, assess how they apply to the development of capitalism in Europe, and examine what they tell us about whether capitalism exists in Africa today and its possible chances for development there.

Weber on Capitalism

Much of the commonly accepted Weberian view of capitalism comes from the reading of and controversy surrounding *The Protestant Ethic*, which stresses specific attitudinal and motivational factors. In fact, his "last theory of capitalism," incarnated in *General Economic History* and *Economy and Society*, is much broader in scope and predominantly institutional in its thrust. The "spirit" elements discussed in *The Protestant Ethic* play merely a small part in the overall picture. A good deal of the misperception of Weber's views is due to the damage inflicted by Talcott Parsons, who selectively introduced Weber to and interpreted him for English-language, particularly American, social science.[4]

In his broadest usage of the term, Weber defined capitalism as "the provision of human needs by enterprise, which is to say, by private businesses seeking profit. It is exchange carried out for positive gain, rather than forced contributions or traditionally fixed gifts or trades."[5] Weber made it very clear that forms of capitalism have existed in a wide variety of historical eras and places, that economies can be partly capitalist, and that an economy or epoch can be considered capitalist "only as the provision for wants is capitalistically organized to such a predominant degree that if we imagine this form of organization taken away the whole economic system must collapse."[6] Clearly, then, early modern Europe and Africa today cannot in this sense be considered capitalist. In contradistinction to modern, rational, productive or industrial capitalism based on the "rational permanent enterprise," he referred variously to "commercial capitalism," "political capitalism," "booty capitalism," "adventurers' capitalism," "traditional capitalism" and "patrimonial capitalism." Above all, he stressed that modern capitalism does not necessarily develop from extensive trade or accumulation. He used the cases of early modern Spain and India during Roman times as examples. Recently, Robert Brenner strongly criticized Wallerstein's confusion on this point; it is a central weakness in world system, dependency and underdevelopment theory.[7] As Brenner indicates, these Marxian-rooted perspectives have simply inverted Adam Smith's focus on trade, the market and division of labor. Unequal exchange does not rule out the development of capitalism any more than extensive extraction of surplus value or accumulation necessarily induces capitalism. Brenner's more orthodox Marxist focus on the nature of labor and the class relations that produce it is important and constitutes one central element of Weber's broader conceptualization of capitalism and its development.

Ira Cohen notes that "Weber's writings clearly indicate that he was influenced both positively and negatively by the conceptions of capitalism developed by Smith and Marx,"[8] but that neither Marx's views on labor-capital relations and the surplus theory of value nor Smith's emphasis on the central role for trade and the market became dominant aspects of Weber's perspective. They are necessary but not sufficient elements of his definition and conceptualization. As Bottomore stresses, "The real distinctiveness of Weber's view of capitalism is to be found in the broad perspective which he adopts, and in what that perspective leads him to highlight or obscure."[9] Likewise, the views of both Marx and Smith were greatly influenced by their focus on England as the primary example of capitalism and its development. While Weber saw England as important, he was greatly influenced by the experience of Germany and to a somewhat lesser extent by those of France and Russia. The result was that Weber gave much more weight to the role of the state, which, of course, he was theoretically more disposed to do than either Marx or Smith.[10] A key point here is precisely that the role of the state was central to the development of capitalism in Europe and not just for the "late developers" in the Third World today.[11]

In fact, Weber argued that the development of the modern state, with its attendant state system, and the rise of capitalism in Europe are conceptually analogous processes of consolidation and expropriation and that historically they took place in tandem. Neither necessarily created or is reducible to the other.[12] Unlike the current Wallersteinian paradigm, however, Weber stressed that it was the national state, not a generalized world system of exchange and production, that accounted for the rise of the contextual factors that facilitated the development of modern capitalism. According to him,

> it was a question of competing national states in a condition of perpetual struggle for power in peace or war. . . . Out of this alliance of the state with capital, dictated by necessity, arose the national citizen class, the bourgeoisie in the modern sense of the word. *Hence it is the closed national state which afforded to capitalism its chance for development.*[13]

In particular, Weber stressed the eventual intense bureaucratization of the national state in Europe, which distinguished it from the thin bureaucratization of empires, such as those in China, that did not produce modern capitalism.[14] In the African context it is crucial, then, how strong bureaucratic characteristics of the state become. Weber also clearly took international forces and processes into account, as the above quotation indicates, but he did so in quite a different manner than Wallerstein. He focused on competition—political, military and economic—between national states in a state system, and not on a world system powered by transnational forces, particularly economic ones.

For Weber "the idea of rationality is a great unifying theme," an "*idé-maîtresse*" of his work.[15] This notion of rationality has caused a great deal of misunderstanding, because Weber used the term in complex and multiple ways and readers have not paid careful attention to this fact.[16] The notion of rationality is central to Weber's view on the development of both the modern state and capitalism:

> Thus modern capitalism, for Weber, is defined by the rational (deliberate and systematic) pursuit of profit through the rational (systematic and calculable) organization of formally free labor and through rational (impersonal, purely instrumental) exchange on the market, guided by rational (exact, purely quantitative) accounting procedures and guaranteed by rational (rule-governed, predictable) legal and political systems.[17]

Crucial to this notion of capitalism (as well as that of state bureaucracy) is the distinction between formal and substantive rationality. Formal rationality orders actions purely on the basis of means-ends calculus with regard to universally applied abstract principles, laws and rules. Substantive rationality orders actions in relation to specific value preferences.[18]

Weber was very careful to point to the substantive irrationalities of capitalism (exploitation and other negative aspects), while he stressed its formal rationality as compared to other types of economies.[19] The tensions that result from the clash of these two types of rationality in capitalist economic forms lead to conflict and struggles which variously affect its development, depending on the outcomes. Hence these outcomes cannot be predicted. Weber was careful to point out, however, that not all or necessarily even the most important of these conflicts are class conflicts. Unlike Marx, Weber was willing to analytically consider other forms of conflict, again to take a broader view. Marx's notion of capitalism is focused very heavily on labor, labor power, labor value and class conflict; Marx turned "his conception of labour into a systematic theory of the historical development of human society." Despite this, Bottomore notes that Marx's "theory of classes was even less fully elaborated than was his theory of economic crises" and that "it may be suggested that Marx's notion of the increasing polarization of society and the growing intensity of class conflict should be seen as the formulation of a 'tendency' whose working out in practice is inhibited by various 'counter-tendencies.' "

Weber was as interested in the nonclass factors as the class ones. He had a much more ambiguous view of classes, noting the importance of other bases of social action and that class action is not by any means a universal phenomenon. As Bottomore points out, Weber's "emphasis upon the competitive struggle in which individuals and a plethora of interest groups are engaged is clearly intended to contest the idea of a polarization of social interests between 'two great classes,' increasingly locked in conflict over the whole structure of society."[20] For Weber, class conflict was not a central element in his conceptualization of the *development* of modern capitalism; other factors were more important.

For Weber, this "rational" form of capitalism became dominant only in Europe around the middle of the nineteenth century, but its roots are deeply buried in the socioeconomic and political context of early modern Europe.[21] Key to this conceptualization of rational capitalism is calculability, that is, not only the intent, capability, or willingness to use it, but also a calculability nexus or context of social, economic, technical, institutional and attitudinal factors which facilitate its presence and use:

> To be sure, calculability is not the only element in Weber's conception of the rationality of the modern social order. Weber also stresses the increasing significance of specialized knowledge; the steady erosion of customary, religious and ethical restraints on behavior; the regulation of social life through abstract, general norms; the increasingly instrumental orientation of action in all spheres of social life; the systematic self-control bequeathed to modern society by puritan asceticism; the devotion to impersonal purposes that defines the ethic of vocation; the development of increasingly powerful techniques for controlling

men and nature; and the growing impersonality of relations of power and authority. Yet each of these elements is closely related to calculability and thus to enhanced means-ends rationality; each furthers in a general way the *purposeful, calculated achievement of any and all substantive ends.*[22]

In addition to the two major strands to this development—one in production and the other in the state—there is also a less important attitudinal strand, the one that received so much attention in *The Protestant Ethic.* Of particular importance for the develoment of modern capitalism are expanding knowledge and the depersonalization of the structures of power and authority in both the political and economic arenas. As we shall see later, Weber felt that it was difficult for modern capitalism to develop a dynamic of its own in the context of patrimonial political systems; what did flourish were certain kinds of "patrimonial capitalism" and "adventurers' capitalism, oriented to the exploitation of political opportunities and irrational [economically non-productive] speculation."[23]

Weber thus developed a largely institutional, as opposed to idealist, theory of capitalism, with a central role for the state in it. He delineated six key elements facilitating the emergence of modern capitalism, which undergird the rationalization of both the state and the economy:

1. private appropriation by entrepreneurs of all the means of production, separation of the workers from the means of production;
2. formally free labor, but compelled to sell its labor;
3. rational technology based on calculation and knowledge, especially mechanization;
4. market exchange not burdened by irrational restraints;
5. calculable law in both adjudication and state administration;
6. a rational monetary system and the general commercialization of economic life.[24]

These elements are supported by an economic ethic that is methodical and nondualistic or particularistic, as well as an accompanying demagification or "disenchantment" of life, and a viable transportation and communications system.[25]

The logic of Weber's position "is first to describe these characteristics; then to show the obstacles to them that were prevalent in virtually all societies of world history until recent centuries in the West; and, finally, by the method of comparative analysis, to show the social conditions responsible for their emergence."[26] For example, in precapitalist Europe:

> The labor force was generally unfree. . . . Technologies of mass production hardly existed. The market was generally limited either to local areas or to long-distance trade in luxuries, due to numerous near-confiscatory tax barriers, unreliable and varying coinage, warfare, robbery, and poor transportation. And legal systems, even in literate states, tended to be characterized by patrimonial or magical-religious procedures, by differential application to dif-

ferent social groups and by different localities, and by the practices of officials seeking private gain. Reliable financial transactions, including the operation of a banking system relatively free from political interference and plundering, were particularly handicapped by these conditions.[27]

The similarity between much of this configuration and the situation in large parts of Africa today is striking.

The rise of the modern bureaucratic state is a central factor for Weber in the institutional underpinnings of the rise of modern capitalism. As Collins notes, "The state is the factor most often overlooked in Weber's theory of capitalism. Yet it is the factor to which he gave the most attention."[28] It rose out of the political imperatives of domination (war and interstate competition externally and domination and extraction internally) and the state formation processes and struggles which they generated, and this new state form helped, slowly and unevenly, to break down the political and economic barriers to the rise of capitalism and to facilitate the development of the six elements listed above.[29] Increased trade, greater accumulation and surplus value extraction, and better control over a freer labor force were not sufficient. As part of a political logic, these states attempted to pursue mercantilist policies in order to increase their strength internally and externally. "One might even argue," according to Collins, "that the bureaucratic state was the proximate cause of the impulse to rationalization generally—above all, via the late seventeenth- and eighteenth-century spirit of enlightened absolutism, which set the stage for the industrial revolution."[30]

Weber's view on the nature and rise of capitalism is broader and more rounded than that of either Marx or Smith. It stresses the context and the conjuncture of factors *and* the relative weight or balance between them. The presence of a key element when some of the others are missing or the undue weight of one or two could have very negative effects on the development of capitalism. This is particularly true of the role of the state, which can either foster or hinder the development of capitalism, or even do both simultaneously in different arenas.[31] It can, for example, reinforce noncapitalist social groups or classes, skew accumulation and investment, impose a climate of arbitrariness and unpredictability which weakens the calculability nexus. Much of the energy of the rising bourgeoisie in France, for example, was siphoned off into the venality of office and land acquisition— the search for status and position to go with its increasing wealth.[32] Here, as in Africa today, the nature and ease of accumulation and well-rooted processes of the search for status, power and social legitimacy are particularly important.

Because the specific configuration of the conjuncture is determined by the outcomes of actual struggles and conflicts, this view is clearly nondeterministic, nonevolutionary. Capitalism does not have to grow out of any particular conjuncture of elements. The important point is the relationship between the various outcomes of these complex, ongoing sociopolitical, economic and intellectual struggles and their impact on the factors which

Weber delineated as crucial to the nature and rise of capitalism. As Collins appropriately stresses, this is indeed a conflict theory of capitalism, not a static ideal-typical one, and a much broader one than either the Marxist or Smithian versions and their derivatives.[33] This point will be pursued later as we look briefly at the differing trajectories of African states. This perspective is also nonlinear, insofar as Weber noted the very uneven rate and spread of the elements of rationalization and combinations of them.[34]

Weber also stressed that there were numerous historical cases where capitalism did not develop out of a conceivably favorable conjuncture of factors. Andreski notes that "Weber's explanation of the arrest and decline of the ancient capitalism rests upon his distinction between unproductive or parasitic capitalism (which he calls 'irrational') and productively or industrially ordered capitalism (which he calls 'rational')." From the historical examples that Weber used, Andreski extracts the following general proposition: "New forms of production and trade (i.e. industrially oriented capitalism) develop only where the business class is too strong to be fettered and exploited but not strong enough to accumulate wealth by extracting it from others, and where, in consequence, production and trade offer to the members of this class the most promising road to satisfactory livelihood or enrichment."[35] Historical cases of patrimonial capitalism abound where the state became the easiest avenue of extraction and access to power. Such a structure of opportunity has rarely been conducive to the development of modern capitalism—direct extraction is too easy and productive investment too difficult. Central here are the particular balance or weight of key elements facilitating or inhibiting the development of modern capitalism and the nature and availability of various forms of upward mobility. The latter has much to do with the nature of classes, especially opportunity structure, permeability and closure. As we shall see in the discussion of patrimonial capitalism, the arbitrariness of the state is also a key factor which inhibits the growth of capitalism.

In a critique of Wallerstein, Robert Brenner notes that, "The original emergence of capitalist development is, therefore, incomprehensible as a phenomenon of 'money,' 'trade,' 'the production of commodities' or of 'merchant capital.'" He goes on to say that, "From this perspective, it is impossible to accept Frank's view, adopted by Wallerstein, that the capitalist 'development of underdevelopment' in the regions colonized by Europeans from the sixteenth . . . is comprehensible as a direct result of the incorporation of these regions within the world market, their 'subordination' to the system of capital accumulation on a world scale."[36] Brenner argues persuasively for a focus on the class struggles in rural Europe over labor and property. Weber would have agreed with the correctness of this position, but would have found it only one element in the much larger configuration sketched above. Weber also asserted that the "accumulation of wealth brought about through colonial trade has been of little significance for the development of modern capitalism. . . . It is true that the colonial trade made possible the accumulation of wealth to an enormous extent, but this did not further the specifically occidental form of the organization of labor."[37] He uses the example of early modern Spain, as well as an earlier historical example of India, which "proves that such an importation of metal [bullion] will not alone bring about capitalism. . . . The greater part of this precious metal disappeared into the hoards of the rajahs instead of being converted into cash and applied in the establishment of enterprises of a rational capitalist character."[38] In the contemporary African context, the case of Nigeria comes to mind in this regard.[39]

The Development of Capitalism in Europe:
The State and the Historical Record

The role of the state in the development of capitalism in Europe "was a crucial background determinant for all the legal and institutional under-pinnings of capitalism"[40] that were listed above. This role was both extensive and ultimately limited. The state attempted to do many things intentionally via its policies of mercantilism; it succeeded in accomplishing only a few of them. The major legacy was a more indirect one; the cumulative impact of the development of the modern bureaucratic state, which took place slowly and unevenly, was felt most strongly in the areas of law and administration, particularly in the slow decline in arbitrariness and in the transportation and infrastructure realms, which facilitated market exchange and production.

As E.L. Jones indicates, probably the greatest *eventual* achievement of the European state was "the progress in bringing political arbitrariness to heel," in decreasing uncertainty and increasing the calculability nexus in a variety of direct and indirect ways. He cautions, however, that "greater security was won very slowly": "We should exaggerate neither the pace nor the permanency with which a risk-free environment was supplied, nor yet the demand for it."[41] Part and parcel of this was "a slowly declining liquidity preference," central to which was the "reduction of thoughtless behavior by those in authority." Policy became "more constructive—intermittently no doubt, but always laying down useful precedents"[42]

> What was important instead was the slow pruning away of roughness and risk, so that entrepreneurs might not merely maximise profits but retain them too. . . . The economy became regulated by economic rather than political decisions. This emphasis on the withering away of arbitrariness, violence, custom, and old social controls, seems to leave little scope for direct assaults on the old order.[43]

Jones quite correctly reminds us that these consequences did not come about because of the goodness of the rulers and their concern for their subjects, but rather that "national purpose in the *anciens régimes* was largely a cloak for ruling interests," that there was little "cherishing of human capital," and that "security of life, property and investment were not security of employment, income and health." He also reminds us that these things "remained nevertheless essentials for development, parts of it by definition" and that "for all these reservations, the modernising effect of state action is clear."[44]

Like Jones, Hindess and Hirst, despite their Marxian roots, also point to the autonomous importance of the actions of the state and to the eventual "displacement of dominance from the political to the economic level."[45] The point is that in much of the European transition to full capitalism the political level did predominate, and that only with the complete development of capitalism was this dominance shifted more toward the economic level. This is an interesting point for two Marxists to make. This process led slowly and unevenly to a shift by rising bourgeois elements from demanding special protection and favor, which allowed some increased certainty and calculability, to relying increasingly on the generalized presence of Weber's contextual factors, which in turn allowed the full flowering of the development of modern capitalism. As this shift took place over time, key bourgeois elements began to *expect* a viable calculability nexus without having to "pay" for it each time via patron-client ties and patrimonial administration, and they increasingly demanded it from the state as their class weight, presence and power accumulated. As Weber indicated, this is the difference between the presence of some of the contextual facilitating factors of modern capitalism and their becoming the dominant elements of a capitalist *system*. For Africa the political level is still clearly dominant, although the existence of second economies and the development of a more coherent true bourgeoisie in a country such as Kenya, for example, *might* indicate that important early changes are taking place. Internal economic processes are badly skewed by "overdeveloped," "overdominant," but "under-developed" and "soft" states. In early modern Europe "overdeveloped" and "soft states" also existed, as seen very clearly in the record of mercantilist efforts, to which we now turn.

In Europe the state also played a more direct role in the development of modern capitalism. Alexander Gerschenkron was one of the first to stress the increasingly important role for the state, both direct and indirect, in the development of capitalism taken by "late developers" or "follower societies." What many people tend to forget is that his "late developers" were European states; he focused primarily on pre-Soviet Russia and Germany and to a lesser extent on France. It should be remembered that after England all other states were "followers" and that in most of these cases the state played a very significant role. The heavily statist policies of mercantilism and the existence of "parastatal" sectors were the norm; they are not a new phenomenon of the Third World. In fact, much of the statist legacy of colonial rule for states in the Third World can be directly traced to the statist past of the European colonizers themselves. What Gerschenkron says about Russia holds for much of the rest of Europe—that "the state . . . assumed the role of the primary agent propelling the economic progress in the country."[46] His assessment of these policies also probably holds for contemporary Latin America, with its record of nearly a century of statist efforts at economic development: "There is no doubt that the government as an *agens movens* of industrialization discharged its role in a far less than perfectly efficient manner. Incompetence and corruption of bureaucracy were great. The amount of waste that accompanied the process was formidable. But, when all is said and done, the great success of the policies pursued . . . is undeniable."[47] Jones' assessment of the European record follows in the same vein.[48] Peter Evans has made similar judgments about statist efforts at capitalist development in Brazil and the Third World more generally.[49] Whether such an assessment will hold for Africa is still clearly impossible to predict, but the World Bank might want to take another look at the historical record, especially since its counter-factual arguments about the private sector in Africa are not as sound as it makes them appear.

Weber made a very important point in this context which pertains to Africa: that there is a strong historical link between cases of patrimonial rule and the establishment of "all kinds of fiscal enterprises and monopolies" and that capitalism developed out of only one of them. He points to Egypt, the late Roman Empire, the Near and Far East, and "the public enterprises of the rulers at the beginning of modern times [in Europe]."[50] Capitalism appeared only in the last case. In short, there is no necessary link between statist economic policies and the eventual development of modern capitalism. We will come back to this point in the next section.

Regarding European mercantilism, Weber noted that by and large the results of the direct efforts of European statesmen were meager; for example, "neither the period of Colbert nor of Frederick and Peter succeeded in turning their countries into industrial states." There were both economic and political reasons for the failures. On the political side the primary "retarding factor was again the arbitrariness of patrimonial rulership." Weber pointed out that "the economically interested groups behind the royal monopolies and the industries which were imported, founded or protected" were often "members and favorites of the royal family, courtiers, military men and officials grown rich, great speculators and adventurous inventors of 'systems of political economy.' . . ." He pointed to the importance of foreign capital, personnel and technology in many of these statist efforts. Weber also indicated that these state activities eventually became "one of the major issues in the struggle between the monarchy and the rising bourgeois classes." His final assessment, however, was that these efforts "played a very important part in creating some of the essential conditions for . . . the later autonomous capitalistic development."[51] With this theoretical and historical background, we now turn to a discussion of these issues in the African context.

Africa and the Development of Capitalism

Given the discussion so far, how capitalist is Africa? I think the appropriate answer is "not very." Certainly there is not much modern capitalism as Weber defined it: the calculability nexus is very weak; state arbitrariness,

instability, corruption and inefficiency are very high; patrimonial, not bureaucratic, administration and adjudication are the norm; the personalization
of power and authority structures, political and nonpolitical, is pervasive;
entrepreneurs, both domestic and foreign, do not control all the means of
production, especially in the rural areas as important restrictions on the
market use of these factors remain; liquidity preferences remain high and
investment patterns lean heavily toward speculation and the short term;
technologies remain rudimentary and not easily transferable; important
restrictions on a free labor market continue to exist;[52] markets are not well
developed and economic, political and social impediments continue to exist,
and in many cases formal markets are actually shrinking, while *magendo*
economies grow into much of the gap; noncapitalist modes of production
remain very important; only partial incorporation into the world economy
is the norm; national financial, banking and monetary systems are quite
unsophisticated; and transportation and communications infrastructures,
already weak, are disintegrating in many areas of the continent.

If there is very little modern capitalism in Africa now and most of the
factors which facilitate its development remain weak or nonexistent, how
likely is Africa to become significantly capitalist in the near future? I think
the answer is "not likely." Certainly international trade alone will not develop
capitalism in Africa, nor further underdevelop it for that matter. The above
discussion ought to make it abundantly clear that internal obstacles to the
development of capitalism in Africa are at least as important as those
imposed by the world capitalist economy and international state system, if
not more so. And the political and social obstacles are at least as important
as the economic ones, if not more so. If the record of socialism in Africa
is weak and modern capitalism does not exist, what does? The answer is
early syncretic economies with very mixed modes of production, noncapitalist
social logics, patrimonial administrative states with their own political logics,
mercantilist economic policies and patrimonial, not modern, capitalism.

Frederick Cooper is quite right to stress the fact that "capital has not
invariably won the battles it fought in the first and second occupations of
Africa—to make production predictable and orderly throughout the continent. . . . The march of Africans into the world economy does not appear
to follow a straight line." Both Africa's precolonial and colonial rulers "had
long stumbled on the problem of systematically controlling the productive
activities of their subjects"; it was difficult to redefine the organization of
labor and production.[53] Africa clearly remains only partially capitalist, despite
the impact of roughly 80 years of direct colonial domination and 25 years
of neocolonial influence. Goran Hyden raises a similar argument when he
takes issue with the commonly asserted "notion that capitalism has totally
submerged everything pre-capitalist in Africa, because it has destroyed the
pre-colonial modes of production. . . ." According to him, "One cannot
argue that the destruction of the pre-colonial modes of production in Africa
automatically meant the disappearance of everything pre-capitalist." In fact,
he argues that in the postcolonial period market forces have weakened and

what he calls "pre-capitalist" (noncapitalist, actually, in order to avoid any teleological or necessarily evolutionary implications) forces have increased in strength.

Hyden maintains, correctly, that "it has been too readily assumed that the prevalence of capitalism at the global level has been the solely important force in setting the parameters of development in Africa." His focus, not inappropriately, rests primarily on the rural sector "where the bulk of the rural producers possess their own land, use very simple technologies, and are only marginally [partially would be more accurate] incorporated into a market economy; their dependence on the macro-economic system . . . is very limited [just limited would be more accurate]." Both Cooper and Hyden stress the importance of straddling and point to at least the possibility of "exit options."

Hyden sums up by saying that "most African countries are still only in the early phase of transition from pre-capitalist formations to capitalism."[54] It would be more accurate to state that noncapitalist economies or nonmodern forms of capitalism remain very important in Africa. Weber, in his constant use of a variety of historical comparative referents, pointed to many situations in which "mixed," not "dual," economies, possessing elements of commercial and patrimonial capitalism, did not develop into modern capitalism.

Society, Social Logic and Capitalism

In the context of Zaire, S.N. Sang-Mpam discusses "peripheral capitalist societies" (it would be more accurate to say peripheral societies with some capitalist elements), which he says are "dominated by a historically specific capitalist mode of production." While overstating the case a bit, he elaborates the nice notion of a "disarticulated socio-economic structure":

> Its characteristic features can be summarized. First, they are economic and include: (1) lack of integration and interdependence in the economy from geographical, sectoral, and input-output viewpoints; (2) sectoral inequality in terms of productivity and specialization of material production; (3) partial commodification of (socio-)economic production and the stagnant reproduction of economic activities; (4) exiguity of the internal market; and (5) external economic domination and strong dependence of most of the economic activities on the world market. Second, the features are social and include: (1) oscillation of social classes and groups between capitalist relations of production and precapitalist relations; (2) the detachment of most social behaviors and activities from the market; (3) the marginal position of indigenous social classes in the structure of ownership of the means of production and in the process of capitalist reproduction; and (4) the distortion, lack of distinctiveness and lack of the type of "organized cohesion" of class structure present in advanced capitalist countries. The failure of the capitalist mode of production to become exclusive has other effects. Inherent in the disarticulated socio-economic structure are such well-known persistent phenomena as "tribalism," conservatism in the face of changes in the forces of production, competing forms of "traditional" ideologies etc.[55]

This configuration is very similar to my historically grounded notion of the mosaic state and its syncretic economy, and it is important to note its lack of compatibility with Weber's characteristic elements of modern capitalist societies.[56] As we shall see, Sang-Mpam links his notion to the concept of an "overdominant state."

Sara Berry describes a powerful socioeconomic logic, important in much of Africa today, which is relevant to such a "disarticulated" social structure. This socioeconomic logic results in "a pattern of economic development in which the growth of transactions tends to outpace the growth of production, and which favors the proliferation of small-scale enterprises and low levels of labor productivity" and serves "to increase uncertainty and inhibit productive investment."[57] It is worth quoting this argument at some length:

> In short, property rights were politicized rather than privatized in many parts of colonial and postcolonial Africa, and strategies of accumulation were directed toward building up power over resources rather than increasing productivity.... Commercialization occurred within a framework of conflicting legal and political principles and practices, in which people often sought to strengthen their access to markets and purchasing power by fostering relations of loyalty and dependence. This is turn affected the use of economic resources in two ways. First, to the extent that access to land, labor, credit and commercial opportunity was predicated on ties of kinship, traditions of common origin, relations of patronage, and so forth, such social relations became objects as well as instruments of accumulation.... Second, the strategies which people used to gain access to productive resources sometimes interfered with effective management of production itself.[58]

> Such patterns were reinforced by the uncertainties and unevenness of commercialization, by incomplete privatization of property rights, and by growing state interventionism in the post colonial period, all of which channelled resources into maintaining and defending access to resources rather than developing their productive potential.[59]

Such socioeconomic logic is not particularly favorable to the development of the facilitating factors that Weber linked conceptually and historically to the rise of modern capitalism.

The Nature of the African State:
A Powerful Political Logic

What kind of state is linked to this form of socioeconomic structure? There is a state-level political logic analogous to the socioeconomic logic described by Berry, and the two kinds of logic powerfully reinforce each other in ways that do not enhance the development of modern capitalism. Elsewhere I have elaborated the concept of the patrimonial administrative state.[60] Increasingly, observers have pointed to the authoritarian, arbitrary, highly personalistic, inefficient, corrupt, prebendal, and rentier nature of this state form. It tends to reinforce the disarticulated nature of society and the economy, including its deeply rooted noncapitalist, syncretic characteristics. Just as this state form has not served socialism all that effectively in Africa, it may also not serve the development of capitalism all that well, at least for quite some time.[61] As we shall see below, there is a major difference between the developmental statism of most of the Asian and Latin American newly industrializing countries (NICs) and the poorly developed and ineffective statism prevalent in much of Africa today.[62]

The similarity of this African state form to that of early modern Europe discussed above is striking. Many analysts have stressed the important colonial legacy of "the mercantilist capitalism of the colonial state" and the fact that the "state sector was already well developed" by the colonial powers, which has carried over to both the "nurture" and "parasitic" capitalisms of the postcolonial period.[63] It is important to emphasize that this colonial legacy is deeply rooted in Europe's own statist past. The "African capitalist state" today does need to be distinguished "from the [*contemporary*] model Western state,"[64] but it certainly has important similarities to the model Western state's historical predecessor. It was this historical predecessor that the colonial powers imposed on Africa, albeit in a slightly more bureaucratized form.[65] One of the main points here is that the record of the *development* of capitalism in Europe is indeed germane to similar issues in the contemporary African context.

The inherited colonial state has been patrimonialized in the postcolonial era:

> The realities of the public service in the African countries after independence, therefore, came soon to resemble the patrimonial system with its tension between the inviolability of tradition and the supremacy of sanctioned arbitrariness rather than the bureaucratic system with its tension between the equity of the rule of law and the equity of the case. Thus, the problem, facing the attempts to establish a "development administration" was not really the persistence but the disappearance of bureaucratic norms and principles. With patrimonialism taking over, the scope for administrative reform along the lines argued by local and expatriate professionals was severely reduced.[66]

This is not to say, however, that this state form has "no structural roots in society."[67] This clearly ignores the impact of marketing boards, formal and informal taxation and other forms of extraction. Peasants, after all, do straddle. As in early modern Europe, the state is authoritarian and extractive, but its control is ultimately limited, especially in regard to attempts to redefine existing relations of production. In Europe this was made very clear by the limited substantive impact of mercantilist efforts, just as in most of Africa today. Sang-Mpam says the state is "overdominant"; it would be more accurate to say that it is quasi-omnipresent, but not anywhere near omnipotent. The power of the state is not unlimited, but rather unsupervised.

Crawford Young stresses the "decay," "decline" or "progressive 'dequalification' of the state" in Africa as a result of which "the impersonal institutions of the once-potent colonial state now lie in ruins." This "crisis of the state" is thus characterized by "the erosion of its probity, competence, and credibility." Corruption (a key patrimonial characteristic) "has become a defining feature of the state." The decline in competence of the state is measured by the decline in "its ability to transform allocated public resources into intended policy aims" (also a key characteristic of patrimonial administration in early modern states). He notes that this is particularly true in the rural areas and correctly points to agriculture and infrastructure.[68] In fact, there are two conceptually distinct but interrelated processes at work: the progressive patrimonialization and functional contraction of the inherited colonial state structure, and the normal cycles of political control and extraction characteristic of early modern state formation. These processes have now been accelerated by the economic and fiscal crises of African states since the mid-1970s (in themselves key manifestations of their patrimonial character).

The colonial state imposed the administrative structure of an authoritarian state on Africa. African rulers subsequently patrimonialized it. The Europeans brought a more fully developed and modern administrative structure to Africa, a structure which was the end result of European developments. Consequently, it was more fully organized, systematized and formalized than the structures which were exported by the Spanish monarchy to Latin America. The colonial state of Latin America was exported from Europe midstream, so to speak, and as a result it was much more a patrimonial state than the colonial apparatus imposed in Africa. The patrimonialization of this apparatus by the Africans, however, has reduced the effectiveness of the state, making it more early modern in character. For example, the existence of more state "services" in Africa than in colonial Latin America is one legacy of the later colonial state. But there has been a very real functional, if nor formal, contraction, not to say atrophy, of these services. Many of them barely operate at all, and in this sense the state produces only a few more "services." In addition, the functioning of these additional services is oriented more toward control and extraction than mass welfare.

The authority of the African state often resembles a sort of authoritarian bragging which drowns in an often mocking passivity. As Young notes, there "is a prime contradiction of the contemporary state; it is at once hard and distant, soft and permeable. In its habits and operating modes, the state reflects the inertial perpetuation of its colonial past; in its command style, the domination that gave it birth persists."[69] As in early modern Europe and nineteenth-century Latin America, the centralizing patrimonial state in Africa is a Leviathan, albeit a lame one.

Mercantilism: The Political Economy of African States

The economic policies of most African regimes usually take, in substance if not in rhetoric, an intermediary position, rejecting both the free-market operation of classical *laissez faire* capitalism and the centralized, total state planning and control of command socialism. Their political economy is what Weber described as "political capitalism," or "patrimonial capitalism," what historically has been referred to as mercantilism, in which the state has an important, but not all-encompassing, role.

Mercantilism, both historically and now in African states, has been closely associated with state formation and a search for sovereignty—not with revolutionary change or welfare goals. Mercantilist policies are specifically designed to aid in the formation of stronger states, to help achieve unity, to centralize and concentrate power and to struggle against internal particularism and external dependence. Mercantilism is not primarily an economic phenomenon: it is an attempt to force economic policy into the service of power as an end in itself.[70]

Like their early modern European predecessors, most African states today are centralizing, but distinctly limited, authoritarian patrimonial-bureaucratic states. They have low levels of development and penetration and limited coercive and implementation capabilities. Politics is highly personalized, and a ruling class is emerging, with the gap between the rulers and the ruled increasing. Mercantilist states are not welfare states: state power and the interests of the ruling group—not mass welfare or basic societal change— constitute the central focus of state policy. In many African countries welfare-oriented development policies are discussed at great length, but development policies that augment state and ruler power are the primary focus of implementation efforts. These states have predominantly agricultural economies characterized by low levels of development and technology, a central role for trade and enclaves of capitalist commerce, manufacturing and extraction.

In the basic mercantilist equation of African state formation the key element in the search for sovereignty and unification is power, the basis of power is wealth, and the foundations of wealth are foreign exchange and economic development. The crucial link between foreign exchange and economic development is external trade. Trade is pivotal to the mercantilist political economy because, in a period of relatively limited internal markets and low levels of economic development, it is the major source of foreign exchange. Thus, because it constitutes the foundation of state power and the ability to raise the level of economic development, African mercantilist states seek to augment their supply of foreign exchange by attempting to increase the volume, terms and types of trade. Development projects, in addition to fostering the well-being of the ruling group, are designed primarily to expand the control capabilities of the state, increase exports, regulate imports and promote economic autarky.

African mercantilist states attempt to maintain a partially open, partially closed approach to penetration by external economic groups. The ruling group or class can increase state power and further its own interests (and the two reinforce each other) by encouraging regulated investment and development of new enterprises by external groups. Mercantilism is opposed to *laissez faire* or autonomous capitalism, but not to political capitalism. As in early modern Europe, African mercantilism may provide a favorable framework for the early development of politically regulated and controlled capitalism in Africa.[71]

The African mercantilist state has played an important role in the economy. Mercantilist policies result in a mixed condition of state-regulated and coordinated capitalism and some state enterprise in the parastatal sector. The goal is not, however, the extensive state ownership and operation of the economy characteristic of socialism. The role of the state emphasizes direction and regulation, with some direct investment in state enterprises. The state seeks to encourage trade; regulate imports and exports; grant subsidies, monopolies, and incentives for manufacturing and extractive industries; search for new mineral deposits; improve the transportation and communications infrastructure; promote inward technology transfer; establish some state enterprises and participate in others; and foster a unified internal economy.

Such is the *intent* or *thrust* of African mercantilist policies; they are reinforced by the statist economic legacy of the colonial period. Successful implementation, however, is another matter. Like their European predecessors, African neomercantilist states do not engage, despite the rhetoric, in effective large-scale economic planning. Although there is much talk about and promulgation of economic "plans," they are seldom implemented in a serious way. Planning is indicative at best. Again, like early modern European mercantilist states, African mercantilist states often seem to be in serious financial difficulty—even on the brink of bankruptcy. Regular sources of revenue are not adequate or are poorly organized; extensive borrowing and debt are common; corruption is rampant; scarce resources are squandered by ruling groups.[72]

A key characteristic of the limited patrimonial-bureaucratic states of early modern European mercantilism, as of African mercantilism today, was the enunciation of elaborate and ambitious policies that were scarcely implemented. That these African states are not fully developed modern bureaucratic states is vividly attested to by the general failure of their implementation efforts. This is particularly true in regard to the parastatal sector, which reflects larger African realities.[73] The ineffectiveness of the parastatals is most vividly demonstrated by the very limited success of socialist attempts at development in Africa, but it also applies to most other African states.[74] Echoing Weber, Eli Heckscher's assessment of early modern European mercantilism might well apply to contemporary Africa: "The ability of mercantilist statesmen to achieve what was required by their programs was very limited. . . . Generally it may be said that mercantilism is of greater interest for what it attempted than for what it achieved. It certainly paved the way for its successors."[75] In the medium run, most African states, whatever their rhetoric and alleged development strategy and whether in reality they are weaker or stronger versions of mercantilist states, will achieve at best moderate rates of growth and development.

Class, Accumulation and the State

An increasing number of observers agree with Cooper that in Africa "the weakness of class formation may be as essential to stress as its importance." The point is that it is both. Many would also agree with him that most African states have a dominant, albeit weak, ruling or political class and that it has a class project of self-aggrandizement:

> But it is not a project that has been altogether successful, and the very difficulties of transforming privileged access to resources into accumulation of productive capital have often fostered the tendency of this class project to take the easier forms of urban real estate speculation and compradorism. The class basis of state action has been compromised by the particularistic power base of its members and the high stakes of state control.[76]

This reinforces the points made earlier about the balance between contextual factors and the importance of the structure of opportunity. Because of the nature of this class and its project, I have suggested that we stop referring to it as a national bourgeoisie; this term is simply historically misleading.[77] Hyden correctly notes that "the assumption that there is a dominant class in power capable of ensuring the reproduction of capitalism in Africa must be seriously questioned." It is less true, however, that "the existing inequalities are not crystallizing into class consciousness."[78] Class consciousness is increasingly important; what is lacking is significant class organization and thus weak and inchoate class politics, other than by the political class. Here the importance of the relationship between class and clientelism needs to be stressed. Sang-Mpam shows that patron-client politics in Zaire, for example, helps to consolidate the position of the ruling class. This type of politics does not take place *only within* the dominant class, however. Nelson Kasfir argues persuasively that patron-client politics occurs between the ruling class and other emerging classes and that, in fact, it helps to mitigate some of the negative consequences for the ruling class of the increasing class consciousness of its subjects, as well as some of the emerging class conflicts that Brenner finds so central to the development of capitalism in Europe. As Lemarchand emphasizes, there are also external patrons and clients.[79] Sang-Mpam, Hyden and others have argued correctly, I believe, that the centrality of this type of politics reinforces many of the noncapitalist aspects of both the economy and politics, rather than fostering their redefinition.

The state in Africa, directly or indirectly, has certainly become the major avenue of upward mobility and accumulation. As Cooper notes:

> The point is not that the existence of advanced capitalist countries and powerful corporations makes domestic accumulation impossible—the alternative paths are crucial, for example, in Brazil . . . —but that it presents choices to a ruling class which allow it to accumulate much wealth and some capital without a direct assault on the autonomy of the cutivators. . . . African kings . . . like their modern-day counterparts—found that external relationships can be easier to develop than internal control and that those relations can bring in wealth even if they provide little basis for continued growth or security.[80]

In a sense, this important point might also be made about the impact of the early colonial exploration and empire building on early modern states in Europe, where it was easier to go outside than to tackle the multiple and deeply rooted internal obstacles to new forms of production. In fact, the outcome of the early mercantilist efforts tends to verify this supposition. Ultimately, the pressures to redefine political and economic relationships came from internal struggles and conflict by a wide variety of types of actors—that is, not only classes, which are the focus of Brenner's analysis—and from interstate relationships between the European states themselves. The latter took place only partly in the colonial areas. What Leys says about Africa today holds quite well for early modern Europe as well and is very congruent with Weber's views on capitalism:

> What capital is interested in is not development, but its own expansion.
> . . . The emergence of such conditions has something to do with stages of
> growth. . . . But it also has to do with politics, and it is the *political* power
> of domestic capital that is at least as important as its capacity to organize
> production on its own. . . . Such power is, of course, never limitless. . . .
> But the emergence of African states capable of sustaining the conditions for
> capitalist growth—a measure of reliability in public administration, social
> control without repression so severe as to jeopardize stability, a nonarbitrary
> application of commercial and criminal law, and so on—is importantly con-
> ditioned by the political power exercised by a domestic class with substantial
> capital of its own at stake.[81]

Clearly, then, as Hyden notes, "pumping money into the state machinery . . . in present circumstances cannot be expected to make much difference unless certain conditions are met."[82] Many of these points about accumulation illustrate the importance of Hindess and Hirst's notion of the displacement from the economic to the political and Ravenhill's and Leonard's emphasis on the importance of political, rather than economic logic.[83]

Patrimonial Capitalism: The Dominance of Political Logic

Most of the points already discussed in this section on Africa are inherent in Weber's use of the term "patrimonial capitalism"—the juncture between patrimonial states and certain forms of capitalism. What I would like to do here is to discuss some of the possible variations of forms within patrimonial capitalism, as well as its major historical trend. Weber made it clear that patrimonialism is compatible with many different types of economic structure. For example, he noted that it is "compatible with household and market economy, petty bourgeois and manorial agriculture, absence and presence of capitalist economy."[1091][84] As Weber emphasized, the rela-tionship between patrimonial rule and capitalism is not a deterministic one, but it does have a general negative historical trend. He indicated that "the spirit of the ancient economy" was linked to "accumulated wealth as a source of rent, not as acquisitive capital." There was also a related link between patrimonial rule and the establishment of "all kinds of fiscal enterprises and monopolies." These "emerged, on a sometimes very extensive scale, in Egypt, the late Roman empire and in the Near and Far East; the public enterprises of the rulers at the beginning of modern times were similar."[1097] Parastatal sectors are obviously not a new thing and are clearly compatible with patrimonial states. Weber underlined the fact that only in the last case did a form of patrimonial capitalism develop into modern capitalism. Now, of course, we also have the post-Weber historical example of Latin America, where some of the nineteenth-century patrimonial states of the region have developed significant elements of modern capitalism, while others have not. Hence there is no necessary evolution through stages.

In this regard, Weber differentiated between what he termed the "negatively privileging" and "positively privileging" aspects of economic policy under patrimonial rule."[1097–1098] On the one hand, "the wide latitude of the ruler's unrestricted discretion can reinforce the anti-traditional power of capitalism in a given case, as it happened in Europe during the period of absolutism."[1094] Thus, these "positive privileges . . . played their last and most important role in the age of mercantilism, when the incipient capitalist organization of trades, the bureaucratic rationalization of patrimonial rulership and the growing financial needs of the military, external [foreign affairs] and internal administration revolutionized the financial techniques of the European states." Weber reminds us, however, that "the bureaucracy" of this period "was still as patrimonial as was the basic conception of the 'state' on which it rested." As we indicated earlier, even here Weber felt that the results were meager, at least in all but the very long historical run. These state enterprises were supported by "members and favorites of the royal family, courtiers, military men and officials grown rich."[1098] He notes that "both traditionalism and arbitrariness affect very deeply the developmental opportunities of capitalism. Either the ruler himself or his officials seize upon the new chances of acquisition, monopolize them and thus deprive the capital formation of the private economy of its sustenance, or the ubiquitous resistance of traditionalism is reinforced by them so as to hinder economic innovations that might endanger the social equilibrium."[1094] Or both may happen simultaneously as is the case in many African countries today, certainly in Zaire. Since under patrimonialism "the important openings for profit are in the hands of the ruler and his administrative staff. . . . Capitalism is thereby either directly obstructed . . . or is diverted into political capitalism. . . ."[238]

Thus, "as a rule, the negative aspect of this arbitrariness is dominant":

> because—and this is the major point—the patrimonial state lacks the political and procedural *predictability*, indispensable for capitalist *development*, which is provided by the rational rules of modern bureaucratic administration. Instead we find unpredictability and inconsistency on the part of the court and local officials, and variously benevolence and disfavor on the part of the ruler and his servants. It is quite possible that a private individual, by skillfully taking advantage of the given circumstances and of personal relations, obtains a

privileged position which offers him nearly unlimited acquisitive opportunities. But a capitalist economic *system* is obviously handicapped by these factors, for the individual variants of capitalism have a differential sensitivity toward such unpredictable factors. Wholesale trade can tolerate them most easily, relatively speaking, and adapt itself to all changing conditions . . . and the formation of trade capital is feasible under almost all conditions of domination, especially under patrimonialism.

It is different with *industrial* capitalism. . . . [It] must be able to count on the continuity, trustworthiness and objectivity of the legal order, and on the rational, predictable functioning of legal and administrative agencies. Otherwise those guarantees of predictability are absent that are indispensable for the large industrial enterprise. They are especially weak in patrimonial states [1094–1095; the second and third emphases are mine].

Here, then, "two bases of the rationalization of economic activity are entirely lacking; namely, a basis for the calculability of obligations and of the extent of freedom which will be allowed to private enterprise."[238] Finally, Weber stressed that, under patrimonialism, the enormous "opening for bribery and corruption would be the least serious effect if it remained a constant quantity, because then it would become calculable in practice. But it tends to be a matter which is settled from case to case with every individual official and thus highly variable."[239] This affects both the indirect role of the state in the development of modern capitalism and its direct role via regulation and the parastatal sector.

Patrimonial capitalism in Africa could still go either way—that is, maintain variants of the current situation or move in the direction of the development of modern capitalism. I do not believe that the tipping point into some semi-sustained move toward productive capitalism has yet been reached anywhere in Africa. It appears to be different in the comparatively much more bureaucratic environment of key Latin American NICs, such as Brazil and Mexico, where there is now a much more favorable calculability nexus and attendant facilitating factors and a more effective role for the state.[85] There is a real difference between the two types of economic statism. Peter Evans makes this point in his nice comparison between Brazil of the "tripé" and Nigeria. He notes that it is inappropriate to refer to Nigeria as "the Brazil of Africa":

To call Nigeria the "Brazil of Africa" underlines the differences between the two continents as much as it does the similarities between the two countries. In an African context the structure of the Nigerian economy may appear relatively advanced; in a Latin American context it would appear anachronistic. From the role of the state to the position of the multinationals, the structure of the Nigerian elite is in many ways more suggestive of the period of classic dependent development in Brazil and Mexico. In both Brazil and Mexico the central state apparatus has succeeded in imposing its authority on regional elites. In Nigeria this process is just beginning. The degree of regional integration that characterizes contemporary Nigeria resembles that of Mexico in the days before PRI or Brazil during the old republic.[86]

Nineteenth- and early twentieth-century Latin America is indeed a more relevant comparative referent for Africa today than the contemporary NICs.

By Way of Conclusion:
Trajectories and Marginalization

Weber stressed that "in the interest of his domination, the patrimonial ruler must oppose . . . the economic independence of the bourgeoisie." This did not mean that the ruler succeeded, as the result emerged "everywhere according to the outcome of the resultant historical struggles."[87] In other words, different countries followed different paths as the result of concrete conflicts between real actors, the outcomes of which could not be fully predicted. Thus there is nothing mechanistic or deterministic about Weber's views on state and class formation or the development of capitalism. The same holds for Africa today. The paths that different countries take are determined by the presence and balance of facilitating factors, opportunities and struggles between rulers, emerging classes, status groups, organizations and particularistic forces, both internally and externally. As Cooper points out, "Africa itself is heading in different directions."[88] For both Young and Iliffe, Kenya and Nigeria are examples of nurture capitalism. Young sees Zaire as a form of perverted capitalism in which its "peculiar configuration of power . . . led all participants in capital transactions . . . to ensure that profits accrued at the point of the exchange . . . ,"[89] while Iliffe sees Zaire and Zambia as manifestations of parasitic capitalism; Young also sees Gabon as one version of enclave capitalism.

A few countries have undergone important economic changes within the context of the existing patrimonial administrative state. Not having abundant mineral resources, Ivory Coast has focused on the rural sector, where a distinct agricultural capitalism has emerged. An Ivorian planter class has developed and diversified outward from coffee production to palm oil, cocoa, cotton, sugar and pineapples. Of particular interest, especially given Berry's assessment of agriculture in western Nigeria,[90] is that there has been an important shift from family-based labor to relatively large-scale, mostly migrant wage labor—about half of it from the poor north of the country and the other half from other places in West Africa. The significant shift here is not to mechanization but to an increased calculability fostered by the new types of labor. Weber made a similar point for early modern Europe. As Collins says,

The "green revolution" which preceded (and made possible) the industrial revolution was not a process of mechanization (agricultural mechanization took place only in the late nineteenth century) but was, more simply, the application of capitalist methods of cost accounting to hereto traditional agriculture. Thus, it is the shift to the calculating practices of the capitalist market economy which makes technological innovation itself predictable, rather than as previously, an accidental factor in economic life.[91]

Compared to Nigeria, Ivory Coast has had a much more limited opportunity structure, but it has taken much better advantage of it. For Nigeria, with its oil bonanza, the opportunity structure has been almost too easy. Unlike Kenya, however, Ivory Coast has made little effort to foster a national capitalist bourgeoisie in the manufacturing sector. The role of foreign capital is much more important and much less restricted than in Kenya. The parastatal sector in Ivory Coast is much less significant, although there is still a strong statist thrust. These changes, in conjunction with the maintenance of long-term political stability and a better-than-average infrastructure by African standards, have provided Ivory Coast with a more advantageous bargaining position with foreign firms, lenders and donors. This relatively favorable balance of factors has placed it in a stronger position than most other African states.[92]

Kenya, likewise, has undergone important changes, although, like Ivory Coast, it too is clearly still a patrimonial administrative state. As in Ivory Coast, the agricultural sector has become increasingly capitalist and productive. On the manufacturing side, foreign confidence, relative political stability and decent infrastructure have all been maintained, but Kenya has pushed more vigorously than Ivory Coast in developing an indigenous true bourgeoisie, albeit one heavily linked to the state. In both Ivory Coast and Kenya a basic balance of factors has allowed these changes to take place and take root. This is not to say that there are no problems; there are. How one assesses them, however, depends on the model of capitalist development that one uses as a comparative referent—a historical one based on European or Latin American experience, for example, or some conceptually constructed model of "balanced" or "humane" capitalist development, which is not well rooted in historical reality.[93]

Nigeria, on the other hand, is a case of an African patrimonial state which has not maintained a beneficial balance of facilitating factors for the development of early capitalism. From "nurture capitalism" in the 1960s, Nigeria moved by the late 1970s to a form of "pirate capitalism," in which the oil boom seemed to aggravate all of the negative consequences of the patrimonial administrative state. Agriculture was neglected, corruption reached staggering heights and what investment did take place was not particularly productive in either the parastatal or private sector. As a result, unproductive debt has soared and foreign confidence has plummeted. Nigeria, like early modern Spain, has little to show for its enormous earnings.[94]

Whatever variant of early modern capitalism an African country has, as Leys points out, "like early capitalism everywhere," it is "painful, wasteful, and ruthless." His final assessment rings true: "It would be as mistaken to think that capitalism is in the process of developing all the countries of Africa as it is to suppose that it has not developed, and cannot develop, any of it."[95]

So far I have said little about foreign capital and the role it plays in Africa. I do not want to quibble here with the now large dependency literature about the pernicious effects of foreign "merchant, monopoly, and finance capital," but I do want to point out that the barriers and obstacles (e.g. political arbitrariness) discussed here affect foreign capital, too. One result of this, as I have argued elsewhere, is an involuntary marginalization of much of the continent which is under way within the world economy.[96] For, as Cooper has indicated, "Multinational corporations have considerable power, above all to choose the kind of state they need to cooperate with. . . . They do exercise some choice over the battleground. . . . Whether Africa plays a significant role in the shift in manufacturing markets in Europe and North America is doubtful. . . ." This holds for "finance capital" too. And as Hyden points out, for Western businessmen "Africa has become the black pit that swallows their money with little or no return."[97] From this point of view and the theoretical and historical view of this paper, a blunt statement by Cooper rings true: "The laments of international organizations and development economists about the intractable backwardness of Africa is not a conspiratorial attempt to conceal the pillage of Africa, but a reflection of the fact—although they would not put it this way— that Africa is an underexploited continent."[98] Clearly, what happens to Africa will be the combined result of the international market and state system, internal socioeconomic structure and the state. From what I can see, Africa has, at least so far, reaped few of the alleged benefits of "late" or "follower" development; nor is its current dismal situation predominantly the result of its dependent position in the world economy or its relationship to dominant countries in the international state system.[99] If, and there is no certainty of it, Africa develops some systematic form of modern capitalism, it will have to tackle many of the elements and processes that Weber conceptualized about and pursued comparative historical sociology to investigate.

There is clear evidence now of the increasing scale and texture of long-standing second economy phenomena in Africa. Much of this economic activity is composed of various forms of commercial capitalism, which are attempting to operate outside of both the formal market and the state. There is less evidence of productive activity based on significant new investment. The bulk of the second economy is still oriented toward survival and coping with a deteriorating socioeconomic, ecological and political situation. Signs do exist, however, that second economy activity could begin to redefine certain types of patron-client relationships away from the political logic of the state toward a social logic of accumulation and production outside the state, especially as the opportunity structure of some groups becomes increasingly restricted due to growing state weakness, declining state resources and increasing ruling class closure. Is this activity significant enough to indicate a displacement from the political to the economic? I doubt it, at least for quite some time. It is also far from clear that the calculation nexus of the second economy is such as to allow it to expand and transform itself into more sophisticated and long-lasting forms of capitalism or produce social groups that will seek to influence or take control of the state and transform it.[100] Much the same can be said for the existing tertiary sector of the formal economy. Speaking of artisans in western Nigeria, Berry notes that "investments in expanding and diversifying their businesses and in real estate reflect and reinforce the prevailing trend toward tertiary rather than industrial expansion in the Nigerian economy, just as cocoa farmer's investments in more farms or in rural trade reinforced rather than transformed the structure of the rural economy."[101]

Pessimism and optimism depend on where you stand—Ghana last year or nineteenth-century Latin America. For Africa, my short- and medium-term perspectives are highly pessimistic; my long-term perspective is guardedly optimistic. One thing that we must beware of is what I call the "Fault of Analytic Hurry"—the desire to rush things along, whatever the path, to see things as real before they actually are, to attribute substantive weight to social processes, institutions and actors that do not possess it. This has been one of the major problems with the analysis of class factors in Africa for quite some time now. It could apply just as easily to bureaucratization, the significance of *magendo* economies, the spread of the market, or any of the other elements of the configuration discussed above in regard to the development of modern capitalism. Analysts cannot hasten or control social processes; change is slow, incremental, uneven, often contradictory from a given analytic point of view, and dependent on the outcome of unpredictable socioeconomic and political struggles. At the same time, we cannot afford not to look for changes. As Iliffe's favorite African proverb says, "He who waits for the whole animal to appear, spears the tail."[102] And our models must match our reality. "In the present state of knowledge," as Jones reminds us, "we must resist the notion that any simple model will account for the whole developmental process."[103] We must retain a sense of the historical complexity involved. The brutal death of the voluntarist view of the state in Africa is but one pertinent example.[104] Lastly, we must not hope too unduly for any coming revolution that will be the salvation of the continent, because, as Cooper puts it, drawing on Skocpol, "It is easier to explain why peasants might want to rebel than how they might succeed." He also reminds us that "ending dependency is likely to press harder on the poor rather than easier—the history of early capitalist development in Europe hardly suggests otherwise."[105]

> My colleagues chide me for painting such a bleak picture. There must be a silver lining—there could be an upbeat ending to Mwasi's story. . . . Yet the struggles are becoming even more complex. How to educate one's children when schools are venal? How to exist when food is in short supply, medication cannot be found, and income is eroded by inflation unimaginable in the United States? How to maintain one's moral integrity and sense of purpose in Zaire's society today?
>
> —Jan Vansina, "Mwasi's Trials"[106]

Notes

1. Jan Vansina, "Mwasi's Trials," *Daedalus*, 111, 2 (Spring 1982): 69.

2. On the economic crisis see John Ravenhill, *Africa in Economic Crisis* (London/ New York: Macmillan/Columbia University Press, 1986); Robert J. Berg and Jennifer

Seymour Whitaker, *Strategies for African Development* (Berkeley: University of
California Press, 1986); Tore Rose, ed., *Crisis and Recovery in Africa* (Paris: Organisation
for Economic Co-operation and Development, 1985); Rupert Pennant-Rea, *The
African Burden* (New York: Twentieth Century Fund, 1986); Richard Sandbrook,
The Politics of Economic Stagnation in Africa (Cambridge: Cambridge University
Press, 1985); Colin Leys, "African Economic Development in Theory and Practice,"
Daedalus, 111, 2 (Spring 1982): 99–124; Crawford Young, *Ideology and Development
in Africa* (New Haven: Yale University Press, 1982); Jerker Carlsson, ed., *Recession
in Africa* (Uppsala: Scandinavian Institute of African Studies, 1983); Timothy M.
Shaw, *Towards a Political Economy for Africa: The Dialectics of Dependence* (New
York: St. Martin's, 1985); Henry F. Jackson, "The African Crisis: Drought and
Debt," *Foreign Affairs*, 63, 5 (Summer 1985): 1081–1094; and Adebayo Adedeji,
"Foreign Debt and Prospects for Growth in Africa During the 1980s," *Journal of
Modern African Studies*, 23, 1 (March 1985): 53–74.

3. John Ravenhill, "Introduction" in his *Africa in Economic Crisis*, p. 26.

4. See Randall Collins, "Weber's Last Theory of Capitalism: A Systematization,"
American Sociological Review, 45 (December 1980): 925–942; Jere Cohen, Lawrence
E. Hazelrigg and Whitney Pope, "De-Parsonizing Weber: A Critique of Parsons'
Interpretation of Weber's Sociology," *American Sociological Review*, 40 (April 1975):
229–241; Tom Bottomore, *Theories of Modern Capitalism* (London: Allen and Unwin,
1985); Max Weber, *General Economic History* (New Brunswick: Transaction Books,
1981); *Economy and Society* (Berkeley: University of California Press, 1978); and *The
Protestant Ethic and The Spirit of Capitalism* (New York: Scribner's, 1930).

5. Collins, "Last Theory," p. 927, abstracted from Weber, *General Economic
History*, pp. 275–276, 354–355.

6. Weber, *General Economic History*, p. 276.

7. Robert Brenner, "The Origins of Capitalist Development: A Critique of Neo-
Smithian Marxism," *New Left Review*, 104 (July–August 1977): 25–92.

8. Ira J. Cohen, "Introduction to the Transaction Edition: Max Weber on Modern
Western Capitalism," in *General Economic History*, p. xxiv.

9. Bottomore, *Theories*, p. 31.

10. Anthony Giddens, *Studies in Social and Political Theory* (New York: Basic
Books, 1977), pp. 185–188. In this regard, Bottomore notes that: "Marx was not
able to pursue with anything like the same thoroughness his proposed study of the
social and political context of capitalist development—that is to say, to analyse
capitalism as a historically evolving total society—and it is in this sphere especially
that attempts have been made, since the end of the nineteenth century, to extend
his theory" ("*Theories*," p. 19).

11. See Dietrich Rueschemeyer and Peter B. Evans, "The State and Economic
Transformation: Toward an Analysis of the Conditions Underlying Effective Inter-
vention," in P.B. Evans, D. Rueschemeyer, and T. Skocpol, eds., *Bringing the State
Back In* (New York: Cambridge University Press, 1985), pp. 44–77.

12. Skocpol makes a similar Weberian point; she stresses the *interdependence*
between the two spheres; *States and Social Revolutions* (Cambridge: Cambridge
University Press, 1979), p. 22. Also see Otto Hintze, "Economics and Politics in
the Age of Modern Capitalism," in F. Gilbert, ed., *The Historical Essays of Otto
Hintze* (New York: Oxford University Press, 1975), pp. 422–452; and Aristide R.
Zolberg, "Origins of the Modern World System: A Missing Link," *World Politics*,
33, 2 (January 1981): 253–281.

13. Weber, *General Economic History*, p. 339, emphasis added. Also see Collins,
"Last Theory," p. 932. Collins considers Wallerstein's viewpoint to be much more

compatible with Weber's conceptualization than I do; see his "Last Theory," pp. 939–941.

14. For an assessment of Weber's views on China from the perspective of recent scholarship see Stanislav Andreski, *Max Weber's Insights and Errors* (London: Routledge and Kegan Paul, 1984).

15. Rogers Brubaker, *The Limits of Rationality: An Essay on the Social and Moral Thought of Max Weber* (London: Allen and Unwin, 1984), p. 1. Also see Stephen Kalberg, "Max Weber's Types of Rationality," *American Journal of Sociology*, 85, 5 (1980): 1145–1179; Arnold Eisen, "The Meanings and Confusions of Weberian 'Rationality,'" *British Journal of Sociology*, 29, 1 (1978): 57–70; and Wolfgang Schluchter, *The Rise of Western Rationalism: Max Weber's Developmental History* (Berkeley: University of California Press, 1981).

16. Andreski, for example, clearly does not understand Weber's notion of rationality; see his *Weber's Insights*, pp. 58–82.

17. Brubaker, *Rationality*, pp. 1–2.

18. Ibid., p. 36.

19. Ibid., pp. 40–42.

20. Bottomore, *Theories*, pp. 5, 14, 16, 29. For Weber's views on class see *Economy and Society*, Chap. 4. Schumpeter took an even more jaundiced view than Weber of the significance of class factors in the development of capitalism; see Joseph A. Schumpeter, *Capitalism, Socialism and Democracy* (London: Allen and Unwin, 1976). Bottomore notes that "where Schumpeter's theory diverges most radically from Marxism is in its rejection of the idea of class struggle as a major factor in the development, and eventual decline of capitalism" (*Theories*, p. 44).

21. For an interesting debate on the roots of modern capitalism see Jere Cohen, "Rational Capitalism in Renaissance Italy," *American Journal of Sociology*, 85, 6 (1980): 1340–1355; and R. J. Holton, "Max Weber, 'Rational Capitalism,' and Renaissance Italy: A Critique of Cohen," and Jere Cohen, "Reply to Holton," both in *American Journal of Sociology*, 89, 1 (1983): 166–187.

22. Brubaker, *Rationality*, p. 37.

23. Weber, *Protestant Ethic*, p. 76.

24. Collins, "Last Theory," p. 928; Weber, *General Economic History*, pp. 275–279.

25. Weber included the development of citizenship as a key variable in the rise of modern capitalism; I do not believe that it is a necessary factor. Weber linked it very closely to the nature of the bourgeoisie, and I think it is possible to have the qualities of a bourgeoisie necessary to the development of modern capitalism without a viable citizenship, although having it probably facilitates the speed of the transformation. See Weber, *General Economic History*, pp. 315–337; and Collins, "Last Theory," pp. 932–933. In addition, Weber put less weight on the significance of entrepreneurship than Schumpeter did, choosing instead to focus on the contextual factors that would allow it to flourish. I think more direct emphasis on entrepreneurship is warranted.

26. Collins, "Last Theory," p. 928. A key difficulty with Weber's conceptualization of the rise of modern Western capitalism, one that is central to any attempt to apply it to Africa, is that it does not show how modern capitalism arises out of the slow and uneven emergence of the "prerequisites" or "preconditions," as Collins calls them. It is both a historical and an analytic problem. How much of a given factor must exist? What mixture of the partial presence of several factors is sufficient? What relationship exists between the various factors that facilitates their emergence?

Clearly, modern capitalism did not develop in Europe only when all the "preconditions" were lined up.

27. Collins, "Last Theory," p. 930.

28. Ibid., pp. 931–932.

29. The state may be viewed as a ruling organization that competes for power with other political, economic and social organizations and groups. The state as a ruling organization is a compliance structure. Weber called the state a compulsory political organization with a territorial basis (*Economy and Society*, p. 56). It is important to note that this is not a functionalist view of the state, a view common to both Marxist and many liberal perspectives, although the functions are rather different in the two. The state is not here because it is to perform certain functions for society, as in the liberal version, or to foster the development of capitalism and facilitate the rise and power of the bourgeoisie as a class. Any state, and the "functions" it performs, is the outcome of concrete sociopolitical and economic struggles. See Thomas M. Callaghy, *The State-Society Struggle: Zaire in Comparative Perspective* (New York: Columbia University Press, 1984), Chaps. 1–3; and Randall Collins, "A Comparative Approach to Political Sociology," in R. Bendix, ed., *State and Society* (Boston: Little, Brown, 1968), pp. 42–67.

30. Collins, "Last Theory," p. 932.

31. See Andreski, *Weber's Insights*; and John Hall, "Capstones and Organisms: Political Forms and the Triumph of Capitalism," *Sociology*, 19, 2 (May 1985): 173–192.

32. See Barry Hindess and Paul Q. Hirst, *Pre-Capitalist Modes of Production* (London: Routledge and Kegan Paul, 1975), p. 306.

33. See Randall Collins, *Conflict Sociology* (New York: Academic, 1975).

34. Anthony Giddens, *Capitalism and Modern Social Theory* (Cambridge: Cambridge University Press, 1971), p. 127.

35. Andreski, *Weber's Insights*, pp. 141–142.

36. Brenner, "Origins," p. 83.

37. Weber, *General Economic History*, p. 300.

38. Ibid., p. 353.

39. See Sayre Schatz, "Pirate Capitalism and the Inert Economy of Nigeria," *Journal of Modern African Studies*, 22, 1 (1984): 45–57, and note 94 of this essay.

40. Collins, "Last Theory," p. 931. For relevant sources for this section see: Douglass C. North and Robert Paul Thomas, *The Rise of the Western World: A New Economic History* (Cambridge: Cambridge University Press, 1973); C.M. Cipolla, *Before the Industrial Revolution: European Society and Economy, 1000–1700* (London: Methuen, 1976); Jan de Vries, *The Economy of Europe in an Age of Crisis, 1600–1750* (Cambridge: Cambridge University Press, 1976); Maurice Dobb, *Studies in the Development of Capitalism* (London: Routledge and Kegan Paul, 1963); David Landes, *The Unbounded Prometheus* (Cambridge: Cambridge University Press, 1969); John Nef, *Cultural Foundations of Industrial Civilization* (New York: Harper Torchbooks, 1960); Goran Ohlin, "Remarks on the Relevance of Western Experience in Economic Growth to Former Colonial Areas," *Journal of World History*, 9 (1965): 30–38; Charles Tilly, ed., *The Formation of National States in Western Europe* (Princeton: Princeton University Press, 1975); Skocpol, *States and Social Revolutions*; W.W. Rostow, *How It All Began: Origins of the Modern Economy* (New York: McGraw-Hill, 1975); Robert Wesson, *The Imperial Order* (Berkeley: University of California Press, 1967) and *State-Systems* (New York: Free Press, 1978); Immanuel Wallerstein, *The Modern World System: Capitalist Agriculture and the Origins of the European World-Economy in the Sixteenth Century* (New York: Academic Press, 1974) and *The*

Modern World System II: Mercantilism and the Consolidation of the World Economy,
1600–1750 (New York: Academic Press, 1980); Perry Anderson, *Lineages of the*
Absolutist State (London: New Left Books, 1975); Robert L. Heilbroner, *The Nature*
and Logic of Capitalism (New York: Norton, 1985); Joseph Strayer, *On the Medieval*
Origins of the Modern State (Princeton: Princeton University Press, 1970); and William
M. Reddy, *The Rise of Market Culture: The Textile Trader in French Society 1750–*
1900 (Cambridge: Cambridge University Press, 1984); also see Callaghy, *State-Society*
Struggle, Chaps. 2 and 3.

41. E.L. Jones, *The European Miracle: Environments, Economies, and Geopolitics*
in the History of Europe and Asia (Cambridge: Cambridge University Press, 1981),
pp. 93, 92, 95. Also see Albert O. Hirschman, *The Passions and the Interests: Political*
Arguments for Capitalism before Its Triumph (Princeton: Princeton University Press,
1977).

42. Jones, *European Miracle,* p. 94.

43. Ibid., p. 235.

44. Ibid., p. 237.

45. Hindess and Hirst, *Pre-Capitalist Modes,* p. 307, and Chap. 6 generally.

46. Alexander Gerschenkron, *Economic Backwardness in Historical Perspective*
(New York: Praeger, 1962), p. 17.

47. Ibid., p. 20.

48. Jones, *European Miracle,* p. 135.

49. Peter Evans, *Dependent Development: The Alliance of Multinational, State,*
and Local Capital in Brazil (Princeton: Princeton University Press, 1979). Also see
Rueschemeyer and Evans, "State and Economic Transformation"; and Albert O.
Hirschman, "The Turn to Authoritarianism in Latin America and the Search for
Its Determinants," in David Collier, ed., *The New Authoritarianism in Latin America*
(Princeton: Princeton University Press, 1979), pp. 61–98.

50. Weber, *Economy and Society,* p. 1097.

51. Ibid., pp. 1098, 1099, 1098, 241.

52. See Bill Freund, "Labor and Labor History in Africa: A Review of the
Literature," *African Studies Review,* 27, 2 (June 1984): 1–58. Because this piece focuses
rather narrowly on labor-related matters, Freund gives the impression that major
changes have taken place regarding this crucial factor of production; I believe this
to be an incorrect impression. See Sara Berry, "The Food Crisis and Agrarian
Change in Africa: A Review Essay," *African Studies Review,* 27, 2 (June 1984): 59–
112, and idem, *Fathers Work for Their Sons: Accumulation, Mobility, and Class*
Formation in an Extended Yoruba Community (Berkeley: University of California
Press, 1985), in which she provides a much more balanced and nuanced look at
many of these issues.

53. Frederick Cooper, "Africa and the World Economy," *African Studies Review,*
24, 2/3 (June/September 1981): 51, 31.

54. Goran Hyden, *No Shortcuts to Progress* (Berkeley: University of California
Press, 1983), pp. 29, 6–7, 29–30, 71, 24.

55. S.N. Sang-Mpam, "Peripheral Capitalism, the State and Comparative Public
Policy" (Conference paper, October 1984), pp. 21, 16. Also see his "Peripheral
Capitalism, the State and Crisis: The Determinants of Public Policy in Zaire, 1965–
1980" (Ph.D. diss., University of Chicago, 1984).

56. Callaghy, *The State-Society Struggle,* Chaps. 1–3.

57. Berry, *Fathers Work,* pp. 82–83.

58. Berry, "Food Crisis," pp. 92–93.

59. Ibid., p. 96.

60. Thomas M. Callaghy, "The State as Lame Leviathan: The Patrimonial Administrative State in Africa," in Zaki Ergas, ed., *The African State in Transition* (London/New York: Macmillan/St. Martin's, 1987), pp. 87–116. The "Lame Leviathan" piece should, ideally, be read in conjunction with this chapter in order to obtain the full elaboration of the argument, which cannot be presented here.

61. See Richard Joseph, "Class, State, and Prebendal Politics in Nigeria," in Nelson Kasfir, ed., *State and Class in Africa* (London: Frank Cass, 1984), pp. 21–38.

62. See note 49 above.

63. Crawford Young, *Ideology and Development in Africa* (New Haven: Yale University Press, 1982), pp. 188–189.

64. Ibid., p. 188.

65. See Callaghy, *State-Society Struggle*, Chaps. 1–3.

66. Hyden, *No Shortcuts*, p. 77.

67. Ibid., p. 19.

68. Crawford Young, "Zaire: Prospects for the Future" (Paper presented to the Conference on Zaire, Department of State, August 24, 1982), pp. 3–5.

69. Crawford Young, "Patterns of Social Conflict: State, Class, and Ethnicity," *Daedalus*, 111, 2 (Spring 1982): 94.

70. See Eli R. Hecksher, *Mercantilism* (London: Allen and Unwin, 1935); Charles Cole, *Colbert and the Century of Mercantilism* (Hamden, CT: Anchor Books, 1964); and Walter E. Minchinton, ed., *Mercantilism: System or Expediency?* (Lexington: Heath, 1969).

71. See note 40 above.

72. See Thomas M. Callaghy, "The Political Economy of African Debt: The Case of Zaire," in Ravenhill, *Africa in Economic Crisis*; and Adedeji, "Foreign Debt."

73. Ernest J. Wilson III, "Contested Terrain: A Comparative and Theoretical Reassessment of State-Owned Enterprise in Africa," *Journal of Commonwealth and Comparative Politics*, 22, 1 (March 1984): 22. Also see R. Sobhan, "Public Enterprises and the Nature of the State, *Development and Change*, 10 (1979); C. Frank, "Public and Private Enterprise in Africa," in G. Ranis, ed., *Government and Economic Development* (New Haven: Yale University Press, 1971); and Ernest J. Wilson III, "The Political Economy of Public Corporations: The Politics of Energy Parastatals in Zaire and Nigeria" (Ph.D. diss., University of California, 1978).

74. See Carl G. Rosberg and Thomas M. Callaghy, eds., *Socialism in Sub-Saharan Africa: A New Assessment* (Berkeley: Institute of International Studies, 1979).

75. Eli R. Heckscher, "Mercantilism," in *Encyclopedia of the Social Sciences* (New York: Macmillan, 1937), IX, p. 339.

76. Cooper, "Africa," pp. 20–21.

77. See Thomas M. Callaghy, "Absolutism, Bonapartism, and the Formation of Ruling Classes: Zaire in Comparative Perspective," in Irving L. Markovitz, ed., *Studies in Power and Class in Africa* (New York: Oxford University Press, 1987), pp. 95–117.

78. Hyden, *No Shortcuts*, pp. 60, 22.

79. Sang-Mpam, "Peripheral Capitalism"; Nelson Kasfir, "State, Magendo, and Class Formation in Uganda," in idem, *State and Class*, pp. 84–103; and "Class, Political Domination and the African State," in Ergas, *African State*; Brenner, "Origins"; and René Lemarchand, "The State, the Parallel Economy, and the Changing Structure of Patronage Systems," in this volume.

80. Cooper, "Africa," pp. 45, 52. Also see John Iliffe, *The Emergence of African Capitalism* (London: Macmillan, 1983), pp. 68, 76–78.

81. Leys, "African Economic Development," p. 113.

82. Hyden, *No Shortcuts*, p. 79.

83. Hindess and Hirst, *Pre-Capitalist Modes*; Ravenhill, "Introduction"; David Leonard, "What is Rational When Rationality Isn't?" *Rural Africana* (Spring-Fall 1984): 99–113; also see Berry, *Fathers Work*, for many fine examples of these phenomena.

84. Since this quotation and those that follow are from Weber, *Economy and Society*, the page numbers are indicated in brackets.

85. See note 49.

86. Evans, *Dependent Development*, p. 309.

87. Weber, *Economy and Society*, p. 1107.

88. Cooper, "Africa," p. 49.

89. Young, *Ideology*, p. 251.

90. See Berry, *Fathers Work*, Chaps. 1, 3–4.

91. Collins, "Last Theory," p. 929.

92. On Ivory Coast see Young, *Ideology*, pp. 190–203; P. Foster and A. Zolberg, *Ghana and the Ivory Coast: Perspectives on Modernization* (Chicago: Chicago University Press, 1971); Bonnie Campbell, "The Ivory Coast," in John Dunn, ed., *West African States: Failure and Promise* (Cambridge: Cambridge University Press, 1978); Samir Amin, *Le Développement du Capitalisme en Côte d'Ivoire* (Paris: Minuit, 1967); Lynn Krieger Mytelka, "The Limits of Export-Led Development: The Ivory Coast's Experience with Manufactures," in John Gerard Ruggie, ed., *The Antinomies of Interdependence* (New York: Columbia University Press, 1983).

93. On Kenya see Young, *Ideology*, pp. 203–219; Colin Leys, *Underdevelopment in Kenya* (Berkeley: University of California Press, 1974); Joel Barkan, ed., *Politics and Public Policy in Kenya and Tanzania*, 2nd edition (New York: Praeger, 1985); Nicola Swainson, *The Development of Corporate Capitalism in Kenya 1918–77* (Berkeley: University of California Press, 1980); Gavin Kitching, *Class and Economic Change in Kenya: The Making of an African Bourgeoisie* (New Haven: Yale University Press, 1980); Steven Langdon, "The State and Capitalism in Kenya," *Review of African Political Economy*, 8 (1977): 90–98.

94. On Nigeria see Young, *Ideology*, pp. 219–238; Sayre Schatz, *Nigerian Capitalism* (Berkeley: University of California Press, 1977), and "Pirate Capitalism"; Joseph, "Class, State"; Gavin Williams, ed., *Nigeria: Economy and Society* (London: Rex Collings, 1976); Berry, *Fathers Work*; Wouter Tims, *Nigeria: Options for Long-Term Development* (Baltimore: Johns Hopkins University Press, 1974); Keith Panter-Brick, ed., *Soldiers and Oil: The Political Transformation of Nigeria* (London: Frank Cass, 1978); I.W. Zartman, ed., *The Political Economy of Nigeria* (New York: Praeger, 1983); and Thomas J. Biersteker, *Multinationals, the State, and the Control of the Economy: The Political Economy of Indigenization in Nigeria* (Princeton: Princeton University Press, 1987).

95. Leys, "African Economic Development," pp. 105, 115.

96. See Callaghy, "Political Economy."

97. Cooper, "Africa," p. 51; Hyden, *No Shortcuts*, p. xi.

98. Cooper, "Africa," p. 52.

99. See Gerschenkron, *Economic Backwardness*.

100. See Lemarchand, "Patronage Systems"; Naomi Chazan, "Patterns of State Incorporation and Disengagement in Africa"; and Janet MacGaffey, "Economic Disengagement and Class Formation in Zaire"; all in this volume. Also see Janet MacGaffey, "Fending-for-Yourself: The Organization of the Second Economy in Zaire," in Nzongola-Ntalaja, ed., *Myths and Realities of the Zairian Crisis* (Trenton:

Africa World Press, 1986), and "How to Survive and Get Rich: The Second Economy in Zaire," *African Affairs*, 82 (1983): 351-366; and Kasfir, "State, Magendo."

101. Berry, *Fathers Work*, pp. 159-160, and the remainder of Chap. 6, "From Peasant to Artisan."

102. Iliffe, *African Capitalism*, p. 5.

103. Jones, *European Miracle*, p. 238.

104. See Callaghy, "Lame Leviathan."

105. Cooper, "Africa," pp. 53, 56.

106. Vansina, "Mwasi's Trials," pp. 69-70.

4

States Without Citizens: An Emerging African Phenomenon

John A.A. Ayoade

Until recently, 1960 was regarded by most Africans as their *annus mirabilis*, for the colonial edifice was thought to have begun its final journey to extinction in that year. But since about 1966 it has been apparent that the jubilations over political independence were premature and misplaced because the hopes of independence have not materialized. It has become clear that economic independence is a prerequisite of political independence. However, the success of any feasible strategy to turn around Africa's economic decline depends on the availability of external financing, and if Africa has antagonized possible foreign donors through political independence, then the achievement of real independence will be difficult. In any event, the process of independence generated unrealistic expectations, which launched postcolonial African states into both political and fiscal bankruptcy.

In a way, Africans could not have avoided the crisis of the state, because they perceived the state in Africa as an imposition, on the one hand, and as an instrument for satisfying the needs of the people, on the other. Thus, the philosophical alienation from the colonial state engendered by the independence movements not only resulted in political disengagement, but also gave rise to and sustained suspicion of the state. Yet African political leaders portrayed it as an *infinitus thesaurus*. Thus, in most cases the state in Africa progressed from the "Mother Theresa" or Welfare State through the Never-do-well State to the Expired State. It is this rapid transition from buoyancy at independence to bankruptcy within a quarter century that has made the African state a unique phenomenon.

It appears that the concept of OLOF (Optimum Level of Functioning) can be borrowed from the field of Community Nursing to explain the phenomenon of the pathology of the state in Africa. OLOF, the best possible functioning, all things taken into account, is derived from a holistic perspective and deals with the whole client environment. It affords the investigator an opportunity to look at factors that positively influence

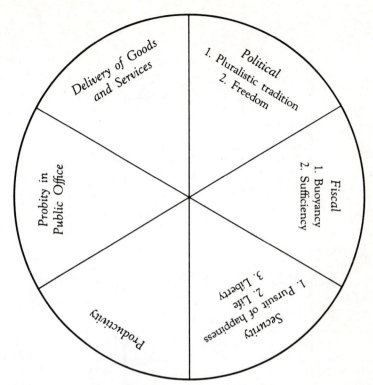

Figure 1 Optimal Level of Functioning (OLOF).

function, as well as those that negatively affect it.[1] The characteristics of a state at an optimum level of functioning are indicated in Figure 1.

However, the boundaries of abilities and potentials of a state also indicate the relationship between Negative Functional Indicators (NFI) and Positive Functional Indicators (PFI). These indicators constitute the Continuum of Function (Figure 2),[2] so that the probable level of functioning of a state can be measured. The NFI, presented in general terms in Figure 2, can be specified with some examples, including an expanded secret police system, crowded jails, heavy foreign debt, a high crime rate, considerable unemployment and sociopolitical insecurity. The NFI represent different stages of the paralysis of the state. For example, stress overload symptomizes an Infected State, which gradually becomes a Never-do-well State when the stress overload worsens and the state shows overt negative symptoms. If the trend is not reversed, a Bed-ridden State results, so that the state functions by fits and starts, and the people, out of necessity, attempt to establish their own autonomous, alternate governments. Such communities have to provide their own security and utilities. And when the state degenerates to the level of disability it goes into a coma, leaving its effectiveness to hinge on the precarious probability of resuscitation. While the state of

102

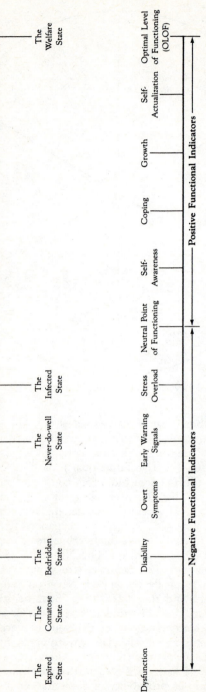

Figure 2 Continuum of Function. Developed from Sarah Ellen Archer and Ruth P. Fleshman, *Community Health Nursing: Patterns and Practice* (North Scituate: Duxbury Press, 1979), p. 38.

coma lasts, people relieve themselves of their obligations to the state and elevate alternate governments established in the Bed-ridden State to competing governments. At this stage those who can afford to do so will engage the services of armed retainers and equate right with might. This is a near-state of nature that is surpassed only at the level of the Expired State, which is characterized by political dysfunction that produces social and territorial disintegration. This is the state that Chad has now reached. The state, as formerly constituted in Chad, is extinct, giving rise to all sorts of makeshift arrangements lacking central coordination and decision-making rules. The state has lost its monopoly on force and has become the object of law by individuals and groups who have succeeded it. In contrast, the strong state is not only the repository of legitimate coercive force, but also the guardian, promoter and beneficiary of accepted rules of behavior, regularized relationships and social coherence.[3]

Whenever the political elite cartel succeeds in possessing the state, political brittleness develops, giving rise to a soft state in which there is a shrinkage of competence, credibility and probity.[4] State agencies become involuted mechanisms, such that material means fall short of policy ends. This gap gradually engenders a legacy of doubt, insofar as the incapability of the state results in the deflation of state credibility. More often than not, such a situation is compounded by the routinization of corruption in public life, which detracts from the minimal legitimacy a government requires for routine functioning.[5]

Unfortunately, the period of political incapability of a state paradoxically coincides with greater public demands, thus creating a feeling of demand overload that tends to exasperate the political elite cartel. This becomes an excuse for curtailing the rights of the people and disregards the notion that "for a government to deny individuals of their constitutional rights is to be guilty of an unconstitutional action, and to invite citizens to do the same, thus doubly breaching political authority."[6] It is no surprise, then, that Justice Brandeis, in his dissenting opinion in Olmstead vs. the United States (1928), concluded that "crime is contagious. If the government becomes a lawbreaker, it breeds contempt for law; it invites every man to become a law unto himself; it invites anarchy."[7] To some extent, here lies one of the causes of state pathology in Africa. It is the aim of this paper to examine the causes and course of state pathology, which is becoming a characteristic of the African state system.

The Bondage of Independence

At the risk of sounding simplistic, it is valid to say that colonialism irreversibly changed the course of African political history. The colonial period dichotomized African societies into the government and the people, such that an adversarial relationship was established between the two. Thus, the people felt they were being haunted by the government, against which they had to act if and when they could. This dichotomy was fortified by the fact that the colonial government was externally imposed and sought to undermine the traditional political leadership. This congenital dichotomy became the original sin that destroyed colonialism.

The nationalist movements in Africa questioned the legitimacy of an imposed government and promised the people a better deal under a democratic indigenous government. Furthermore, the state was portrayed as an external imposition which would be converted after independence into a veritable instrument for providing all the needs of the people. The nationalists thus generated philosophical alienation from the colonial state for the purpose of political disengagement and by so doing ostracized the state. Postcolonial politicians therefore had to reintegrate the state with the society and make the postcolonial state acceptable to the people.

Nationalist agitation was characterized by almost one-sided political speechifying, resulting in the mobilized political participation of a large segment of the colonial peoples. At different stages it was characterized by a false ideologization of empirical data and mere plebiscitary mobilization of support. Unlike autonomous participation, it resulted in the premature political engagement of the people and was manifested as political ectopia. Independence thus became problematic, since the premature incorporation of the people into politics resulted in excessive demands for redistribution and necessitated a return to departicipation.[8] The adversarial relationship between the state and the people that developed in colonial times worsened when the claims of the citizenry to the privileges of the state outstripped the obligations of the citizens to the state.

The postcolonial politician therefore found himself, of necessity, as the champion of the very state he had maligned, and poured venom on the strategy of opposition that he had effectively adopted. In his effort to realign the state with the society he adopted contradictory policies. He used state resources to placate the people, thereby creating a false impression about the affluence of the state. Thus, independence was viewed as capable of effecting a magical transformation of postcolonial society. People were promised amenities in return for political support, and these were sometimes provided at relatively no cost to them.

However, because the state had been undercut by the nationalist movement and easily suffered political overloading in the postcolonial period, the growth of government responsibilities was not matched by an equivalent growth in its capabilities.[9] Yet the weakened state was expected to provide more and more facilities. This paradoxical situation resulted from the attempt of the inheritors of the postcolonial state to outbid their colonial predecessors by exaggerating the benevolence of the state. In turn, a demand overload developed, and easily resulted in a crisis of rising expectations under conditions of declining state legitimacy. The inheritors encouraged the growth of public spending by emphasizing the benefits, rather than the costs, of the welfare state as if benefits are costless. This was an effect of separating politics from economics and ignoring the fact that if democratic politics entails giving people what they want, sound economics necessitates telling them what their resources can provide.[10]

African politicians have behaved as if they do not understand that no government can legislate to meet infinite wants with a finite national product. Postcolonial African politicians have not been content to act as custodians of established programs; they want to preside over new ones. They therefore have resorted to deficit promising, which places continuous demands upon the national product. And since they have not been expected to balance their books at the end of every fiscal year, the costs of their promises have been surfacing after them.

It is no surprise, then, that many African countries had fallen into the debt trap by the mid-1970s. By December 1983 Nigeria had an outstanding and disbursed debt of $11.7 billion which was 17.2 percent of its GNP and 109.1 percent of its exports of goods and nonfactor services. Ghana faced a more difficult period. By the same date it was indebted to the tune of $1.3 billion, which was 6.4 percent of its GNP and a huge 127.3 percent of its export of goods and nonfactor services. In December 1985 Ghana raised the minimum wage by 28.5 percent to ninety cedis per day, which with the devaluation was equivalent to $1.00. This has really meant a paralysis of the working class, which for almost a decade had been migrating to neighboring countries, particularly Nigeria. The continuing decline of per capita GDP growth rates in Ghana also confirms the infirmity of the economy. In 1961-1970 the per capita GDP growth rate was −0.3 percent; 1971-1979, −3.5 percent; and 1980-1984, −5.4 percent.

Unlike Ghana, Nigeria has been suffering from the pains of prosperity, which account for the excess of spending zeal that marked the boom and bust economic conditions in 1979-1983. From 1973 petroleum began to ease the capital constraint of Nigeria. Foreign exchange earnings by the sector rose from N5.7 billion in 1974 to N12.25 billion in 1980, i.e. 96.09 percent of the country's total exports. In fact, in 1982 oil exports amounted to a huge 98.6 percent of its total exports.[11] This created what Teriba calls a "fiscal illusion" and accounts for what Marinho aptly calls "quantum myopia," insofar as schemes and projects not only were in megaproportions but were also replicated without a sound economic basis.[12] Thus, at the height of its oil boom (1979-1983), Nigeria earned more foreign exchange (N43.0 billion) than in all of the preceding 21 years (1958-1979).[13] But surprisingly, during the very same period (1979-1983) it acquired more domestic and foreign debts than the cumulative debt ever owed previously. The total external indebtedness during these four years amounted to N24 billion, compared to a total of N5 billion incurred between 1960 and 1979.[14]

For Nigeria and many of the other African countries, reliance on such resources as minerals is reliance on nonreplenishable assets. Although natural resources confer a generous resilience, it must be understood that such a resilience is an inverse function of time. Thus, what Nigerians experience now as privations and frustrations may be the signature tune of a reality when factories and warehouses become relics of an aborted civilization.

The level of mismanagement in Nigeria in 1979-1983 has perhaps only been equaled by that in Zaire from 1975 to date. The GDP in Zaire rose around seven percent annually in real terms from 1968 to 1974, and the country was one of the most attractive investment prospects in Africa. It is a leading copper and cobalt producer, the world's largest supplier of industrial diamonds, and rich in coffee, timber and palm produce. But from 1975 the phenomenon of Mobutu turned it around. Zaire embarked on a spending orgy, such that by the tenth anniversary of the ascendancy of Mobutu debt repayments reached 60 percent of its export earnings. This fiscal crisis of the state dates back to the halcyon days of the mid-1970s copper boom and was catalyzed by gross financial irresponsibility in public life. At the highest levels corruption funds the system of political patronage. And at the lower levels it has permeated the very fabric of a society where the official monthly salary of most workers cannot properly feed a family for a week, thus crippling the productive potential of working Zairians. Consequently, in September 1983 there was a massive 77.5 percent devaluation of the zaire, necessitated by the huge debt that Zaire had incurred. In fact, by the end of 1983 the country had an outstanding and disbursed debt of about $4.5 billion, which amounted to 103.1 percent of the GNP. This debt also amounted to a huge 276.3 percent of its exports of goods and nonfactor services.

In addition, a network of about 88,000 miles of usable roads inherited at independence in 1960 has shrunk to about 12,000 miles, of which only 1,400 are paved.[15] The consequent high freight costs have been largely responsible for farmers receiving no more than 20-40 percent of the retail value of their produce. Although Zaire has attempted to comply with International Monetary Fund prescriptions for economic recovery and classified agriculture as the priority of priorities, the prospect of self-sustaining growth remains in doubt because of agriculture's daunting handicaps. These, according to Patti Waldmeir, include low budgetary allocations, relatively slow renewal of private investment, woefully inadequate credit and extension facilities and, worst of all, a transportation infrastructure crippled by years of neglect.[16] The resultant invalidation of the Zairian economy has created political brittleness that has marginalized the state in the delivery of essential services.

Generally, most African countries have exhibited a lack of efficiency in capital allocations, and the waste in government fiscal operations has neutralized the advantages of the fiscal transfusions of foreign loans. But perhaps the biggest setback is that the African countries are not credit-worthy, and the extension of international credit without collateral has done more harm than good. An utter lack of transparency in fiscal matters, a placatory posture in resource allocations and the spending of loan funds on luxury items have plunged most African countries into an abyss. Such conditions quickly turn risk into failure, and perhaps the way out, following Sharkansky, is for the state to deliver goods by learning "to do more with less,"[17] rather than doing less with more as the situation now stands. Africa cannot continue to use foreign loans to finance consumption instead of investment.[18] The state should stop operating as a bribe-ring of the state bourgeoisie to dull mass demand. It should assume the leadership and guardianship of the people.

Postcolonial Bureaupathology

Nationalists identified the fact that Africans were excluded from colonial bureaucracy on racial grounds. Further, nationalist ideology equated public-service jobs with amenities that ought to be allocated to the people. In practice, the state in Africa constituted an important resource as an employer, as well as an attractive one for those with access to its upper-echelon positions.[19] This created a new perception of the public service.

At independence Tanzania and Cameroon, among others, did not contain any institutions of higher learning. Zambia had only 36 university graduates and Malawi only 33. Countries such as Ivory Coast, Gambia, Senegal and Somalia had an illiteracy rate of over 90 percent.[20] Hence, there was a dearth of human capital. The absence of a highly trained corps of civil servants capable of providing responsive and efficient government gave rise to institutional decline in the postcolonial era.[21] The solution to such a problem is generally either to employ expatriate experts or to develop domestic staff resources. While the logic of independence makes the first alternative a contradiction, the fact that the gestation period for domestic staff resources is long cannot be overlooked. Nonetheless, the latter option was adopted in Africa, with all its consequences.

Almost all African countries experienced a rapid increase in both the number of civil servants and the rate of localization. In 1967 the Tanzanian civil service had 65,708 established posts. This figure increased to 101,182 in 1972, 191,046 in 1976, and 295,352 in 1980,[22] exceeding the 5.75 percent annual growth rate established by Parkinson's Law. The expansion rate of 13.3 percent was also far in excess of the 3.88 percent growth rate of the GDP between 1966 and 1976. Similarly, it outstripped the 2.84 percent rate of increase of total national wage employment.[23] The expansion of the civil service posts was fastest shortly after the Arusha Declaration of 1967 and continued to rise precipitately after the administrative decentralization in 1973/1974. While it is easy to say that the rise in the number of civil servants meant a higher demand on the national product, it is not easy to assess the effect of the creation of a political service in 1964. In that year the political-administrative dichotomy ended when civil servants were allowed to become members of the Tanganyikan African National Union. In fact, in 1972 legislation was passed allowing civil servants to contest elections without prejudicing their civil service status.[24]

Similarly, in Zambia the number of civil servants increased. Between 1963 and 1974 it increased by 265 percent, while emoluments increased by 328 percent. Between December 1975 and December 1977, when employment in the private sector declined from 120,260 to 98,730, employment in the civil service increased from 124,260 to 126,260 and from 116,150 to 128,350 in the parastatals.[25]

The civil service suffered a phenomenal increase after independence because it had been perceived in colonial times as the seat of political power. Thus, a civil service post was valued as a worthwhile political investiture. In addition, the civil service was seen as a domain of privilege, made even more attractive by high cash returns. It was therefore a high political risk to exclude any section of the community. Consequently, the civil service exploded at the seams.

Quite apart from the numerical expansion, average earnings were 60 percent higher in the parastatal sector than in the private sector in 1977. In addition to the civil service, the army has been equally overestablished, and there is hardly any reasonable explanation for the soldier-people ratio. For example, one wonders why Swaziland requires 6.9 soldiers per 1,000 inhabitants and Kenya only 0.8.[26] But quite apart from being overestablished, African armies are hardly productive. It is no surprise, then, that Dumont says "the Zambian army is good at spending ever-increasing sums of money, but doesn't know how to produce on an economic basis."[27]

Almost without exception, by 1985 African civil services were characterized by overstaffing. Thus, Pierre Biarnes maintains that Senegal's 70,000 civil servants and 35,000 in the parastatals is too heavy a burden for such a small country to bear.[28] Perhaps this is an outcome of the state having become a resource. It is in this vein that one can explain the rate of localization in spite of an initially weak technocratic base. Between 1963 and 1968 the number of Zambians in central government employment rose from 1357 to 7509. In Tanzania the rate of localization was even faster. In 1961 there were only 1170 Tanzanians (i.e., 26.1 percent) out of a total of 4452 in established senior and middle-level posts. By December 1972 this figure increased to 11,988, a huge 94.1 percent of the total civil service.[29] Even in Zaire where the rate of localization has been fairly low, Paul Cheeseright notes that the figure of 20,442 Belgians in Zaire in 1975 had dropped to 14,282 by the end of 1984.[30]

A high rate of localization in a situation of scarce expertise raises the problem of efficiency. McNamara argues that "the weaknesses in the political and administrative decision-making systems are a function of this problem."[31] Although by 1968 only 20 percent of the Tanzanians holding administrative officer positions possessed the prerequisite qualification of a recognized university degree, Mutahaba has argued that their jobs were repetitive and required practice rather than a high level of education. As far as he was concerned, nongraduates were actually better suited to administer development since the socio-cultural gap between them and the general Tanzanian public was narrower. Andreski, however, completely debunks the inferiority of the African successor class, at least in the universities, although he has reached the same conclusion about their incompetence. He states very pointedly that

> although many African dons are abler than their British predecessors (who were often people who could never have got equivalent jobs at home), their work is much worse because they devote most of their time to political

intrigues, and having arrived, no longer bother about intellectual matters. To a large extent this happens because the prizes of politics are too glittering and seemingly too attainable to be resisted; but secondly, because once an educational institution becomes riddled with nepotism and cut-throat politics, even people with no taste for this game have to take part in it for the sake of keeping their jobs.[32]

Andreski, however, also agrees with Mazrui, who distinguished between intellectuals and those who are intellectually engaged when he concluded that those who compose the new African elite are not intellectuals but graduates. Similarly, the new African states are governed by either officers or graduates or both.[33] While it is true that independence would have meant even less than it does now if the bureaucracy had remained tethered to the colonial metropolis, the wrong choice was made between incremental and precipitative development of the bureaucracy. As a consequence, a weak bureaucracy was saddled with the difficult task of consummating independence.

It is highly likely that the most critical aspect of this bureaupathology has been the creation of what an astute Ghanaian has called the "Afropean" class, whose members formerly criticized the very colonial European privileges which they have now inherited and protect. The inherent contradiction that they represent has produced not only envy, but also ambition stimulated by the reality of incredible careers made through the process of decolonization.[34] By and large, members of this class are not as well educated as their subordinates, a situation which makes them uneasy in their new incarnation. This status anxiety sometimes results in repression which, more often than not, leads to an unnecessary diversion from the affairs of state.

The contradictions resulting from the status anxiety of the bureaucracy leadership has often resulted in a decrease in labor discipline or productivity, as well as moral disorientation that tends to make bureaucracy chaotic. Many African countries have had to grapple with the problem of discipline in public life. For quite some time Kenya has been waging a relentless battle against drunkenness, while General Obasanjo, the former head of the Nigerian state, in his famous Jaji Address identified indiscipline as the source of all Nigerian problems. Perhaps the moral disorientation that we have identified above is an unintended consequence of the delinkage of society from the state at independence, as well as a symptom of general indiscipline. In any event, it has resulted in massive corruption that has paralyzed the public household.

Such corruption can be divided into two types: solidaristic and egoistic graft. Some public functionaries justify graft in order to redress perceived group economic disequilibrium; this is solidaristic graft. For example, in Nigeria the north has perceived the south as controlling the economy, and a large number of bad financial deals have been rationalized as a form of restoring economic equilibrium. Egoistic graft also occurs when the individual enters into a shady deal for personal enrichment per se. In both cases politicians and bureaucrats use the state to reward themselves and their

supporters with jobs, contracts, public monopolies and illicit income. The
state is thus incapacitated to produce goods and services for the mass of
the population.[35] This situation alienates the general public from the state,
thus making it an orphan.

The successor bureaucrats, however, unite to exploit the rural dwellers.
For example, Dumont contends that in Zambia in the late seventies a mere
$10 per capita was spent annually in the rural districts, while subsidies to
lower the cost of basic foods in the cities amounted to as much as $30
per head in 1978.[36] Similarly, the Third National Development Plan of
Zambia 1966–1971 allocated 14 million kwachas to rural dwellings containing
60 percent of the population, compared to 283 million kwachas to urban
dwellings.[37] It is this kind of discrimination against the rural areas that the
Ghanaian People's National Revolutionary Defence Council has called "ur-
bantheid" and decried.

The relationship between the urban and rural areas in Tanzania has not
been nearly as bad. Rural areas have been given priority and the peasants
have pride of place.[38] But it is also true that in Tanzania foreign exchange
is earned by the rural areas and spent by the towns. For example, in order
to buy a bureaucrat an ordinary car costing Sh 60,000 in 1979, a peasant
was required to work 6,000 days for very little pay.[39] There is some truth,
therefore, in the assertion that independence is for townspeople and that
the state was set up for the benefit of its capital city, its political and
economic leaders and its bureaucrats.[40]

The disillusionment underlying the above statement and general disenchantment in postcolonial Africa have reverberated recently in Nigeria. For
instance, Governor Sam Mbakwe of Imo State wondered whether a return
to colonial rule should be considered by Nigerians as a viable option. The
disillusionment was stated even more forcefully by General Obasanjo, who
said:

> Although in a different context, Nigeria was ruled and governed from amal-
> gamation to independence by colonial military administrators. And barring
> other ills of that period, and they were many, the administration established
> and preserved considerable stability and consistency. If such stability and
> consistency had not been tarnished with economic exploitation, social depri-
> vation, cultural oppression and political exclusion, the period might have been
> hailed as glorious.[41]

Quite apart from the absence of class justice in the rural-urban division
and the "two-tier" towns that have been mushrooming, wages in the public
sector have continued to undercut private enterprise. Wages in the public
sector have been forcing up wages in the private sector, and occasionally
the private sector has been coerced to comply with pay hikes. Wage increases
in the public sector, however, have not necessarily been related to productivity,
which is—or should be—the prime consideration of the private sector.
More often than not, wage increases in the public sector have been granted
as part of an election package deal.[42] The effect of the forced incorporation

of the private into the public economy has been the limitation of choice, which properly belongs to the individual.[43] This erosion of choice has been complicated by the fact that expansion in the public economy has no direct relation with expansion in the national economy. In fact, in most African countries the public economy has expanded at the same rate by which the national economy has contracted. But some African countries, such as Zaire and Nigeria, have come to realize the futility of this situation and have been seriously contemplating privatization of public holdings. This would result in the direct correlation of the size of the public sector with the capabilities of the government and political systems and, over time, with the salience of politics and the levels of political participation.[44]

The creation of morbid states is not only attributable to the precipitate accession of the postcolonial bureaucrats to office. The age and rate of career advancement of the indigenous pioneer bureaucrats have created immense problems that have dampened morale. The successor bureaucrats underwent very rapid career advancement and, due to their generally young age there has been a very low turnover rate in the civil service. Consequently, they have become an organizational bourgeoisie that has established an authoritarian, patrimonial administrative structure to ward off challenges from second-generation bureaucrats whose career advancement would have to be slower. This has sometimes reduced productivity and at other times resulted in the inordinate expansion of the service. And sometimes those who believe they are victims of career retardation have appropriated elements of social surplus through the state apparatus. This has inevitably resulted in the gradual incapacitation of the state.

In other places escape from arrested careers has taken the form of demands for either structural or lateral expansion of the service. The synonymity of these demands with the career requirements of the bureaucrats therefore indicates that in most of these countries the state exists for the bureaucrats. But in addition, these autonomist demands have sometimes been instruments for the regional redistribution of income, particularly in plural societies. Examples can be found in Katanga/Shaba Province, southern Sudan and eastern Nigeria. These examples illustrate the attempt to balance the political rewards of a region with its economic contributions to the nation.

The Dialectics of Popular Participation

In the nationalist period the nationalists set in motion the phenomenon of mobilized participation, which in the Gramscian fashion was aimed at enlisting mass energies in the struggle for ideological hegemony. This occurred because the nationalists were political entrepreneurs or constituency creators who were impatient with autonomous participation but precipitated political participation by appealing to the inalienable rights of all people to independence. As the paramount Chief of Basutoland, Prince Bereng, said in 1963, "we desire it [independence] as a nation and are entitled to it as human beings."[45] The consequence of mobilized participation in most African countries was an unusually high degree of political penetration and activation by European standards. Thus, political parties were formed. These nationalist parties had the advantage of being able to plead a congruence of interests with the generality of the colonized peoples. It was therefore easy to isolate the colonial administrators, who were synonymous with the colonial state. This ultimately resulted in a dichotomy of society and government as well as society and state.

Apart from creating a state-society dichotomy, the nationalist era also emphasized rights and denounced duties and obligations to the state. This worked well as a strategy of decolonization because it incapacitated the colonial state. The nationalists questioned the legality of taxes and demanded higher wages and better service conditions.

Independence moved the nationalists from marginal to central roles in the administration of their states. For a while the political speechifying of the preindependence era continued simultaneously with the celebratory rhetoric of independence. A new form of ideological socialization emerged in order to transform the colonial state into a nation. Its purpose was to create normative identification with the state through a network of universalistic rules. In effect, this meant the reversal of the process of dichotomization of the state and society which had been forcefully set in motion in the independence period. It also meant a redemption of the state from its previous pariah status. Unfortunately, the reconciliation of the state with society and its restoration had to take place according to the terms set down by the triumphant political class that inherited power at independence. Thus, while there was a desire to endear the state to the people, it was also insisted that the state is coterminous with its leaders, who perceived the state as their political earning. Therefore, neither state-society reconciliation nor the restoration of the state was pursued honestly. It is, however, necessary to examine the modalities that failed. They include the homogenization of diverse political views and interests through single-party structures, the espousal and propagation of new political ideologies, and the sacralization of political leaders.

At the end of the first quarter century of independence in Africa less than ten percent of the countries show trappings of the multipartism that preceded independence. In some of them, such as Lesotho, Nigeria and The Gambia, political parties other than those in power are tolerated but not approved. The success of the opposition Basutoland Congress Party in the Lesotho general elections on January 27, 1970 showed that victory for an opposition party can be likened to political trespassing in Africa. Similarly, the opposition party in Sierra Leone in 1967 committed the crime of victory. And in 1983 Nigeria spent a colossal N764 million (about $916.8 million) to conduct a highly disputed election that awarded victory, but not legitimacy, to the government party. In most African countries the following view of a member of the Basutoland National Party prevails: "How can we lose the match? The ball is ours; the jerseys are ours; the field is ours; the linesmen are ours; and, more important, the referee, too, is ours."[46]

Only Mauritius has shown ample tolerance for the opposition. The founding father, Seewoosagur Ramgoolam, lost gracefully to the opposition party in 1982. The multiparty system has also worked in Botswana. But apart from the few exceptions, the reality has been the mushrooming of single-party regimes. Several pious reasons have been adduced by proponents of the single-party system. It is, however, most likely that the phenomenon emerged because of the high personalization of office by the initial postcolonial leaders. These leaders fabricated justificatory ideologies appropriate to the spirit and mood of the postcolonial societies. They claimed there was a need to balance political independence with an autochthonous ideology. Consequently, most postcolonial regimes embraced the ideology of African socialism.

The immediate postcolonial political leadership in Africa apparently adopted socialism as a strategy of decolonization. It was seen as a feasible strategy because colonialism was perceived as a capitalist enterprise by the metropolitan nations. Thus, colonialism could have been confronted only by an ideology that is equal and opposite. But it would have been suicidal for the African nationalists to adopt an exclusionary ideology at a time when they needed the support of all and sundry. Therefore, the option of African socialism was preferred to Marxism-Leninism, which would have confronted African traditional culture and emphasized classes.[47] Consequently, single-party systems developed on the understanding that opposition is alien to African culture. The single parties have performed the task of political education admirably, such that Africans under these regimes are highly politically literate. The case of Tanzania, which exemplifies this situation, has been vividly described as follows:

> Partly because of his [Nyerere's] approach and the importance placed on education where a conscious effort is made to infuse the youth with the egalitarian ideal, Tanzanians are among the most politically literate people anywhere. The visitor is often enthralled by a taxi driver or a photographer going into the nuances of world diplomacy or the stumbling block Reagan's constructive engagement poses to the liberation struggle in South Africa.[48]

Unfortunately, the inclusionary ideology of African socialism was contradicted by the exclusionary single-party *modus operandi*. Thus, the people were mobilized through independence movements which initially sought legitimacy by extolling African communalism but after independence opted for a departicipatory process in an extremely politicized state. The leadership had aimed at a plebiscitary mobilization of support, which the people mistook for an offer of real participation. This contradiction resulted in a split between the leaders and the people in Africa. The political leaders, for their part, believed the achievement of independence guaranteed their position, while the people regarded their leaders' actions as a breach of trust. The single-party system and the concurrent assumption of a "divine" status by the leaders blocked the exhaust system for the easy discharge of political toxic waste. The leaders exonerated themselves from legal sanctions, and citizen political liquidity preference diminished. In these circumstances most African states consolidated at a zero growth point or less.

This is not to say that there has been no interaction between the state and the society. In fact, the political leadership has continued to spin out new ideologies that reinterpret the state and their persons. This very process of establishing the synonymity of the leaders with the state produces "sacred" leaders too "divine" to be challenged, who bask in bemedaled uniforms and gilded palaces, that in their splendor symbolize state-society dichotomy. This era of the "man-gods" in Africa has been characterized by long political careers, in which the containment of dissent has been the only visible preoccupation of the state. Consequently, the political arena has contracted through mass political departicipation set in motion by the single-party system, which has paradoxically thrived on populism. Politics has therefore degenerated into "riding the tiger," such that long tenures in political offices more often than not symptomize a political dilemma. In fact, long stays in office tend to correlate positively with bad governments, and the leaders' fear of reprisals necessitates the elimination of potential successors. Hence, a paradoxical situation has emerged whereby regime stability coexists with political instability in which the state suffers political incapacitation.

The dilemma of the disengagement of African political leaders from office has not been easy to resolve. Nonetheless, Leopold Senghor of Senegal, for example, produced a model of disengagement in which the president selects his successor and retires. In this way, Senghor passed on political power to Abdou Diouf. Similarly, Ahmadou Ahidjo passed on power to Paul Biya in Cameroon, probably with some regret, and Julius Nyerere passed it on to Hassan Mwinyi. Perhaps the strangest species of the Senghorian model so far has been that of Sierra Leone, where Siaka Stevens relinquished power to Major-General Joseph Momoh, who, until his inauguration as the president, was the commanding officer of the Sierra Leonean army. In a way it was a voluntary, peaceful blending of the civil and the military in the government, possibly to preempt a military takeover. It is also ironical that Siaka Stevens, to whom the military had handed over power in the civilian restoration of 1970, voluntarily handed over political power to the military in 1985.

The situation has not been better in those states where frequent changes of government, particularly through coups, have taken place. Such frequent changes not only prevent the normal growth of government, they also result in political-cultural discontinuities. Each new government discredits the previous one, sometimes not unjustly, but not because it will have a better record of performance. The result of this continual process of deprecating political leaders who made themselves coterminous with the state adds up to giving the state a pariah status in the society. Consequently, when government becomes ineffective—as it often tends to become, given the combination of factors that we have enumerated—the value of the state is further reduced, sometimes to a point where it hinders the development of the society.

Insofar as change has acquired a momentum of its own in many African countries and the denigration of predecessors is the obvious justification of successors, government in Africa has become a high-risk domain. Unfortunately, almost as a rule, each succeeding government has tended to be worse than its predecessor, so that there has been a gradual deterioration of the government and of course the state. The net effect of the deterioration of the state is that it has become more and more difficult to attract competent, responsible people to government in Africa. Consequently, the quality of government has been getting worse, rather than better.

People escape the dire consequences of state decay by recoiling inwards and establishing voluntary neighborhood governments. In this way they provide their own utilities and security. There are therefore two levels of governments: the general constitutional government, and the local informal government. The latter is based on levies and necessitated by the incompetence of the general *de jure* government. The per capita cost of government is therefore high, because people pay taxes to the *de jure* government, from which they have learned not to expect any services, and levies to a nonconstitutional *de facto* government, which provides essential services. It should be noted that possibilities of clashes between both governments exist because the latter, which is effective, must operate under the regime of the former, which is incompetent.

Conclusion

The state apparatus in Africa has suffered a gradual and sustained diminution of authority. In the immediate postcolonial period this was attributable to the successful defamation of the state by the leaders of the independence movements. The ideology of independence weakened the state system because the faults of the state *qua* state were confused with those of colonialism. Thus, the state was convicted as an alien apparatus for the oppression of the people. Consequently, the people dissociated themselves from the state, which they have continued to perceive as an adversary.

Paradoxically, the state has also been seen as the prime distributor of benefits, and thus the people have been mobilized, to an extent, by an emphasis on the benefits to be derived from the state, without regard for the costs. The inability of the state to match this requirement has created a credibility gap, which has necessitated the delinkage of the people from the state.

As if that were not enough, the Santa Claus syndrome has also resulted in an overestablished civil service, which in terms of technical expertise remains underbureaucratized. Thus, the unit cost of government has increased by about the same proportion that the quality of social service delivery has declined. This situation has engendered immense frustrations because a government may be omnipresent, but it is not omnipotent. Such frustrations have more often than not been confronted by the political class, which has deodorized these political cesspools with populist ideologies of doubtful logical integrity. Expectations have been raised simultaneously as participation has narrowed. The result has been a vicious form of paternalism.

In order to revitalize the African states, the image of the state will have to be repaired so that it is endeared to the society. But that process will require the disempowerment of the invalid state, rather than its reempowerment. The overstretched state must contract to an optimal level of functioning. This will facilitate the political reorientation of society and provide an understanding of the agenda of the state. Africa can no longer afford to meet present exigencies through temporary expedients.

It is, however, not sufficient to reform the system. System reform must be complemented with leadership engineering. This view was appropriately emphasized by General Obasanjo when he wrote:

Until 1979, I was by virtue of my training and upbringing what you might call a systems man. I believe that if a system is good and well-founded, any person with average ability could make it work. I changed my belief after watching the rapidity with which the system was perverted and destroyed and the depth to which rot set in within a short space of time.[49]

The process of leadership engineering must reverse the elite cartel nature of leadership and emphasize dedication and service to the nation. This will make it possible to convert the vote into a means of mass-interest articulation, rather than a means of gaining support. It will also halt the practice of extending political rights while social and civil rights are freely curtailed. This reconstruction of political authority and the limitation of the state to its legitimate duties will dissolve the current state-society dichotomy and scarcity of hope.

Notes

1. Sarah Ellen Archer and Ruth P. Fleshman, *Community Health Nursing: Patterns and Practice* (North Scituate: Duxbury Press, 1979), p. 37.

2. Ibid., p. 38.

3. Donald Rothchild and Michael Foley, "The Implications of Scarcity for Governance in Africa," *International Political Science Review*, 4, 3 (1983): 313.

4. Crawford Young, "Zaire: Is There a State?" *Journal of African Studies*, 18, 1 (1984): 80–81.

5. Ibid., p. 81.

6. Richard Rose and Guy Peters, *Can Government Go Bankrupt?* (New York: Basic Books, 1978), p. 236.

7. Quoted in Jethro K. Lieberman, *How the Government Breaks the Law* (New York: Stein and Day, 1972), p. 15.

8. Ruth B. Collier, *Regimes in Tropical Africa: Changing Forms of Supremacy 1945-1975* (Berkeley: University of California Press, 1982), p. 21.

9. Rothchild and Foley, "Implications of Scarcity," p. 318.

10. Rose and Peters, *Can Government Go Bankrupt?*, p. 20.

11. F.R.A. Marinho, "Nigeria: A Regenerative Economy or Vegetative Existence," mimeo (1985 University of Ibadan Alumni Lecture, June 14, 1985).

12. Ibid.

13. Ibid.

14. Ibid.

15. *Financial Times Survey*, July 9, 1985.

16. Ibid.

17. Ira Sharkansky, *Wither the State?* (Chatham: Chatham House, 1979), p. 3.

18. A.W. Clausen, *Priority Issues for 1984* (New York: The World Bank, 1984), p. 9.

19. Morris Szeflel, "Political Graft and the Spoils Systems in Zambia—The State as a Resource in Itself," *Review of African Political Economy*, 24 (1982): 7.

20. Robert S. McNamara, "The Challenges for Sub-Saharan Africa," Sir John Crawford Memorial Lecture (Washington, D.C., November 1, 1985), p. 30.

21. Ibid.

22. Rwekaza Mukandala, "Trends in Civil Service Size and Income in Tanzania 1967–1982," *Canadian Journal of African Studies*, 17, 2 (1983): 253.

23. Ibid., p. 254.

24. Gelase Mutahaba, "The Effect of Changes in the Tanzanian Public Service System upon Administrative Productivity 1961–72," *African Review*, 5, 2 (1975): 204–205.

25. Szeflel, "Political Graft," p. 6.

26. Peter S. Heller and Allan T. Tait, *Government Employment and Pay: Some International Comparisons* (Washington, D.C.: International Monetary Fund, 1983), p. 28.

27. René Dumont, *Stranglehold on Africa* (London: André Deutsch, 1983), p. 53.

28. Ibid., p. 185.

29. Mutahaba, "The Effect of Changes," p. 204; cf. Mukandala, "Trends in Civil Service Size," pp. 253–254.

30. *Financial Times Survey*, July 9, 1985.

31. McNamara, "Challenges for Sub-Saharan Africa," p. 30.

32. Stanislav Andreski, *The African Predicament: A Study in the Pathology of Modernization* (New York: Atherton Press, 1968), p. 141.

33. Ibid.

34. Ibid., p. 56.

35. Dumont, *Stranglehold on Africa*, p. 51.

36. Ibid., p. 85.

37. McNamara, "Challenges for Sub-Saharan Africa," p. 9.

38. Dumont, *Stranglehold on Africa*, p. 102.

39. Ibid., p. 157.

40. Ibid., p. 179.

41. O. Obasanjo, "Nigeria: Which Way Forward," *Daily Times*, August 7, 1985.

42. John A.A. Ayoade, "Federalism and Wage Politics in Nigeria," *Journal of Commonwealth and Comparative Politics*, 13, 3 (1975): 282–289.

43. "Introduction: Multiple Approaches to Measurement and Explanation," in Charles Lewis Taylor, ed., *Why Governments Grow, Measuring Public Sector Size* (Beverly Hills: Sage, 1983), pp. 11, 20.

44. Karl W. Deutsch, "The Public Sector: Some Concepts and Indicators," in Taylor, *Why Governments Grow*, p. 26.

45. Quoted in M. Khaketla, *Lesotho 1970: An African Coup Under the Microscope* (Berkeley: University of California Press, 1972), p. 55.

46. Ibid., p. 206.

47. "Introduction," in Carl G. Rosberg and Thomas M. Callaghy, eds., *Socialism in Sub-Saharan Africa: A New Assessment* (Berkeley: Institute of International Studies, University of California, 1979), pp. 1–11.

48. Sully Abu, "Farewell to Mwalimu," *The Guardian* (Nigeria), October 27, 1985, p. B4.

49. Obasanjo, "Nigeria," p. 5.

PART THREE

The Changing State in Africa: Societal Perspectives

5

Patterns of State-Society Incorporation and Disengagement in Africa

Naomi Chazan

State-Society Relations: The Problematics

The dynamics of power and political configurations in postindependence Africa have become increasingly perplexing and elusive. An array of seemingly disparate and frequently contradictory socioeconomic and political activities appear to be occurring simultaneously. Political apathy intermingles with activism, resistance with fatalism. People are leaving their homes and their countries in search of sustenance, while at the same time dependency on government grows. Ambitious programs of structural adjustment have been undertaken and long-range economic plans designed, yet parallel markets are burgeoning and a good deal of local production is unrecognized and unrecorded. State structures are extensive and instrusive; they are also often weak and ineffective. Processes of social differentiation are taking place in conjunction with and separately from the formal institutional apparatus. The continent encompasses a variety of states, each exhibiting varying degrees of stateness.[1]

The difficulties inherent in grasping these realities lie perhaps less in the intricacies of the processes at hand than in the limitations of existing analytical frameworks. State-centric approaches have stressed the centrality of the state as a historical actor, the key collective agent of macropolitical processes.[2] This perspective views the state as the central organ for the extraction and distribution of resources, the determination of binding principles for society, and the maintenance of external and internal security, social harmony, and political and economic well-being.[3] These approaches look at political process (domestically and externally) from the top down. The unit of analysis is the state; the level of analysis in the first instance is national; the object of analysis, inevitably, social and economic trends. Explanations for present conditions in Africa are lodged in the state, state policy and reactions to state actions.

Fascination with the notion of state autonomy and state failure has peaked, however, precisely when events in Africa have directed attention to the study of economic deterioration and decline.[4] While arguments cast in this mold may be skillfully mustered to help account for regressing conditions,[5] they are far less useful in illuminating ongoing processes and directions of change.

Society-based approaches, in contrast, have sought to focus more squarely on survival strategies in changing economic and political circumstances. Starting from a societal vantagepoint, work carried out in this vein has explored how specific social groups define their identity and interests, how they mobilize their resources and construct alliances to pursue their goals, and how they cope with their fickle environment. This mode of analysis has generated a good deal of research in recent years, most of which highlights the internal dynamics of socioeconomic relations in small-group settings.[6] Especially insightful are the detailed studies of peasants and workers and, most recently, of the informal economy.[7] Society-centered approaches thus do not consider participation in the state as axiomatic or necessarily desirable.[8] Specific social constellations measure their affiliations and the degree of their involvement in light of their concerns, capacities and needs.

Society-rooted research examines political and economic processes from the bottom up. The unit of analysis is the specific social group or local community; the level of analysis is the micro collectivity; the object of analysis is socioeconomic process as well as political dynamics. Explanations for the present situation on the continent are offered in terms of social predilection, action and behavior.

Societal perspectives of political life in Africa do go a long way toward correcting some of the excesses of state-centric analyses. Because they are conceived and conducted at the micro level, however, they frequently run the risk of minimizing, or even ignoring, activities emanating from the state. In the ongoing quest for uncovering the regularities and flexibilities of coping mechanisms, insufficient attention is paid to the impingement of macro forces. As a result, societal analyses have encountered difficulties not only in delineating the boundaries of the groups whose behavior they wish to trace, but also in identifying the various overlapping manifestations of social and political action.

The contemporary African political experience defies the neat classificatory schemes devised to capture its multivariate texture. The message emanating from the continent in recent years is one of constant movement, of straddling the dichotomies of its observers.[9] There is a growing awareness that the major challenge facing students of African politics at this juncture is to directly confront the many interchanges between state and society and to tease out their political significance. By concentrating on the web of relations and the networks of interactions it might be possible to attain a better understanding of the rhythm of unfolding processes and to overcome the intellectual confines that have given birth to the disparate images of African politics today.

Recognition of the relativity of state-society relations is a precondition for coming to terms with the issue of state reordering. The purpose of this paper is to take the first steps in this direction by mapping out the key dimensions of state-society relations in Africa. It looks closely at how social groups and formal institutional networks interconnect, and attempts to outline the main functional, human, situational and symbolic facets of these exchanges.

State and society are conceptualized in these pages as two intersecting and potentially independent variables with political process as the dependent variable. Thus, the state entity does have an existence of its own, and its actions may have a profound bearing on social organization and economic enterprise. Social groups, similarly, maintain an institutional and resource base which permits them to act independently as well as conjointly with structures in the public domain. These political, social and economic fields may intertwine in a multiplicity of ways.[10] The manner of articulation of these spaces is central to tracing political flows.

The state, therefore, is no longer viewed as the sole magnet of social, economic and political exchange. It constitutes merely one of many possible foci of social action.[11] If state institutions, resources and values appeal to specific social constellations, they will ally themselves with state policy and act in accordance with its guidelines. If, however, state interventions adversely affect the well-being of these groups or reduce their prospects for advancement, then they will work to minimize their exposure and vulnerability to these forms of interference. Constantly shifting social reactions to the state and to each other at various (local, regional, national and transnational) levels assume center stage. The dynamic combinations of social confrontations with constantly changing circumstances may help to account both for the heterogeneity of African political processes and the multitude of directions they are taking.[12]

Relationships between the state and social groups in Africa may vary from total indifference to complete immersion.[13] Incorporation of social groups and the public domain is one pole in this dynamic; disengagement from the state, that point at which it is no longer integrating,[14] constitutes the other. Links between the state and other socioeconomic arenas vacillate dramatically along this range. Since these associations follow divergent lines and involve many distinct considerations, multiple combinations of disengagement and incorporation have evolved.

The main contention of this analysis is that politics, power and control are not of necessity coterminous with the state. Politics, the competition for access and control over resources, takes place well beyond the narrower public domain in African countries. Power—the capacity to control resources—and authority—the right to do so—may legitimately be vested in local social structures as well. Power vectors and the search for empowerment take on different meanings in this context.[15] Political variables retain their centrality in explicating unfolding processes; they are not, however, necessarily state-centric. The form a given state takes is a function of the scope of its institutional capacities, the extent of its ties to society, and the kind of resources it controls. Only by looking at the various dimensions of political interaction is it possible to identify specific varieties of states and degrees of stateness on the continent.[16]

Such an approach may help clarify analyses of ongoing processes. For example, it can shed light on why seemingly strong states do not achieve their declared goals and why policy preferences are expressed in such divergent ways at the local and national levels.[17] If state structures are undergoing a process of disaggregation, then the quality and substance of state-society linkages may provide vital clues to the direction of reaggregative trends. Also, the differentiation between power, politics, regime and the state may assist in refining policy options and suggest less conventional— and perhaps more viable—formulae for the remolding of formal structures on the continent. This perspective, therefore, may delineate new areas for research and furnish an additional impetus to the most fundamental challenge at hand: the need to review and possibly revise prevailing concepts and concomitant theory in order to better unravel the dynamics of political process and change.

Dimensions of Incorporation and Disengagement

Societal relations with the state in Africa have centered on four critical questions: what is the substance of exchanges between social groups and the state? Who interacts with whom, and under what circumstances? Where do various activities take place? And what meanings are attached to these ties? Africans have provided many answers to these questions over the years. Each of these responses illuminates a separate element of the mechanisms of state-society incorporation and disengagement, and each possesses distinct implications for understanding political constellations and flows.

Substantive Dimensions

The first aspect of state-society ties refers to what people do in relationship to their state. It exposes the manifold activities individuals and groups conduct and the degree to which these actions do or do not take place within the civic realm. These patterns depend on the institutional capacities of the state apparatus, the resources it controls and distributes and the manner in which it implements policy, as well as the existence of alternatives in these areas. Association with, or dissociation from, the state in specific fields is therefore an outgrowth of conditions that prevail as a result of the uses to which state power is put.

Activities along this axis are shaped by perceptions of what state roles are and how they are being fulfilled.[18] The state in this sense is viewed as a public bureaucracy or administrative apparatus charged with maintaining external security, internal order, economic activity and ideological-cultural cohesion.[19] Relations with the state can be determined by looking at actions in the economic, political and sociocultural spheres.

Economic links with state operations have been the most pronounced and best documented. At independence African leaders promised rapid improvements in the quality of life. They nurtured the hope of economic development, more education, expanded health facilities and a better standard of living. Realities a generation later did not live up to the promises of yesteryear in most of these areas.

Initially, African states attempted to centralize development efforts. "Almost everything that the new states do in the name of development means the intention at least of forcing the diversity of remote rural lives into an iron grid of title documents, accounts, censuses and tax lists—words and numbers."[20] African governments have not, however, usually been able to transform their material base.[21] Although they control liquid revenues and mineral resources and have promoted the commodity economy, their reach has rarely extended to the point of production.

There are many reasons for the current economic malaise permeating the continent. The changing structure of production and exchange plays a certain role. So, too, do demographic considerations, migration patterns and social concerns. Africa's dependency on world prices for its primary products, the rising cost of imports, lately the intervention of the World Bank and the International Monetary Fund regimes, and the region's unequal incorporation into the global economy also help to explain the present situation. Changes in the environment, natural disasters and ecological conditions are contributory factors.[22] But it is increasingly apparent that much of the responsibility lies with the failure of governments. Inadequate and irrelevant policies, meager incentives, poor distribution mechanisms and rampant inefficiency and corruption have combined to skew distribution patterns, alter production and limit accumulation.[23]

Economic relations with the state today reflect various modes of coping with scarcity. Activities of a totally incorporative nature are still carried out by small groups of people in most states. These individuals do not have access to any alternative resources and are usually reliant on the state for their maintenance (mostly in the form of salaries). They expect state agencies to make commodities available at reasonable prices and to furnish essential services.[24]

Most people, however, mix engagement in the formal economy with a variety of other economic activities outside the domain of state institutions. Many individuals maintain economic ties with the state but make do with less. They have learned to cope with chronic shortages. They have altered their consumption patterns, shifting from scarce imported products to local goods. Frequently they have had to change their use of time in order to search for necessary commodities at reasonable prices. Other initiatives have surfaced: some independent backyard cultivation is taking place in many areas; almost every salaried person moonlights, and barter techniques are widespread.[25] In the rural areas there is a move from export to food crops. These activities are a form of adjustment to state policies and they are widely practiced. Nevertheless, they are conducted within the state orbit and do not signal either a change in the relationship between the market and the state or an attenuation of the close interconnection between state and society in the sphere of social services.[26]

A second manifestation of economic separation of state and social groups involves the introduction of different techniques, mostly centered on the construction of a parallel, or informal, economy. One of the first marks of the emergence of an informal economy is smuggling, a topic on the agenda of every African administration.[27] For many people, smuggling is a way of life. Throughout West Africa primary goods are smuggled across frontiers in exchange for basic necessities such as soap, sugar and kerosene. In Ghana cocoa smuggling is still widespread. In the early 1980s Ghanaian manufactured cloth was best purchased in Abidjan and Lomé.[28] "Anything can be smuggled into Nigeria, including human beings."[29] In East Africa, Kenya has become a regional market and the main source of much-needed supplies. In general, smuggling is divided between that type which seeks to satisfy the demand for imported luxury goods and that which is carried out to acquire basic needs.

Hoarding and black marketeering are closely allied to smuggling. Hoarding is generally induced by shortages and usually, popular myths notwithstanding, does not affect price fluctuations.[30] Black markets are also a reaction to the lack of availability of certain products. They generally spring up around growing demand and are controlled not only by retailers and wholesalers but also largely by food producers.[31]

The parallel system, or second economy, in many parts of Africa has gradually developed its own institutions, revenues and rules of the game. Although much of the shadow economy is concerned with trade, many productive activities take place within its boundaries. Petty manufacturing is one mainstay of the parallel market. In Accra, for example, 80 percent of the salaried workers are also engaged in the informal sector.[32] In most urban areas an entire apprenticeship system supports these activities.[33] And in many instances agricultural and nonagricultural occupations are combined as people attempt ". . . to diversify their options—both economically and institutionally."[34]

The initial capital for these activities is frequently provided by monies siphoned off from the formal economy. Corruption, bribery and embezzlement are essential features of the parallel market. However, as informal structures are solidified and reproduced, capital is also being accumulated and reinvested in this sector independently. Thus, while in some countries parallel markets— *magendo* in Uganda and Zaire, *kalabule* in Ghana—are associated with state officials, in others this same phenomenon may be taking on autonomous trappings. A distinction between the informal economy ("activities [which] are supposedly controlled by the state but . . . either evade this control or involve illegal use of state position")[35] and the nonformal economy (which ignores the state and operates beyond its reach) is beginning to emerge.

The informal economy is a complex response to either opportunities presented by state engagement in the market or the inadequacies and frailties of state economic structures. The growth of the informal economy may be due to the continuity of historical patterns, the inability of the formal economy to absorb demands, problematic exchange controls, purposeful efforts by the state to delink social strata from the sphere of its responsibility, and/or responses of particular social groups to adversity and loosening state control. It is concerned with the revision of patterns of accumulation and distribution, and has internal as well as external roots and consequences. It is perhaps the prime example of the aggregation of individual solutions to problems which have not been adequately handled on the macro level.[36] Annual estimates show the increasing importance of parallel market activities throughout the continent.[37]

Nevertheless, parallel economies can still only be understood in relative terms. Although they may have their own independent existence in many respects, these systems of necessity also have ties with state economic activities. The informal economy is about linkages.[38] It flourishes at the fringes of the formal economy. Most families are engaged in both economies simultaneously.[39] Their activities, however, provide a clear indication of the tendency of individuals and groups and of state agencies to distance themselves from each other in order to maintain standards of living and to provide essential social services. The by-passing of formal networks and their legal constraints is therefore a sign of the tenuous nature of relationships between the state and specific social groups.

Economic detachment between state and society is clearly exhibited in processes of economic self-encapsulation. These activities manifest either a lack of incorporation in the state or withdrawal from contact with it in the economic sphere. This trend is usually grounded in processes of ruralization, not only a shift from public to private occupations but also a move from town to village. Such mutual detachment is accompanied by a renewed emphasis on food production and subsistence agriculture. Some farmers never cultivated market crops, and those who do sometimes reorder their priorities to regain a modicum of self-sufficiency.[40]

The quest for self-reliance is also apparent in the resurgence of village industries, the creation of new crafts at the local level, and the subsequent elaboration of alternative marketing networks.[41] Local ingenuity is an important catalyst in these circumstances. Minds are taxed to find new reservoirs of water; different cultivation techniques; other sources of grain, fertilizer and farming implements; and even much needed skills and expertise. Economic enclosure has implied a change in the scale of production and exchange, but not necessarily an atavistic withdrawal from the contemporary world.

Processes of self-encapsulation thrive as a response to abject poverty, to the total breakdown of formal production mechanisms. Local communities can and do function without governments, although it is rare to find instances of completely isolated economic systems in contemporary Africa. In Kenya *harambee* self-reliance has usually come hand-in-hand with increased demands on the state.[42] In Cameroon few villages can claim that they have a fully developed exit option.[43] Even in Tanzania some economic contacts persist between remote villages and the state.[44] Thus, what withdrawal does indicate with a great deal of force is the pervasiveness of market-related activities which refer to the state only tangentially and sporadically.

The most tangible sign of economic disengagement from the state is physical escape from its territory. This process of economic outward migration is generally of two sorts: the emigration of highly skilled professionals and the exodus of urban and rural manual labor. In many parts of Africa migration as a response to the constraints of poverty has deep historical roots. For example, the Makonde in northern Mozambique have used escape techniques as a way of dealing with problems in their political economy throughout this century.[45] In West and Southern Africa and in the Horn, population movements offer continuous and painful corroboration of political and economic instability on the one hand, and the quest for survival, on the other.

Physical escape is an act of abandonment. It constitutes a complete, albeit at times temporary, divorce from the official economy. Migration not only has become more commonplace, but also, ironically, it has created new pressures on the already stretched resources of population absorbing states. The process of economic detachment from the state has consequently spread uncertainty throughout wide areas of tropical Africa. This is particularly true in areas of abject poverty, where local resources have been limited and options narrowed. In these situations helplessness sets in and dependence of social groups on the state actually grows.

There are manifold manifestations of processes of economic incorporation and disengagement between state and society throughout the continent. The state comprises only one of many economic arenas. Precapitalist configurations intermingle with markets, state-controlled spheres and, most recently, autonomous capitalist networks.[46] The economic field is therefore syncretic: both domestic forces and outside intervention have combined in recent years to reorient relations in this crucial sphere. Because of the heterogeneity of these activities and their fluidity, the state does not control all resources and expertise, and power concentrations do exist beyond its reach. This symbiotic economic relationship between the formal, the non-formal and the informal economies consequently has important implications for political relationships.

Political exchanges between the state and social groups complement and refine economic connections. At independence the postcolonial African state sought to translate the control it inherited into centralized power.[47] Programs of bureaucratic expansion were initiated in virtually every African country, often to the detriment of participation, representation and efficiency. In some instances force has been used to compensate for malfunctioning institutions. In other cases those in office have manipulated, distorted and diverted public structures for their own personal use. "Many West African governments represent in themselves the single greatest threat to their citizens, treat the rule of law with contempt, and multiply hasty public schemes designed principally for their own private and collective enrich-ment."[48] In these conditions, many African states have faced a crisis not only of legitimacy and authority, but also of power.[49]

The political performance of African states in the past few years has varied widely. Nevertheless, few states can boast, especially in the present economic environment, a record of steady state consolidation. Indeed, "scarcity . . . underlines and exacerbates the main problems of governability in Middle Africa—namely social incoherence, overdeveloped state structures, insufficient state legitimacy, and inadequate state coercive power."[50]

Political associations with the state are in part reactions to specific regimes. They are also in part reflections of power distribution within society. Incorporative activities in the political realm are, of course, common. Ongoing efforts in such places as Nigeria and Ghana to devise formulas for meaningful political participation are merely one example. But in most cases the absence of participatory opportunities has generated complex forms of politicization not always directed at the state center.

Dissatisfaction with political affairs at the national level had bred, at least in the first instance, a mixture of disaffection and dissent. Disaffection has frequently been expressed as apathy—fatalism and studied indifference.[51] Cynicism has sometimes been transformed into dissent. Expressed first in the form of complaints and then as political opposition, these sentiments serve as a constant reminder of the precarious position of those in national office. As dissent grows, its overt manifestations are concretized: strikes, demonstrations and military takeovers have occurred in all corners of Africa. These actions, as long as they are sporadic and open, nevertheless convey a sense of attachment to the state and concern with its composition and policies.[52]

Many political activities in Africa carry a greater measure of ambivalence. They reflect malintegration (where state consolidation processes have not been encompassing) or the beginnings of disintegration (where greater interaction was apparent in the past). The alteration of patron-client networks serves as one example. Brokers and mediators have continuously interceded between the local community and the state rubric. In Tanzania and Kenya legislators have served as crucial linkage structures between their constit-uencies and the central government.[53] In some military settings patrons have provided the essential funnel to the soldiers-politicians.[54] For many years these webs of patrons and clients have dispensed their own justice and at the same time, when convenient, cooperated with the rulers and attempted to take advantage of state mechanisms and resources.

Patron politics relates to, but is not dependent exclusively upon, the state. In fact, the institutionalization of patronage tends to deplete and impoverish the political and financial center.[55] It can also survive and thrive, under certain conditions, without recourse to the state.[56] The relationship between patronage and the state is hence not always fixed, and patronage itself is undergoing change.

If the political context and meaning of patronage is ambiguous at best, nonformal political action is even more inconclusive. Informal political frameworks blossomed during the early years of independence as substitutes for more formal political structures and as ongoing mechanisms for meaningful competition and exchange. They enabled some participation in smaller settings and effectively pressed specific demands on the government of the day.[57] Informal associations continue to proliferate in the 1980s. They do not, however, necessarily interact with the state or accept its directives. They, like the patrons that often stand at their head, have frequently nurtured autonomous power bases. Political activities of this sort accentuate the intermittent ties between state and society. Their appearance is an indication that the state is not always in a position to exercise systemic power.[58]

Rampant abuses of state power and/or massive power vacuums at the center have engendered more explicit manifestations of political disengagement. Some of these activities have been explicitly disruptive, focusing on organized resistance to specific regimes. In Zaire and Uganda, Ghana and Mozambique, Angola and Guinea, armed groups, usually controlled by, if not composed of, political exiles, have presented severe challenges to the validity of the official power structure. They have been buttressed by populist, antiestablishment movements domestically. Some of these activities have concentrated on undermining the integrity of the state framework. Many countries in the Sahel belt and the Horn of Africa are beset by civil wars initiated by separatist movements. In these cases internal fragmentation is the political corollary of intense poverty. Disengagement has also been expressed less violently, but perhaps more fundamentally, by a quiet, sustained and embracing political detachment. Here traditional institutions have been reinvigorated, revamped and sometimes replaced by new local authority structures.[59] Whatever the precise method, political activity of this sort ignores the state, questions its validity and relegates its political functions to other settings.

These passive and active forms of political interaction between the state and social groups highlight the diffuseness of power arrangements in many African countries. They also support conditions for an admixture of external intervention and possible internal atomization.[60] Both these tendencies are apparent in Africa today. While few states have actually collapsed or are likely to do so, few can lay claim to effective power concentrations backed by authority and not only force.

Political relations between state and society in Africa fluctuate wildly. They also vary in intensity, insofar as some are violent, some active, and others subdued. This diversity of forms of political action should not, however, obscure their ambiguous quality. To be sure, "at a minimum we have seen that the threat of anarchy is unfounded."[61] On the other hand, state consolidation is, at best, tenuous. In between these two poles a variety of political phenomena are discernible which underscore the equivocal nature of attachments to the state. Indeed, the political field in most African states is a mosaic reflective of the syncretic nature of economic relationships. The avenues of access and control are not always clear, precisely because the locations of desired resources are neither monolithic nor cohesive.

Sociocultural facets of state-society interaction confirm these trends. In the political and economic spheres, most states in Africa have at least made an effort to engage large portions of their populations. Attempts to construct a national culture and social cohesion—rhetoric aside—have been few and far between. In a small number of isolated cases a new normative system was designed with a view to establishing an innovative ideological order. The example of Tanzania stands out in this regard, alongside the less successful experiments of Kwame Nkrumah, Leopold Sedar Senghor, and Ahmed Sekou Touré. Even the most elaborate of these gestures has usually met with a wall of disinterest and indifference. When cultural engineering has been particularly intrusive, alienation sets in.[62] Few African states can lay claim to cultural incorporation with their societies on any significant scale.

Indeed, people in most parts of the continent are still clearly affiliated in lineages, familial networks, chiefdoms, secret societies and local communities. Around these frameworks specific norms of behavior have evolved. These are endowed with meaning insofar as the types of activities they entail are rationalized, justified and conceptualized. Patterns of deference; attitudes toward seniority; values related to cooperation, friendship, reciprocity and hierarchy; concerns about social maintenance and even development: all these and more have been formulated and subsequently revised on the basis of historical, customary and contextual considerations. Local cultural patterns, each with its own distinctive flavor, combine to form unique symbolic networks which sustain daily life and only sporadically articulate official ideologies.[63]

In some instances new realms of meaning have developed in response to the normative vacuity at the state core. For example, in countries such as Nigeria and Uganda organized crime networks, buttressed by their own peculiar values, have reached alarming proportions. In other settings spiritualism, new belief systems, magic and cult activities are on the rise. Music and popular literature have provided an important channel for the articulation of new cultural forms as well as for the continuing elaboration of existing symbolic world views.[64]

Normative interaction between states and social groups has displayed vast disjunctures and irregularities, reflective of the sporadic nature of links in this sphere. Here disparities are especially noticeable and, more significantly, points of intersection less well-defined.

Economic, political and cultural interconnections between states and social groups in contemporary Africa manifest varying rhythms and alternating foci of articulation and autonomy. Multiple combinations of incorporation and disengagement in these interacting, but hardly overlapping, fields are everywhere in evidence. These actions provide a good foundation for understanding the substance of state-society relations and lay the groundwork for grasping the topics around which conflict and competition revolve. By themselves, however, they do not explicate the quality of these interactions.

Human Dimensions

The second aspect of state-society ties refers to the relationships between specific social groups and those who occupy state office. It focuses on the organization of the actors (and not only on the activities) within, alongside and beyond the domain of public institutions. Social forces relate to the official structures of government partly in terms of the amount of access they have to state resources and their wielders and partly in terms of the social composition of officeholders.[65] The types of contact between various social organizations thus help to determine the web of relations within a given territorial setting. They delineate the structure of exchanges, the nature of differentiation, the precise composition of diverse coalitions and the degree of societal cohesion.[66]

The human axis of state-society relations is molded by a notion of the state as a social entity which embodies a clearly delineated structure of human interactions.[67] In this perspective, while the state does not coincide with social divisions, it is deeply immersed in social conflict. The relationship between the ruling class and the government structure is one of affinity, not necessarily of coincidence.[68] The state, therefore, ". . . is nothing other than a product of social relations, an entity of social power."[69] In order to understand processes of incorporation and disengagement in this vein, it is necessary to look at the changing relationships between social groups along occupational, cultural, religious and gender lines.

Colonialism was accompanied by the introduction of new criteria for social stratification and class differentiation in Africa. Economic control associated with the colonial state and proximity to the administrative apparatus became important factors in social mobility. "Because the state bourgeoisie is the internally dominant class, and because powerful social formations autonomous from the state are relatively lacking, the link between state and class in Africa is quite different from that which has evolved in the western state."[70] Therefore, with independence, there emerged in each African country a bureaucratic stratum defined by its ability to control resources accruing to the state.[71] The state, through these managers, played a crucial role in the reproduction of social relations.

Over the years, however, the relationship between social stratification and the state has lost some of its definitive character. Economic scarcity, to be sure, has frequently accentuated social cleavages and, in extreme cases, has bolstered the propensity of managerial groups to prey on the countryside and deplete its resources. Evidence of this trend can be garnered from the actions of elites in Ethiopia, Nigeria, Zaire and Ivory Coast. On the other hand, technocrats and wage earners in the public sector have been the first to suffer from price fluctuations, inflation and economic malaise. It is this group that has taken advantage of its position to establish a foothold in the parallel economy and to uncover new sources of accumulation independently of the state.

The close association between the dominant class and governmental structures in Africa may be undergoing significant change. It is quite possible that this group has lost some of its initial cohesion. While a social segment attached to the state exists in every African country, in many parts of the continent a competing and indigenous capitalist bourgeoisie is emerging.[72] This latter group has transnational links, bypasses state frontiers and possesses its own sources of capital. Indeed, it may benefit from disarray in the ranks of state bureaucrats.

If the relationships among the individuals who make up the public domain are not clear-cut, their links with other horizontally defined strata in recent years are even more difficult to assess. Specific groups of workers, traders, farmers and artisans, although tied in various ways to each other and the market economy, have always had an ambivalent connection with government decision makers. Indeed, depending on the perspective from which they are viewed, these organizations may be seen either as autonomous entities with defined interests, traceable structural properties, a fair amount of historical continuity, and at least some control over their own resources; or alternately as social aggregations identified in terms of each other. Thus traders, strategically located at the interface of production and exchange, have been affected by government distribution measures and fiscal policies. They have also been able to capitalize on the opportunities presented by the expansion of parallel markets and consequently enhance their options.[73] It is these forces which are central to understanding contemporary processes of social reorganization.

Specific groups of farmers—frequently referred to in undifferentiated terms as peasants—have consistently been defined, in part, by their ambiguous links with those in national office. The shaping of many farmer interests prior to independence was, undoubtedly, a function of the penetration of the market economy and of colonial efforts to manipulate the countryside.[74] At the same time, because of their direct access to land and their mode of cultivation, these same groups have maintained a large measure of autonomy and flexibility.[75] Different relations between land, labor, the market and central institutions helped to mold distinct agglomerations of rural culti- vators.[76] In recent years rural production units have redefined their position vis-à-vis the market and the state when official programs have threatened their food self-sufficiency and official actions have encroached on their productive resources.[77] These units interlock with each other (especially since social differentiation in the countryside has intensified) in manifold ways. Rural dwellers, while exhibiting many common concerns, nevertheless cannot be neatly lumped into one category: the analytical disaggregation of the concept of the peasantry is a precondition for understanding the multiple patterns of social organization at the local level.

Salaried employees, especially semi-skilled and skilled workers, although often most directly affected by the actions of state rulers, have remained firmly, albeit reluctantly, within the state realm. Most wage earners are tied to the public sector. Although they have repeatedly voiced their discontent not only with their specific situation but also with the system that has generated these conditions, workers have very few options other than to maintain an uneasy alliance with state managers.[78] Individuals, it is true, can desert, withdraw or revolt. But the main methods by which organized groups voice discontent range from demonstrations and strikes to the more common adoption of lethargic work practices, perpetuating inefficiency, staging accidents and sabotaging equipment.[79] Since these actions are directed at gaining a greater share of public resources, they encourage incorporation and conflict, rather than disengagement or indifference.

The picture of class relations in many parts of Africa lacks a cohesive structure. In those places where state resources are the object of major competition and conflict, public institutions continue to constitute an important determinant of class formation and class relations.[80] But in most instances the focus on the macro sociological processes of social differentiation tends to obscure the fact that "the 'soft' state is the inevitable product of a situation where no class is really in control and dominant enough to ensure the reproduction of a given macro-economic system."[81] Farmers see the state as both oppressor *and* ally; workers seek to reap some of its rewards yet avoid its reach. State institutions provide one arena for competition, but not all forms of social conflict revolve around its resources or symbols. Specific groups interlock and intertwine differentially while protecting their own political spaces.[82]

Another way of looking at large-scale social processes in Africa has been through the lens of ethnicity. The emergence of a broad ethnic political consciousness in many locations throughout Africa was related to the extension of central control. In the same way that state construction was connected with the crystallization of new class forces, ethnicity has been seen as another manifestation of the expansion and consolidation of state power.[83] In Nigeria, Zanzibar, Ghana and Kenya, ethnicity has surfaced as a response to government action.[84]

Ethnically defined groupings have persisted and flourished in many parts of Africa because they have been proven to be effective channels for the extraction of state resources. In most instances ethnic demands have been of low intensity when benefits have accrued from association with the state.[85] But, "just as ethnicity can be organized, it can be *dis*organized."[86] In conditions of dwindling resources, ethnic and class tensions coexist and intersect, indicating equivocal, but nevertheless ongoing, relations with state managers.[87] In situations of unequal distribution, ethnicity tends to intensify and ethnic links are viewed as vehicles for access to common resources. At this stage demands for ethnic autonomy may increase and ethnicity may be counter-integrative.[88] When poverty becomes widespread, the forms of ethnic identification multiply and the social distance between cultural groups may grow. As broad ethnic coalitions cease to be effective tools for economic interaction within the state framework, specific communities, variously defined, become substitutes for state structures. Migration also implies ethnic mutation. In some cases ethnic identities are altered, in others they are reconfirmed.[89] In all these instances, however, competition between social groups is also expressed, albeit not exclusively, through culturally delineated structures.

Both ethnicity and class thus emerge as rather blunt tools to convey the variety of social organization and arenas which exist and interact throughout the continent. Daily socioeconomic, and consequently political, relations take place within and between specific trade unions, professional associations, local geographic collectivities, kinship networks, chieftancies, farmers and government officials. Although ethnicity and class help to conceptualize lines of coalition and conflict—and hence of interpenetration and dependence—as seen from above, they do not, in and of themselves, illuminate the dynamic areas of interchange between specific, tangible social structures. Some of these activities relate to central policies and institutions, while others remain separate and distinct.

The relationship between religious groups and state managers is a case in point. Religious movements have embodied, especially during the twentieth century, combined cultural, ideological, social and even economic responses to specific situations. They have been eminently political, but not necessarily involved in national politics.[90] This mixture of politicization and religious exploration has been highlighted by the religious resurgence that has permeated the continent in recent years. Some groups, mostly Islamic, have intensified their connections with state officials in some countries, such as Senegal, Sudan and, to some extent, Nigeria and Somalia. Here public institutions have assumed religious trappings and shed many of their secular characteristics.[91]

In other cases religious communities have supplied important channels for the expression of discontent with state authorities. A return to religious beliefs, apparent in Christian as well as Muslim quarters, may also reflect disaffection with the activities and behavior of those charged with operating central institutions. Islamic nationalism in northern Nigeria has become an important channel for dealing with capitalist penetration and social dislocation.[92] In Senegal the strong Mouride marabouts have become the spokesmen for farmer interests; they have transformed themselves into trade union leaders of a new sort.[93] In Ghana the clergy have been at the forefront of protest against a succession of arbitrary rulers. Some religious communities, moreover, have created alternative constructs of a totally independent sort and maintain next to no contact with government officials. In southern Africa churches have provided the settings for autochthonous groupings of the devout.[94] In West Africa and the Sahel fundamentalist Islamic sects have sprouted up in Senegal, Niger, northern Nigeria and Mali. In these areas an Islamic network may be entirely remolding political allegiances.[95] In all of these instances religious militancy is highly political, but only somewhat linked with state political affairs.

Cultural, occupational and religious groupings also intersect with gender. Women's organizations in Africa have brought sex solidarity associations to the fore in recent years. Although some attempts have been made to involve women in state-linked activities, as a group females have been systematically neglected and underrepresented in central institutions.[96] Even strategies purportedly designed to improve the lot of women have usually resulted in their further marginalization. In some countries in West Africa where women have gained prominence in commerce, they have been hounded when economic conditions have deteriorated. In East Africa gender has become an important predictor of political involvement: public ". . . life is increasingly differentiated on the basis of sex."[97]

The peripheralization of women has frequently enhanced their sense of community. Women, perhaps more than any other social category, have resisted incorporation and remained aloof from state links. The victimization of women by the state has fueled a conscious assertion of independence.[98] This gender-based withdrawal, however, has not shielded women from the exigencies of scarcity. Sex-related inequities increase under conditions of poverty. Women exemplify processes of disengagement from state centralism in Africa in recent years because the distinction between the public (state) and private (household) spheres is also a gender division.[99]

The human dimensions of state-society links vacillate widely. Social organization in most African countries has a web-like quality: specific groups sometimes interact with each other or with public officials, yet at times remain detached and maintain only minimal vertical ties. Each social structure may reflect a set of organizing principles which ". . . may act alone, may reinforce, or may work against each other, depending on the social situation."[100] Lateral transactions may be growing, but these only sometimes intersect with the official domain. Indeed, both the extent of contact and the structure of social differentiation indicate a lack of social cohesion around groups associated with central governments. Social links and conflicts are nevertheless not incoherent: they do reflect a pattern of interlocking organizations established to pursue particular interests. The state-centric view is too limited a lens through which to examine the dynamic of contact and conflict, autonomy and interdependence, coalition building, and the actual construction of social hierarchies. Politics is taking place within and between multiple frameworks that extend far beyond the public realm.

Spatial Dimensions

The third aspect of state-society ties refers to the location of the various activities of specific groups. It concentrates on the settings of social and functional interactions and their connection with the formal geographic boundaries of the state. The spatial facet of incorporation and disengagement sheds light on where power is held—on the organization of political spaces.

State-societal relations in this sense derive from a notion of the state as the key arena of decision making and social interchange.[101] From this vantage point the state is perceived as a territorial concept within which activities take place and social groups interrelate. To understand state-society relations in spatial terms it is important to specify various preferred loci of operation and their interconnection with the territorial parameters of the state.

The smallest units of exchange are the household and the village community. These entities do have other domestic and international contacts, but usually they operate mostly on their own within their rural or urban settings. The rural collectivity in twentieth-century Africa has always maintained a large measure of flexibility, even if it has hardly been isolated from other national and external currents. Local producers have continued established patterns of cultivation and social organization. At the same time they have adjusted to the intrusion of the market, learning to take advantage of opportunities, place demands on policy makers and avert implementing measures that may harm their interests. To many people in the countryside, in fact, the state—be it colonial or postcolonial—constitutes an intrusive device from which they can possibly reap benefits, but over which they have little influence.[102] Rural communities therefore carve out different modes of operation at different levels: they tend to augment connections which will improve their own well-being and are extraordinarily protective of the legitimacy and power they have garnered over the years. They shun contacts which may limit their scope of autonomy and at the same time make demands, especially for infrastructural improvements (e.g. clean water supplies, latrines, feeder roads, electrification) that may augment their resources. They thereby underline the centrality of the local arena and its organizational modes, while simultaneously being drawn into, and seeking to manipulate, ties at other levels as well.

Urban contexts, in contrast, have generally been associated with the state arena. Most African cities grew up around the seat of colonial administration and became the locus of the market economy. After independence rural-urban migration was taken as a significant sign of processes of state-society incorporation. Africa's towns seemed to provide the framework for involvement in the state nexus: they were the main setting for new processes of social differentiation, political participation and capitalist growth.[103]

As urbanization has increased, however, the nature of links between the cities and the state has become more complex. Not all urban dwellers have moved to the city to escape the confines of rural life; many have sought other ways to enhance their status at home. Large numbers have been involved in the informal and nonformal sectors. Residents may enjoy superficial amenities; they do not necessarily have greater access to desired resources. And poverty has taken on particularly pernicious characteristics in the metropolises of Africa.[104] The relationship between the town and the state is therefore quite different today from in the past. The macro economic rationality of the urban household stands in contrast to bureaucratic roles. The professional structure of cities is constantly changing. Just as the relationship between the city and the countryside is undergoing change, so too, are spatial links within the urban areas. There may be a growing dislocation between the state and its towns; at the same time separate spaces are being constructed in these settings as well.[105]

Regions and geographically defined cultural entities also sometimes constitute key loci of activity and interaction. Regions (or states in Nigeria) are ostensibly administrative creations and hence integrally tied to the state apparatus. But as with other internal structures, Africa is replete with examples of efforts by regional groupings to disengage from overreliance on the state. Richer subunits are in a position to profitably do so, and more disadvantaged regions, previously heavily dependent on state ties, have frequently sought other—sometimes external—connections to increase their margin of maneuverability.[106]

The spatial importance of the African state as a central arena for societal interaction is mitigated by external as well as domestic forces. The boundaries of African states are highly porous. When convenient, they are ignored by individuals and groups. Continental agglomerations and international contacts (with states and multinational bodies) also affect the exclusivity of the state sphere.

Specific social organizations pursuing their own interests interact differently at various possible levels of exchange. The state is hardly the sole vertical magnet of diverse and situationally distinct social groups. The definition of social, political and economic space involves the construction of a series of interlocking blocks, each of which contains areas of separation, horizontal bonding and vertical meshing. These densely constructed structures have chains of associations both domestically and internationally. The adhesive that bonds them together varies. They do not of necessity have direct contact with each other. There is, consequently, a great deal of fluctuation around the situational preeminence of the territorial framework of the state today. The three-dimensional architecture of power (physically and conceptually) illuminates directions of flows and pinpoints diverse locations of concern and interconnection. In situations of fluidity and uncertainty, boundaries are being redefined and social, economic and cultural spaces reorganized.

Symbolic Dimensions

State-society relations cannot be fully comprehended without some reference to symbols and values—to the organizing principles governing these ties. This final facet of state-society links focuses on the meaning behind these exchanges and on the rules which guide them. It derives from the tendency to conceptualize the state as a normative order, as the primary source of binding values.[107] State-society links in this sense center on the justifications employed for contact or, conversely, for disengagement.

Broadly speaking, linkages between social groups and the state can be entertained for reasons either of utility or identity.[108] Subjective identification with the state is sometimes based on historical-cultural reasons. The historical roots of most African states, however, are not particularly deep. The colonial experience, or the shared memories of a prolonged liberation struggle, has some bearing on common identities, but usually these are accompanied by more profound historical connections associated with other arenas.

Identity with the state may also revolve around religious and mythical considerations. Until recently, however, most African leaders underlined the secular quality of the state entity. Only in those countries where efforts have been made to align the state with the religious community have these principles for affiliation carried much weight.[109]

At independence most African countries favored a national-communal interpretation for drawing social groups into the state orbit. The notion of the nation-state, with its imported myth of unity of consciousness, provided the model upon which ideologies were constructed and normative models were elaborated.[110] Intriguing philosophical efforts were made to inject a notion of a humanistic national community into the territorial boundaries of the postcolonial state.[111]

Conceptual designs of this sort have not been able to effectively draw on solidarity ties with more clearly defined sociohistorical entities at the substate level. Neither have they been able to avert charges that they are none other than normative exercises designed to perpetuate the position and status of ruling elites.[112] The obverse of identity with the state is either normative detachment, apathy or rationalization in more particularistic terms. Some groups never did respond to efforts at value mobilization. Some have become disenchanted. And others explain ties in terms of fulfillment of other goals. It is not that the state does not have any normative meaning for most Africans, but that its significance in this regard is usually not central. Struggles over resources are also struggles over the symbolic supremacy of variously derived survival techniques.

Justification for some forms of interaction may also be formulated on the basis of instrumental considerations. From the perspective of specific social groups, certain associations with the state are supported in utilitarian terms: the public domain can furnish needed goods, desired services and scarce resources. Those purveying such ties can gain authority and possibly greater legitimacy. Many groups that link up with each other and the state do so because they think it is worthwhile. When ideological disarticulation takes place either because public institutions have very little to offer or because specific groups feel exposed to state whims or materially deprived as a result of inequitable distribution practices, these actions can be explained in normative terms on grounds of utility.[113] From the perspective of the state, acceding to dictates from abroad (lately from the IMF and the World Bank) may be rationalized along similar lines, with pains being taken to underline that pragmatic acquiescence does not imply the surrender of ideological commitment. Even internally, the propensity of state officials to divest themselves of responsibility is explained usually in practical, and not moral, terms.

The reasons given for disengagement and incorporation help to explain some of the apparent anomalies in state-society relations. Engagement in activities at odds with declared interests may be given symbolic justification at different levels. More to the point, however, gradually the identification of interests, their organization and their structuring are assuming a normative dimension as well. In this underresearched area, new forms of ideological articulation are being devised and rules of interaction laid down. Some combination of interest and values is present.[114] "Integration is then about identity and organization, consciousness and action, including a range of relationships between a sense of difference and the state or political whole."[115]

Fundamental codes in which public institutions are merely one element are emerging. They illuminate the meaning behind the variegated interactions of discrete groups occupying specific locations in contemporary Africa.

Patterns and Implications

This analysis has attempted to delineate the major dimensions of state-society relations in contemporary Africa. It has suggested various ways of looking at the fluid phenomena associated with incorporation and disengagement. Attachments of social groups and state structures have vacillated widely along substantive, human, spatial and symbolic lines. An admixture of indifference, attraction and distaste underlies these contacts.

The intricacies of these dynamic movements help to unravel issues of statehood, stateness and state variety on the continent. The degree of cohesion of state and society in Africa points to various degrees of stateness. The centralization of African states today is constantly being questioned. The thoughts, links and actions of individuals and social groupings continuously belie the abstract model of fully integrated and functionally effective entities. Some observers have consequently been tempted to dismiss the significance of states in Africa. Others have argued that, however enfeebled, there are still no substitutes for the state.[116] The reality, in all probability, is both far more complicated and tenuous. The boundaries between state subsistence and state extinction are hardly clear-cut. In this amorphous middle ground, states do continue to matter in most parts of Africa. This paper has attempted to show that the nature of African states is an outcome of the rhythm of relations between social entities and public institutions and officials. The nature of states—rather than their actual existence or dissolution—is an empirical question that can be answered through a close analysis of various avenues of linkage.

The overall trend appears to be toward a redesigning of political arrangements to conform less to imposed models and more to the dynamics of interchange as they are manifested in specific areas. The organic state concept of the first generation of African leaders is giving way to a more locally defined interactive notion of statehood. The public domain is being reconceptualized not in terms of official structures, but in terms of the points of intersection between various existing power vectors. It is at these locations that politics take place, and around these foci that authority is accumulated and support garnered. The absence of coincidence between formal institutions, power networks and political actions suggest that African countries may be reorganizing themselves in heterogenous ways away from the strict constructions of centralized organs.

Differential patterns of incorporation and disengagement in Africa point to the existence and elaboration of many different kinds of state entities in recent years.[117] Thus, while most of these states do evince some patrimonial elements, in some cases formal institutions are cohesive, differentiated and enjoy varying degrees of support, while in others they boast less internal coherence and backing.[118] In each instance it is necessary to map out the topics and actors, as well as the symbolic and spatial relationships, which appear on the ground. These may yield various patterns ranging from mutual closure to diffuse and uncoordinated exchanges lacking common direction or purpose. In most cases, however, forms and rules of interaction are being worked out. The tracing of modes of concentration and diffusion of power networks relies heavily on the identification of channels of organization and agency in order to trace unfolding processes over time.

"Incorporation and disengagement can obviously occur in the same country in various combinations at different times and have different effects on various groups and social spheres."[119] In short, variable interactions make political processes in Africa a veritable laboratory for the readjustment or reorganization of the hegemonial predilections associated with the postcolonial regimes in the past.

Awareness of the conjunctural nature of contemporary political formations is a preliminary step in the reformation of channels of political interchange. The reconsideration of institutional structures, rules of interaction, means and methods of governance, and degrees of competition and cooperation both externally and domestically, must take into account the flow of transactions and the directionality and meaning of specific interchanges. In this connection the critical question is how new linkages can be constructed or existing ones revised to rearrange economic, social, political and normative ties within existing state boundaries in order to enhance good government.

Answers to this question cannot be put forward without further probing constantly shifting processes of incorporation and disengagement and reflecting on their effects. This involves greater emphasis on the mechanics of transactions, the factors affecting them, and the formulation of criteria to uncover their changing shape over time. The relative weight of various tendencies toward incorporation and disengagement at given historical moments must be evaluated, and perhaps a more appropriate conceptual and theoretical terminology devised.

The reorientation of political analysis away from the official and visible and toward the interactive and dynamic may assist in breaking away from the narrow confines of formalistic frameworks. It may also redirect research concerns and their practical ramifications to better reflect the rhythm of ongoing political processes in Africa.

Notes

The research for this paper was supported by the Harry S. Truman Research Institute for the Advancement of Peace, the Hebrew University of Jerusalem. Katya Azoulay assisted in gathering material for the paper. Irene Eber, Victor Azarya, Jane I. Guyer and Donald Rothchild commented on the draft and suggested critical revisions. My appreciation for their help is considerable.

1. See Otwin Marenin, "The Managerial State in Africa" (Paper presented at the Twenty-Eighth Annual Meeting of the African Studies Association, New Orleans, November 1985).

2. Crawford Young, "The African Colonial State and its Political Legacy," in this volume. Also see Thomas Callaghy, *The State-Society Struggle: Zaire in Comparative Perspective* (New York: Columbia University Press, 1984).

3. On the separation between various public domains see Peter Ekeh, "Colonialism and the Two Publics in Africa: A Theoretical Statement," *Comparative Studies in Society and History*, 17, 1 (1975): 91-112. For a similar view see Nelson Kasfir, "Introduction: Relating Class to State in Africa," *Journal of Commonwealth and Comparative Politics*, 21, 3 (1983), esp. p. 16. For an overview of the concept see J.P. Nettl, "The State as a Conceptual Variable," *World Politics*, 20, 4 (1968): 559-592.

4. Victor Azarya, "Reordering State-Society Relations: Incorporation and Disengagement," in this volume.

5. Richard Sandbrook, *The Politics of Africa's Economic Stagnation* (Cambridge: Cambridge University Press, 1985).

6. Goran Hyden, *No Shortcuts to Progress: African Development Management in Perspective* (Berkeley: University of California Press, 1983), p. 191.

7. For some recent examples see Janet McGaffey, "How to Survive and Get Rich: the Second Economy in Zaire," *African Affairs*, 82 (1983): 351-366, and Nelson Kasfir, "State, *Magendo* and Class Formation in Uganda," *Journal of Commonwealth and Comparative Politics*, 21, 3 (1983): 84-103.

8. Jane I. Guyer, "Comparative Epilogue," in her *Feeding African Cities: Studies in Regional Social History* (Manchester: Manchester University Press, 1987), p. 27. Also see Jean-Francois Bayart, "Les Societés Africaines Face à l'Etat," *Pouvoirs*, 25 (1983): 23-39.

9. Thomas Callaghy, "The State and the Development of Capitalism in Africa: Theoretical, Historical and Comparative Perspectives," in this volume. Also see Richard Joseph, "The Crisis in African Governance and Development: Implications for the Social Sciences" (Discussion Paper, Walter Rodney Seminar, Boston University, December 1985).

10. Jean-Francois Bayart, "La Revanche des Societés Africaines," *Politique Africaine*, 11 (1983): 95-127.

11. Adrian Leftwich, *Redefining Politics: People, Resources and Power* (London: Methuen, 1983), esp. Chap. 1.

12. See Sara Berry, *Fathers Work for their Sons* (Berkeley: University of California Press, 1984), p. 6 and elsewhere.

13. For an overview see John Lonsdale, "States and Social Processes in Africa: A Historiographical Survey," *African Studies Review*, 24, 2/3 (1981): 139-225.

14. Bernard Schaffer, "Organization is not Equity: Theories of Political Integration," *Development and Change*, 8, 1 (1977): 19-44.

15. Thanks to Jane I. Guyer for clarifying this point.

16. Otwin Marenin, "The Managerial State in Africa: A Conflict Coalition Perspective," in Zaki Ergas, ed., *The African State in Transition* (London: Macmillan, forthcoming).

17. This raises questions also echoed in Jonathan Barker, "Political Space and the Quality of Participation in Rural Africa: A Case from Senegal," University of Toronto, Development Studies Program, Working Paper No. 4 (July 1984).

18. This is a functional view of the state. For differing analyses in the same vein compare Theda Skocpol, *States and Social Revolutions: A Comparative Analysis of France, Russia and China* (London: Cambridge University Press, 1974) and Robert H. Jackson and Carl G. Rosberg, "Why Africa's Weak States Persist: The Empirical and the Juridical in Statehood," *World Politics*, 37 (1982), esp. pp. 10-17.

19. Stephen D. Krasner, "Approaches to the State: Alternative Conceptions and Historical Dynamics," *Comparative Politics*, 16, 2 (1984): 224.

20. Keith Hart, *The Political Economy of West African Agriculture* (London: Cambridge University Press, 1982), p. 105.

21. Goran Hyden, *Beyond Ujamaa in Tanzania: Underdevelopment and an Uncaptured Peasantry* (London: Heinemann, 1980), pp. 3–4.

22. An excellent summary may be found in Michael F. Lofchie and Stephen K. Commins, "Food Deficits and Agricultural Policies in Tropical Africa," *Journal of Modern African Studies*, 22 (1982): 1–25.

23. The problematics of policy are discussed in Carl K. Eicher, "Facing Up to Africa's Food Crisis," *Foreign Affairs*, 60, 1 (1982): 153–174. For a particularly sharp critique of government inefficiency see John Howell and Christopher Stevens, "Agriculture: Why Africa Cannot Feed Itself," *African Business*, 24 (1980): 55–64; and Rene Dumont and Marie-Francine Mottin, *Stranglehold on Africa* (London: Andre Deutsch, 1983).

24. This was felt very strongly in Nigeria in the mid-1980s, where there were many expectations from the government and the crisis was recent. In Ghana 65 percent of wage employees are in the public sector.

25. Victor Azarya and Naomi Chazan, "Disengagement from the State in Africa: The Experience of Ghana and Guinea," *Comparative Studies in Society and History*, 29, 1 (1987): 107–131.

26. Donal Cruise O'Brien, "Des Bienfaits de l'Inégalité: L'Etat et l'Economie Rurale au Sénégal," *Politique Africaine*, 14 (1984): 35.

27. "Smuggling: Scourge of Africa," *New African* (May 1983): 11–16. For details also see Catharine Newbury, "Survival Strategies in Rural Zaire: Realities of Coping with Crisis," in Nzongola-Ntalaja, ed., *The Zaire Crisis: Myths and Realities* (Trenton: Third World Press, 1986).

28. Claire Robertson, "The Death of Makola and Other Tragedies," *Canadian Journal of African Studies*, 17, 3 (1983): 475.

29. "Smuggling: Scourge of Africa," p. 16. Most recently, in a reversal of past trends, goods have been purchased in Ghana and then brought illicitly into Nigeria, because of higher prices in the latter country.

30. Kodwo Ewusi, "The Determinants of Price Fluctuations in Ghana, 1955–1975," University of Ghana Discussion Paper 2 (1977) p. 3.

31. Assefa Bequele, "Stagnation and Inequality in Ghana," in Dharam Ghai and Samir Radwan, eds., *Agrarian Policies and Rural Poverty in Africa* (Geneva: ILO, 1983), pp. 240–245.

32. Angelo Barampama, "Secteur non Structuré en Afrique: Cacophonie de la Survie et Lueurs d'Espoir," *Genève-Afrique*, 22, 1 (1984): 46.

33. Pierre Mettelin, "Activites Informelles et Economies Urbaine: Le Cas de l'Afrique Noire," *Mois en Afrique*, 223/224 (1984): 57–71.

34. Sara S. Berry, "Custom, Class and the Informal Sector: Or Why Marginality is not Likely to Pay," African Studies Center, Boston University, Working Paper No. 1 (1978), pp. 16–17.

35. Janet MacGaffey, "Economic Disengagement and Class Formation in Zaire," in this volume.

36. Barampama, "Secteur non Structuré," p. 45.

37. Ernesto May, "Exchange Controls and Parallel Market Economies in Sub-Saharan Africa: Focus on Ghana," World Bank Staff Working Papers No. 711 (Washington, D.C., 1985), p. 7, gives precise figures for Ghana.

38. See A. Morice, "A Propos de l'Economie Populaire Spontanée," *Politique Africaine*, 18 (June 1985): 114-124.

39. Richard Stren, "L'Etat au Risque de la Ville," *Politique Africaine*, 17 (1985): 82.

40. Jonathan Barker, "Can the Poor in Africa Fight Poverty?" *Journal of African Studies*, 7, 3 (1980): 161-166. The fullest discussion of this issue may be found in Hyden, *Beyond Ujamaa in Tanzania*.

41. Merrick Posnansky, "How Ghana's Crisis Affects a Village," *West Africa*, 3306 (December 1, 1980): 2418-2420. A good overview may be found in Roy Preiswerk, "Self-Reliance in Unexpected Places," *Genève-Afrique*, 20, 2 (1982): 36-64.

42. Frank Holmquist, "Class Structure, Peasant Participation, and Rural Self-Help," in Joel D. Barkan and John J. Okumo, eds., *Politics and Public Policy in Kenya and Tanzania* (New York: Praeger, 1979), p. 178.

43. Peter Geschiere, "La Paysannerie Africaine est-elle Captive?" *Politique Africaine*, 14 (1984): 13-33.

44. Some good examples may be found in Don Hasset's Ph.D. thesis on Tanzania, Cambridge University, 1984.

45. Edward A. Alpers, "'To Seek a Better Life': The Implication of Migration from Mozambique to Tanganyika for Class Formation and Political Behaviour," *Canadian Journal of African Studies*, 18, 2 (1984): 367-388. Also see A.I. Asiwaju, "Migrations as Protest: The Example of the Ivory Coast and the Upper Volta Before 1945," *Journal of African History*, 17, 4 (1976): 577-594.

46. Naomi Chazan, "The Demise of the State in Ghana: Disintegration and Endurance" (Paper prepared for the International Conference on State and Society in Africa, Oaxtupec, October 1983), pp. 1-2.

47. Raymond D. Duvall and John R. Freeman, "The State and Dependent Capitalism," *International Studies Quarterly*, 25, 1 (1981): 106.

48. Hart, *West African Agriculture*, p. 104.

49. Ali Mazrui, "Political Engineering in Africa," *International Social Science Journal*, 35, 2 (1983): 279-294, Robert H. Jackson and Carl G. Rosberg, "Popular Legitimacy in African Multi-Ethnic States," *Journal of Modern African Studies*, 22, 2 (1984): pp. 177-198; Kiflé Selassie Beseat, "Convaincre, Contrôler ou Contraindre? Systèmes et Mecanismes de Contrôle de Pouvoir en Afrique," *Presence Africaine*, 127-128 (1983): 79.

50. Donald Rothchild and Michael Foley, "The Implications of Scarcity for Governance in Africa," *International Political Science Review*, 4, 3 (1983): 315.

51. Fred M. Hayward, "Rural Attitudes and Expectations About National Government: Experiences in Selected Ghanaian Communities," *Rural Africana*, 18 (1972), esp. p. 58.

52. For one example see Robin Cohen, "Resistance and Hidden Forms of Consciousness Amongst African Workers," *Review of African Political Economy*, 19 (1980): 8-22.

53. Frances Hill, "Peoples, Parties, Politics: A Linkage Perspective on African Party States," in Kay Lawson, ed., *Political Parties and Linkage: A Comparative Perspective* (New Haven: Yale University Press, 1980), p. 222; Joel D. Barkan and John J. Okumu, "Linkage Without Parties: Legislators and Constituents in Kenya," in Lawson, *Political Parties and Linkage*, pp. 289-324.

54. For one example see John Dunn, "Politics in Asunafo," in Dennis Austin and Robin Luckham, eds., *Politicians and Soldiers in Ghana, 1966-1972* (London: Frank Cass, 1975), pp. 164-213.

55. A good case study is Frank Holmquist, "Toward A Political Theory of Rural Self-Help Development in Africa," *Rural Africana*, 18 (1972): 60–80.

56. Naomi Chazan, "Ethnicity and Politics in Ghana," *Political Science Quarterly*, 47, 3 (1982): 461–485. For an excellent discussion of the transition from patronage to prebends see Rene Lemarchand, "The State, the Parallel Economy, and the Changing Structure of Patronage Systems" in this volume.

57. Naomi Chazan, "The New Politics of Participation in Tropical Africa," *Comparative Politics*, 14, 2 (1982): 169–190.

58. Hyden, *No Shortcuts to Progress*, p. 45.

59. Harry Silver, "Going for Brokers: Political Innovation and Structural Integration in a Changing Ashanti Community," *Comparative Political Studies*, 19, 2 (1981): 253–263.

60. I. William Zartman, "Issues of African Diplomacy in the 1980s," *Orbis*, 25, 4 (1982), esp. pp. 1029–1032.

61. Irving Leonard Markovitz, *Power and Class in Africa* (Englewood Cliffs, N.J.: Prentice-Hall, 1977), p. 346. For an excellent general discussion of exit and voice see Albert O. Hirschman, *Exit, Voice and Loyalty: Response to Decline in Firms, Organizations and States* (Cambridge, Mass.: Harvard University Press, 1976).

62. Reactions to Mobutu's "authenticity" or Acheampong's notion of "national redemption" are cases in point.

63. Norman N. Miller, *Kenya: The Quest for Prosperity* (Boulder: Westview, 1984), p. 126; and Hyden, *No Shortcuts to Progress*, call this phenomenon the "moral economy" or "the economy of affection." This concept, however, is unspecified and murky: it requires specification and disaggregation. I owe thanks to Jane I. Guyer for clarification of this point.

64. Azarya and Chazan, "Disengagement from the State."

65. Chazan, "New Politics of Participation."

66. For a detailed view of these issues see Kwame Ninsin, "Three Levels of State Reordering: The Structural Aspects," in this volume.

67. Joel Samoff, "Class, Conflict and the State in Africa," *Political Science Quarterly*, 97, 1 (1982), esp. p. 123. Also see G. Van Benthem van den Bergh, "The Interconnection between Processes of State and Class Formation: Problems of Conceptualization," Institute of Social Studies Occasional Papers No. 52 (The Hague, August 1975), p. 15.

68. Claude Ake, *A Political Economy of Africa* (London: Longman, 1981), pp. 126–129.

69. Peter Anyang Nyongo, "The Economic Foundations of the State in Contemporary Africa: Stratification and Social Classes," *Presence Africaine*, 127/128 (1983): 187. For another view see I. William Zartman, "Social and Political Trends in Africa in the 1980s," in Colin Legum et al., eds., *Africa in the 1980s* (New York: McGraw Hill, 1979), pp. 69–119, and Schaffer, "Organization is not Equity." Also see Issa G. Shivji, "The State and the Dominated Social Formations of Africa: Some Theoretical Issues," *International Social Sciences Journal*, 32, 4 (1980): 730–742.

70. Crawford Young, "Patterns of Social Conflict: State, Class and Ethnicity," *Daedalus*, 16, 2 (1982), p. 82. Also see Richard L. Sklar, "The Nature of Class Domination in Africa," *Journal of Modern African Studies*, 17, 4 (1979): 531–552.

71. Abner Cohen, *The Politics of Elite Culture: Explorations in the Dramaturgy of Power in a Modern African Society* (Berkeley: University of California Press, 1981) calls this a power cult and provides one example from Sierra Leone. For a Zairian analysis see Wyatt McGaffey, "The Policy of National Integration in Zaire," *Journal of Modern African Studies*, 20, 1 (1982): 87–105.

72. Colin Leys, "African Economic Development in Theory and Practice," *Daedalus*, 16, 2 (1982): 121. John A.A. Ayoade, "States Without Citizens: An Emerging African Phenomenon," in this volume, suggests that the lack of internal cohesion in the civil service may be due to the fact that as a group the bureaucracy is overestablished but under bureaucratized.

73. The activities of market women in Ghana are a case in point. See Robertson, "The Death of Makola."

74. For an excellent analysis consult M. Catharine Newbury, "Ubureetwa and Thangata: Catalysts to Peasant Political Consciousness in Rwanda and Malawi," *Canadian Journal of African Studies*, 14, 1 (1980): 97–114.

75. Martin Klein, ed., *Peasants in Africa: Historical and Contemporary Perspectives* (Beverly Hills: Sage, 1980). Also see Joshua B. Forrest, "Defining African Peasants," *Peasant Studies*, 4, 4 (1983): 242–249.

76. For a breakdown of these groups see Sandbrook, *Politics of Africa's Economic Stagnation*, p. 59.

77. See Jonathan Barker, "Can the Poor in Africa Fight Poverty?" *Journal of African Studies*, 102, 3 (1980): 164.

78. Richard Jeffries, *Class, Power and Ideology in Ghana: The Railwaymen of Sekondi* (London: Cambridge University Press, 1978).

79. For one case study see Jeff Crisp, *The Story of An African Working Class: Ghanian Miners' Struggles, 1870–1980* (London: Zed Press, 1984).

80. Kasfir, "Relating Class to State," p. 4.

81. Hyden, *No Shortcuts to Progress*, p. 63. Also see his "La Crise Africaine et la Paysannerie Non Capturée," *Politique Africaine*, 18 (June 1985): 93–113.

82. These points are stressed by Berry, *Fathers Work for Their Sons*; and Frank Holmquist, "Defending Peasant Political Space in Independent Africa," *Canadian Journal of African Studies*, 14, 1 (1980): 157–167.

83. Young, "Patterns of Social Conflict." Also see Pierre L. van den Berghe, "Class, Race and Ethnicity in Africa," *Ethnic and Racial Studies*, 6, 2 (1983): 221–236.

84. For some examples see Larry Diamond, "Class, Ethnicity and the Democratic State: Nigeria 1950–1966," *Comparative Studies in Society and History*, 25, 3 (1983): 459–489; M. Catharine Newbury, "Colonialism, Ethnicity and Rural Political Protest," *Comparative Politics*, 5, 3 (1983): 253–280; and David Brown "Who Are the Tribalists? Social Pluralism and Political Ideology in Ghana," *African Affairs*, 322 (1982): 37–70.

85. Donald Rothchild and Victor Olorunsola, "Managing Competing State and Ethnic Claims," in Donald Rothchild and Victor Olorunsola, eds., *State Versus Ethnic Claims: African Policy Dilemmas* (Boulder: Westview, 1983), pp. 10–11.

86. Robert Bates, "Modernization, Ethnic Competition and the Rationality of Politics in Contemporary Africa," in Rothchild and Olorunsola, *State Versus Ethnic Claims*, p. 166.

87. The following analysis is based on Naomi Chazan, "Ethnicity in Economic Crisis," in Dennis L. Thompson and Dov Ronen, eds., *Ethnicity, Politics, and Development* (Boulder: Lynne Rienner, 1986), pp. 137–158. Also see Michael G. Schatzberg, "Ethnicity and Class at the Local Level: Bars and Bureaucrats in Lisala, Zaire," *Comparative Politics*, 13, 4 (1981): 461–478.

88. Martin O. Heisler and B. Guy Peters, "Scarcity and the Management of Political Conflict in Multicultural Politics," *International Political Science Review*, 4, 3 (1983): 327–344.

89. A superb case study may be found in Ulrich Braukamper, "Ethnic Identity and Social Change Among Oromo Refugees in the Horn of Africa," *Northeast African Studies*, 4, 3 (1983): 1–15.

90. See Terence O. Ranger, "Religious Movements and Politics in Sub-Saharan Africa," ACLS/SSRC Joint Committee on African Studies paper (Presented at the Twenty-Eighth Annual Meetings of the African Studies Association, New Orleans, November 1985).

91. Mar Fall, "L'Etat Sénégalais et le Renouveau Récent de l'Islam: Une Introduction," *Mois en Afrique*, 219/220 (1984): 154–159.

92. Paul Lubeck, "Conscience de Class et Nationalisme Islamique à Kano," *Politique Africaine*, 1, 4 (1981), esp. pp. 31–40.

93. Donal Cruise O'Brien, "La Filière Musulmane: Confréries Soufies et Politique en Afrique Noire," *Politique Africaine*, 1, 4 (1981): 7–30.

94. Margaret Peil, *Consensus and Conflict in African Societies* (London: Longman, 1977), p. 239.

95. Christian Coulon, "Le Reseau Islamique," *Politique Africaine*, 9 (1983): 68–83. O'Brien, "La Filière Musulmane," p. 29, disagrees.

96. Achola O. Pala, "La Femme Africaine Dans Le Développement Rurale," *Cahiers Economiques et Sociaux*, 16, 3 (1978): 306–333; *Review of African Political Economy*, 27/28 (1983), special issue on Women in Africa.

97. Marc Howard Ross and Veena Thadani, "Research Note: Participation, Sex and Social Class: Some Unexpected Results from an African City," *Comparative Politics*, 12, 3 (1980): 327.

98. For an example from Southern Africa see Pauline Peters, "Gender, Developmental Cycles and Historical Process: A Critique on Recent Research on Women in Botswana," *Journal of Southern African Studies*, 10, 1 (1983): 100–122.

99. Kathleen Staudt, "Women's Politics and Capitalist Transformation in Subsaharan Africa," W.I.D. Working Paper No. 54 (1984).

100. Kasfir, "Relating State to Class," p. 6.

101. The notion of the state as an arena is summarized in Skocpol, *States and Social Revolutions*, pp. 1–24.

102. Hart, *West African Agriculture*, p. 105, makes this point forcefully, but it is highlighted in most local studies.

103. For one case study see Michael A. Cohen, *Urban Policy and Political Conflict in Africa: A Study of the Ivory Coast* (Chicago: University of Chicago Press, 1974).

104. Richard Sandbrook, *The Politics of Basic Needs: Urban Aspects of Assaulting Poverty in Africa* (London: Heinemann, 1982).

105. Stren, "L'Etat au Risque de la Ville," pp. 85–87. Also see his "The Ruralization of African Cities" (Paper presented at the Twenty-Eighth Annual Meetings of the African Studies Association, New Orleans, November 1985).

106. Donald Rothchild, "Comparative Public Demand and Expectation Patterns: The Ghanaian Experience," *African Studies Review*, 22, 1 (1979): 127–147.

107. Krasner, "Approaches to the State."

108. Walter Barrows, *Grassroots Politics in an African State: Integration and Development in Sierra Leone* (New York: Africana, 1976).

109. Libya may constitute one such example.

110. Yves Person, "L'Etat Nation et l'Afrique," *Mois en Afrique*, 190–191 (1981): 27–35.

111. For some insights see Ali A. Mazrui, "The Reincarnation of the African State: A Triple Heritage in Transition from Pre-Colonial Times," *Presence Africaine*,

127/128 (1983): 114–127, and Codjo Huenu, "La Question de l'Etat et de la Nation en Afrique," *Presence Africaine*, 127/128 (1983): 329–347.

112. A scathing critique of elite ideology may be found in Ekeh, "Colonialism and the Two Publics."

113. Walter Barrows, "Comparative Grassroots Politics in Africa," *World Politics*, 26, 2 (1974): 283–297.

114. Otwin Marenin, "Essence and Empiricism in African Politics," *Journal of Modern African Studies*, 19, 1 (1981): 28.

115. Schaffer, "Integration is not Equity," p. 38.

116. Hyden, *No Shortcuts to Progress*, p. 19; Rothchild and Foley, "The Implications of Scarcity," p. 314.

117. René Lemarchand, "Quelles Indépendences?" *Mois en Afrique*, 205/206 (1983): 19–37.

118. See Callaghy, "The State and the Development of Capitalism."

119. Azarya, "Reordering State-Society Relations," this volume.

6

The State, the Parallel Economy, and the Changing Structure of Patronage Systems

René Lemarchand

Peasants avoid it, urban workers despise it, military men destroy it, civil servants rape it and academics ponder the short- and long-term results. There can be no gainsaying the importance of the state in Africa as both an empirical phenomenon and an analytic category; yet, by a curious twist of fate, just as the concept of the state has gained an unprecedented vogue among Africanists, its reality seems to have dissolved into a host of invertebrate species which for the most part defy categorization. Has the state suddenly become conspicuous by its absence? Or has a new type of state system emerged from the ashes of its predecessor, forcing us to reconsider our initial assumptions about the character of the postcolonial state?

The current fascination with the state is not merely an intellectual fad. It reflects in part a sense of perplexity over the metamorphoses that have accompanied the transplantation of Western state models in tropical soils and a genuine effort to come to grips with the basic issues raised by the emergence of African state systems. To what degree have the characteristics of the colonial Leviathan been inherited by African states? To what extent are the emergent institutions of governance shaped by the societal matrix in which they are embedded? How much autonomy can the state claim for itself while denouncing the ills of international dependency? And if the conditions of internal autonomy lie in the capacity of the state to act as a "mediatory institution" (to borrow Donald Rothchild's phrase), what enters into the mediating process, and with what consequences for the mediator?

By virtue of the circumstances of their birth and colonial heritage, African states belong to a kind of conceptual borderline area where the encounter of traditional and modern institutions generates its own perverse effects, most notably "political decay." In the regnant Huntingtonian paradigm of the 1970s the decay of "developing" state institutions was singled out as the inevitable concomitant of rapid political modernization.[1] But inasmuch as decay appeared to persist even in the absence of political mobilization, attention shifted to other types of explanatory variables. The hijacking of state autonomy by class interests became the stock-in-trade of neo-Marxists.[2] Because the debate about class threatened to lead to an impasse, mainstream analysis drew attention to alternative modes of explanation, some focusing on "institutionalized corruption" (Gould), others on the vagaries of "personalized rule" (Jackson and Rosberg), and still others on "the arbitrariness of patrimonial leadership" (Callaghy). With the rehabilitation of state-centered paradigms, a fresh effort is now being made to bring these several variables into some kind of coherent conceptual framework, an effort for which Thomas Callaghy deserves considerable credit.[3] The aim, in essence, is to encourage maximum comparability, in terms of time and space, of phenomena which have generally been treated as unique, and in so doing to initiate a new debate about the relevance of the "state as a variable." Thus, the not entirely rhetorical question raised by Crawford Young—is there a state?[4]— confronts us once again with the problem of sifting out the epiphenomenal from the more enduring traits of African state systems.

If there is any validity to Huntington's arresting thesis that "the absence in America of a state in the European sense" carries with it "a promise of disharmony,"[5] in the African context disharmony translates into a range of pathological dysfunctions for which there are few plausible equivalents in the United States.[6] The most enduring manifestation of such "dysfunctions" has been the decline of state capabilities, a phenomenon nowhere more painfully evident than in "the shrinkage in the competence, credibility and probity of the state."[7]

What follows is an attempt to explore the roots of the phenomenon in light of the changing structure of patronage systems. In part because they focus attention on the informal means of persuasion (and coercion) built around the selective allocation of state resources, and because they bring to light the increasingly important role of the "parallel economy" in the reordering of state-society relationships, patronage mechanisms provide a convenient point of entry into the evolving (and involuted) configurations of African state systems. The other side of the coin, in Waterbury's terms, is that the concept of patronage "offers all the analytic frustrations common to most attempts at categorising social action and human motivation."[8] There is, for one thing, the problem of differentiating patronage from related cases of political influence, notably "tribute" and "prebends" (or corruption), a task made all the more frustrating by the tendency to use normative criteria as the only guide to definition. Compounding the problem of definition is the classic dilemma of assessing the explanatory power of a concept which doubles as a descriptive device: is patronage (or tribute or corruption) merely a symptom of something more fundamental, or can it be viewed as the analytic key that enables us to make sense of otherwise untractable political realities?

In the following section we try to clarify these issues in light of traditional and contemporary forms of patronage or, more accurately, by looking at patronage as distinct from "tribute" and "prebends." We then turn to a discussion of the recent transformation of African patronage systems seen from a political economy perspective. Finally, an attempt is made to show the relationship between systematic bureaucratic corruption and the emergence of parallel economies, and the impact of both on the reordering of rural dependency relationships.

Some Preliminary Distinctions:
Tribute, Patronage and Prebends

Among revisionist interpretations of African politics none has been more instrumental in demonstrating the centrality of political patronage than the "machine model." First brought into academic discourse by Aristide Zolberg and subsequently elaborated upon by Henry Bienen (among others),[9] the model posits as its central element a type of political organization strikingly similar to the American machine, in which support is generated through the distribution of material incentives (i.e., patronage jobs) rather than through an appeal to ideology or principle. With the discovery of the machine model, many of the standard dichotomies previously used to explicate the dynamics of African politics—e.g., "mass" vs. "patron" parties, "revolutionary-centralizing" versus "pragmatic-pluralistic" regimes—were quickly consigned to oblivion and rarely resurrected. Although the concept of patronage continues to offer significant analytic leverage where machines are still in motion (e.g., Senegal, Ivory Coast, Zimbabwe, Kenya), the machine model admits to many variations.[10] Political machines, as we all know, operate on the basis of short-run material benefits; the exchange process normally involves the trading of tangible rewards for votes and other forms of support. Yet political support may come at a discount where rural notables are cast in the role of saintly figures (as in Senegal) or retain enough legitimacy and trust to inspire respect and affection. Depending on the context in which it operates, patronage may take on very different connotations from those generally associated with self-interested exchanges; it may partake of the quality of "gift-giving" (in the Maussian sense of the term) and summon a level of trust unknown among urban clienteles.

For the sake of clarity, the concept of "patronage" needs to be distinguished at the outset from those of "tribute" and "prebends," even though in practice they often interact and interpenetrate each other in more or less complex ways. All three involve certain types of self-interested exchange. Yet they each tend to develop within specific institutional frameworks and are sustained by radically different normative orientations. They can best be seen, therefore, as diagnostic features of the changes taking place in the wider sociopolitical environment.

As one form of generalized exchange, tribute operates in a context of trust based on expectations of reciprocity; the obligation of the chief, subchief or notable to reciprocate the gifts and services offered by his clients is inscribed in their shared value system; yet the element of self-interested rationality entering into this relationship cannot be ignored. While status differences help set the rate of exchange between patron and client (subject to frequent recalculations, depending on economic contingencies and other factors), the principle of exchange is itself legitimized by the structure of the environment and the nature of the commodities exchanged. This is central to the argument set forth by Daryll Forde and Mary Douglas in their discussion of "primitive economics": "The obligation to distribute income is supported by two factors. One . . . is the constant menace of want. Everyone is aware of his own insecurity and consequent dependence on his neighbours. The second is the technical difficulty of conserving goods for future consumption."[11] In these conditions the chances of gross economic disparities among individuals are significantly lessened by the obligation to repay gift for gift, which might conceivably be viewed as an investment strategy designed to enhance one's future security, as well as by the limited absorptive capacity of the recipient. As Max Gluckman once observed, "there are limits to how much porridge a man can eat"; there are no limits, however, to the amount of money one can stash away in a Swiss bank.

The element of trust is equally important to help us discriminate between traditional and modern forms of generalized exchange. In traditional societies trust is a necessary (but not sufficient) condition for the payment of tribute to or the performance of services for a chief or patron; in the context of machine politics, on the other hand, the ability to allocate patronage is what motivates trust.

The extent to which colonial rule has contributed to the erosion of social trust and deference between patrons and clients, chiefs and subjects lies beyond the scope of this discussion.[12] Suffice it to note that colonial rule has accelerated the shift from traditional clientelism to political patronage in the modern sense in a variety of ways, and most decisively by providing the conditions for popular participation in electoral politics. With the rise of nationalist machines, the vote emerged as a critical political resource in the hands of the masses, a resource which could be traded for material rewards of all kinds, ranging from schools and piped water to scholarships and jobs.[13] As new inducements entered the political arena, the texture of politics also changed, with bargaining tending to eclipse social trust as the dominant style of machine-based reciprocities. Another difference relates to the identity of the beneficiaries: while one can cite countless examples of traditional authority figures capitalizing on their social status to deliver the votes of their constituents, in general it is the modern-day politicians and westernized elites who have supplanted the traditional patrons as the key recipients of patronage resources. Moreover, the substitution of public goods for individual prestations has tended to widen the access of the electorate to the benefits of the machine. Finally, the rapid enlargement of the scope of political exchange, in response to the expanding size of the electorate, must be viewed as a critically important feature of machine-based patronage systems. Just as control of the state unlocked patronage resources on an unprecedented scale, the expansion of the vote, along with the need to achieve a measure of political cohesion in the midst of social fragmentation, economic inequalities and ecological discontinuities, engendered powerful pressures to widen the ambit of patronage.

Ironically, the very same factors that have conspired to expand the scope of patronage have often led to its demise. Where patronage coalesced with ethnicity, the struggle for state resources only served to unleash violence. For example, the extent to which marketing boards were used as a source of patronage for ethno-regional interests in Nigeria is well established, as is indeed the contribution of "the convoluted collaboration of government, party, public corporation and private business"[14] to the eventual breakdown of the federation in 1967. Competition over patronage resources may produce factional splits among bureaucrats and politicians that have little to do with ethnicity but whose effects can be just as devastating. The point, at any rate, is that in a number of cases and for a variety of reasons, including the part played by ethnic and fractional pressures in skewing distributive patterns, the machines failed conspicuously in the performance of their integrative functions. Many simply ran out of steam and lost their clienteles; others retooled themselves into coercive instruments in the hands of Mafia-like bureaucracies. Almost everywhere the limitations placed on political participation led to a rapid demobilization of the citizenry. As the rules of the game changed to the advantage of the incumbents, so did the character of political exchange.

With the dismantling of political machines, patronage moved into new circuits—the army or paramilitary organizations, administrative and corporate channels, and a variety of fluid networks of patron-client ties based on kinship or regional ties. These and other changes in the overall structure of patronage systems will be discussed at greater length in the following pages. What must be stressed here is the rapid spread of cynicism and corruption that has accompanied the decline of electoral politics.

The distinction between patronage and corruption is notoriously vague, if only because of the judgmental and normative elements which normally enter into definitions of corruption. Nye's definition of corrupt behavior— that "which deviates from the formal duties of a public role (elective or appointive) because of private-regarding . . . wealth or status gains"[15]—does not necessarily exclude patronage from such behavior, but it does focus attention on the extent to which corruption deviates from legal norms.

The appropriation of state resources for personal gain, rather than for amassing public support, is a crucial aspect of the corruption syndrome. Here the concept of "prebend," borrowed from Max Weber,[16] seems especially appropriate. Stripped of its etymological connotations, it refers to the personal benefits drawn from the appropriation of public office—in the same way that in medieval Europe canons drew prebends from ecclesiastical lands. In the context of prebendal politics the state emerges as the proprietory state par excellence or, to use Terisa Turner's expression,[17] as a "market" where officeholders compete for the acquisition of material benefits. The relevance of the prebendal pattern for the analysis of Nigerian politics during the Second Republic has been convincingly demonstrated by Richard Joseph; behind the countless deals and rip-offs and institutionalized theft of state property that have given Nigerian politics their distinctive mafioso style lies "the justifying principle that the offices of the state may be competed for and then utilized for the personal benefit of office-holders as well as that of their reference or support group."[18] This characterization applies equally well to the dominant style of politics in Zaire and, to a lesser extent, in Kenya.

As the foregoing makes clear, the boundaries between tribute, patronage and prebends are frequently effaced by empirical realities. Seldom do we encounter situations where one type eclipses another. Disentangling their interconnections is one of the most arduous tasks facing the analysis of political exchange. What does seem reasonably clear, however, is that these shifts and interconnections among political exchange systems cannot be explained by reference to their own structural characteristics; they are the symptoms, not the cause, of the more fundamental transformations taking place in political arenas.

With these observations in mind, let us now turn to an examination of the political economy of patronage systems. The key emphasis here is on the evolving patterns of interactions between African economies and the allocation of patronage resources.

The Political Economy of Patronage Systems

Since the advent of independence in the 1960s three major trends have altered the structure of African patronage systems and in most cases have led to their atrophy or elimination.

Where political departicipation has been effectively enforced (which includes the vast majority of African states), the result has been a drastic shrinkage in the scope of the machine pattern. In the absence of electoral pressures, patronage operations have centered increasingly upon certain key sectors of the civil service, the army and the police; "cronyism," with or without any discernible pecking order, has tended to flourish, giving an entirely different quality to the style of machine politics.

Additionally, access to patronage resources is becoming more intricately tied up with the penetration of the world economy into African arenas. This has contributed to the acceleration of the previous trend in two major ways. The sharp and persistent drop in international commodity prices has greatly reduced the pool of patronage resources available to the state, a phenomenon nowhere more evident than in Zaire and Zambia, where the fall in copper and other mineral prices has severely affected their fiscal revenues and foreign earnings. The deterioration of agricultural commodity prices has had similar effects in many other states. Furthermore, the sheer complexity and multiplicity of commercial transactions attendant upon the penetration of international capitalism has introduced a host of opportunities for all kinds of corrupt behavior, ranging from the embezzlement of foreign exchange and currency manipulations to kickbacks, bribes and other mal-versations. Multinational corporations, international lending agencies, emergency relief organizations, metropolitan-based *sociétés de développement* and the like figure prominently in the patterns of exchange through which external resources are funneled into African circuits. As the periodic disclosure of African scandals makes abundantly clear, the benefits involved in these transactions are considerable and are concentrated in fewer and fewer hands, some of them foreign.

Finally, in many rural areas patrons have ceased to patronize. The elimination of patronage incentives from the countryside, along with their replacement by a kind of free-for-all system in which local officials, military men and security spooks are given a blank check to use their prerogatives (and weapons) as they deem fit, has already been the rule for some years in such countries as Zaire, Uganda and Chad. This pattern is most likely to persist and expand. How to avoid, circumvent or mitigate the preda-ciousness of the state is the central dilemma confronting the rural masses. The issue lies at the heart of the new patterns of dependency emerging within the perimeters of the "parallel economy."

These observations are of course subject to major qualifications related to the political context and economic structure of individual states. In those rare instances where electoral pressures and party competition are still in existence, the scope of patronage politics is relatively extensive, as in Senegal and Zimbabwe; on the other hand, where electoral competition is nonexistent or elections resemble plebiscites, as in Zaire, patronage hardly goes beyond the confines of the presidential clique. Again, the incidence of ethnicity as a variable in political recruitment may circumscribe the allocation of benefits to specific groups (e.g. the Shona in Zimbabwe, the Kikuyu in Kenya, the Tutsi in Burundi) or subgroups.[19] Nor is the externally oriented pattern of patronage operations observable in Nigeria, Zaire or Kenya all that significant in states where external dependency relations are minimal. Rather than looking for deviant or exceptional cases, a more fruitful approach to an understanding of variations and similarities is to look at patronage systems from a political economy perspective, taking into account specific forms of interaction between the polity and the economy. Especially relevant here are: (1) the impact of state expansion on the availability of patronage resources; (2) the feedback effect of bureaucratic corruption on the economy; and (3) the involvement of foreign business interests in the structure of patronage systems.

Patterns of State Expansion

That the availability of patronage resources tends to vary in proportion to the size of the public sector is almost axiomatic; a corollary of this is that the size of bureaucratic prebends also increases in proportion to the penetration of the economy by the state. While the first proposition suggests that patronage systems will be most extensive where nationalization has been most thorough, the second suggests the existence of significant con- straints on the expansion of patronage benefits.

"*L'étatisation de la société mene à la privatisation de l'Etat.*" Elbaki Hermassi's pithy statement[20] captures the essence of the mechanism behind the involution of patronage networks: policies designed to enhance the control of the state merely tend to speed up the privatization of state resources. Rather than promoting the deployment of public resources for patronage purposes, *étatisation* has often had the opposite effect: favoring the accumulation of prebends in private hands.

That the scale of prebendal accumulation tends to vary in proportion to the size of the nationalized sectors is well established. In states like Sierra Leone, Zaire and Nigeria, where state control is relatively extensive, bu- reaucratic corruption absorbs the lion's share of public resources; in Zim- babwe, by contrast, where the mining and manufacturing sectors, along with commercial farming, are still privately controlled, the scope of corruption is far more limited and normally subject to exposure and public sanctions. Local corruption is by no means unheard of in Zimbabwe;[21] yet there is no parallel for the endemic and massive bureaucratic corruption at the highest levels that has been reported in Lagos and Kinshasa.

More often than not nationalization has led to enormous losses of state revenue, due to corruption as much as to sheer ineptitude in the imple- mentation of nationalization policies. This has drastically reduced the size of the investment pie and created severe opportunity costs from the standpoint of rural development efforts.

Directly or indirectly, rural stagnation is largely associated with the failure of nationalization schemes, as evidenced by the cases of Tanzania following the adoption of the Arusha Declaration in 1967, Zaire following the disastrous Zairianization decrees of 1973–1975, and Nigeria following the oil boom of the late 1960s and 1970s. The reason for this is that state-centered patronage often tends to deflect rural development policies from their original goals. One example among others is the highly unorthodox lending procedure that came to characterize the African Farming Improvement Funds (AFIF) in Zambia. Though intended to "promote better conditions for African farmers through improved marketing and farming of agricultural produce," for the most part the AFIF loans were channeled into the pockets of southern politicians and civil servants to feather their rural nests and help their friends in the countryside:

> Loans were made without any enquiry as to how far arrangements had been made for the purchase of the properties concerned, without any enquiry as to whether the persons concerned were African farmers, whether they were farming in the province concerned. . . . Most of the loans were made to persons who were members of the Board or who held positions in Government or Public Service.[22]

The Southern Province African Farm Improvement Fund (SPAFIF), in particular, was mainly used to offset the growing political influence of northern politicians (mostly Bemba) in the United National Independence Party (UNIP), which in turn prompted a Bemba-based faction to bolt UNIP and form the United Progressive Party (UPP). Besides sharply aggravating factional tensions within UNIP, the SPAFIF scandal revealed how, in the words of one observer, "policy designed to broaden the base of the public enjoying access to state resources can be highjacked in the interest of private accumulation. . . . Funds contributed by, and intended for the benefit of peasant producers were appropriated by high level officials for the purchase of private farms on state land."[23]

Feedback Mechanisms

There is more, however, to corruption and inefficiency than a diversion of public revenue into private hands; both tend to generate their own feedback mechanisms through which vast new opportunities emerge for further embezzlement, thus perpetuating rural stagnation and bureaucratic corruption.

Neglect of the rural sectors has drastically altered patterns of trade, with food imports accounting for an increasingly large share of the national budgets. The food crisis has generated unprecedented poverty in the countryside, as well as unprecedented accumulation of wealth at the top. Several factors account for this paradoxical situation. For one thing, the transactions involved in the importation of food commodities have substantially enlarged the scope of opportunities for bureaucratic corruption. The widely publicized Dikko affair in Nigeria[24]—culminating in one of the most bizarre cases of international intrigue—is a case in point. The involvement of the former Minister of Transportation (Amaru Dikko), along with the former Minister of Finance (Victor Masi) and several other disreputable characters, in a series of illicit rice deals said to involve frauds and kickbacks amounting to $1 billion is an appalling commentary on the scale of the profits made possible by the existence of food scarcities; it also reveals the complexity of the international connections that lie in the background of the scandal.

Though practiced on a lesser scale, overinvoicing of food imports has been a standard feature of the Zairian brand of kleptocracy, along with kickbacks on the sale of imported commodities. Less well known than the Nigerian rice scandal, but just as suggestive of how the food crisis has enhanced opportunities for corruption, are the entry-port fees collected by Ethiopian authorities on shipments of emergency food aid to drought-stricken areas, which, according to one report, amount to $28 million a year (or $12.60 on every ton of grain).[25] Finally, passing reference must be made to the covert payments made to Sudanese officials in return for their cooperation in evacuating thousands of Falasha Jews to Israel. Clearly, the implications of hunger for the analysis of corruption can be detected in various and complex ways, and at many different levels.

Triangular Partnerships

Just as bureaucratic corruption has a feedback effect on African economies—by deflecting investment priorities away from agriculture, enhancing
the role of imported commodities, heightening the need for foreign exchange
and strengthening external dependencies—commercial capitalism tends to
shape patronage systems in specific ways. The most richly documented
example of this phenomenon is the "triangular relationship" that developed
in Nigeria during the oil boom, roughly between 1966 and 1976, involving
the participation of multinational corporations, local middlemen and "state
compradors." For the former, as Terisa Turner observes, "bribe-bidding is
a logical means of seeking competitive advantage"; for middlemen, whose
prime function is one of brokerage, i.e. to facilitate the contact of foreign
businessmen with state representatives, commissions are the normal reward,
and these are generally shared with the "collaborating state comprador";
the latter, whose "gatekeeping function" entails "opening the gate" for the
entry and exit of commodities, collects fees from both foreign businessmen
and local bureaucrats.[26] Out of these mutually rewarding transactions
developed a pattern of exchange made all the more complex by the
competitiveness existing at all three levels and by the "deals" that presumably
took place between the Nigerian National Oil Corporation (NNOC), the
Petroleum Advisory Board and the Ministry of Finance's Petroleum Division.
As Turner points out, "Instability is endemic in the struggle among middlemen
for patronage, and in the competition among officials of state for control
of decisions. In these circumstances politics is a form of business through
which actors seek influence in the state . . . in order to secure advantages."[27]
A lucrative business to be sure, but not only for Nigerian actors.

The active involvement of foreign elements in the corruption syndrome
carries important implications. The obligations they incur for gaining access
to African markets go far beyond the realm of business. In return for
services rendered (or not rendered), foreign businessmen have often served
as the critical links in the chain of personal connections through which
specific political objectives have been reached. The Dikko affair, though
unique for its tragicomic quality, is only one example among others; the
recent history of Zaire and Gabon is equally instructive in this respect.

The case of Gabon presents an interesting variation on the triangular
pattern discussed above in that two elements in the triangle are French,
with the third bringing into Gabonese hands a unique combination of
economic wealth and political clout.[28] Given the preferential status enjoyed
by French business interests in dealing with Gabonese officials (the so-called
chassé gardee privileges) and the "closed," oligopolistic structure of the
Gabonese market, there is little need for African middlemen. What French
business interests and Gabonese officials need most are security guarantees
to make sure that the conditions of their mutually profitable relationship
are firmly secured. This safety net is serviced by the French state. It consists
of a dense network of French-sponsored security and intelligence gathering
organizations,[29] strategically placed military and political advisers, some of

them better described as mercenaries, and the "good offices" of the French Embassy. Thus, the third element in the Gabonese triangle—the French state—consists not of one but of several components. What holds them together (most of the time) and brings them into close working relationships with business interests and Gabonese officials are the shared material benefits arising from this triadic partnership. For example, the substantial tax breaks accorded to Elf, the major French parastatal in charge of drilling, prospecting and commercializing Gabon's oil resources, are repaid in the form of a transfer of ten percent of petroleum sales to the Provision pour Investissements Diversifies (PID), which in turn serves as a thinly disguised slush fund at the disposition of Bongo and key members of his entourage. Although French security and paramilitary personnel are technically on the payroll of the Gabonese government, salaries, kickbacks and gifts all originate from the same source, i.e. the business sectors, with Elf at the top of the list.

The substantial campaign contributions made by Elf-Gabon to the Rassemblement pour la République (RPR) in 1980[30] is entirely consistent with the overwhelmingly Gaullist orientation of the French "estate" in Gabon and indeed with Bongo's metropolitan sympathies. But it also suggests a wider dimension to the pattern of reciprocities analyzed above. The most arresting feature of the Gabonese case lies in the continuing strength of a powerful informal political machine entirely dedicated to serving the interests of Gaullist notables and politicians both within and outside Gabon. More surprising still is the extent to which, even after independence, this machine has effectively mobilized the resources and sympathies of Gabonese officials on behalf of Gaullist interests and political objectives. This phenomenon is traceable to the postwar years when a number of French *resistants*, most of them associated with the Free French, were given access to a vast store of patronage positions in Gabon. Some were recruited in the colonial administration, while others made a fortune in timber, commerce and industry. Intimate bonds of friendship developed among French expatriates and administrators, and these ramified widely into metropolitan-based Gaullist milieux. The remarkably smooth transition to independence (which almost had to be forced upon the Gabonese, since Leon Mba, Gabon's first president, insisted on *departementalisation* as the preferred alternative!) paved the way for the incorporation of Gabonese elements into the machine. Under Bongo, however, the system underwent profound alterations: a single party state was introduced and the internal opposition dismantled; a large number of corporate posts were Africanized and the share of the Gabonese state in corporate profits derived from oil, manganese and timber increased dramatically after 1973; and a large proportion of this wealth was now used by Bongo to lubricate his own machine. The shoe is now on the other foot: rather than Gabonese elements being incorporated into the Gaullist machine, as was the case in the years immediately following independence, it is the Gabonese state which now uses its patronage to finance the campaign of Gaullist candidates in metropolitan France, to hire French military advisers and mercenaries, to set the terms of contractual agreements with French corporations, and eventually bring pressure to bear on the French government. That so little of Gabon's vast resources is invested in development, and so much in "managing" metropolitan connections, is not the least of the ironies of the Gabonese patronage system.

What makes the case of Gabon unique is the resilience and wide-ranging metropolitan ramifications of the Franco-Gabonese nexus; on the other hand, it is illustrative of certain features of the "foreign estate connection" which are broadly applicable to much of French-speaking Africa, as well as to Nigeria and Kenya.

The contribution of foreigners to the corruption syndrome can be analyzed at several levels. (1) At the technical level: foreign "accomplices" are in a position to offer the managerial skills, outside contacts and clout that are of critical importance for Africans to cash in on corporate bribes, illicit foreign exchange transactions, rake-offs, laundering operations of one kind or another, and so on; in states like Gabon, the CAR and Zaire expertise on "how to beat the system" (and its opponents) has often been proffered by foreigners who were themselves on the receiving end of the line. (2) At the psychological level: the foreign presence sets certain standards of affluence and conspicuous consumption which, among junior civil servants, can only be emulated by having recourse to corrupt practices. Prebends, in short, are the quickest route to opulence. (3) At the political level: in specific instances foreigners have played an important role in countering or silencing criticism of their African "patrons" in their home countries, in monitoring and relaying sensitive information, and in handling "delicate missions," sometimes (as in Gabon) involving the physical elimination of political opponents. This foreign-based network makes the pursuit of corruption at home safer than it would otherwise be, but it also creates expectations of rewards for services rendered. These expectations are usually met by enlarging the scope of prebends and privileges, thus giving further impetus to personalized favors, rip-offs and kickbacks.

Even though these realities are seldom articulated by Africans, the extent to which the foreign estate contributes to the survival of thoroughly unpopular regimes is well understood by their domestic opponents. The exceptional violence unleashed against European residents of Kolwezi during Shaba II captured the full force of the animosity released by their presence in one of Zaire's key industrial towns.

Although we have already underscored the relationship between the expansion of the prebendal state and the stagnation of the agricultural sectors, let us now take a closer look at the significance of the parallel economy for an understanding of state-society relations in the rural areas.

The Parallel Economy and the Restructuring of Rural Dependency

With the expansion of the informal, or parallel, economy a new social field has come into being in which capitalist and precapitalist modes of production intersect in complex ways. This shadowy world provides the setting for the proliferation of transient and instrumental ties between civil servants and their intermediaries, on the one hand, and the rural masses, on the other. The exigencies of economic survival are motivating a growing number of rural Africans to enter into this nexus of dependency; the opportunities for material gain are causing these networks to penetrate into bureaucratic and governmental spheres.

Parallel economies are not new to Africa. As precapitalist enclaves they persisted and flourished in the interstitial spaces of the colonial state. Their recent expansion and growing significance as an informal exchange system, however, cannot be properly grasped unless attention is paid to the weakening of state institutions that has accompanied the shift from patronage to prebends. Whether the prebendal state claims a Marxist or capitalist orientation has very little to do with the spread of the informal sectors; the phenomenon, after all, is just as noticeable in Marxist Angola as in capitalist Zaire. The important point to stress is the thoroughly negative impact of prebendal policies on rural producers. To the extent that prebendal states have enough authority left to initiate and implement policies, these are primarily intended to increase the volume of prebends at the center, to the detriment of the countryside. Thus, overvalued exchange rates, high taxes on agricultural exports and the subsidization of food imports are standard policies associated with prebendal states, to which must be added the inefficiency and corruption which normally attends the operation of marketing agencies and parastatals. The result has been the placement of enormous burdens on the producers of cash crops and food crops; selling or smuggling through informal networks is the most rational course to avoid economic strangulation. In addition, where the prebendal state proves incapable of generating the fiscal resources needed to pay the salaries of civil servants and military men, it is likely that the latter will be heavily involved in smuggling and black-market activities. They may even take the initiative in priming the pump of the informal economy.

To recapitulate, almost everywhere in Africa informal economies have come into being in response to the convergence of two distinctive sets of pressures: (1) the pressures from below, reflecting the growing vulnerability of the peasant sectors to the urban-oriented-cum-corrupt policies and practices of the prebendal state; and (2) the pressures originating from those elements in the civil service and the army who feel that they have no other option but to make the most of this situation—either as protectors or mediators of the rural communities or, if these roles fail to yield the expected returns, as predators.

It is hardly a matter of coincidence that parallel economies have flourished most extensively where the prebendal syndrome is most conspicuous, assuming in some instances the status of a "dominant submode of production," to borrow Reginald Green's felicitous phrasing.[31] As Green's painstaking analysis of *magendo* makes clear, the phenomenon is most fully developed in Uganda, but it is also becoming prominent, if not dominant, in such states as Zaire, Angola, Chad, Senegal and Sudan. In 1981 approximately two-thirds of Uganda's monetary GDP went into the parallel economy; in 1971, according to one estimate, 60 percent of Zaire's revenues "were lost or directed to other purposes than the official ones";[32] in 1985 more than half of Senegal's peanut harvest was smuggled into neighboring states, mainly the Gambia, representing a loss of Fr. 200 billion in tax receipts.[33]

For the vast majority of Africans, involvement in the parallel economy is a survival strategy tailored to conditions of extreme scarcity. Although one cannot discount the contribution of natural calamities to the spread of informal economies, the state, rather than nature, is seen as the main source of aggression. Disengagement from the state is the major preoccupation of most rural inhabitants, even though it is not always feasible. Circumventing the predators through clientelistic ties with local patrons is one aspect of this strategy (best illustrated by the case of Senegal); another is to work out some kind of modus vivendi with the predators in the hope that their predaciousness can thereby be mitigated (as has often happened in Uganda and Zaire). Whether one strategy prevails over the other depends on the distribution of economic vulnerabilities and the availability of local patrons to minimize the incidence of such vulnerabilities. The first of these variables helps us identify those sectors where the quest for some kind of protection or patronage is most likely to arise; the second tells why, in the vast majority of cases, this protection fails to materialize.

The depth and distribution of socioeconomic vulnerability is in part a function of state policies (or the absence of such policies) and in part the result of social dislocations that have followed in the wake of acute and prolonged crises (as in Zaire, Uganda, Chad, Sudan and Mozambique).

Where pricing and marketing policies have caused a sharp drop in producer prices and rural incomes—as is now the dominant trend almost everywhere in Africa, with the qualified exception of Zimbabwe—the tendency has been to use the parallel economy against the state. The smuggling of cash crops is the standard practice to avoid economic exploitation by the state. Countless examples can be cited of large-scale smuggling operations involving coffee (Uganda and Zaire), cocoa (Ghana) or groundnuts (Senegal). In Senegal alone as much as 300,000 tons of groundnuts found their way out of the country through informal channels, presumably with the active cooperation of the Mouride establishment.[34] The picture which emerges is one in which the Islamic brotherhoods set themselves up as a contre-pouvoir against the sociétés d'état, not only offering the peasants a higher price (CFA frs. 80 per kilo of groundnuts as against CFA frs. 60 paid by the state) but also providing the contacts and transportation facilities necessary to effectively conduct smuggling activities. In the absence of such supportive networks, countering the depredations of the state becomes far more problematic. Whereas in Senegal the brotherhoods are still in a position to offer effective sources of patronage (but for how much longer?), the types of dependency recorded in settings as diverse as Zimbabwe, Rwanda and Zaire suggest a far more oppressive relationship.

The most vulnerable sectors in Zimbabwe are the landless peasants and squatters (to which must be added ex-guerrilla fighters). The combination of large-scale commercial farming, mainly under white control, and communal farming has done little to improve the conditions of Zimbabwe's 950,000 subsistence peasant farmers and 9,000 small-scale farmers. For the landless, squatting is the normal survival strategy, but in this case survival comes at a cost. Economic exploitation is nowhere more severe than among those squatters[35] that have been reduced to the status of an unpaid labor force on small-scale holdings.[36] In northern Rwanda, where land hunger has been sharply aggravated by development schemes favoring large landowners and state officials (the two are often the same), the result has been to stimulate the growth of a rural proletariat whose livelihood depends on the starvation wages paid by their landed patrons.[37] In Zaire, despite or because of the introduction of a policy of liberalization aimed at decontrolling agricultural prices, removing import taxes on farm inputs and organizing new sources of rural credit, oppression and economic exploitation are still the rule in much of the countryside. Land-grabbing operations, according to one observer, are becoming "increasingly common in the east of the country,"[38] in violation of traditional land rights and with no legal recourse available to displaced owners. The situation reported in the Lufira Valley appears fairly typical: "Chiefs continue to function as intermediaries in the system, profiting from the labor of prisoners put to work in their fields; they sometimes direct their policemen to use corporal punishment, and the practice is considered normal by officials."[39] Difficult though it is at times to identify the aggressors, oppression is here traceable to specific state policies or to the inability of the state to control the perverse effects of the parallel economy.

On the other hand, there is also considerable evidence to show that the state has a stake in the perpetuation of the secondary economy, as when state officials act as privileged partners in the management of economic exploitation. The cases of Uganda and Zaire are instructive in this respect, in addition to being richly documented.

In Uganda and Zaire the atrophy of the state translates into acute poverty and plundering activities on a major scale. At the root of this situation lies the inability of the state to maintain a viable economic infrastructure and provide agricultural and pastoral inputs, the widespread disruption of transportation facilities, the absence of public services, the rising cost of consumer commodities, and so forth, all of which have led to dramatic increases in levels of rural poverty. But it also reflects the inability of the state to provide a minimum of security. In fact, it is the state and its local agents—*agents d'execution* (an appropriate designation), military men, police officers and security officials—who often create the very conditions of insecurity that make for dependency upon their caprice and good graces. The inability of the state to pay its employees means that official tolerance of plunder and extortion is the nearest equivalent of patronage. Exoneration of legal sanctions is the cheapest way to reward local officials.

In these circumstances the state often acts as the mediator through which retreat from the official economy is made possible. On the basis of a careful analysis of the Zairian situation, Janet MacGaffey concludes that "the political-administrative class takes advantage of position in the state apparatus to participate heavily in profiteering activities; its members are unable to exert a monopoly but they attempt to do so, primarily by using personal relations among themselves to restrict the access of others to resources."[40] Emizet Kisangani's analysis of the involvement of Zairian officials in the illegal sale of ivory and poaching activities in national parks shows the extensiveness of these networks and the competition among state officials attempting to control the procurement and commercialization of ivory.[41] A similar pattern can be detected in the smuggling of coffee, gem diamonds and gold, the hoarding of food resources for purposes of speculation, and the organization of local manufacturing activities. Much the same kind of situation has been reported in Uganda, although questions arise as to the depth of state involvement in *magendo* activities. According to Reginald Green, the hierarchy of *mafutamingis* and *magendoists* includes "no more than a tiny fraction of corrupt politicians," but then he goes on to note that the one form of public sector corruption that has contributed most directly to the parallel economy involves "accepting *magendo* payments for allocating goods (by public sector firm management personnel *as well as by officials and politicians*) and for passing dubious papers (e.g., tax, contract, billing)."[42] One can reasonably speculate that the forms and levels of official participation tend to vary with the nature of the transactions occurring in the informal sectors. In her penetrating discussion of the various forms of malpractices associated with *kalabule*, the Ghanaian variant of *magendo*, Naomi Chazan notes that "embezzlement activities aimed at diverting monies and goods from the formal to the informal economy" require greater "proximity to the state apparatus" than smuggling and hoarding;[43] yet the latter have also been known to involve official connivance at the highest levels (as in Kenya and Zaire).

Beyond a certain threshold, however, official proddings are no longer needed. The informal economy institutionalizes itself to the point where it becomes self-perpetuating; traders and *traffiquants* are drawn into its vortex by necessity. Just as the disintegration of legal and statutory norms makes clientelistic accommodation the only path to survival, the erosion of the formal economy leaves no other choice but to operate through informal channels. Once institutionalized, the system generates its own normative code and informal power hierarchies, but these leave little room for traditional forms of clientelism or political patronage—only for transient "deals" based on self-interest and opportunism.

Civil violence in these conditions is the normal outcome of impoverishment and oppression; yet seldom is "defensive mobilization," to use Tilly's term,[44] effective in breaking the system. Although oppression may bring out unsuspected capacities for resistance, in most instances these are quickly absorbed into ethnic or factional nets and brutally repressed. This, at least, is the pattern which suggests itself when one looks at the disturbances in southern Chad, the simmering factional struggle in Uganda, the endless civil war in Sudan, and the periodic explosions of rural violence in the Shaba province of Zaire.

The historic parallel that comes to mind is that of the Mediterranean world in the fifteenth and sixteenth centuries, as portrayed by Fernand Braudel:

> Pauperization and oppression by the rich and powerful went hand in hand. . . . The Mediterranean in the sixteenth century, though hot-blooded enough, for some reason never managed to bring off a successful revolution. It was not for want of trying. . . . But there (was) no final cataclysm. . . . For these disturbances broke out regularly, annually, daily even, like mere traffic accidents which no one any longer thought worth attention, neither principals nor victims, witnesses nor chroniclers, not even the states themselves.[45]

The parallel takes on added salience in light of recent attempts to conceptualize African states as patrimonial polities. In such polities, as Weber reminds us, "the political administration . . . is treated as a purely personal affair of the ruler, and political power is considered as part of his personal property"[46]—a state of affairs which applies not only to the Mediterranean world but preeminently to seventeenth-century France.

The parallel with early modern Europe stops where the parallel economy begins. Despite some notable exceptions, and contrary to what Thomas Callaghy argues in his otherwise excellent analysis of contemporary Zaire,[47] the parallel economy puts a very different construction on the notion of a "political aristocracy" solely dependent upon the state for its status and material wealth. It shows that class formation may also take place on a substantial scale outside the state, a point which emerges with reasonable clarity from the works of Reginald Green and Janet MacGaffey. "The expansion of the second economy," MacGaffey argues, "has provided a means for class formation outside the state, since it offers opportunities for capital accumulation independently of the state."[48] She goes on to note that

> the various activities of the second economy have been one source of the opportunities for capital accumulation that has resulted in the emergence in recent years of a small commercial middle class of substantial business owners. These individuals have invested in productive as well as distributive enterprise and in real estate; they enjoy a middle class lifestyle and are giving their children a secondary and even university education. They are thus reproducing themselves as a class.[49]

Does this mean that the parallel economy serves as the engine that is transforming the political aristocracy pattern into a class-based society, with all the tensions and antagonisms which the term implies? Viewed from the top of the social pyramid, this is indeed the picture which appears to be emerging, with growing tensions between the state bourgeoisie (or aristocracy) and the bourgeoisie tout court. Looked at from the perspective of the masses, however, nothing like a class consciousness has thus far crystallized in any permanent form or fashion. How the rural masses perceive their condition and act on these perceptions cannot be reduced to one single analytic category, whether it be class, ethnicity or clientelism. And even if agreement could be reached on which of these categories happens to be dominant at any given time and place, this would hardly be sufficient to explain political action or inaction. Identities do not materialize in a social void, any more than they are mobilized in a political vacuum. Ultimately, what needs to be explained is a different level of social reality: the inequalities of power arising from state transformations. Just as the emergence of the prebendal state has paved the way for the institutionalization of the parallel economy, both have in turn created conditions of profound and permanent inequalities in African societies.

Notes

1. Samuel Huntington, *Political Order in Changing Societies* (New Haven: Yale University Press, 1968).

2. For some recent examples see Pierre Jacquemot, "Le Proto-Etat Africain: Quelques reflexions autour de l'Histoire Contemporaine du Mali," *Revue Tiers Monde*, 24, 93 (Jan.-March 1983): 127-141; and Pierre Francois, "Class Struggles in Mali," *Review of African Political Economy*, 24 (1982): 22-38.

3. Thomas M. Callaghy, *The State-Society Struggle: Zaire in Comparative Perspective* (New York: Columbia University Press, 1984).

4. Crawford Young, "Zaire: Is There a State?," *Canadian Journal of African Studies*, 18, 1 (1984): 80-82.

5. Samuel Huntington, *American Politics: The Promise of Disharmony* (Cambridge, Mass.: Harvard University Press, 1981).

6. In this context "disharmony" is of course a euphemism for chaos (Chad, Uganda, Equatorial Africa), semi-anarchy (Sudan, Mozambique, Angola) or prolonged stagnation (Zaire and Nigeria); the term "dysfunction" covers such uncomfortable realities as civil violence, state coercion, administrative ineptitude, fiscal impotence, rampant corruption and nepotism. Although our discussion focuses primarily on the internal roots of such dysfunctions, this is not meant to minimize the significance of exogenous forces, including military invasions and armed raids from neighboring states. This is made all too clear by the recent histories of Chad, Mozambique, Angola and Botswana.

7. Young, "Is There a State?"

8. John Waterbury, "An Attempt to Put Patrons and Clients in Their Place," in Ernest Gellner and John Waterbury, eds., *Patrons and Clients in Mediterranean Societies* (London: Duckworth, 1977), p. 329.

9. See Aristide Zolberg, *Creating Political Order* (Chicago: Rand McNally, 1966); and Henry Bienen, "One Party Systems in Africa," in Samuel Huntington and Clement Moore, eds., *Authoritarian Politics in Modern Society* (New York: Basic Books, 1970), pp. 99-127.

10. See René Lemarchand, "Political Clientelism and Ethnicity in Tropical Africa," *The American Political Science Review*, 66, 1 (March 1972): 68-90.

11. Daryll Forde and Mary Douglas, "Primitive Economics," in George Dalton, ed., *Tribal and Peasant Economies* (Austin: University of Texas Press, 1971), p. 21.

12. For an excellent treatment of this dimension see James C. Scott and Benedict Kerkvliet, "How Traditional Patrons Lose Legitimacy," in Steffen W. Schmidt et al., eds., *Friends, Followers and Factions* (Berkeley: University of California Press, 1977), pp. 439–457.

13. The implications of electoral politics for an understanding of machine patterns are brilliantly analyzed by James Scott in "Corruption, Machine Politics and Political Change," *American Political Science Review,* 63, 4 (December 1969): 1142–1158; and in his *Comparative Political Corruption* (Englewood Cliffs, N.J.: Prentice-Hall, 1972).

14. Douglas Rimmer, "Elements of the Political Economy," in Keith Panter-Brick, ed., *Soldiers and Oil: The Political Transformation of Nigeria* (London: Frank Cass, 1978), p. 148.

15. Joseph Nye, "Corruption and Political Development: A Cost-Benefit Analysis," *American Political Science Review,* 61, 2 (June 1967): 416. The limits of the usefulness of Nye's definition are hinted at in Morris Szeftel's comment that "there is clearly a difference between using a clientelistic link to obtain state contracts or public office, on the one hand, and stealing government funds or taking bribes, on the other." This difference, however, cannot be readily inferred from Nye's definition; although most observers would intuitively grasp its significance, the distinction between "patronage" and "graft" makes it even clearer. Again, to quote from Szeftel: "It might be useful to consider patronage to involve the dispensing of state resources to third parties in return for political support of some kind, while graft would involve the use of state resources for personal advantage by officials." Morris Szeftel, "Political Graft and the Spoils System in Zambia—the State as a Resource in Itself," *African Review of Political Economy,* 24 (1982): 5. Szeftel's definition of "graft" is largely synonymous with our use of the term "prebends" as distinct from "patronage" and "tribute."

16. "We wish to speak of 'prebends' and of a 'prebendal' organization of office wherever the lord assigns to the official rent payments for life, payments which are somehow fixed to objects or which are esentially economic usufruct from land or other sources. They must be compensations for the fulfillment of actual or fictitious office duties; they are goods permanently set aside for the economic assurance of the office." Max Weber, "Wirtschaft und Gesellschaft," in H.H. Gerth and C. Wright Mills, eds., *From Max Weber: Essays in Sociology* (New York: Oxford University Press, 1958), p. 207. For recent applications of the concept see Richard Joseph, "Class, State and Prebendal Politics in Nigeria," *Journal of Commonwealth and Comparative Studies,* 21, 3 (November 1983): 21–38; and Jacquemot, "Le Proto-Etat Africain." According to Jacquemot, "la constitution d'une nouvelle couche de prébendiers" was a fundamental cause of political decay in Mali under Modibo Keita, revealing "le proto-état en deliquescence" (p. 133).

17. Terisa Turner, "Commercial Capitalism and the 1975 Coup," in Panter-Brick, *Soldiers and Oil,* pp. 166–200.

18. Joseph, "Class, State and Prebendal Politics," p. 30.

19. In a number of cases the real struggle for patronage appears to involve ethnic subgroups. Thus, the key to an understanding of ZANU politics in Zimbabwe lies in the ongoing competition among Zezuru, Karanga and Manyika, all related to the wider Shona aggregate. Similarly, the Hima-Ruguru polarity in Burundi appears far more significant at this time than the more widely publicized Hutu-Tutsi cleavage; and the same applies to Kenyan politics, where competing factions tend to cut across the basic Luo-Kikuyu fault line. Commenting on the case of Kenya, Joseph Karimi and Philip Ochieng note that during the succession crisis that followed Kenyatta's death "the main characters among the *dramatis personae* on both sides

were Kikuyu, non-members of the Kikuyu community playing in the main only supporting roles." (Joseph Karimi and Philip Ochieng, *The Kenyatta Succession* [Nairobi: Transafrica, 1980], p. 8).

The recent history of Uganda provides a particularly tragic illlustration of the consequences of factional competition over spoils. In October and December 1982 an estimated 80,000 Banyarwanda were driven out of their homes in southwest Uganda. Approximately half moved to Rwanda, while others moved to refugee settlements elsewhere in Uganda. Behind this human tragedy lies a vicious struggle between the so-called syndicate and scientists factions in the Uganda Peoples Congress (UPC), identified respectively with the Minister of State in the Office of the President, Chris Rwakasisi, and Efrain Kamuntu, Minister of Finance. From the evidence available it would appear that the expulsion of Banyarwanda was a calculated move on the part of Rwakasisi, designed to give added leverage to his own faction against that of his opponent, both in his home district (Mbarara) and at the center. As one observer noted, "In this instance it seems clear that both local and national (factional) interests were accommodated by a single action. The pretext for this action, both locally and nationally, is the assertion that 'Banyarwanda' (loosely defined) aided Idi Amin, benefited from his rule and now attempt to undermine President Milton Obote's government" (Jason W. Clay, *The Eviction of the Banyarwanda* [Cambridge, Mass.: Cultural Survival, 1984], p. 8).

20. In the course of a rejoinder at the Georgetown conference on North Africa Today: Issues of Development and Integration, April 22–23, 1982, Washington, D.C.

21. A notorious case involved the Mayor of Gweru, Patrick Kombayi, whose "wrong-doings" ranged from the use of public money for the purchase of four gold chains (amounting to a total of $44,850) to "very unethical business practices" (such as the awarding of tree-cutting contracts to "Comrade and ex-combatant Sledge Hammer") and the placement of women (the "Amazons") on the municipal payroll in exchange for "supporting the Mayor in demonstrations" and other (undisclosed) services. The case was debated at length in the Zimbabwe House of Assembly in June 1983. See *Parliamentary Debates, House of Assembly*, Vol. 7, No. 4, Harare, (June 19, 1983), pp. 66–79.

22. Republic of Zambia, *Report of the Commission of Inquiry into the Allegation Made by Mr. Justin Chimba and Mr. John Chisata*, Lusaka, May 1971, quoted in Morris Szeftel, "Corruption and the Spoils System in Zambia," in Michael Clarke, ed., *Corruption* (London: Frances Pinter, 1983), p. 175.

23. Ibid., p. 177.

24. See Patrick Smith, "Anatomy of the Rice Scandal," *New African* (April 1985).

25. *The Christian Science Monitor*, May 20, 1985.

26. Turner, "Commercial Capitalism," pp. 167–170.

27. Ibid., p. 172.

28. The information in this paragraph and the next is drawn in part from interviews conducted in Gabon (1973) and in part from Pierre Péan, *Affaires Africaines* (Paris: Fayard, 1983). The Péan book contains one of the most astonishing exposés ever printed on the Franco-Gabonese connection. The publication of the book almost severed the connection.

29. These are essentially extensions of the now defunct Gaullist-oriented, metropolitan-based Service d'Action Civique (SAC) and the Service de Documentation et de Contre-Espionage (SDECE), now known as the Direction Générale de la Sécurité Extérieure (DGSE).

30. For further details see Péan, *Affaires Africaines*, p. 335.

31. Reginald H. Green, "Magendo in the Political Economy of Uganda: Pathology, Parallel System or Dominant Sub-Mode of Production?" Discussion Paper No. 64 (Institute of Development Studies, University of Sussex, 1981).

32. Janet MacGaffey, "How to Survive and Become Rich amidst Devastation: The Second Economy in Zaire," *African Affairs*, 82, 328 (July 1983): 351. For a fascinating account on the significance of the informal sector in Angola see A. Morice, "Commerce Parallele et Troc à Luanda," *Politique Africaine*, 17 (March 1985): 88-104. See also E. Archambault and X. Greffe, *Les Economies Non-Officielles* (Paris: La Découverte, 1984).

33. Mireille Duteil, "Senegal: Le contre-pouvoir des marabouts," *Le Point*, May 20, 1981.

34. Ibid.

35. The term "squatter" in this context covers many different types of social categories, described in one newspaper article as including "wage earners; abandoned farm laborers, some who qualified for resettlement and some who did not; people from surrounding communal areas who again could be subdivided into those qualifying for resettlement and those who did not; displaced people from Mozambique; and vagrants." (*The Herald* [Harare], December 23, 1983.)

36. As one report put it, "black farmers in Zimbabwe are the worst violators of the minimum wage in the agricultural sector. . . . The veteran trade unionist Cde Dickson Ndawana told the *Herald* that the new minimum wage of Z$55.00 a month which became effective in September 1983 was not being paid. . . . He said that during the rainy season many farmers forced their workers to work overtime without pay . . . and [that] most people are living under horrible conditions in the farms. Our repeated appeals to employers to improve houses have fallen on deaf ears of people who think they still are living in Rhodesia, he said." (*The Herald* [Harare], December 23, 1983.)

37. For specific examples, see René Lemarchand, "The World Bank in Rwanda." Occasional Paper (Bloomington: Indiana University Press, 1982).

38. Catherine Newbury, "Dead and Buried or Just Underground? The Privatization of the State in Zaire," *Canadian Journal of African Studies*, 18, 1 (1984): 113.

39. Brooke Grundfest Schoepf and Claude Schoepf, "State, Bureaucracy and Peasants in the Lufira Valley," *Canadian Journal of African Studies*, 18, 1 (1984): 90. How "liberalization" under Mobutu is contributing to rural development through the parallel economy is nowhere more graphically expressed than in the comments of a Zairian trader: "The President announced the creation of an agricultural bank, ostensibly for peasants. . . . A big wheel takes an empty farm and corrupts the expert (who supplies him with) a favorable assessment of the farm value. . . . He gets 3 million at the SOFIDE bank; then he gives it to his brother-in-law to trade in gold and diamonds to make the money yield the most rapid profit. Even this would be alright if he then invested the profit inside the country. But the big men are not investing. . . ." (Ibid., p. 93).

40. MacGaffey, "How to Survive," p. 363.

41. Emizet Kisangani, "A Social Dilemma in a Less Developed Country: The Massacre of the *Loxodonta Africana* in Zaire." (Paper prepared for the Common Property Resource Management Conference, National Academy of Sciences, New York, March 26, 1985). The author shows how the decision to abolish the Bureau National de l'Ivoire, ostensibly to "liberalize all ivory activities," not only failed to create small private hunting groups, but ended by shifting control over elephant hunting and the ivory trade to the hands of "the presidential clique, the presidential brotherhood and a few members of the new aspirant bourgeoisie." He goes on to

cite "a strange case involving the Governor of Upper Zaire and his police commissioner": both were arrested in July 1981 on charges of ivory smuggling, "but the truth was that (they) had double-crossed the Zairian President and his son Niwa, who were also involved in that operation to the tune of an estimated $25 million." (Ibid., p. 17.)

42. Green, "Magendo in the Political Economy," p. 7.

43. Naomi Chazan, An Anatomy of Ghanaian Politics (Boulder: Westview, 1983), p. 196.

44. Charles Tilly, From Mobilization to Revolution (Reading, Mass.: Lexington, 1978), p. 73.

45. Fernand Braudel, The Mediterranean and the Mediterranean World in the Age of Philip II, Vol. 2. (New York: Harper, 1975), p. 735.

46. Max Weber, Economy and Society, quoted in Callaghy, The State-Society Struggle, p. 70.

47. Callaghy, The State-Society Struggle, passim.

48. MacGaffey, "How to Survive," p. 362.

49. Ibid., p. 363.

7

Economic Disengagement
and Class Formation in Zaire

Janet MacGaffey

Economic disengagement from the state in what is variously known as the second, parallel, informal, underground, black or irregular economy exists on an increasingly large scale in most countries of the world. The second, or parallel, economy has been defined in several ways but is here taken to consist of those economic activities that are unmeasured and unrecorded. Some of its activities are illegal; others are not illegal in themselves but are carried out in a manner intended to avoid taxation or in some way deprive the state of revenue.[1] These activities are supposedly controlled by the state, but they either evade this control or involve illegal use of state position. By this definition the second economy is as much a political phenomenon as an economic one. It is a manifestation of class struggle, as well as of coping strategies for dealing with the depredations of the state and of economic exigency. This approach provides a framework for comparison of second economies in different parts of the world. Variations in their forms in particular countries can be seen to reflect different stages of the development of capitalism or socialism,[2] different processes of class struggle and different adjustments to economic hardship.

The literature on postindependence Africa has stressed the importance of the state for class formation, but evidence of increasing disengagement from the state indicates a change in this pattern. This paper will show some of the ways in which accumulation taking place outside the state is causing this change.

In Zaire the rapid expansion of the second economy is related to the nature of the Zairian state and ruling class, and to the particular form of Zairian capitalism. The penetration of capitalism is incomplete in the Zairian economy, and noncapitalist modes of production persist in articulation with it. The ruling class is not a true economic bourgeoisie; it is one that loots the economy and collapses effective administration. It is thus unable to exercise the control over production necessary to maintain its dominance and must resort to consolidating its position by participating in the more lucrative activities of the second economy. It cannot, however, prevent others from doing so, too, and therefore cannot close its boundaries; nor, by virtue of its administrative and economic incompetence, can it monopolize other opportunities that may arise for capitalist development.

Zaire's second economy consists of various forms of illegal production, or of production for illegal distribution, and of more widespread distributive activities. Distribution includes smuggling and other forms of illicit trade; barter; theft; speculation, hoarding and middleman activity; and bribery, corruption and embezzlement.

We will first describe the nature of the Zairian state and ruling class to show why and how this class consolidates its position through participation in the second economy. An account of Zaire's form of capitalism and the limitations to its domination will provide the context for a discussion of the resistance of petty producers to this domination and to the predatory activities of the state-based class. This resistance, possible because of access to the means of production available in noncapitalist systems, takes the form of the organization of a system of production and distribution outside state control, providing an alternative to proletarianization. Some second economy activities have occasioned shifts in the balance of the class struggle; others have been sufficiently lucrative to allow considerable capital accumulation and the emergence of a small but significant commercial middle class independent of political position. This class sector invests in enterprises producing for the local market as well as export and, unlike the state-based class, is a nascent, truly capitalist bourgeoisie.

The Nature of the State

In Zaire after independence the power of the new dominant class was based on control of the state, rather than of production, and on partnerships with foreign business interests that owned large mining and agricultural enterprises. The country produced raw materials for export and depended on the developed capitalist countries for capital, technology and manufactured goods. Thomas Callaghy characterizes the Zairian state as mixed patrimonial-bureaucratic and authoritarian.[3] He asserts that, although international assistance has helped to consolidate the regime in Zaire, its nature is neither predominantly determined by nor the result of its place in the international capitalist system, but rather is "the result of the complex interplay of historical and contemporary exogenous and endogenous political and economic forces and actors."[4]

Callaghy shows that Zaire is a patrimonial state in which the president's increasingly centralized authority is highly personalized. The president is supported by officials and administrators to whom he grants power, privileges and material goods in return for their support, loyalty and obedience. This pattern is replicated downward through a patronage system. The regime has a democratic facade, but the single party, the Mouvement Populaire de la Révolution (MPR) is not so much a political machine as a mere propaganda element of the state apparatus. President Mobutu's personal power is such that no distinction exists between the man and his political role or between his personal finances and those of the state.

Under patrimonialism, personal rulers and their followers maintain their support and influence through their access to state resources, which are disbursed as rewards for political support through a network of patron-client relations. As Nelson Kasfir puts it: "The fundamental distinction between a patrimonial and a rational-legal (or what is ethnocentrically called a 'modern') state is whether or not offices may be appropriated for personal wealth. In a patrimonial state there is no sharp distinction between the public and private domains."[5] Kasfir goes on to show the result of this use of patronage by state officials to strengthen their class interests.

> Since patronage depends on material rewards, the system must generate adequate and perhaps increasing economic benefits. But financing patrimonial state apparatuses creates special problems because the political requirements of control and reward undercut the rational prerequisites of economic activity. Although the appropriation of office *may* support vigorous entrepreneurial activity, the state inevitably becomes less effective in generating public revenue and therefore less able to maintain the positions out of which patrimonial control can be sustained.[6]

In the absence of a rational-legal state structure, one cannot count on impartial authority, technical competence and reliable communications. In these conditions it is extremely difficult for individuals to pursue rational economic goals. Postcolonial rulers of African states have not maintained the effectiveness of administration that existed at independence and differ greatly in the levels of wealth they control. The distinction is drawn between dominant states that have a reliable administrative apparatus, participate extensively in economic activities, and can enforce government policies because of popular acceptance of the state's right to exact obedience to its rulers, and weak states that are unable to collect taxes, provide social services, settle disputes or control the military. In the latter the absence of law and order and predictable administration leads to a decline in state revenues, thereby reducing the opportunities for class formation through the state.[7]

Zaire in some ways exhibits marked characteristics of a weak state. The huge scale of the second economy is evidence of its inability to collect many of the taxes due to the state from commerce and imports and exports. In addition, less than 50 percent of the Contribution Personelle Minimum (CPM), the successor of the colonial head tax, finds its way into the state's coffers.[8] The provision of social services is abysmally poor; public health services are practically nonexistent; the economic infrastructure is in a state of gross decay; education suffers because teachers are seldom paid and often have to be bribed to pass children through the system, which anyway lacks books, classroom furniture and even blackboard chalk. Further, the population is subject to continual harassment from police and the military in the form of extortion of money and actual violence, and a corrupt brand of justice prevails instead of the rule of law and citizens' rights. The need of members of the state-based class to squeeze wealth out of their position in the state apparatus in order to maintain the patronage system, which is an important basis for their power, contributes further to the weakening of the state administration, decreasing its revenues and creating acute scarcities.

For all its weaknesses, however, the Zairian state also has its strengths. The Mobutu regime has stayed in power for an impressively long time. While foreign assistance, among other factors, has contributed to this longevity it also reflects the strength of the state's mechanisms of political control. The regime cannot adequately regulate the behavior of the military, but it does monopolize most exercise of force and operate efficient security networks. The state-based class certainly extracts resources, but mechanisms for their distribution do not work as well as those in most African states. In many respects the Zairian state seems to operate efficiently solely to help the predatory class to plunder the economy, and not when public interest is at issue.

Seen in this light it does not seem particularly useful to label the Zairian state as either strong or weak. Taking the state to be the organization of domination within a particular territory, we must seek the historically contingent factors that explain its particular strengths and weaknesses and show the means by which domination operates at a specific time. Three of the most relevant historical factors which explain the present situation in Zaire are the nature of Belgian colonialism, which kept Africans out of government and provided only a low level of education; the handing over of political, but not economic, control at independence; and the country's position in the world economy, a result of the colonial experience. Another factor of great importance is Zaire's immense natural riches. But in order to properly understand the particular organization of domination currently in existence and the concomitant relations between the state and society, we must examine the nature of the post-independence dominant class.

This state class, the regime's main internal support, is called a "political aristocracy" by Callaghy. Loyalty to Mobutu is the ultimate requirement for entry and continued membership. Mobutu rules through this "political nobility" of his chosen men and patrimonial instruments, and they engage in true court politics. This class is a political aristocracy and not an economic bourgeoisie, for its power, values and economic base result from its relationship to the state. It is composed of three main groups. The first group comprises the "presidential family": the president's close advisers and relatives; all top-level administrative, political and military officials and foreign advisers; and all council members. Within this group, power and material perquisites are enormous, and almost unlimited for those closest to the president. The second group consists of middle-level administrative and military officers in Kinshasa, while the third is made up of the remaining territorial administrators and military officers in the regions.[9] Members of the political aristocracy increasingly use state position to gain access to resources with which to amass vast sums of wealth through second economy activities.

The Limited Domination of Capitalism

The form of capitalism the Zairian political aristocracy engages in is aptly described by John Iliffe as "parasitic capitalism": state power is used to acquire private property and businesses, so that surplus is channeled into the "pockets of a parasitic bourgeoisie whose wealth and business interests derive from their political and administrative positions."[10] This situation is a long way from producing the conditions necessary for the complete development of capitalism, as discussed by Callaghy in this volume. In Zaire those with political position have used the power of their office to seize control of the economy and, by means of the Zairianization measures of 1973–1974, to acquire manufacturing, wholesale and retail businesses and plantations. However, they have neither managed their enterprises in a rational capitalist fashion nor invested their profits in expansion of their businesses and improved production, but rather have expended their wealth on conspicuous consumption, foreign holdings and real estate. The virtually unlimited power of those at the top has allowed them to plunder the natural riches of their country and to amass vast fortunes. Indeed, they have behaved like parasites sucking the lifeblood of the economy for their own benefit. As a result, the official economy has declined: both agricultural and industrial production have dropped, the national debt stands at over $5 billion, the economic infrastructure has deteriorated, and inflation and shortages are rampant.

Faced with this decline of the official economy, ordinary people have organized their own system of production and distribution, economic infrastructure and means of acquiring foreign exchange, thereby creating a second economy outside the state. An important factor in this disengagement from the state is the incomplete penetration of capitalism in Zaire and the persistence of noncapitalist modes of production, though modified and subordinated, in articulation with the capitalist mode.

Some scholars assert that capitalism has destroyed the conditions of reproduction of these noncapitalist modes and argue that the term "artic-ulation" is thus inaccurate.[11] This point of view, however, disregards the empirical realities of lineage, hunter-gatherer and tribute-based societies in Zaire. The view taken here is that so long as access to land is determined by kinship or tribute relations, these modes of production, though affected by capitalism through commodity production, will nevertheless continue to reproduce themselves; their relations of production may be *modified* to varying degrees, but not destroyed. In this situation both petty producers and rural and urban wage laborers are not completely separated from the means of production but have access to land and other resources; they do not constitute a free labor force because they have an alternative means of subsistence.

The control of capital over production and distribution thus varies from one region of the country to another and over time. In investigating the limitations of the domination of capitalism, we need to focus on the struggle being waged over the appropriation of surplus from the direct producers and workers, on

> relations between capital and labor in the sphere of production, and hence the dynamics of internal class differentiation as these relations change. This position . . . implies that capitalist production does not presuppose, as a universally necessary condition, that capitalism exercises direct control over the production process, with labor separated from effective ownership in the means of production.[12]

An important result of the inability of capitalism to monopolize the appropriation of surplus from noncapitalist modes of production has generally been ignored, however. This limitation to capitalist domination, in conjunction with a weakening in the functioning of the state apparatus, makes it very difficult for the dominant class to reproduce existing relations of production, since opportunities arise for accumulation and socioeconomic mobility. Some scholars have emphasized that noncapitalist modes lower the cost of reproduction of the capitalist work force by helping to support wage laborers and operating in place of welfare benefits. Cooper, however, makes the point that perhaps these "very processes that cheapen the *physical* reproduction of the workforce might make *social* reproduction—the extension of capitalist relations of production—all the more difficult."[13]

Cooper criticizes structural Marxists such as Meillassoux and Wolpe for failing to grasp that capital has difficulty in obtaining steady, reliable work from laborers who retain access to land and from workers who bring resources back to the countryside or devote them to petty trade or production in the city; these workers have posed serious challenges to capital and the state.[14] Such challenges are manifested in the expansion of the second economy. Much has been written about *how* surplus is appropriated in the conflict between state and peasant, in the articulation of modes of production and in the informal sector of small, unenumerated urban enterprises, but the question of *who* exactly appropriates this surplus has received much less attention, although its implications for class formation are profound. It is this question that we propose to explore here.

If the control of capitalism over production and distribution and the appropriation of surplus is thus limited, then the following question arises: what are the limitations on complete disengagement from the state and total withdrawal into autonomy, and what restraints does capitalism exercise over such withdrawal? The answer, as Henry Bernstein persuasively argues, lies in the dependence of simple commodity producers on the products of capitalism.[15]

Simple commodity production is a form of production in which the household, or another unit of production, produces use values for its direct-consumption needs, as well as commodities which are sold for cash to buy other needed items, such as tools, seeds, clothing, kerosene and household utensils. Simple commodity producers retain control over the means and organization of production and, therefore, are not proletarians. But they are in varying degrees dependent on the exchange of commodities for the reproduction of the producers and the unit of production. The independence of the producers is thus circumscribed not only at the level of exchange through prices, but also at the level of production. Falling prices for commodities produced, relative to those bought, result in reduced levels of consumption or intensified commodity production or both. Capital can thus put a "squeeze" directly on production by forcing the household, or another unit, to intensify its labor to keep up the supply of commodities necessary for its reproduction.[16] The more commodity relations and a cash income become conditions of reproduction, the more powerful the control that capital can exercise, albeit still without the need to organize and supervise the production process.[17] The monetization of elements of the cycle of reproduction of small commodity producers "through the substitution of commodities and the corresponding withdrawal of labor from use-value production, provides scope for the mercantile and political agents of productive capitalism to intensify commodity relations."[18]

Forms of resistance to this squeeze include attempts to withdraw at least partially from commodity production or to find alternative sources of cash, such as migration for wage labor, and evasion of imposed terms of exchange through smuggling and other forms of illicit marketing in order to realize higher returns on labor.[19]

The development of Zaire's second economy exemplifies all these forms of resistance. On the other hand, some individuals realize higher returns on labor in second economy activities and accumulate considerable wealth. The possibility of such accumulation is a significant factor in class formation outside the state. Some of the wealth accumulated in second economy activities has been invested in businesses that have contributed to the emergence of a small, commercial middle-class owning productive enterprises.

The Development of the Second Economy and the Process of Class Struggle

In the control of capitalism over petty producers, the terms of trade between rural and urban areas by which the price squeeze operates are crucial:

> The terms of trade between "town" and "country" are the locus of struggle between the emergent class forces in industry and agriculture as the capitalist transformation proceeds. These terms of exchange, in a significant sense, hold the key to class control over the pace and direction of the accumulation process. . . . Control of the price system, and hence the intersectorial terms of trade, is the absolutely strategic mechanism for achieving involuntary reallocations of resources between different sectors and social classes.[20]

In Zaire in the 1960s the political upheaval and collapse of the government after independence and the unreal value of the Congo franc resulted in the rapid development of fraudulent export trade on a massive scale. Pierre Dupriez provides a detailed account of three different types of export fraud in this period, showing the mechanisms by which each one primarily furthered the interests of different class sectors in achieving reallocation of resources.

After independence the rapid development of export fraud resulted from the difference in the official rate of exchange of the Congo franc and the parallel market rate. For example, a kilo of coffee selling at BF 30 in Antwerp realized CF 90[21] to the producer selling by way of the legal export trade, but as much as CF 210 if illegally exported.[22] Numerous traders took up this profitable illegal commerce, organizing trade networks throughout the country, and taking advantage of the weakened administrative and border controls caused by the political troubles of this period.

The first type of fraudulent export described by Dupriez is that of palm oil from Mayombe and Lower Zaire. Production was largely dependent on the purchase of palm fruits from petty producers and, in some areas, palm kernels for palm kernel oil as well. When a difference existed between the official rate of exchange, which determined the prices paid by the oil-exporting firms, and the rate on the parallel market, which determined the price paid by traders, producers could choose between selling palm fruits to the companies or making oil themselves and selling it and palm kernels to traders. Generally, palm kernels were fraudulently exported and palm oil sold in the domestic market.

Demand in the domestic market increased because of a fall in the production of high-acidity oil in many areas. High-acidity oil of lower quality than that exported was used locally. Oils for export, with an acidity of only 5 percent, were produced by the big companies, but the law compelled them to reserve a portion for internal markets. When they were unable to supply the local demand, additional oil came from independent producers. Thus, increased domestic demand from urban centers resulted in competition in purchasing palm fruit between the big oil companies and traders and broke the monopsony previously held by the companies. In this competition the big companies were at a disadvantage because their prices were tied to the official rate of exchange, while the traders, selling in towns where the demand exceeded the supply, could easily offer higher prices to producers. Kasai, in particular, in areas wealthy from diamond smuggling, supported high prices. By 1965 the price of oil per kilo paid to petty producers was CF 30, up from CF 17 in 1963.

With two competing markets available, petty producers could gear their activities to yield and income. Hand methods of oil extraction produced only 10 percent of oil, in contrast to the 17 percent extracted by machinery, but the difference in price between the two markets compensated for the difference in yield.[23] In 1958 oil production by hand was not worth the labor, whereas by 1963 it was widespread. However, the producers always reserved some fruit to sell to the palm oil companies, because so long as they kept up a regular supply, the companies recognized them as cutters and gave them the right to buy goods at the significantly lower prices charged in the company stores.[24] In addition, the companies maintained the roads which enabled the traders to go to the villages.[25] Hence, petty producers were dependent on capitalism for goods and the necessary infrastructure of roads, and therefore were still constrained to supply capitalist enterprise.

Thus, two buying circuits developed: the official one, in which palm fruits were collected by the companies for processing in factories, and the unofficial one, in which oil (processed in the villages) and palm kernels were bought by traders to be sold on the internal market or fraudulently exported. In 1962 about 15 percent of the production of North Mayombe was fraudulently exported.[26] Dupriez shows how each circuit also distributed consumer goods at different prices. In the official circuit they were sold cheaply in company stores, at prices related to those of palm fruit bought from the small producers and set by the official rate of exchange. In the unofficial circuit the prices of consumer goods were higher. They were sold by traders who bought them from the countries to which they smuggled palm kernels, and prices were dependent on the parallel market currency rate.

Whichever of these circuits was the most advantageous at a particular time took a larger share of production. The devaluation of November 1963 doubled the prices offered in the official circuit, giving it an advantage over the unofficial circuit; this advantage disappeared after March 1965, when the difference between official and parallel market rates of exchange increased rapidly. Thereafter the oil companies began to cut back on the sale of consumer goods, previously a source of advantage. There was great elasticity in this situation because producers could shift from one circuit to the other to maximize their income.[27]

The breaking of the monopsony of the oil companies and the growth of unofficial commercial circuits led to an increase in palm fruit production because areas outside the official circuits (e.g. near the Angolan border) began commercial production in response to the increase in demand. The quantities were not very large; nevertheless, small-scale producers clearly benefited from the creation of unofficial circuits, while the state was deprived of export income.[28]

The significance in terms of class control of the accumulation process of this fraudulent export trade in palm oil was the decreased control of capitalism. The price squeeze relaxed because of competing buyers, and incomes of producers and local traders rose, opening up possibilities for upward mobility.

The second type of fraud identified by Dupriez mostly benefited the foreign-planter class in the 1960s, but in the 1970s a shift occurred in the process of class formation and struggle as foreigners were dispossessed of their assets and nationals displaced them as beneficiaries in a profitable trade.

Due to the troubled political situation in Oriental and Kivu provinces in 1960-1961, coffee and tea, important export crops of these regions, could not be exported in the usual way. The political isolation and distance of the foreign planters who grew these crops from the control of the central government allowed them to organize an export system of their own through smuggling, principally to the east. Intermediaries organized export through Uganda and Tanzania, sometimes under cover of license to barter from local authorities, but usually by crossing frontiers illegally with the collusion of customs officials or, when necessary, by using armed force.[29]

Details of the scale and organization of this trade are given in one account from North Kivu, a principal route for illegal export of agricultural products to Uganda. In 1963 a European customs expert filmed a caravan of 500 men with armed guards, transporting products bought by *les trafiquants Ismaeliens*. These Asians, in cooperation with local chiefs, organized the export trade in coffee, tea, papain, foodstuffs and imported consumer goods. It was estimated in January 1962 that official exports represented only 25 percent of local agricultural production.[30] Robusta coffee and palm oil were exported to the north in this way, as were Arabica coffee and tea to the south. Cinchona, papain, gold and cassiterite were also part of this trade.

The positive outcome of this illegal trade was that plantation production was maintained when it might have otherwise collapsed with the breakdown of the official export system; the negative result was again the loss of state revenues. This type of fraud in the 1960s principally benefited foreign planters and intermediaries, who hardly contributed to the expansion of the local economy, but rather repatriated profits to their countries of origin.[31]

However, with the Zairianization measures of 1973-1974, nationals took over the profitable coffee sector from foreigners. Although those with political connections acquired most large plantations, some were acquired by businessmen and women without position in the state. In addition, many small-scale producers took to growing plots of coffee, often smuggling out their crop or selling it for a good price to traders for illegal export after the price rise of 1976.[32] Rapid accumulation in this and other forms of illegal trade was a factor in the shift from class formation through the state toward the emergence of a small, commercial middle class of individuals who did not hold political positions and were relatively independent of politics.

The third type of fraudulent export that developed in the early 1960s, and the most profitable, was that of diamonds from Kasai. The diamond-mining companies reduced and even ceased production for a period of time, putting many people who were experienced in the extraction and sorting of diamonds out of work. They found it easy to continue their work in the river beds in the dry season; traders then bought the stones from the villagers and organized networks to smuggle them out of the country. Dupriez estimates that diamond smuggling in 1964 amounted to 10-12 million carats,[33] which means that as much as 81 percent of Zaire's official diamond production was fraudulently exported. At that time diamonds were the country's third most valuable export, and the loss in revenue could have amounted to as much as eleven-and-a-half million zaires.[34] This scandalous state of affairs had somewhat improved by 1966, after the authorities had succeeded to some degree in enforcing anti-smuggling measures.

Illicit diamond digging and trade during this period resulted in an enormous accumulation of wealth for some participants in these activities. It was widely reported at the time that one reason why it was so difficult to stop these activities was that the highest authorities and those who were in charge of prevention were themselves the biggest smugglers. We do not know very much about the traders and intermediaries. Some of them were the "*Sénégalais*,"[35] who established efficient, illicit export networks for diamonds, gold and other commodities. But diamond miners, intermediaries and traders from the local population also profited. The trade raised their incomes and the demand for food, and the high prices at which foodstuffs could be sold stimulated production of palm oil in lower Zaire and fish in Kivu, from where it was imported by air.[36]

Participation of State Personnel

By the late 1960s, as we have seen, state personnel were fulfilling their needs for the perquisites of office over and above their salaries by smuggling diamonds on a large scale. By the mid-1970s they were further consolidating their class position by increasing their wealth and means for patronage through an enormous expansion of their involvement in other second economy activities. The principal illegal activities to which a position in the state or the army or employment in a large capitalist enterprise provides access are bribery, corruption and embezzlement; smuggling and fraudulent export; and speculation and middleman activity.

Bribery, corruption and embezzlement on an enormous scale are widespread in Zaire and have been described in detail elsewhere.[37] A survey of government personnel in Lubumbashi in 1982 reveals the principal ways in which officials regularly supplement their inadequate salaries: corruption, embezzlement, pay-offs, forgeries of official signatures and seals, sales of false documents of certification, illegal taxation, use of spouses for commerce and other unauthorized practices, overcharging on document fees, usury, second jobs, and cultivation and sale of foodstuffs.[38] David Gould documents several more ways: false bills and profit-margin cheating on the allowed rate of profit by business; import, export and excise stamp fraud; distribution of merchandise quotas; postal and judicial fraud; and extortion at military barricades.[39] Embezzlement includes direct payroll theft, often by padding payrolls with fictitious names. In addition, position in the state apparatus is used to acquire commodities such as cobalt, gold, diamonds, ivory and coffee for smuggling and fraudulent export. I have given details of the enormous scale of these activities and of the wealth amassed in them elsewhere.[40]

Newspapers and government reports, as well as hearsay, supply abundant evidence of the expansion of speculation and middleman activity by state personnel from the mid-1970s onward. As one annual report complains:

> It is necessary to point out the appearance in commerce of a class of intermediaries, extremely powerful and rapacious, who dangerously restrict the distribution circuits. There are magistrates, directors of the JMPR, managers of the wholesale houses, state functionaries but especially political and administrative officials (sub-regional and zone commissioners). These intermediaries use their power to seize for themselves all the merchandise to the detriment of the real merchants who must content themselves with the crumbs. . . . The complicity between these intermediaries and the managers of the wholesale houses means that the latter become, in the long run, untouchable and uncontrollable. Merchandise is thus sold at triple, quadruple or more than its original price.[41]

The report deplores the dwindling power of the economic affairs office in the face of the collaboration of higher authorities in these activities.

Government personnel, military officers and others with official position, however, generally try to avoid participating in such activities in their public official capacity. They frequently use intermediaries, have a spouse or relative act as a front for their operations, or use certain words and gestures that in popular usage refer to the second economy, in order to avoid open involvement in defrauding the state. Although in the patrimonial state the distinction between public and private domains is blurred and officials do not always bother to disguise the ways in which they act to deprive the state of its revenues, the fact that they often do take pains to disguise such actions reflects an ideology of public morality still retained in Zaire, albeit in increasingly hollow form, for its necessary part in upholding the authority of the state.

Officials make use of their position to obtain the vouchers through which commodities are hoarded and used for speculative distribution through middleman activity. Goods are obtained by voucher at official, controlled prices; these vouchers are then sold, often several times, and each time for a higher price; by the time the goods are collected and sold to the consumer, they cost many times the official price. In Kinshasa in 1978–1979 there was a 258 percent difference between the official price of consumer goods and their actual market price.[42] In accumulating wealth by these means, members of the political aristocracy consolidate their position and maintain their supporting networks of dependents and clients.

All these activities, however, also contribute to further serious weakening of rational, effective administration and to a continuing decline of the economy, so that shortages increase, agricultural and industrial production decline, prices spiral higher and wages become more and more derisory. The index of real salaries was only 16 percent by 1977 and only 6 percent by 1979 of what it had been in 1960.[43] In terms of purchasing power, in 1979 an unskilled laborer had to work for five days to buy a kilo of rice,

116 days for a sack of manioc, seven for a kilo of dried beans and three for a loaf of bread.[44]

Resistance to the Predatory State and Opportunities for Capital Accumulation

The second economy expanded in the 1970s because, as conditions worsened, people responded to the depredations of the political aristocracy and took advantage of the weakening of administration and control to organize an independent system of production and distribution outside state control. They obtained foreign exchange by smuggling, appropriated commodities from capitalist enterprises, and made their own arrangements to compensate for the lack of infrastructure. Since I have given details of the organization of this system elsewhere,[45] I will only outline it briefly here.

There are three kinds of production for the second economy. First, there is small-scale production, by small-scale rural producers with access to land under relations of production in noncapitalist modes or by urban dwellers engaged in craft manufacture using simple tools, or by those who steal the means to set themselves up in production. Production is also carried out in organized enclaves either by illicit gold or diamond miners or by groups, often followers of particular religious sects, who have withdrawn to subsist autonomously in areas out of reach of the government. Finally, commodities produced by capitalism may be appropriated for distribution in the second economy.

Second-economy distribution takes place through private channels that are unlicensed and untaxed; through barter, replacing a formal transaction that would have earned revenue for the state if carried out as an official transaction; and by smuggling and fraudulent export. Commodities so distributed include food crops, fish and game; export crops such as coffee, tea, cotton, palm oil and papain; ivory, gold and diamonds; cobalt; and various imported goods.

By such means, rural and urban dwellers devise strategies to survive Zaire's stringent conditions: urbanites who cannot live on their wages organize supplies of foodstuffs from rural areas, sending kerosene, salt, soap, cooking oil and other items that are unobtainable or unaffordable in rural areas to kin who send them manioc, rice, plantains, beans and other staples in exchange. The second economy, therefore, represents disengagement from the state in order to escape the excessive appropriations of the ruling class. It is also significant for class formation, because some of its activities allow considerable accumulation. The possibility of amassing wealth depends on access to resources such as land and its fertility, proximity to mineral or other natural resources and location with regard to truck routes or frontiers. For some rural and urban workers the activities of this economy provide a favorable alternative to wage labor and thus the means to avoid proletarianization.

Indications that this process has taken place come from several sources. Government reports from the early 1970s onwards have complained about workers deserting plantations because they could make better money from their own cultivations or by fishing or hunting. In 1977, for example, many workers deserted the Lever plantations because their salaries, at Z 28 a month, were too low. In 1979–1980 business owners in Kisangani complained that workers in their commercial agricultural ventures were deserting to dig gold, at which they were said to make as much as Z 200 a month, instead of their former wages of Z 40–60. One maintained that the number of her workers had dropped from 200 to 40. An official with coffee and citrus plantations outside the city complained that his workers from among the local Bakumu people only showed up irregularly because they could make more than their Z 2 per day wage by fishing. In town and on plantations wages have been so low that the only reason many people continue in wage employment is to retain the accompanying health and housing benefits.

The gold trade provides an even more lucrative alternative to wage labor for those who are able to enter it. In 1980 soldiers were reported to have sold their uniforms and arms and abandoned the military camp at Watsa completely in order to enter the gold trade.[46] In the same year in Kisangani an employee left a job in a hotel to become a gold dealer because of the poor pay and long hours. Profits in the gold trade were high: he bought gold in 1979 at Z 30, the *likuta* (a small coin) weight in Bunia, a town northeast of Kisangani, and sold it in Kisangani for Z 50–65 (from which he had to deduct transportation costs and payoffs to the police). He also traded in ivory, bought at Z 80 a kilo in the interior and sold in Kisangani for Z 120. In North Kivu it is widely recognized that the gold trade is the basis for the recent expansion of businesses of Nande traders. As one of them said: "You get gold, take it to Nairobi and sell it for dollars or Kenyan shillings, which you put in the bank. Then you buy merchandise and take it back to Zaire, having all the necessary purchase documents to cross the border."

Capital accumulated in the second economy has been one factor in the emergence of a small, commercial middle class in Upper Zaire and North Kivu of businessmen and women who do *not* hold a position in the state and who are relatively independent of politics. One must say "relative" because some sort of political influence or connections is necessary to get anything done in Zaire.

In Kisangani, the principal city of Upper Zaire, accumulation in unlicensed trade and other second economy activities has been a factor in the founding and expansion of productive, manufacturing and distributive enterprises, which have been the basis for the new commercial middle class.[47] Its members make up 22 percent of substantial business owners in the city.[48] They enjoy a middle-class life-style and constitute a nascent true bourgeoisie since, in contrast to the political aristocracy, they invest their profits in expanding their enterprises and managing them effectively. Their investment in inheritable productive property and real estate and their emphasis on the education of their children indicate that they are reproducing themselves as a class.

Nande traders in Kivu, Zaire's easternmost region, conduct long-distance trade, exporting vegetables grown in the temperate climate and fertile soils of the highland zones of Beni and Lubero in North Kivu to Kisangani by truck and then downriver to Kinshasa by boat. In exchange they import manufactured goods, fuel, building materials and beer from Kisangani's breweries. Shortages of goods, transportation difficulties and other problems have been offset by the profits of the illegal gold trade and of coffee smuggling to East Africa.

North Kivu and Upper Zaire are the two principal coffee growing regions of the country. After independence many Nande grew small patches of coffee on lineage land or bought it from the producers and sold it for export; smuggling and illegal trade, however, were much more profitable than licensed trade at official prices, especially after the rise in coffee prices in 1976. Some of the capital rapidly accumulated in this coffee trade or illegal gold trading was invested in legitimate businesses; as these prospered, profits were invested in productive enterprises in the official economy, such as ranches producing meat and dairy products for local consumption, or coffee, tea and cinchona plantations, as well as in expanding wholesale, retail and transportation enterprises.

Conclusion

The economic disengagement from the state represented by the activities of the second economy enables people to survive the hardships of high prices, low wages and scarcities. For some people, however, these activities are more than coping strategies: they allow the accumulation of wealth, sometimes on a very considerable scale. Not all of the wealth accumulated in the second economy is invested in productive enterprises and the expansion of business concerns in the official economy, but some of it is, and the potential exists for more. Such investment has been one factor in the emergence of a nascent, indigenous capitalist class, a new sector of the dominant class that is not based on position in the state and is thus distinct from the political aristocracy. This new class is the beginning of a true economic bourgeoisie, as yet small and with an undetermined future. One ground for optimism about its long-term prospects is the weakness of the political aristocracy's control over economic processes and opportunities, very evident in the recent huge expansion of second economy activities.

Notes

I am indebted to the editors and the participants in the Hebrew University Workshop on the Reordering of the State in Africa for stimulating discussions on the issues of this paper and to Tom Callaghy, Crawford Young and Jane Parpart for their specific comments.

1. This definition is taken from Edgar L. Feige's study of the underground economy in the United States, "How Big is the Irregular Economy?" *Challenge: the Magazine of Economic Affairs* (Nov.-Dec. 1979).

2. Gregory Grossman describes the "illegal economy" of the socialist U.S.S.R. in terms that can be matched point for point in peripherally capitalist Zaire. See his "Notes on the Illegal Private Economy and Corruption," in *Soviet Economy in a Time of Change* (A compendium of papers submitted to the Joint Economic Committee Congress of the U.S., 1 1979), pp. 836–846.

3. Thomas M. Callaghy, *The State-Society Struggle: Zaire in Comparative Perspective* (New York: Columbia University Press, 1984), p. 142.

4. Ibid., pp. 48–49.

5. Nelson Kasfir, "Relating Class to State in Africa," *Journal of Commonwealth and Comparative Studies*, 21 (1983): 14.

6. Ibid., p. 15.

7. Ibid., pp. 9–10.

8. Callaghy, *The State-Society Struggle*, pp. 370–371.

9. Ibid., pp. 184–186.

10. John Iliffe, *The Emergence of African Capitalism* (Minneapolis: University of Minnesota Press, 1983), p. 81.

11. Henry Bernstein, "Notes on Capital and Peasantry," *Review of African Political Economy*, 10 (1977): 60–73.

12. David Goodman and Michael Redclift, *From Peasant to Proletarian* (New York: St. Martin's Press, 1982), p. 54.

13. Frederick Cooper, "Urban Space, Industrial Time and Wage Labor in Africa," in idem, ed., *The Struggle for the City* (Beverly Hills: Sage, 1983), p. 29.

14. Ibid., p. 16.

15. Such dependence is part of Bernstein's argument that capitalism destroys the reproduction of these noncapitalist modes. Clearly, it is a matter of degree, but his viewpoint posits an unreal degree of isolation of precapitalist African societies which, in fact, were often dependent on trade for items crucial to the maintenance of their relations of production; cf. Claude Meillassoux, *Anthropologie économique des Gouro de Côte d'Ivoire* (Paris, Mouton, 1964).

16. In Marxist terms this is the production of absolute surplus value.

17. Bernstein, "Notes on Capital and Peasantry," pp. 64–65. This situation represents the formal subsumption of labor under capital: "Capital subsumes the labor process as it finds it, that is to say, it takes over an existing labor process, developed by different and more archaic modes of production. . . . This stands in striking contrast to the development of a *specifically capitalist mode of production* (large scale industry etc.); the latter not only transforms it also revolutionizes their actual mode of labor and the real nature of the labor process as a whole. It is in contradistinction to this last that we come to designate as the *formal subsumption of labor under capital* . . . the takeover by capital of a mode of labor developed before the emergence of capitalist relations" (Karl Marx, *Capital*, I [New York: Vintage Books, 1976], p. 1021).

18. Goodman and Redclift, *From Peasant to Proletarian*, pp. 88–89.

19. Bernstein, "Notes on Capital and Peasantry," p. 69.

20. Goodman and Redclift, *From Peasant to Proletarian*, p. 75.

21. The value of the Congo franc at independence in 1960 was CF 100 = BF 100 = $2. Its value declined rapidly thereafter and was subject to frequent fluctuations:

November 6, 1961	CF 130 = BF 100	$1 = CF 65
November 9, 1963		
purchase	CF 300 = BF 100	$1 = CF 150
sale	CF 360 = BF 100	$1 = CF 180
June 24, 1967	CF 1000 = Z 1 = $2 = BF 100	

(Fernand Bézy, J.Ph. Peemans, J.M. Wautelet, *Accumulation et sous-développement au Zaire 1960-1980* [New Louvain: Presses Universitaires de Louvain, 1981], p. 75). By February 1980 the new unit of currency, the zaire, was equal to $.34. The unofficial and realistic rate was Z 1 = $.20.

22. Pierre Dupriez, "Les Relations économiques extérieures (du Congo)," in *Indépendence, inflation et développement: l'économie Congolaise de 1960 à 1964* (Institut de Recherches Economiques et Sociales, Paris: Mouton, 1968), p. 674.

23. The price in Congo francs to oil-exporting societies was 120 in 1958, 160 in 1963, 380 in 1965; on the uncontrolled market it was 132, 434 and 619, respectively, to producers, and in 1965, 900 to intermediaries (Ibid., p. 676).

24. In North Mayombe in 1963 rice cost CF 14 a kilo in the stores of a big company, CF 20 in stores in town and CF 40 in stores in the interior supplied by traveling traders. A kilo of salt was CF 5.5, 20 and 25, respectively. Dried fish was CF 50 from the company but CF 180 in town; cotton cloth CF 40 compared to CF 75 a meter (Ibid., p. 721, n. 49).

25. Ibid., pp. 674-677.

26. Pierre Dupriez, "Eléments du commerce extérieure de la république du Congo," *Cahiers Economiques et Sociaux*, I (1962): 78.

27. Dupriez, "Les Relations économiques extérieures," pp. 677-679.

28. Ibid., p. 679.

29. Ibid.

30. Jean-Claude Willame, *Les Provinces du Congo. Structure et Fonctionnement*, Centre d'Etude Politique no. 3 *Cahiers Economiques et Sociaux* (1964): 28.

31. Dupriez, "Les Relations économiques extérieures," pp. 680-681.

32. A world shortage of coffee caused by frost in Brazil, drought and floods in Columbia and the Angolan civil war caused prices to rise from BF 40 a kilo in 1975 to BF 92 in 1976 and BF 240 in March 1977.

33. Dupriez, "Les Relations économiques extérieures," p. 682.

34. Zaire's five most valuable exports in 1964 (in thousands of zaires) were: copper (76190), palm oil (17588), diamonds (14341), coffee (13808), cobalt (9333). (Bézy et al., *Accumulation et sous-développement*, pp. 222-224).

35. A general term for West Africans and those from other parts of Central Africa.

36. Dupriez, "Les Relations économiques extérieures," p. 683.

37. Mukenge Tshilemalema, "Les hommes d'affaires Zairois: du travail salarié à l'entreprise personelle," *Canadian Journal of African Studies*, 7, 3 (1973): 455-475; David J. Gould, *Bureaucratic Corruption and Underdevelopment in the Third World: the Case of Zaire* (New York: Pergamon, 1980); and Michael G. Schatzberg, *Politics and Class in Zaire* (New York: Africana, 1980).

38. Nsaman O. Lutu, "Le Management face à la crise de l'administration publique Zairoise," *Zaire-Afrique*, pp. 276.

39. Gould, *Bureaucratic Corruption*, pp. 138-149.

40. Janet MacGaffey, "How to Survive and Get Rich: The Second Economy in Zaire," *African Affairs*, 82 (1983): 351-366; idem, "Fending for Yourself: the Organization of the Second Economy in Zaire" in Nzongala-Ntalaja, ed., *The Crisis in Zaire: Myths and Realities* (Trenton, N.J.: Africa World Press, 1986).

41. *Rapport Economique Régional, Haut Zaire* (1976).

42. Mubake Mumeme, "Crise, inflation et comportements individuels d'adaptation au Zaire: solution ou aggravation du problème?" *Zaire-Afrique* (May 1984): 266-267.

43. André Huybrechts and Daniel Van der Steen, "L'Economie: structures, évolution, perspectives," in J. Vanderlinden, ed. *Du Congo au Zaire 1960-1980* (Brussels: CRISP, 1981), p. 241.

44. Mubake, "Crise, inflation et comportements individuels," p. 268.

45. MacGaffey, "Fending for Yourself."

46. Jean-Claude Willame, "Système de survie et fiction d'état," *Canadian Journal of African Studies*, 18, 1 (1984): 86.

47. Janet MacGaffey, *Entrepreneurs and Parasites: The Struggle for Indigenous Capitalism in Zaire* (Cambridge: Cambridge University Press, 1987).

48. Callaghy's assertion in his *The State-Society Struggle*, p. 188, that I do not attempt to show the relative size of this class is based on a misreading of my dissertation ("Class Relations in a Dependent Economy: Businessmen and Businesswomen in Kisangani, Zaire." Bryn Mawr College, 1981). The relevant information appears on pp. 108–110.

8

State Responses to Disintegration and Withdrawal: Adjustments in the Political Economy

Victor A. Olorunsola
with Dan Muhwezi

As a strategy, withdrawal from the state by individuals, groups or communities is predicated on the central assumption or conclusion that their lot in the state is gloomy or likely to be so in the future. Specifically, withdrawal from the state may be seen as a viable alternative under any of the following conditions: the economic performance of the state is perceived as hopelessly poor, considerable skepticism abounds regarding the capacities or resolve of the state vis-à-vis development, individuals and various groups do not feel confident that the state is interested in improving their condition, or there is a lack of confidence in the state's commitment to foster development for all its citizens. This alternative, they believe, will at worst minimize the negative impact of the state economy on them. Similarly, governments that feel the political system has undertaken state-centric economic strategies that are totally out of proportion with state resources, both human and material, may seek the path of withdrawal. Such withdrawal may be manifested in privatization, judicious efforts to reduce citizens' expectations from the state, slow shedding of previous state promises or an overall shrinkage in the economic parameters of direct state action. The state may withdraw in order to extricate itself from policies of previous governments that new leaders consider ineffective or ill-advised.

It seems to us that the phenomenon of withdrawal from the state may take several forms or patterns, which are partly dependent on the central assumptions made about the state's capacities, resolve, performance record and overall effectiveness, as well as the way in which citizens or various groups perceive their prospects to effect change through the ruling class and its institutions.

While generalizations may be dangerous at this stage, one can perhaps discuss at least a few apparent patterns of withdrawal. First, there is a pattern of withdrawal propelled from the top down, in which the state, for a number of reasons, seeks to alter the degree of dependency on the governmental apparatus. This pattern can be called "self-propelled disengagement." Secondly, there appears to be a pattern whereby the state grudgingly and haltingly disengages as a result of varied and persistent cues from its citizens and groups. This pattern can be referred to as "bottom-up state withdrawal."

In any event, due to several factors, adjustments have been contemplated, attempted variously and in some cases effected by African states throughout their relatively short histories. In this paper the cases of Tanzania, Nigeria and Zaire, which have exemplified various patterns of adjustment and currently approximate two patterns of state withdrawal, will be examined.

Tanzania

Beginning with the Arusha Declaration, Tanzania has made a number of adjustments in its political economy. However, from the outset it must be stated that the state's economic performance record has not been satisfactory. Tanzania is one of the poorest states in Africa. According to the World Bank, its per capita income stands at about $280. In the last decade food production showed a per capita negative growth rate of 1.3 percent per year. In 1974 and 1977 Tanzania had to import large amounts of food, which depleted its foreign reserves. In 1978 gross international reserves—in months of import coverage—stood at 0.9.[1] In these circumstances, let us look at major or minor adjustments, if any, that have been undertaken.

The national executive of the Tanganyika African National Union (TANU) adopted the Arusha Declaration in 1967. According to Nyerere, this declaration marked a turning point in the political economy of Tanzania.[2] It explained the meanings of socialism and self-reliance and their relevance to Tanzania. More specifically, it announced the nationalization of the "commanding heights of the economy," which included the major financial, manufacturing and trading institutions. Through the "leadership code" it called for a halt to the accumulation of private wealth by the leaders of the party and government. It signaled the state's desire to emphasize rural development and prescribed *Ujaama* as a strategy for attaining that goal. Briefly, then, it was a policy statement aimed at making Tanzania a socialist and self-reliant nation.

Why this apparent major thrust? Diverse reasons abound. Some scholars argue that the declaration was an adjustment to diminishing resources; others see it as an attempt to turn away from previous organizational arrangements considered unsalutary to development. The first explanation is somewhat credible if one considers, for example, that at this juncture in time, Tanzania had severed relations with Great Britain, West Germany and the United States, which had been its major foreign-aid donors. This suggests Tanzania's need to readjust its domestic policy to accommodate the vacuum left by these former donors. In short, Tanzania needed to look within itself for a substantial portion of its development resources. Hence, as Coulson observed, a policy emphasizing self-reliance seemed to be an adjustment in the right direction.[3] Moreover, the private sector had become more capital intensive and rural unemployment was becoming increasingly critical. Therefore, a policy that emphasized hard work, underscored the need for investment in rural areas and minimized the role of industrial investment appeared logical. In addition, it seems there were civil servants who indulged in excessive materialistic accumulation and were inclined to abuse and exploit their position for personal gains. In a country where public resources are extremely scarce, a leadership code curbing such materialism is a seemingly necessary adjustment. However, the second explanation is not without considerable merit.

In post-Arusha Declaration Tanzania two major adjustments—decentralization and villagization—have been particularly important. One could argue that these were adjustments in the political economy following disappointing results in a number of Ujaama villages and very low communal production in rural areas. Nyerere believed that Ujaama villages could be created and maintained by the people. However, despite the government's explicit rural development orientation, apparent in rural water supply programs and expansion of primary school education and health facilities, the response of the peasantry to government and party calls for the creation of cooperative or communal production units remained limited.[4] Some of the major objectives to which Tanzania's rural development strategy had been directed included: (1) establishing self-governing communities, (2) making better use of rural labor, (3) taking advantage of the economies of scale to increase production, (4) avoiding exploitation, and (5) increasing the standard of living of the peasants.[5] Yet the peasants seemed reluctant to take advantage of these villages, while the civil service showed little sign of becoming an active agency of development.[6] Against this background Nyerere declared that "it is time for the party to take control of its instruments."[7] He further announced a policy of administrative decentralization in which the civil service was to be the party's main instrument. Decentralization was seen as a means of increasing efficiency in the civil service and of allowing meaningful citizen participation. According to Mwapachu: "the regional administration was to move from its original law and order and revenue allocation function into a more development-based management function with the people."[8] Thus, decentralization was a preparatory move, or strategy, for the villagization which came into effect in 1973.

The debate about the effect of compulsory villagization has yielded various opinions. Some believe that it significantly affected agricultural production. Michael Lofchie, for instance, observes that some peasants were moved from their traditional residences to new villages in the middle of planting, growing or harvesting seasons, which resulted in the loss of entire crops.[9]

Hyden argues that disruptions in agriculture resulting from the movement of people were of a temporary nature.[10] He concedes that some temporary dislocation occurred, as peasant farmers concentrated on producing food crops to meet their most immediate needs in their new environment. However, he refutes the argument that villagization was the principal cause of the decline in Tanzania's agricultural production. He contends that drought was the main culprit, but also claims it was a "blessing in disguise" since it facilitated the movement of people.

Before we examine the impact of decentralization and villagization, let us address the issue of participation. Since independence, a series of schemes, including the 1972 administration decentralization, have been adopted to strengthen popular participation in the planning and implementation of rural development.[11] However, it seems that each decision has taken planning further away from the rural constituents and made mass participation in rural development increasingly difficult. Although one of the stated goals of decentralization is to encourage peasants to participate in the development process, the evidence suggests that it has led to the simultaneous and ironic elimination of important channels of citizen participation as illustrated by the abolition of the elected district councils in 1972.[12] Nyerere argues, however, that the establishment of elected village councils has given peasants an opportunity to determine their own development.[13]

The Village and Ujaama Villages Act replaced the village development committee with the village assembly, which in turn elected a village council of no more than 25 members. By institutionalizing the village assembly as the ultimate authority and the village council as its executive arm, the act presumably encouraged a certain amount of self-government in villages, and it was viewed as the precursor of more extensive popular participation in the development of rural areas.[14] The act did not specify how village leaders were to be selected. In most cases, however, the chairman and the secretary of the local party branch served as the chairman and secretary, respectively, of the council. The selection of council members began with villagers who, as party members, submitted names to the local and regional party for consideration. The names approved by the regional party were returned to the village to be voted on by the villagers.[15] These councils were dominated by official representatives.[16] While district leaders could suspend village leaders, regardless of their manner of election, the village assembly could not recall any village official, except in those cases where a local party branch did not exist.[17]

The village council was a body corporate capable of entering into all kinds of legal arrangements. Important matters were supposed to be presented to the village assembly for discussion and final decision. However, the power of the village assembly appeared to be limited to the election of village officials.[18] Hatfield and Slater found that some committee meetings of the village council were attended only irregularly by the majority of committee members and that committee decisions were not always submitted to the village assembly for approval. Another case, studied by Rutabingwa, shows how a committee ignored the vote of the village assembly, even though in theory nothing major could be done without the assembly's approval.[19] In theory, each village plan was discussed by district personnel and village representatives.[20] It was then presented to the district development and planning committee, which included village representatives. It then moved to the district development committee, which included special interest groups and party officials. Finally, the plan approved was forwarded to regional and national authorities for final approval and financing. Case studies show that most of the development projects originated from the district level or above.[21] Even though given development planning might have originated from village requests, such plans could be overturned by officials in the district or regional offices, or the prime minister's office.[22] Thus, the channels were only for downward communication. Insofar as villagers' proposals were generally long lists of desired projects, with no technical details or priority setting, it is not surprising that only projects proposed by officials had a chance of being implemented.[23]

Let us now examine the specific impacts of decentralization and villagization. Briefly, decentralization meant the end of local district councils. Hitherto, the councils had amassed chronic debts. They were inefficient and corrupt, and there were increasing tensions among councilors, council staff and officers of the ministries in the district.[24] The functions of local district councils, such as primary education, rural health and secondary road maintenance, had been taken over by the central government. Thus, the new arrangement rendered them redundant. Perhaps they were seen primarily as instruments of petit bourgeois power and thus had the potential to undermine party policies. If that were so, their lack of political space in post-Arusha Declaration Tanzania is understandable.

Villagization was also seen as a measure through which capitalist markets could be replaced. Following this policy, middlemen, such as cooperative societies, were removed. In 1976 cooperative unions were formally abolished, and in their place, crop authorities were established. Cooperatives were accused of fostering corruption and inefficiency and of being run for and by wealthy peasants, who were seen as a threat to state policies. State officials were apparently oblivious to the fact that the rural petty bourgeoisie that ran the cooperatives often did so with major peasant support. They did not seem to realize that in the rural context the petty bourgeoisie may have been the only channel through which complaints about state pricing and a host of other state policies could be channeled. Hyden argues that their abolition created an institutional vacuum that complicated the interaction between the government and peasants.[25] It could be argued that these institutional changes provided the government with viable agencies of economic development, in addition to creating channels for employment. If this were so, both the state and the peasants stood to gain.

However, it would appear that some of these state-centric policies frustrated, and at times alienated, peasants. Consider, for example, the fact that despite villagization, peasants resisted collective farming. This suggests that villagization created villages without socialism. Essentially, villagization threatened to undermine the very foundation of the family as the basic economic unit, as well as to eliminate its claim over land and, ultimately, to alienate it from ownership of the tools of production.[26] In any event, the Tanzanian state dropped its insistence on collectivism. To some this does not indicate a major change in policy; rather, it is seen as a practical accommodation to peasant resistance.[27] However, since the new government strategy reintroduced minimum acreage requirements, compulsory weeding under cashew nut trees, cassava growing, etc., it represents a significant tactical shift.

The leadership code and other subsequent policies demanded strict behavior. For example, in the wake of the Arusha Declaration the state froze salaries of high officials in order to reduce income inequalities. In addition, under this code civil servants and party officials could only hold one job and were denied rental properties. The state also abolished some of the privileges previously enjoyed by middle-level and senior officials. For instance, personal transportation, previously provided to principal secretaries and regional directors, was abolished, and loans to public servants to purchase cars were scrapped.[28] These seemingly restrictive policies gave rise to attempts to adopt certain compensatory strategies. In this case, some argue that the restrictions imposed on the bureaucracy generated conditions which made nepotism inevitable. Mutahaba suggests that because civil servants could not support their job-searching relatives for too long on meager incomes, they tended to place these relatives in their institutions or those of their friends.[29] Furthermore, it could be argued that although corruption is an outstanding feature of emerging states, restrictions imposed on the bureaucracy might have made it more inevitable. For example, while personal advances and traveling expenses stood at Sh. 49 million in 1974/1975, they increased to Sh. 60 million in 1977/1978 and to Sh. 222 million in 1980/1981. Moreover, cash unaccounted for, which stood at Sh. 327,000 in 1967/1968, increased to Sh. 43 million in 1977/1978 and then to Sh. 437 million in 1980/1981. We do know that corruption exists even where restrictions such as those mentioned above are not imposed on civil servants and political leaders. However, it seems too coincidental that "cash unaccounted for," "traveling expenses," and the like increased dramatically after policy restrictions. We have been led to believe that corruption may be a method civil servants use to adjust to reduced benefits and to accommodate the needs and demands placed upon them from below.

The Tanzanian state has been retreating somewhat, albeit haltingly. It has formally separated a number of party roles from government roles. This adjustment has been designed to maintain the party as the "watchdog" and to make it the channel through which more reliable and effective policy can flow.[30] In addition, the state has reinstated the cooperatives and district councils. The revival of the district councils was explained as an "extension of incomplete decentralization."[31] One may hazard the guess that the return of the cooperatives was due to dissatisfaction with the crop authorities which had replaced them. In addition, the government has expressed its willingness to encourage private, small-scale economic activity in areas where a range of goods and services cannot be easily or efficiently provided by state enterprises.[32]

Nigeria

For a number of reasons, Nigeria did not pursue a heavily state-centric economic policy between 1960 and 1965. First, the state entity itself was rather fragile and was primarily under the effective control of the conservative wing of the Nigerian People's Congress. Secondly, it did not appear to have the resources which could make it capable of meeting the many formal responsibilities. Although oil was discovered in 1956, it contributed only a minor portion of the state's revenue. Oil output and revenue peaked in 1979, when about 2.3 million barrels per day were being produced. Agriculture provided the mainstay of the economy, but the state's revenue was modest indeed. Thirdly, unlike their Tanzanian counterparts, the Nigerian leaders who held real political power were more aligned with the West and subscribed generally to state involvement at only the lowest end of welfare state orientation. The state targeted its meager resources toward education and establishing needed infrastructures which would not have been provided by either the few Nigerian entrepreneurs or the trading and manufacturing concerns which were primarily owned by foreign interests. Following the Civil War, the state's role was expanded, and it increased its direct involvement in production.[33]

The federal military government declared in the 1970–1974 development plan that "as a matter of general policy, the Government will encourage nationwide equity participation in all manufacturing industries. Shares would be allocated to the Federal Government, the state in which a particular industry is located, other states, and to Nigerian nationals willing to participate in industrial development."[34] Furthermore, it announced that it would hold at least 55 percent of the shares in the iron and steel bar complex, petrochemical industries, fertilizer production and petroleum products, for the government "wants to minimize foreign control over the commanding heights of the Nigerian economy."[35] The government flatly declared that the "uncompromising objective of a rising economic prosperity in Nigeria is the economic independence of the nation and the defeat of neo-colonial forces in Africa."[36]

These assertions have led us to observe that if the government's intentions outlined in this plan were taken seriously they would entail the following processes:

1. growth of the public sector to the point where it dominates the private sector;
2. extensive participation by government in directing growth-producing projects in industry and agriculture;

3. detailed control over the decisions of the private sector;
4. extensive development of the infrastructure by government—roads and communications, education, health, etc.;
5. technical description of how objectives are to be achieved; and
6. consultation on projects at the level of the smallest social units— villages and clusters of villages.[37]

In short, on the face of it, the federal military government sought to become a mobilization system, dedicated to the achievement of economic nationalism.

Perhaps the major adjustment in the political economy of Nigeria is represented by the 1972 Nigerian Enterprises Promotion Decree, which stipulated that as of March 1974 no person other than a Nigerian citizen could be the owner or part-owner of enterprises in 22 selected industries in Nigeria (Schedule I industries). Industries which were affected included small, labor-intensive manufacturing and local service-related enterprises, many of which were already predominantly Nigerian owned. In addition, the decree stated that aliens could not participate in 33 other industries (Schedule II industries) in which the paid-up share capital of the enterprises was less than N200,000 or the turnover of the enterprises was less than N500,000. The enterprises exempted on the basis of their size were required to make available to the Nigerian public up to 40 percent of their total equity. The 1977 Nigerian Enterprises Promotion Decree added 20 more industries to the list of Schedule I industries which were to be indigenized in ownership, while 33 industries were added to the Schedule II list, and the mandatory sale of shares was raised from 40 to 60 percent. Enterprises in Schedule II included banks, shipping agencies and food manufacturers. A third schedule, which included textile firms, technological enterprises and tobacco concerns, was also established. Schedule III industries had to make 40 percent of their equity available to Nigerian subscribers.[38]

According to Gowon, the 1972 Nigerian Enterprises Promotion Decree consolidated Nigeria's political independence. Others view it as an anti-dependency measure.[39] Whichever perception one subscribes to, it represents a diversion from previous policies. Moreover, the restrictions imposed by the 1977 decree were more stringent than those of 1972. It could be argued that the new military leaders were more committed to the ideology of economic nationalism.[40] But it is also plausible that, shaken by the assassination of the head of state, the regime in power utilized this strategy to garner greater support.

Let us focus on the impact of and responses to indigenization. For the Nigerian state, it offered breathing space. Regarding the banking industry, for example, the state was able to control liquidity ratios which the banks had failed to control. Moreover, by opening business avenues to a sizeable number of Nigerians, the state satisfied itself that it was the custodian for its people, as well as provided temporary satisfaction for those (particularly in the business community) yearning for economic sovereignty. The business community was poised to fill the vacuum and seize the opportunity to its advantage.

The responses of the people were seemingly positive. Many Nigerians could obtain loans which they had no access to previously. However, the state remained generally baffled by the criticisms leveled against its equity performance. For example, it was criticized for creating a handful of Nigerian millionaires, while the masses remained essentially untouched. Nonetheless, the government probably accomplished more than that. For instance, commercial banks were enabled to channel a large proportion of their loans to the productive sectors of the economy.

The tactics adopted by those in privileged positions to circumvent the state involved the acquisition of shares without revealing the extent of their purchases. Some people could and did change professions and the order of their names. Many used the names of pets, children and secretaries, with the view to consolidating their holdings through private transfers, which though strictly legal, were contrary to public policy.[41]

Despite the apparent restrictions contained in the decree, transnationals remained eager to invest in Nigeria. For example, the capital flow into Nigeria increased from $305 million to $377 million after the 1972 indigenization decree and averaged about $331 million in the 1970s.[42] However, these corporations adopted different strategies to neutralize the indigenization requirement. Some firms sold shares publicly, in order to prevent huge concentrations of share holding among a small number of Nigerians. Some corporations negotiated extensions to the 1972 and 1977 requirements, or different schedules of completely different exemptions. Others selected board members from different ethnic groups with the intention of "playing Hausas and Yorubas" against each other, hoping that past disputes among different ethnic groups would prevent them from cooperating as Nigerians to manage the company. Still others resorted to bribery, changing voting rules and the use of Nigerians as front persons.

In general, the state derived considerable power and influence from oil revenues and the indigenization policy. But the benefits obtained somewhat unwittingly excluded the masses and thus, to some extent, fostered growth more than development. Organized labor consequently became increasingly restless. The 1975 Udoji awards are seen by some as catch-up wages which labor was able to win by calling numerous strikes in order to protect itself from inflationary pressures.[43] On the other hand, the government argues that since the Udoji awards made the highest percentage increases at the bottom of the scale, they initiated a process for making viable adjustments in the wage and salary structure and provided a real opportunity for addressing the problem of income inequalities.[44] These awards, however, have been held largely responsible for the inflation which ensued. Neither the informal nor the rural sector was able to protect itself to the same degree as organized labor.

The nature and extent of poverty in rural areas is illustrated by Malton's 1981 survey in Kano. The results of this survey cannot be overgeneralized. It is significant to point out, however, that in the three villages surveyed, Malton found "a serious degree of absolute impoverishment among the poorest 30–40 percent of the households."[45] In addition, the work of Ojo et al. revealed a growing number of Nigerians with neither land on which to grow food crops nor income to purchase food.[46] Furthermore, the 1981 basic-needs study of the International Labor Office (ILO) noted that the number of urban poor had doubled in the last decade. The ILO estimated that about four million families in Nigeria were below the poverty line in 1978, representing an increase of over 25 percent since 1973.[47] Hence, the seemingly distributive policies of indigenization and wage increases not only bypassed poor groups, but pushed more people into the poverty ranks. As a result, the rural poor migrated to urban areas in search of better jobs and life-styles, thereby shrinking the agricultural labor force. Agricultural manpower declined from 71 percent of the active labor force in 1960 to 55 percent in 1979,[48] while the percentage of manpower in the services increased from 19 percent (1960) to 27 percent (1979). The decline in the agricultural labor force presented severe problems to the agriculture sector. In general, agricultural output decreased not only relatively but absolutely. Production fell 1.5 percent per annum from 1970 to 1977; food production declined markedly.

We would have expected the rise of wages in the formal sector to increase the supply of employment seekers in urban areas, which would in turn increase the demand for agricultural products, a condition that would have rewarded the rural sector with high agricultural prices. Apparently, however, oil revenues enabled the state to import foodstuffs. The total food import bill, which stood at N 95.1 million in 1972, increased to N 154.8 million in 1974, N 790.3 million in 1977 and N 1.56 billion in 1980.[49] At the same time, the government was reluctant to use oil revenues to raise domestic producer prices for fear of exacerbating inflation. For instance, the millet and sorghum prices offered by the National Grain Board in 1978 were 20 to 50 percent below estimated production costs. With competition from imported foods and deliberate government price policies, the rural sector was further crippled. Once again, the oil revenues bypassed the rural sector.

Let us now focus on the informal sector. Judging from the growth rates of urban centers, there seems to have been a high rate of migration and high birth rate among those already inhabiting the cities. Rural dwellers often move initially to medium-sized cities and then later to large cities. Due to the neglect of the rural sector, migration to urban areas has increased, and this has generated unemployment and underemployment. However, most of the migrants seem to have been absorbed into the informal sector. In a study conducted in Ilesha, Traeger found that informal-sector activities had expanded in terms of the number of people, space and time allocated to them. According to Traeger, expansion in the marketplace, trade and street vending may be a result of overall population increase in the city and/or generally poor economic conditions in which more and more people are entering trade in an attempt to make a living.[50] This finding perhaps explains the growth of the services sector. In addition, Traeger noted changes in terms of the activities or commodities being sold. Her findings tend to support Watts and Lubeck's observations that due to stagnating agriculture there has been a shift from trade in agricultural products to trade in manufactured goods.[51]

The civilian government, which assumed power in 1979, inherited a state totally dependent on the oil sector. Agriculture, which had been the mainstay of the economy, providing 81 percent of export earnings in the 1960s, had dropped to under 10 percent.[52] Oil revenues, however, brought in $26 billion in 1980. The expectations of various groups were high, particularly since a democratically elected government was to assume the role of distributing public goods and services. However, the regime assumed power at a time when resources (i.e., oil revenues) peaked and soon after began to decline. By 1982 oil revenues had plummeted to $10 billion.[53] The continuation of a state-centric policy under such circumstances, and by a political party, created adjustment problems. In the aftermath of party politics, the economy and resources of the state, by default, became more susceptible to the manipulation of political party elites and their supporters, particularly as the political party became the main instrument for operating an essentially state-centric economy. Party loyalists expected, and were often given, positions of power and authority which they used to enrich themselves, their friends and the party. Nonparty and unprivileged groups were disenchanted and felt betrayed. If the state had not been so ubiquitous, the consequences would not have been so dire for other groups. Moreover, to the extent that ethnicity had some impact on the voting behavior of the masses, the dominance of one party—in a system where the winner took all—was a threat to the economic interests and survival of other groups outside the political party in power.

This is not to fault the system because, as I have argued elsewhere, the 1979 constitution was dedicated to the prevention of a society in which only one sector can participate in public goods.[54] However, it is equally true that the operation of the system by the Shagari party created the unmistakable impression among Nigerians who were not party members that it was a "winner take all" system. Before 1979 ethnic affiliation was unashamedly a principal determinant of who got what. The party in the Second Republic became the critical determinant. The analysis of the 1979 election results, however, did not show a radical departure from previous elections: ethnicity remained a relevant variable; ethnicity and voting patterns were very consistent.

In spite of diminished resources and rhetoric about austerity measures, there was no belt tightening with respect to government consumption. The government continued to overcommit oil revenues, and probably did not raise vigorous questions about the execution of its so-called development projects. There was gross mismanagement. For instance, it was noted that "the Central Bank of Nigeria had no actual data on revenues and expenditures in 1981."[55] This immense inefficiency probably made it impossible for the state to make meaningful adjustments in the economy. Corruption was evident almost everywhere. Ultimately, Shagari's promises of a cleanup through the ethical revolution and a tough economic program—which he announced two days before he was ousted from office—came too late. Although the Shagari government cannot be held responsible for the decline in the oil revenues, it is at least culpable for its failure to adjust its programs to meet diminished resources and for the party leadership's failure to demonstrate its commitment to development for all Nigerians.

If Nigeria's Second Republic generated hope for democracy, the military coup d'état of January 1984 gave rise to expectations for fresh adjustments in Nigeria's political economy. Without a doubt, the huge financial reserve which Shagari's government inherited led it to press ahead with expensive development projects, including the construction of a new capital at Abuja. However, the huge reserve quickly disappeared, and foreign exchange and debt-servicing woes appeared. The state of the economy they inherited has led the new military rulers to rethink the government's state-centric posture. The government has now either withdrawn from some of its traditional functions or made serious adjustments in its fiscal and monetary policies—both moves directed at increasing the revenues at its disposal.

In justifying the coup d'état, General Buhari contended that Shagari was attempting to turn Nigeria into a "nation of beggars." He observed that the Nigerian people were worried about the rising prices of items such as rice, sugar, yams and tomatoes. According to the military, "the country was slowly drifting into a dangerous political and economic state." What is particularly interesting to note is that while military leaders acknowledged that "many civil servants had not been paid for several months," they warned "let no one be deceived that workers who have not received their salaries in the past eight awful months will be paid today or tomorrow."[56]

A country which only four years earlier had a healthy financial reserve could not meet its salary obligations! Why? Certainly gross mismanagement and rampant corruption in the face of declining oil revenues incapacitated the state to the extent that it was unable to meet its obligations. Apparently, it was finally recognized that the monocrop of oil had not provided an adequate escape hatch from economic underdevelopment. Therefore, it became necessary to reduce expectations and to specify what the state would and could do. In short, the government was preparing the stage for a withdrawal strategy.

Nigeria in 1984 was still confronted with several economic problems. Export earnings, largely derived from petroleum, remained low; agricultural performance was still poor, while domestic activity depended heavily on imported raw materials. In response to these problems, President Buhari clarified the state's immediate objectives: "to arrest the decline in the economy, to put the economy on proper course of recovery and solvency and to chart out a course for economic stability and prosperity."[57] To this end, various measures were undertaken in the 1984 budget, including a reduction in imports, stimulation of agricultural production and stabilization of prices and incomes. In addition, the government appointed a Projects Review Committee to evaluate the projects in which it was involved. Its strategy was to participate only in those projects which had "immediate beneficial effects."[58] The government also adopted a "tight monetary policy in order to clear the backlog of accumulated trade debts, maintain a reasonable level of external reserves, reduce inflationary pressures in the economy and encourage expansion of domestic output of goods and services."[59] Additionally, the military government slowed down the pace of building the Federal City to that of its original 15-year plan.

The government contended that it would concentrate on agriculture, thereby making Nigeria less vulnerable to the vicissitudes of oil. Accordingly, for example, it reorganized and created the "River Basin and Rural Development Authorities," whose main objective is to focus on the small farmer by means of various incentives, such as easy access to credit, more efficient provision of inputs and higher producer prices. One may not be highly optimistic about this strategy of increasing production, given the record of past programs of a similar nature. However, its small-farmer focus deviates or detours substantially from the former programs of the civilian governments, which tended to place the emphasis on large capital-intensive schemes with only marginal benefits for small farmers. In addition, in some states, such as Kwara, it is "voluntarily compulsory" for government employees to own farms (vegetable gardens). The government's intention to amend the indigenization decree to enable non-Nigerians to own up to 80 percent of the equity in large-scale farming projects clearly demonstrates a shift from previous policies in which the government was to play the major role.

Quite apart from these policies at both the federal and state levels, the Nigerian government has been withdrawing from some traditional functions, such as education. University students are now expected to provide a major portion of their own financial resources. For example, university students must provide for their own meals and pay for their accommodations. To minimize the expenditure on education, some of the states and universities have privatized the cafeteria system. In the new system the students are required to purchase food from private companies granted the concession to run the cafeterias. Secondly, the federal government has established an interministerial committee charged with seeking means to avoid curriculum duplication in universities and studying other cost-cutting measures. Upon the protest of the universities, the Nigerian University Council was asked to look into alternative ways to achieve these ends. Limits on the size of the student population are seriously being considered.

At the secondary school level, students are expected to pay fees. For example, in Oyo the elementary, lower and higher sections of secondary schools are expected to pay $5, $15, and $30 respectively per term. In addition, tax clearances are required to register children in primary schools in all states.[60]

In the long run this withdrawal strategy should have serious consequences for low-income groups in particular and the country in general. The immediate impact, however, has been to encourage squatting in university dormitories. There have also been reports of dwindling numbers of students in rural schools. More seriously, it could be argued that these fees or charges will affect the class composition at all levels of education. If education is an instrument by which those who lack technical and general knowledge skills can participate in a modern economy, if in fact the rural student population continues to diminish, and if only those who can afford a university education go to university, then the fee policy will have serious consequences for development. There is a danger of uneven development and perhaps, ultimately, gross political instability because a substantial part of the population may become alienated. In any case, in Nigeria the present strategy of readjustment is apparently dependent on state withdrawal.

Zaire

Zaire provides a case of a state plagued by continuous economic, social and political crises affecting a growing number of its people. In relative terms, the state's performance in the 1970s was an improvement over that in the 1960s, when its legitimacy was very seriously placed in doubt. However, the situation in the last decade seems to have echoed to some extent that of the 1960s. The two Shaba wars, an overall economic downturn and oppressive state policies have alienated most groups and created conditions which make mass poverty almost inevitable.

Zaire's economic performance, as indicated in other chapters, has been less than satisfactory. In 1982 its per capita income was about $190. It has one of the lowest adult literacy levels (15 percent) in sub-Saharan Africa. On the average the economy experienced a "negative annual growth" rate of about 0.3 percent between 1960 and 1982. In the same time span the inflation rate was about 35.3 percent per year, fueled mainly by government deficits generated by a large external debt and debt servicing. While the total external public and publicly guaranteed private debt outstanding and disbursed stood at $311.1 million in 1960, it rose to about $4,040.3 million in 1982.[61] This has placed Zaire in a rather uncomfortable economic position.

The crises which created conditions for a coup d'état in Zaire seem to have produced further opportunities for concentrating power in the state. In the last decade, however, Mobutu has set Zaire on a seemingly "radical course" in the "quest for national identity and grandeur, and international recognition" under the policy of authenticity.[62] To bolster his campaign for African authenticity, Mobutu declared a policy of Zairianization in 1973. As elsewhere in Africa, Mobutu called for efforts to achieve total economic independence. However, in this case there was a significant difference; whereas in other African countries the state took over economic enterprises, in Zaire they were given to individuals as private property.[63] It is estimated that between 1,500 and 2,000 enterprises were taken over by new Zairian owners, most of whom came from the political establishment, not the merchant class. This giveaway strategy discouraged reinvestment and emphasized salesmanship rather than management. Consequently, there were widespread shortages of most essential items. These conditions led to dramatic price increases and the expansion of the parallel economy. The state retreated from this policy and in 1974 announced measures aimed at nationalizing the businesses which were previously indigenized.

The decision to nationalize was a reaction to the failure of the original policy of Zairianization. Accordingly, the state appointed 100 "delegates-general" to supervise the adjustment of indigenization, *à la* private ownership, to nationalize through public ownership. Unfortunately, only a few businesses were returned to state control. If state control was the prescribed medicine, only a few of the sick patients received it. Thus, economic chaos continued.[64] As another adjustment measure the state denationalized. In 1975, some of the former owners were invited back, and in some cases they took Zairian partners. This arrangement was particularly beneficial to the "political aristocracy," for it enabled them to appropriate wealth without having to perform true "bourgeois functions."[65]

The economic crisis, exacerbated by Zairianization adventures, seriously eroded the regime's credibility. The failure of the regime to maintain reasonable transportation, education and health infrastructures has generally created a mood of cynicism among the populace. Crawford Young argues that the state's vanishing credibility is now more apparent in the periphery than in the center. He offers an appropriate summary of the society's response to the state's poor performance:

> For many, economic survival is sought outside the public realm in the parallel or underground economy. Mercantile networks outside the framework of the state have swiftly grown, with new social classes in gestation built around them. . . . The State bourgeoisie clings ambivalently to the State although only the top layer really prospers. . . . Peasants and the lower end of the urban sector appear passive and resigned, wholly absorbed in the precarious quest for daily survival.[66]

Since the reversal of Zairianization and nationalization, the state has committed itself to expanding the private sector.[67] Zaire, like Benin, Uganda, the Ivory Coast and Ghana, devalued its currency. It has adopted flexible, market-determined exchange rates which, according to the World Bank, have significantly "reduced the parallel markets in their currencies."[68] It also established a National Debt Management Office to ensure coherence in state policies. In addition, in 1982 the state introduced popularly elected councils at the collectivity level and indirectly elected councils at the level of the zone or region. In a highly centralized state, creation of such institutions, however symbolic, represents a significant change. But as Newbury points out, insofar as these councils are manned by teachers, traders and others attached to commercial networks, the establishment of these institutions may be a strategy designed to co-opt the growing power of the trading groups to the state.[69] On the other hand, this move may represent a strategic withdrawal from the countryside, particularly given the diminishing resources and the inept economic performance of the state.

In sum, the state in Zaire has made some adjustments in the political economy, most of which have been directed at enhancing its own power. The economic crisis created spot shortages, which made an underground economy inevitable. Moreover, the continued low economic performance of the state and the pervasiveness of corruption expanded this sector. One would have expected sizeable adjustments from the rural sector, but the coercive arm of the state has rendered the peasants somewhat ineffective as a political group. They are, for now, in the words of Young, "passive and resigned,"[70] absorbed in the drudgery of mere survival.

Conclusion

In this paper very brief and perhaps unavoidably truncated case studies of the attempts of three states to make adjustments in their political economies have been presented. The cases show that all three states, in varying degrees, are now opting for state withdrawal. Perhaps they all arrived at this strategy reluctantly and under some compulsion. Nigeria, under General Buhari, exemplifies a case of state-propelled withdrawal. There may be many reasons for this, but the most paramount reason is related to decreasing resources. Zaire seemingly represents a variant of state-propelled withdrawal, where privatization was instrumentally used to create limited dependency upon the ruling group. Thus, the diminution of the political authority held by the political aristocracy in the urban sectors was prevented, while the peasantry was allowed to seek its survival in the growth of the underground economy. Tanzania under Nyerere represents a case of the bottom-up state withdrawal.

It seems that a declining economy often tends to provide valuable opportunities to reexamine the assumptions upon which a state's economic policy is based. More specifically, then, silent critics of state-centric approaches may be further emboldened to speak out in the face of a poor economic performance of a political economy which has taken a state-centric approach. Indeed, under such circumstances die-hard state-centric advocates may become increasingly less certain about their presumptions. The persistence of a declining economy certainly raises doubts about the wisdom of operational policies, and when deemed appropriate, criticism will be voiced. One may argue, then, that persistently declining economies of African states are instigating reexamination of state-centric approaches. This is indeed the case in Nigeria and likewise seems to be so in Tanzania. It may be a contributing factor in the withdrawal of the state in Zaire, too.

Does this have implications for all states? Are we witnessing the beginning of "state atrophy"? Equally interesting is the evidence that the withdrawal of the state may not be limited to poor, bumbling developing countries: the current administrations of Great Britain, the United States and the People's Republic of China, to mention a few, are all engaged in some variant of state withdrawal strategies. The fear about withdrawal is that it tends to take place either within a strong ideological context or under duress without the benefit of careful thought. While state-centric measures have not borne proper fruits, there is no guarantee that state withdrawal will succeed where state-centric measures have failed.

Notes

1. World Bank, *Accelerated Development in Sub-Saharan Africa: An Agenda for Action* (Washington, D.C., 1981).

2. Julius Nyerere, "The Arusha Declaration: Ten Years After," *The African Review,* 7, 2 (1977): 1-34.

3. Andrew Coulson, *Tanzania: A Political Economy* (Oxford: Clarendon Press, 1982).

4. Goran Hyden, *Beyond Ujaama in Tanzania: Underdevelopment and an Uncaptured Peasantry* (Nairobi: Heinemann, 1980).

5. J. Maeda, "Popular Participation, Control and Development: A Study of the Nature and Role of Popular Participation in Tanzania's Rural Development." (Ph.D. diss., New Haven, Yale University, 1976), pp. 163-165.

6. Frances Hill, "Administrative Decentralization for Development, Participation and Control in Tanzania," *Journal of African Studies,* 6, 4 (1979): 182-192.

7. Julius Nyerere, quoted in ibid., p. 183.

8. Juma Volter Mwapachu, "Operation Planned Villages in Tanzania," *African Review,* 6, (1976): 4.

9. Michael Lofchie, "Agrarian Crisis and Economic Liberalization in Tanzania," *Journal of Modern African Studies,* 16, 3 (1978): 451-475.

10. Hyden, *Beyond Ujaama,* p. 146.

11. Mwapachu, "Operation Planned Villages," p. 1.

12. Hill, "Administrative Decentralization," p. 190.

13. Nyerere, "Arusha Declaration: Ten Years After," p. 12.

14. Hyden, *Beyond Ujaama,* p. 136.

15. Francis Moore Lappe and Adele Becca-Varela, *Mozambique and Tanzania: Asking the Big Questions* (San Francisco: Institute of Food and Development Policy, 1980), p. 91.

16. Louise Fortman, *Peasants, Officials and Participants in Rural Tanzania: Experience with Villagization and Decentralization* (Ithaca: Cornell University Press, 1980), pp. 45-48.

17. Ibid., pp. 57-59.

18. Ibid., pp. 48-50.

19. Ibid., pp. 66-67.

20. Hyden, *Beyond Ujaama,* p. 135.

21. Fortman, "Peasants, Officials and Participants," pp. 74-75.

22. Coulson, *Tanzania,* pp. 319-320.

23. Lappe and Becca-Varela, *Mozambique and Tanzania,* p. 94.

24. Frank Holmquist, "Tanzania's Retreat from Statism in the Countryside," *Africa Today,* 30, 4 (1983): 23-35.

25. Hyden, *Beyond Ujaama,* pp. 132-134.

26. Lofchie, "Agrarian Crisis," p. 470.

27. Ibid.

28. Rwekaza Mukandala, "Trends in Civil Service Size and Income in Tanzania, 1967-1982," *Canadian Journal of African Studies,* 17, 2 (1983): 253-263.

29. Gelase Mutahaba, "The Effect of Changes in the Tanzania Public Service System Upon Administrative Productivity, *African Review,* 5, 2 (1975): 201–207.

30. Holmquist, "Tanzania's Retreat."

31. Ibid., p. 28.

32. Lofchie, "Agrarian Crisis."

33. Paul Collins, "The Policy of Indigenization: An Overall Overview," *Quarterly Journal of Administration* (January 1975).

34. Federal Republic of Nigeria, *The Second National Development Plan 1970-74* (Lagos: Federal Ministry of Information, 1970), p. 145.

35. Ibid.

36. Ibid.

37. James O'Connell, "Political Constraints on Planning: Nigeria as a Case Study in the Developing World," *Nigerian Journal of Economic and Social Studies,* 13 (March 1971): 41–42.

38. Thomas J. Biersteker, "Indigenization in Nigeria: Renationalization or Denationalization?" in I. William Zarman, ed., *The Political Economy of Nigeria* (New York: Praeger, 1983), pp. 189–190.

39. Ibid., p. 188.

40. Ibid.

41. Ibid., p. 191–201.

42. Ibid.

43. Henry Bienen and V.P. Diejomaoh, *The Political Economy of Income Distribution in Nigeria* (New York: Holmes and Meier, 1981).

44. See Victor A. Olorunsola, *Soldiers and Power* (Stanford: Hoover Institution Press, 1977), p. 45.

45. Michael Watts, *The Silent Voice: Food, Famine and Peasantry in Northern Nigeria* (Los Angeles: University of California Press, 1983), p. 487.

46. M. O. Ojo, C. C. Edordu and J. Ayo Akingbade, *Agricultural Credit and Finance in Nigeria: Problems and Prospects* (Lagos: Central Bank of Nigeria, 1981).

47. Michael Watts and Paul Lubeck, "The Popular Classes and the Oil Boom: A Political Economy of Nigeria," in Zartman, *Political Economy of Nigeria,* p. 131.

48. World Bank, *Accelerated Development in Sub-Saharan Africa.*

49. Watts, *The Silent Voice,* p. 485.

50. L. Traeger, "From Yams to Beer in a Nigerian City: Expansion and Change in Informal Sector Trading Activity," unpublished paper (University of Wisconsin-Parkside, 1984).

51. Watts and Lubeck, "Popular Class and the Oil Boom."

52. I. W. Zartman, "Introduction," in idem, *Political Economy of Nigeria,* p. 15.

53. *Newsweek,* January 16, 1984, p. 38.

54. Victor A. Olorunsola in Donald Rothchild and Victor A. Olorunsola, *State Versus Ethnic Claims, African Policy Dilemmas* (Boulder: Westview, 1983).

55. Watts, *Silent Violence,* p. 508.

56. *Time Magazine,* January 16, 1984, p. 25.

57. *West Africa,* May 1984, p. 1009.

58. Ibid.

59. Ibid., p. 1007.

60. *Sunday Times* (Lagos), March 18, 1985.

61. World Bank, *Zaire: Current Economic Situation and Constraints* (Washington, D.C., 1979).

62. Ghislain C. Kabwit, "Zaire: The Roots of the Continuing Crisis," *Journal of Modern African Studies,* 17, 3 (1979): 388.

63. Thomas M. Callaghy, *The State-Society Struggle: Zaire in a Comparative Perspective* (New York: Columbia University Press, 1984).

64. Ibid., p. 192.

65. Ibid., pp. 192, 452.

66. Crawford Young, "Zaire: Is There a State?" *Canadian Journal of African Studies*, 18, 1 (1984): 82.

67. World Bank, *Zaire: Current Economic Situation.*

68. World Bank, *Forward Sustained Development in Sub-Saharan Africa* (Washington, D.C., 1984), p. 35.

69. M. Catharine Newbury, "Dead or Burned or Just Underground? The Privatization of the State in Zaire," *Canadian Journal of African Studies*, 18, 1 (1984): 112–114.

70. Young, "Is There a State?" p. 82.

9

Women and the State in Africa

Jane L. Parpart

In recent years the African state has received considerable attention, but rarely from the viewpoint of gender, which has been subsumed within class, ethnic affiliation or religious persuasion, under the assumption that these identities, rather than gender, define access to the state. This paper challenges that assumption, asserting the particularity of the relationship of women to the state in Africa (and elsewhere) and consequently the need to study gender-state relations, as well as other social divisions, in order to understand both the nature of the state and the place of women in it. We are concerned with women's access to the apparatus of the state, the consequences of their underrepresentation in the state, and the mechanisms women have constructed to cope with their slim hold on the levers of power.

Since economic, social and political power are frequently intertwined in Africa, we shall refer to economic and social realms when discussing political power. It is important to recognize, however, that political power also includes the capacity to force people to do things which may be against their wishes. Authority, while related, is not power, but rather the culturally accepted belief that a person (or persons) have a legitimate right to wield power. This distinction is important in Africa, where women have tended to exert power indirectly, rather than directly, through positions of authority. Women's indirect power has been achieved through a variety of activities, such as withdrawal, calling upon the supernatural, control over food, manipulation of men and collective action. Direct authoritative power held through elected or appointed offices, with its concomitant control over resource allocation, has been less available to women. As a result, despite our concern with female access to authoritative political power, the paper will of necessity examine indirect power or influence as well.[1]

Women and the State in Precolonial Africa

In precolonial Africa women experienced a wide range of relations with the state. In some societies patriarchal authority severely limited women's political and economic power. Women were protected as long as they paid obeisance to patriarchal power. Among the Tswana, for example, women remained legal minors all their lives. Access to land depended on the goodwill of their husband's family. Women were barred from the ward or chiefly court and thus rendered politically powerless. Severe beatings by fathers and husbands received no social censure. Although nominally protected by a web of obligations and dependencies, women who opposed male dominance lived in fear of abandonment and poverty.[2] Shona women also lacked legal rights, being essentially the wards of whichever male they lived with. "Good" women were deferential and obedient to men.[3] Islamic societies, though guaranteeing women certain inheritance rights, constrained many female economic and political activities through *purdah*, or ritual seclusion. Most women had to manage their property through men. In precolonial Mombasa, for example, women rarely held public positions of authority and were prohibited from holding religious offices.[4]

However, in many precolonial societies some women did wield considerable influence and even authority. In these societies women usually controlled certain economic tasks. For example, although men had more authority in hunting and gathering societies, women controlled certain important economic tasks and exerted considerable influence over group decisions.[5] In agricultural societies where women controlled certain productive areas, such as farming, marketing or trading, their power and authority seem to have been largely based on this very control. In matrilineal societies women often had considerable security of land tenure. Among the Tonga in Southern Zambia, for example, although a woman's wealth was often in her brothers' custody, she had her own fields and granary as well as control over grain production. This control over land enabled women to command the labor and allegiance of sons and sons-in-law and facilitated access to political power. Some women even became village headwomen.[6]

Societies that permitted women to accumulate wealth often had political institutions which not only protected them but also enabled them to exert influence. These groups gave women a sense of solidarity and self-worth along with the capacity to protect female interests in the community. Some societies even developed dual-sex systems which gave women a formal role in the political process.[7] In Yorubaland, for example, the *Iyalode* had jurisdication over all women and represented women's concerns on the king's council, an institution otherwise dominated by men.[8] Among the Ewe of Ghana an elected Queen Mother had a council of elderly women as advisers and a linguist to speak for her—exactly as did the male chief. Thus, although women could only speak to the council of male elders through the Queen Mother and the males kept decision making and initiatives in their own hands, women (especially from powerful lineages) had a representative who could seek to influence male councils.[9]

Some women held high political office, either through heredity or election. Their authority never or rarely equaled that of male officials, but they nonetheless wielded considerable power and some authority. The Queen Mother was often an important position, as evidenced by her role among the Asante, Baganda and the Zulu, to cite a few examples. These women not only influenced male-dominated councils; they often had important ritual roles, especially those concerned with fertility and social survival. While women chiefs were rare, they did exist. Among the Mende and Serbro of Sierra Leone, women held chiefships on the same basis as men. As we have seen, influential Tonga women set themselves up as village headwomen. Able women acquired power in a number of African societies. For example, Queen Amina of Hausaland was a famous ruler and warrior in the fifteenth or sixteenth century, and Nzinga of Angola led one of the earliest and most effective resistances against the Portuguese.[10]

Women also exerted power through religious roles. Some women were ritual specialists in women's affairs. The *omu* among the Igbo of Nigeria, for example, used medicines and rituals to ensure the safety and success of the marketplace where women traded. Women were often in charge of puberty rites, marriage ceremonies and other aspects of the life cycle.[11] They acted as mediums and members of spirit possession cults. Some led resistance movements against the early European intruders. Nehanda, a Shona priestess, was hung for her role in the 1896 uprising in Southern Rhodesia. In Kongo a priestess of the cult of Marinda, Dona Beatrice, established her own version of Christianity and led a rebellion against the pro-Portuguese Kongo leadership. This rebellion mobilized discontent so effectively that the Kongo king had her and her infant son burned to death.[12]

Thus, while some precolonial African societies severely constrained women's political and economic power, many others awarded women clearly defined and accepted political roles which permitted them to wield power despite fairly minimal authority. In addition, societies that awarded women political power generally also permitted them some control over the economy.

Women and the Colonial State

For most African women (with the exception of some urban women) the colonial period was characterized by significant losses in both power and authority. Colonial officials accepted Western gender stereotypes which assigned women to the domestic domain, leaving economic and political matters to men. As a result, although many African men suffered under colonialism, new opportunities eventually appeared for them, while women's economic and political rights often diminished. Colonial officials ignored potential female candidates for chiefships, scholarships and other benefits. Many female institutions were destroyed, often more out of ignorance than malice. In Igboland, for example, the male *obi* became a salaried official, while his female counterpart received nothing. Similar reductions in female political power occurred all over Africa during the colonial period.[13]

This loss of political power was frequently associated with diminished access to land and labor power. Colonial development policies focused on men, who were, in the eyes of colony officials, the farmers and producers of Africa. When land rights were reorganized, "legitimate" heads of house-holds, namely men, usually received the land titles. Marcia Wright carefully documents how women in Mazabuka, Zambia, lost both their economic and political power during the colonial period. Similarly, in Western Kenya new property laws reduced women's rights to land. In Zimbabwe and South Africa colonial "reform" resulted in the transfer of women's land to men. Colonial authorities assisted male farmers while often dismissing female farmers as mere subsistence food producers. When colonial officials wanted to encourage African cash crop production, they offered male farmers technical training and assistance but ignored women farmers. As a result, male farmers were more able to accumulate surplus and thus increasingly dominated the rural areas.[14]

Women frequently continued to work on the land, but their control over the products of their labor declined. They often produced cash crops without reaping the profits, while, of course, continuing to grow food and perform domestic duties for their families. Marjorie Mbilinyi reports that in Tanzania "rich peasant wives . . . often lived like poor women, not sharing in the wealth they created."[15] In Zambia, Shimwaayi Muntemba discovered that men "uniformly and consistently returned only a small proportion of agricultural income to their wives, in amounts varying between one-tenth and one-quarter of the total income."[16] In Southern Zambia prosperous farmers gained labor power through polygamy, but wives were often treated "less as partners than as farmhands." Wives still clung to marriage because divorce entailed abandoning all marital property.[17]

Thus, while traditional structures protected most women from absolute starvation, rural life was increasingly onerous for many women during the colonial period. Pushed by patriarchal authoritarianism and rural drudgery, and pulled by rumored economic and social opportunities in the towns, many enterprising women voted with their feet and moved to the urban areas. Despite opposition from government officials and chiefs, many women managed to migrate to towns and once there to support themselves. Of course some found men to support them, but this arrangement was always uncertain, for divorce and desertion were rampant.[18] Most women recognized the need for some economic autonomy. Educational barriers limited opportunities for white-collar jobs, teaching and nursing being the exceptions. All but the most unskilled and irregular wage labor remained a male preserve. Consequently, women were shunted into the informal sector, where they sold goods and services, including their bodies. Some became wealthy, especially the market women in West Africa, but the majority worked long hours merely to survive.[19]

The few success stories should not lead us to underestimate the problems faced by African women in colonial towns, but at the same time we must acknowledge the degree to which women successfully challenged both African and colonial authority in the towns. Ga woman dominated the expanding Ghanaian trading system during the colonial period.[20] The Lagos Market Women's Association (LMWA) was established in the 1920s, and it remained an important political and economic force in Nigeria until its leaders shifted their focus to nationalist politics in the late 1940s.[21] Prostitution provided another avenue of accumulation. Nairobi prostitutes earned enough money during World War I to purchase urban property. In 1943 women (mostly prostitutes) owned 41 percent of the houses in the Nairobi suburb of Pumwani. In Mombasa village women accumulated savings from prostitution and used this money to buy property in both Mombasa and their native villages. Similar patterns existed among the Hausa in western Nigeria.[22]

However, as colonial penetration of African economies intensified in the late 1930s and the "second colonial occupation" increased the need for a stable, disciplined and trained labor force, colonial authorities in the urban areas became more determined to control both the reproduction and production of labor. In collusion with patriarchal African leaders, colonial laws were tightened in order to increase control over women in rural and urban areas. Independent African women posed a threat to both African and European men. The regulation of these women was carried out on two fronts.

First, laws were enacted which made it more difficult for women to subsist independently in urban areas. Houses owned by prostitutes in Nairobi were condemned and razed. Beer production, usually controlled by women, was taken over by the state. Hostile legislation constrained market women's economic opportunities.[23] In Zambia African leaders supported a reinterpretation of customary law which made adultery a criminal offense and enforced harsh fines to curb it, thus limiting women's freedom to change partners. The Urban African Courts, established in 1938, gave rural judges the power to strengthen customary control over urban marriages and consequently to regulate "proud and cheeky" urban women.[24] In Tanzania wives of polygamous marriages were denied legal married status and consequently the rights accorded a wife, especially those related to divorce and inheritance. Yet customary law permitted men to marry several wives. Similar cases existed in other parts of Africa.[25]

Second, colonial officials constrained the advancement of women by limiting their access to education and wage employment. Ga women, for example, lost ground as men gained the education necessary for wage employment and capital accumulation.[26] Throughout the colonial period most African women consistently lagged behind in education and thus failed to acquire the skills needed to participate in the modern economy. When they received training, it usually emphasized domestic skills and preparation to become "better wives and mothers." Few women became qualified for wage labor and even fewer for professional positions. Employed women usually performed low-paying, unskilled jobs connected to the domestic area. Thus, as these regulations took force, the status and potential prosperity of men and women increasingly diverged.[27]

Women struck back against this attack on their economic and political prerogatives, but rarely effected long-term change. It is worth noting, however, that most of the more dramatic female opposition to colonial authority was carried out by women from societies where status differentials of men and women were small enough that it was not unthinkable for women to challenge male authority. Indeed, women often used traditional female methods and organizations to oppose colonial authorities, both black and white. In 1929–1930, for example, Igbo women used the institution of "sitting on a man" (public humiliation of men by a group of women) to protest taxes. In the famous "Igbo Riots" women burned buildings, broke into jails and released prisoners. Officials called in the military, but the fighting continued, eventually leaving 50 women dead and another 50 wounded.[28] Pare women in Tanzania rioted to protest the levying of a graduated income tax in the 1940s. The women organized a 25-mile march to district headquarters, and once there, they stoned colonial officials, demanded settlement of the matter and created so much trouble that a compromise had to be reached.[29] Kikuyu women, who came from a relatively egalitarian society, were instrumental in the 1922 Harry Thuku disturbances.[30]

Women with an independent economic base were the most successful opponents of colonial sexism. In Western Nigeria the Lagos Market Women's Association (LMWA) organized the first mass-based women's interest group in the area. Led by the dynamic Madam Alimotu Pelewura, the LMWA controlled the marketing system and carefully monitored both chiefly and colonial policies in order to protect market women's interests. From 1940 to 1944 the Association openly opposed government price controls, eventually leading to their removal. The Abeokuta Women's Union (AWU) is another example of an influential women's organization. Incorporating a broad spectrum of Abeokuta's female population, from market women to elite members of the Ladies' Club, the AWU could command the support of 80,000 to 100,000 women. The union set about trying to recoup the steady erosion of female power that had occurred during the colonial period when indirect rule had raised men to new heights. In 1946 the AWU launched an attack on indirect rule and that British lackey the Alake of Abeokuta. The AWU organized sit-ins, mass protests, nonpayment of taxes, and even sent its leader, Funmilayo Anikulapo-Kuti, to London to present her case. By 1948 these efforts had succeeded. The Alake resigned, female taxation was suspended and women were given representation in the interim council set up to replace the government.[31] These cases prove that some women successfully mobilized themselves, both in new ways and around traditional institutions, and used their prosperity and influence to counter the colonial threat to their social status.

However, even wealthy and/or well-organized women often lost the battle against colonial patriarchy. Despite their property ownership and low public profile, the malaya prostitutes in Nairobi gradually lost both their property and livelihood through government intervention. Ga women traders were unable to resist government encroachment on their market rights in the 1950s.[32] South African women delayed the hated pass laws for women, but eventually lost out to apartheid.[33] Women had few patrons in the male-dominated colonial state, and even wealthy women could be quashed if various state interests agreed to their destruction.

For most women the colonial state was something to avoid or to deal with indirectly, usually through male patrons. Women had little opportunity to participate in the state as civil servants or, later, as representatives. As we have seen, women's organizations pressured government, but for the most part could effect only limited change. Most women had to work out their solutions on an individual basis. They jockeyed for power within the household, changed husbands, moved to the city, entered trade and fought to improve the lives of their children. Alliances with powerful men and with male-dominated institutions, such as trade unions and separatist churches, provided some support. But for most women economic and social security had to be continually won, because both male-dominated institutions and the state were uncertain allies.

However, these individual and collective protests against colonial domination show that many African women tried to resist encroachment on their rights and that individual women, female political institutions and ad hoc groups of women could mount effective protest against colonial and patriarchal domination. Thus, although women often lost authority and power during the colonial period, the loss was neither even nor linear. Despite efforts to contain them, some women achieved economic prosperity, and many more economic autonomy, even if minimal. Women were thus willing, if often unsuccessful, combatants against colonial and patriarchal domination.

Women and the Nationalist Struggles

African women were often given the opportunity to prove their mettle as political activists during the nationalist struggles. Many responded to the challenge with commitment, enthusiasm and effective collective action. Women played a prominent role in the early nationalist struggles in West, East and Central Africa. In Zambia, for example, women's branches of the nationalist parties (first the African National Congress [ANC] and later the United National Independence Party [UNIP]) organized rural and urban protests. The UNIP Women's Brigade participated in literacy drives to aid voter registration and helped organize town funerals, mass demonstrations, rallies and boycotts to prove UNIP's power.[34] In Cameroon women used a traditional practice, *anlu*, revamped into a well-organized association, to render the paramount chief and his executive council ineffective, to unseat the ruling party, the Kamerun National Congress (KNC), in the 1959 election and to help get the Kamerun National Democratic Party (KNDP) into power.[35] In Nigeria market women's support or rejection of political candidates became a key factor in political life. Oyinkan Morenike Abayomi, leader of women's organizations from the 1920s, established the Nigerian Women's Party (NWP) in 1944 in order to protect women from being cheated by Nigerian men and the government. She believed women, even wealthy women, suffered from lack of representation in government circles and set about to rectify that situation. Ultimately, the party foundered from competition with the more militant Abeokuta Women's Union and the more radical nationalist movements. But Nigerian women continued to be important members of the new nationalist parties.[36] In Guinea women helped Sékou Touré gain power by donating money to the nationalist struggle, providing communication links among the leaders and participating in policy decisions. Guinean women, like many West African women, supported the nationalist struggle with their economic resources and contacts.[37]

Women also participated in more violent liberation struggles. In the Portuguese colonies women fought alongside men, while continuing to perform domestic duties. They bore a double burden in order to bring down colonial rule.[38] Zimbabwean women also carried arms, and women guerrillas had a high status during the liberation struggle. By the end of the war as much as one quarter of the 30,000 Patriotic Front guerrillas were women. Leaders from the different factions declared women's liberation an explicit and integral part of the overall revolution.[39] In South Africa women of all races resisted—and continue to resist—apartheid and racial injustice. The Bantu Women's League of the ANC led the fight against racial injustice in the 1950s. Despite frequent hostility from men both within and outside the ANC, women such as Charlotte Maxeke provided remarkable leadership on women's and black peoples' issues. Today Winnie Mandela provides similar leadership.[40]

Women and the State in Independent Africa

During the liberation struggles women's participation was usually welcomed, and they were promised (and expected) economic and political benefits from independence. These promises, for the most part, have failed to materialize. Some African women are prominent in political affairs, but rarely at the highest levels. Even well-educated women usually occupy the lowest rungs of the political ladder; very few are involved in planning and policymaking. In 1978 a U.N. questionnaire discovered that the mean rate of political participation by women was 12 percent at the local level and 6 percent at the national level. In nonsocialist countries about 5 percent or less of the available political positions are filled by women.[41] In Malawi, for example, there are no women in the three central planning agencies or in any of the ministerial planning units. Women are thus effectively excluded from the planning and planning-related machinery, although a few provide some input from their positions in such traditionally female-dominated areas as home economics, adult literacy, social welfare and health. Representation on lower levels is not much better. Of the 625 wards in Malawi, only 4.8 percent are filled by women, and although some women are active in village affairs, men dominate decision making there as well. In Zambia the Women's Brigade organizers in UNIP have mainly been backstage supporters for male politicians. The few women in high level politics have clustered in traditional female areas, such as welfare and health. Ghanaian market women, even those with considerable wealth, have hardly participated in the independent Ghanaian state.[42]

Despite official support, women in socialist states are not much better off. Women in Guinea-Bissau have had to fight two forms of colonialism: white-Portuguese domination and black patriarchy. Although Samora Machel stated unequivocally that liberation must include liberation for women, Mozambique's economic and political problems, together with its patriarchal traditions, undermined his and Frelimo's efforts. Frelimo group leaders are rarely women. Of the 249 delegates elected to Frelimo's Third Congress in 1977, only 12.2 percent from the provincial level and 7.5 percent on the Central Committee were women. Although women have been encouraged to join the party and some improvements have occurred at the local level, at the national level, where authority and power predominate, women are conspicuously absent. There is no ministry for women, and the only structure that might evaluate development plans for women, the Organization of Mozambican Women (OMW, founded in 1973) is rarely consulted.[43] The Organization of Angolan Women (OMA, founded in 1963) is a respected voice in Angolan government deliberations, but a National Congress meeting recently admitted that despite ostensibly sex-blind policies, "the principle of equality for men and women in society is *not* sufficient to ensure that women are in fact an active element in their country's development or that they participate equally in decision making."[44] Women's demonstrations have been a potent political weapon in Zimbabwe, albeit one that has won powers for men rather than women. The Ministry for Women's Affairs created in 1981 has achieved little, despite nominal government support. Feminists in government have retreated from challenges to gender ideologies and the sexual division of labor and have turned to more reformist goals. Isolated and outnumbered, "feminist leaders have generally been separated out from broader policymaking bodies, allowing other government branches to ignore the differential impact of their policies on women."[45]

Thus, socialist countries advocate political involvement by women but fail to achieve it. Liberal capitalist states promise women equality through the vote, but men continue to dominate. Military governments advocate development but usually ignore women. Meanwhile, the vast majority of poor rural women have no access to the state, and even though middle- and upper-class women have greater access, they rarely enter political life. The African state has become essentially a male preserve. We need to ask the question why.

Barriers to Women in Politics

The lackluster political participation of women in independent Africa is most readily explained by their continued lack of credentials for political and civil service positions, especially formal education and work experience. This is partially a colonial legacy, which has changed depressingly little since independence. Female illiteracy is almost twice that of men. In most African countries the ratio of females to males enrolled in secondary education is less than 35 percent, while the ratio is less than 20 percent at higher levels. Furthermore, available education frameworks continue to shunt women into traditionally female occupations, such as health care (especially nursing), domestic science and primary school teaching. Even more distressing, primary and intermediate school education often fails to prepare girls for any kind of employment, leaving this population with the highest unemployment rate in Africa. Thus, formal education for women in Africa is all too often both insufficient and dysfunctional.[46]

African women are also constrained by their limited economic opportunities. Few hold important economic positions, and with the exception of traditionally "female" occupations, few women are professionals. In the mid-1970s a mere 5 percent of the lawyers, physicians and engineers in Kenya were women; only 6 percent of Nigerian academic staff were women, and they were primarily concentrated in education and the arts. Opportunities for wage labor are few, and even those women with equivalent education and work experience still receive lower wages and slower advancement than men.[47] In the urban informal sector some women have fared better, but here again the majority still eke out a precarious existence. In Yorubaland, for example, while women dominate the open market and many have retail stores, men own the more capital-intensive shops. In Islamic areas *purdah* further hampers women's economic activities.[48] Thus, many women continue to have less access to higher education, job experience and capital accumulation than men, which limits their capacity to compete for jobs that might lead to positions of authority and power within the state.

There are other, more subtle but still important, factors affecting female participation in state affairs. Women are constrained by a sexual division of labor which burdens them with domestic duties whether employed in wage labor or not. This double burden saps women's energies and limits the amount of time and effort available to them to engage in political matters. In rural areas the sexual division of labor has meant more work and less remuneration for African women. Rural women contribute 70 percent of the labor for food production, while remaining solely responsible for food processing. Work in cash crop production is performed with no let up in obligations to produce and prepare food, not to mention child care and other domestic duties. Poor urban women usually work in the informal sector, where they can earn a living while also caring for children and the household.[49] Even middle-class women with household help still have to organize that help and cope with the inevitable crises that disrupt domestic arrangements. Studies of urban working mothers report "fatigue, stress and even anxiety," and high levels of dissatisfaction with child-care arrangements.[50] Limiting family size is still unpopular, and since birth control is rarely available, family planning is difficult. Political life demands both time and energy. Most women cannot cope with both political and family obligations.

Less obvious but also important, Western gender stereotypes and traditional patriarchal institutions have combined to deprive women of political legitimacy. Even where women are legally equal to men, male predominance continues to be assumed. When some women dare challenge this fact, they are sharply rebuked. Witness the recent attack by President Moi of Kenya, who chastised women leaders for "misleading rural women by saying women should be the equal to men." He stated that "to be equal to men was to imply that God had erred after all when he made men the head of the family."[51] One (Tanzanian) MP even stated that "women were meant to serve men and that they can never be equal to men."[52] Similar sentiments have been expressed in Zambia, where in 1982 Prime Minister Mundia advised a new bride that "women graduates should regard themselves as housewives and mothers at home and professionals only at places of work. . . . The husband is the head of the family."[53] In Mozambique, Stephanie Urdang reports that:

> [women] often have to take a bold leap in the present to assert themselves as militants. Often this has to be done against strong pressure from antagonistic husbands. . . . Some men have even resorted to physical restraint, locking their wives in the house to prevent them from attending meetings, and some women have been beaten or thrown out of their homes by husbands for persisting in their regular attendance.[54]

Although rarely official policy, such attitudes pervade the continent and seriously impede women's capacity to undertake political work.

Protests from women are smothered in nationalist or socialist rhetoric that denies the legitimacy of female concerns and exhorts women to accept the inevitable connection between social and sexual justice. Yet at the same time, Zimbabwean revolutionaries, who once linked women's oppression with class oppression, now see government's goal as "helping women become better mothers and citizens within the existing family structures." Mozambican women are constantly reminded that their liberation depends on involvement in the "main transforming task of society;" yet they are advised not to demand changes in the sexual division of labor within the home. And women's bureaus, where they exist, are usually underfunded and underutilized. Linked to the soft underbelly of government, they rarely affect important decisions, and like the aged and infirm, get the leftovers.[55]

Consequences of Underrepresentation in the State

Having established African women's limited participation in government, we are faced with two questions: how does this affect the status of African women, and what, if any, strategies do they employ to deal with this situation?

The most important consequences of underrepresentation for women lie, I believe, in the economic and legal spheres. Although most African countries have awarded women political rights and equal access to education, a gender-biased mixture of colonial and customary law still operates in many countries, especially in matters concerning land, marriage, divorce and inheritance. Given women's lack of involvement in government structures, it is not surprising that state laws reflect male dominance and male-dominated legislatures have been reluctant to undercut patriarchal traditions. Women's groups have lobbied legislatures, but with little success. For example, in 1970 delegates to the Consultation of Women's Rights in Zambia recommended specific legislation to protect women; yet virtually none of it has been passed.[56] Despite official commitment to a socialist, nonsexist society, the Zimbabwean government has refused to change customary land rights in its land resettlement scheme. The Zimbabwean Women's Bureau has protested and women in general have complained bitterly about the scheme, but to no avail. The state has, so far, done nothing, and customary land-tenure practices continue to discriminate against women. Polygamy and *lobola* are still legal in most African countries. Male-dominated parliaments have refused to attack these institutions. In Zimbabwe, for example, government promises to challenge brideprice have evaporated under pressure from male parliamentarians and other leaders.[57] In Tanzania the Marriage Act has reconstituted patriarchal relations of marriage as the legitimate form of state marriage.[58] While legal protection for women varies from state to state, in general women's rights have remained a low priority item despite considerable lobbying from women's groups. This has been especially true for widows, who remain one of Africa's most vulnerable groups.[59]

Even where laws have been changed, states are often unwilling to protect women from sexist traditions. Nigerian widows are still plundered by their deceased husbands' rapacious relatives despite regulations to the contrary.[60] Even women willing to fight for their children find it difficult to win divorce cases, particularly against rich and powerful men. In Zambia, for example, such men are able to flout the law and frequently obtain custody of their children beyond infancy despite the mother's protests. Sexual harrassment at work goes unpunished. Women are denied jobs and opportunities because of their sex, but they can neither prove this nor stop it.[61] The Angolan Women's Organization has cited numerous cases where women were refused jobs because employers did not want to pay for maternity leaves.[62] Tanzanian women workers in the cashew nut industry have struggled in vain to stop the periodic firing of certain categories of women.[63] Women tend to cluster in unskilled, vulnerable wage labor, such as domestic work and small-scale retailing, where they are unlikely to have the resources or leverage necessary to use the legal protection theoretically available to them.[64] This, of course, reinforces female vulnerability and powerlessness. Inadequate representation in government and the consequent inability to exert pressure on legislators make it all the more difficult for most women to defend themselves.

Underrepresentation has important economic consequences as well. Property laws continue to favor men. As we have seen, the Zimbabwean resettlement scheme has perpetuated women's inadequate customary land rights.[65] By allocating land to male family heads, the Land Reform Proclamation in Ethiopia has failed to transform the subordinate status of women. Instead, "land reform has left women dependent on men and under the umbrella of old patriarchal forms." Mozambique's Land Law of 1979 failed to establish, clarify or reinforce women's rights to land.[66] Similar scenarios abound throughout the continent, and according to J. A. Hellen, a student of African land law, women's legal position in relation to land is likely to worsen in the future, particularly if their important role in agriculture is ignored.[67] Thus, the state has made it more difficult for women to acquire and profit from land.

Women's underrepresentation in government has also permitted development planners to ignore women's special needs and concerns. In an atmosphere where such needs and concerns are rarely discussed and where the few female civil servants and legislators find it difficult to raise women's issues, gender-biased planning readily becomes the norm.[68] African governments have often adopted colonial gender biases that relegate women's issues to the private, rather than the public, sphere. Much of women's productive activity in agriculture and trade is not measured by economic planners because it is "for the family." Access to land, credit, agricultural training and education is offered to families on the assumption that women and men have equal access to family resources. Gender struggles within the household are not government's concern. As a result, government policies provide benefits to male heads of households and development plans continue to benefit men more than women.[69] Furthermore, governments frequently ignore women as economic actors and fail to provide them with economic incentives, such as credit, import-export licenses, and tax rebates, so often granted to "well-connected" African businessmen. Even when development plans include women's issues, inadequate representation for women's interests on key decision-making bodies at all levels makes it difficult to change resource allocation patterns.[70]

Women in postindependence African states continue to be prime targets for state abuse. Despite their wealth, Ghanaian market women were scapegoated by Rawlings' "reformists" and attacked as symbols of wealth, while much more affluent businessmen and male bureaucrats escaped. Although the market women fought back and won, Claire Robertson in *Sharing the Same Bowl* documents general economic decline for Ga female traders since independence.[71] Prostitutes, often comprising one of the more prosperous and independent sectors of the female population, also endure frequent attacks by government officials who dislike their independence and see them as safe targets, easily characterized as evil temptresses bent on destroying society's moral fabric. Single women are also frequently branded as prostitutes, making them more vulnerable to arrest and prosecution. The urban woman remains an easy scapegoat who is highly visible and relatively powerless— that is, an obvious target of male dominance and traditional patriarchal values.[72]

Strategies to Cope with the State

Despite their underrepresentation in the state and their difficulties controlling and benefiting from it, African women have not simply acquiesced to state power. They have fought back, both individually and collectively. One common solution has been selective withdrawal. Many women have chosen to avoid the increasingly rapacious, badly run African bureaucracies by withdrawing from politics and concentrating instead on the more immediate issue of survival. Economic matters have become their major concern. Ghanaian market women often ignore conventional politics, preferring to concentrate on their economic associations. Nigerian market women have organized themselves and avoid the government. Many no longer vote, inasmuch as politics is viewed as a man's game.

The state is generally seen as an impediment to progress and is treated as a potential threat, rather than as a source of support. The West African market women have organized to protect themselves *from* the state, not to get closer to it. For example, in 1982 Accra market women withdrew their services until the state returned their control over pricing and the market.[73] Nonetheless, reacting to government differs from attempting to integrate with it. In other parts of Africa the story is the same. Poor Zambian women seem indifferent to participation in national development plans; they are preoccupied with economic survival instead.[74] In Kenya Kathy Staudt has discovered that rural women frequently organize to protect their economic interests but that these organizations usually operate outside the political system. "This autonomy may be an asset in organizational effectiveness but [is] a drawback in extracting the increasingly valuable resources distributed in the policy arena."[75] Everywhere in Africa individual effort and children remain women's most reliable social insurance and consequently their most pressing concern.

It is hardly surprising that many marginal women are also increasingly active in the illegal economy, insofar as it is an arena which deliberately avoids state control. This can be as simple as selling goods without a license. Christine Obbo reports that many poor women in Kampala survive by illegally selling beer, goods and even sexual services, and that some even enter more lucrative illegal activities, such as gin distilling.[76] And Janet MacGaffey describes Zairian women's participation in the flourishing *magendo* economy in their country.[77] Prostitution, of course, remains a common means for escaping patriarchal authority and accumulating wealth.[78] While data for these activities are difficult to acquire, there is no doubt that many women, especially the uneducated, have responded to declining opportunities in the wage economy by moving into the grey area of illegal trade.

The state cannot be entirely avoided, however, and most women employ an age-old strategy to increase their leverage over the state—aligning with powerful men. This solution is more readily available to elite women, who are often either related or married to influential men. But even poor women can gain some entrée to state power through association with powerful male members of their ethnic or regional communities. As Kenneth Little has pointed out, "the acquisition of a well-to-do, much travelled professional husband has become part of the West African women's 'dream.'" For the less fortunate, a politically well-connected nonprofessional is an acceptable substitute.[79] Obbo and Schuster have discovered similar attitudes in Zambia and Uganda, though usually tempered with some cynicism.[80] While this solution fails to alter fundamental sexual inequities, it remains attractive because it can be pursued in a wide variety of circumstances and mitigates the more difficult problem of coordinating collective action against the status quo. It is, of course, quite attractive to elite women, and holds the hope of individual upward mobility to the poor.

Women and the State: New Directions

While the above-mentioned strategies provide some leverage, African women are demanding more. They are becoming increasingly assertive in relation to the state. International concern about the status of women, spearheaded by the United Nations' Decade for Women 1975–1985, and the growing economic crisis in Africa have brought women's issues increasingly to the fore in the last ten years. Conferences, seminars and research projects have been organized. National programs have been devised and women's institutes have been set up.[81] On the continental level the OAU's development plan, the *Lagos Plan of Action*, devotes an entire chapter to women. It recognizes the importance of women in all areas of development and calls for measures to integrate them fully into the development strategies of Africa, including placing more women directly into positions of authority so that women's views and concerns will be incorporated into development planning.[82]

Have these efforts succeeded at all? Data collection on women has improved and some projects are underway, but progress is slow. The impediments discussed above continue to inhibit sexual equality. At recent regional meetings African women leaders and some sympathetic men admitted that advancement has been discouraging and that bold steps must be taken to improve women's status. The Regional Conference on Women and Development, held in Arusha, Tanzania, on October 8–12, 1984, called for better data and development plans that recognize women's diverse circumstances. The assistance educated middle-class women need is very different from that needed by rural women heads of households. Similarly, the policies poor urban women seek are different from those sought by women subsistence farmers. Above all, women must participate in drawing up development plans so that they reflect female realities and provide appropriate services.

But if this is to happen, African women, like women everywhere, must come to their own rescue. The *Lagos Plan of Action*, the U.N. Decade for Women and other women's development projects can only remove some obstacles. Power is rarely abandoned easily, and few men will readily accept changes that are unfavorable (to themselves) in the established power structure and the sexual division of labor. Women have made advances: As the Arusha delegates recognized, "women's visibility to society and their awareness of themselves" has increased.[83] But women will have to make a conscious effort to mobilize female participation in state affairs, especially high-level planning and policy decision making, if further advances are to be achieved.

This need is increasingly being recognized by women all over the African continent. Participants at a recent workshop at Ibadan University's International Institute of Tropical Agriculture, for example, emphasized that programs about women's issues must be "planned by women, organized, interpreted and reported by women on women."[84] Similar statements are being made more and more frequently at international, continental and regional meetings by women's organizations, in markets and at village meetings, especially in the recently turned socialist countries. At the First Congress of the Organization of Angolan Women (OMA) held in 1983, the OMA resolved that "profound changes in social, political and economic structures are the precondition for achieving equality in every sphere." The OMA called on its members to work for "women's full participation in the country's political, economic and social life."[85] Similar statements have been made by Mozambican, Zimbabwean, and Eritrean women's organizations.[86] Women in more capitalist countries have been increasingly outspoken, as well. Kenyan women's organizations recently called for sexual equality in all spheres of Kenyan life. In Nigeria the second annual Women in Nigeria conference, held in April 1983, committed the organization to "engage in research, policy-making, dissemination of information, and action aimed at improving the conditions of women."[87] While none of these resolutions have as yet brought about much change, and impediments continue to inhibit change in both socialist and nonsocialist countries, the resolve of African women for a fairer deal is definitely growing. And that resolve includes the recognition that women will have to become more active in state affairs.

Despite growing consensus among African women, differences of class, ethnicity and region still curtail female solidarity and inhibit effective organization. Political divisions along ethnic or regional lines tend to divide women in a similar manner. Class divisions also endanger female solidarity. Even if some women achieve positions of power and authority within the state, there is a real danger that these women will pursue the rights and prerogatives of women of their class while ignoring the plight of the vast majority of poor women. This is all the more probable in Africa, where the gap between elite and mass living standards is painfully obvious and the fight for resources is a deadly business. This is a danger that cannot be ignored or avoided, for elite women are strategically the most likely to gain access to state power and thus remain crucial participants in the struggle for sexual equality.

On the other hand, several factors draw African women of all classes together. First, as we have seen, the state is not readily accessible to either elite or nonelite women, and women with different backgrounds and education are increasingly understanding this. Protests against women's exclusion from power are being voiced by educated women and the female rural and urban poor alike. Peasant women in Tanzania "speak of their frustration over being excluded from village government," while Tanzanian feminists, such as Marjorie Mbilinyi and Ophelia Mascarenhas, criticize women's underrepresentation at the state level. Not only Arusha delegates are calling for change, but also peasant women of Mozambique and Zimbabwe.[88] The gap between rhetoric and reality is hitting especially hard in the new socialist countries of Southern Africa, where women had expected independence to engender a nonsexist world. They may be discouraged, but they have not given up.

Additionally, divorce and inheritance customs continue to undermine the class position of all but a small number of independently wealthy women. Most women suffer severe economic hardship upon divorce or widowhood. The high divorce rate and ever-present possibility of a spouse's death through accident or disease weaken the class position of elite women and often provide unwanted lessons about sexual inequality. Examples abound, creating anxiety that can lead women to cling to marriage as security but cannot fail to arouse fear and anger about women's vulnerability. It is not surprising that some of Botswana's most ardent advocates of women's rights are divorced female heads of households.[89]

Finally, and most important, over the last fifteen years declining commodity prices and the rising costs of energy and manufactured goods have weakened already inefficient and corrupt African governments. As states have become more corrupt, repressive and inefficient, people have increasingly withdrawn their support. More and more men and women view the African bureaucratic elite with jaundiced eyes. And as state power declines, women's economic power relative to the state is growing. Although those women who depend on elite men lose from the state's decline, most women do not. Women cannot lose power they never had. Meanwhile, the tasks women perform remain crucial for the survival of functioning subunits within shattered states. Women continue to grow the food, trade the goods and perform the household tasks necessary to sustain communities.

Given this reality, it seems reasonable to suggest that the current decline of the African state may benefit African women. Rebuilding weakened, destabilized states may spawn new alliances between the sexes, because attempts to rebuild the state of necessity involve those persons who produce the people and, increasingly, the goods needed to build an effective state in Africa—namely African women. Thus while women can never benefit in the long-run from a destabilized state, in the short-run such a condition may open possibilities for new alliances which strengthen women's positions within the state.

Conclusion

This chapter has shown that by and large African women have a different relationship to the state than men, and that despite ethnic, regional and class differences, women have been consistently underrepresented in African state affairs. This is not to say that women have been treated equally. Ethnic and class differences often affect women's access to the state. In precolonial Africa those societies which gave women a greater opportunity to control land and labor generally awarded women more power, although even this tended to be informal, rather than authoritative. However, during the colonial period Western gender stereotypes combined with patriarchal traditions to facilitate the reduction of female power and autonomy. Although women often fought back and gained economic autonomy in some instances, in general they lost political power during the colonial period.

It is no wonder then that, despite women's active and important role in the nationalist struggles, decolonization was essentially a transfer of power from one group of men to another. Consequently, African women have been underrepresented in the state and have reaped few of the benefits which the state provides. Many women have reacted to this inequity by pulling away from the state, concentrating on economic survival instead. For the most part, these women see the state as an obstacle to be avoided, rather than as a benefactor to be milked. To that end they have employed a wide variety of strategies to ensure their survival in the face of an often hostile, male-dominated state.

Withdrawal has not been the only solution,, however. Increasingly women from different classes, regions and ethnic groups have been speaking out and organizing against sexual injustices in African societies. This ground swell has been spawned by a number of factors: growing awareness of sexual inequality in Africa, revolutionary rhetoric, education, the rise of Western feminism and the U.N. Decade for Women. Revolutionary rhetoric has given women's rights new legitimacy, as has the U.N. Decade for Women. The much publicized plight of Third World women has heightened dissatisfaction with women's underdevelopment and has intensified the commitment of African women to better their lives. And increasingly these women recognize that better access to state power is an essential ingredient of any attack on the status quo.

This renewed activism is all the more important because the current decline of many African states has reduced the power of those who benefit from the state—namely men. The balance of power in shattered economies may be shifting to those people who can provide the necessary reproductive and productive labor for survival. Women, who have learned to live without the state, are well placed to lead this effort. Thus, women's disengagement from the state may provide a source of strength as the state declines. It will be interesting to see whether women can parlay their pivotal role in the current crisis into a more sexually egalitarian future. Given their widespread determination to do so, one can at least hope for such a possibility. But also given the historic tendency for the state to remain a male preserve, equal gender sharing of state power continues to be an elusive goal in Africa and throughout the world.

Notes

1. Jean O'Barr, "African Women in Politics," in Margaret Jean Hay and Sharon Stichter, eds., *African Women South of the Sahara* (London: Longman, 1984), pp. 140-143; Jane Collier, "Women in Politics," in Michelle Rosaldo and Louise Lamphere,

eds., *Women, Culture, and Society* (Stanford: Stanford University Press, 1974), pp. 89–97.

2. Margaret Kinsman, "Beasts of Burden: The Subordination of Southern Tswana Women, ca. 1800–1840," *Journal of Southern African Studies*, 10, 1 (October 1983): 50–54.

3. Gay W. Seidman, "Women in Zimbabwe: Postindependence Struggles," *Feminist Studies*, 10, 3 (Fall 1984): 420.

4. Margaret Strobel, *Muslim Women in Mombasa 1890–1975* (New Haven: Yale University Press, 1979), pp. 62–63, 76.

5. Jane Collier and Michelle Rosaldo, "Politics and Gender in Simple Societies," in Sherry Ortner and Harriet Whitehead, eds., *Sexual Meaning, The Cultural Construction of Gender and Sexuality* (Cambridge: Cambridge University Press, 1981), pp. 275–329.

6. J. Clyde Mitchell, "Land Tenure and Agriculture among the Machinga Yao," *Nyasaland Journal*, 2 (1952): 18–31; and Marcia Wright, "Technology, Marriage and Women's Work in the History of Maize-Growers in Mazabuka, Zambia: a Reconnaissance," *Journal of Southern African Studies*, 10, 1 (October 1983): 73–75.

7. Kamene Okonjo, "The Dual-Sex Political System in Operation: Igbo Women and Community Politics in Midwestern Nigeria," in Nancy J. Hafkin and Edna G. Bay, eds., *Women in Africa* (Stanford: Stanford University Press, 1976), pp. 45–59.

8. Bolanle Awe, "The Iyalode in the Traditional Yoruba Political System," in Alice Schlegel, ed., *Sexual Stratification: A Cross-Cultural View* (New York: Columbia University Press, 1977), pp. 144–195.

9. Jette Bukh, *The Village Woman in Ghana*, Centre for Development Research, Publication No. 1 (Uppsala: Scandanavian Institute of African Studies, 1979), p. 91.

10. David Sweetman, *Women Leaders in African History* (London: Heinemann, 1984), pp. 76–90, 22–27, 39–47; Carol Hoffer, "Mende and Sherbro Women in High Offices," *Canadian Journal of African Studies*, 6, 2 (1972): 151–164.

11. Okonjo, "Dual-Sex," p. 49; and Margaret Strobel, "Women in Religion and in Secular Ideology," in Hay and Stichter, *African Women*, pp. 87–100.

12. Sweetman, *Women Leaders*, pp. 39–54, 91–97.

13. Hafkin and Bay, *Women in Africa*, pp. 1–19; Okonjo, "Dual-Sex," pp. 46, 55–56; Maud Shimwaayi Muntemba, "Women and Agricultural Change in the Railway Region of Zambia: Dispossession and Counterstrategies, 1930–1970," in Edna G. Bay, ed., *Women and Work in Africa* (Boulder: Westview, 1982), p. 85.

14. Wright, "Technology," p. 73; Katherine S. Newman, "Women and Law: Land Tenure in Africa," in Naomi Black and Ann Baker Cottrell, eds., *Women and World Change* (Beverly Hills: Sage, 1981), pp. 125–132; Ester Boserup, *Women's Role in Economic Development* (New York: St. Martin's 1970), pp. 22, 59–61; Kathleen Staudt, "Agricultural Productivity Gaps: A Case Study of Male Preference in Government Policy Implementation," *Development and Change*, 9, 3 (July 1978): 441; and Margaret Jean Hay, "Women as Owners, Occupants, and Managers of Property in Colonial Western Kenya," in Margaret J. Hay and Marcia Wright, eds., *African Women and the Law: Historical Perspectives* (Boston University Papers on Africa, No. 7, 1982), pp. 110–111.

15. Marjorie Mbilinyi, "The Changing Position of Women in the African Labour Force," in Timothy M. Shaw and Olajide Aluko, eds., *Africa Projected: from Recession to Renaissance by the Year 2000?* (London: Macmillan, 1984), p. 175.

16. Maud Shimwaayi Muntemba, "Women as Food Producers and Suppliers in the Twentieth Century: the Case of Zambia," *Development Dialogue*, 1, 2 (1982): 40–41; Muntemba, "Women and Agricultural Change," p. 97.

17. Wright, "Technology," p. 83.

18. A.L. Epstein, *Urbanization and Kinship: The Domestic Domain on the Copperbelt of Zambia 1950–1956* (London: Academic, 1981), p. 291; and Kenneth Little, *African Women In Towns: An Aspect of Africa's Social Revolution* (Cambridge: Cambridge University Press, 1973), pp. 161–165.

19. Christine Obbo, *African Women: Their Struggle for Economic Independence* (London: Zed, 1980), pp. 101, 122–123, 144; Simi Afonja, "Changing Modes of Production and the Sexual Division of Labour among the Yoruba," *Signs*, 7, 2 (Winter 1981): 312–313; and Louise White, "Women's Domestic Labor in Colonial Kenya: Prostitution in Nairobi, 1909–1950" (Boston University African Studies Center, Working Paper No. 30, 1980).

20. Claire C. Robertson, *Sharing the Same Bowl: A Socioeconomic History of Women and Class in Accra, Ghana* (Bloomington: Indiana University Press, 1984), p. 15.

21. Cheryl Johnson, "Grass Roots Organizing: Women in Anticolonial Activity in Southwestern Nigeria," *African Studies Review*, 25, 2/3 (June/Sept. 1982): 137–143.

22. White, "Women's Domestic Labor," pp. 7, 10; Janet M. Bujra, "Women 'Entrepreneurs' of Early Nairobi," *Canadian Journal of African Studies*, 11, 2 (1975): 232–233; Abner Cohen, *Custom and Politics in Urban Africa* (London: Routledge and Kegan Paul, 1969); and Strobel, *Muslim Women*, pp. 138–147.

23. Louise White, "A Colonial State and an African Petty Bourgeoisie: Prostitution, Property and Class Struggle in Nairobi, 1936–1940," in Frederick Cooper, ed., *Struggle for the City: Migrant Labor, Capital, and the State in Urban Africa* (Beverly Hills: Sage, 1983), p. 178; and Robertson, *Sharing*, p. 16.

24. Martin Chanock, "Making Customary Law: Men, Women, and Courts in Colonial Northern Rhodesia," in Hay and Wright, *African Women and the Law*, pp. 60–65; and James M. Ault, Jr., "Making 'Modern' Marriage 'Traditional': State Power and the Regulation of Marriage in Colonial Zambia," *Theory and Society*, 12 (1983): 187–189.

25. Joan May, *Zimbabwean Women in Colonial and Customary Law* (Harare: Mambo Press, 1983); and Jane Rose K. Kikopa, "Law and the Status of Women in Tanzania" (Addis Ababa: UNECA, Research Series E.CN.14/ATRCW/Res/81/04, 1981), p. 5.

26. Robertson, *Sharing*, pp. 16, 142.

27. Kathleen Staudt, "Women's Politics and Capitalist Transformation in Subsaharan Africa," Women in International Development, Working Paper No. 54 (Lansing: Michigan State University, 1984), pp. 6, 9.

28. Judith Van Allen, "'Aba Riots' or Igbo 'Women's War'? Ideology, Stratification, and the Invisibility of Women," in Hafkin and Bay, *Women in Africa*, pp. 59–87.

29. Jean O'Barr, "Pare Women: A Case of Political Involvement," *Rural Africana*, 29 (1976): 121–134.

30. Audrey Wipper, "Riot and Rebellion among African Women: Three Examples of Women's Political Clout," mimeo (1982), pp. 28–30.

31. Johnson, "Grass Roots Organizing," pp. 138–158.

32. White, "A Colonial State," pp. 178–184; and Robertson, *Sharing*, pp. 16–18. The Malaya prostitutes in Nairobi's Pumwani location virtually mimicked marriage. All sales of domestic labor were made inside the woman's residence. This term came from coastal Swahili and referred to a form of prostitution rather than an ethnic group.

33. Cheryl Walker, *Women and Resistance in South Africa* (London: Onyx Press, 1982).

34. Peter Harries-Jones, *Freedom and Labour: Mobilization and Political Control on the Zambian Copperbelt* (Oxford: Blackwell, 1975), pp. 23–43, 64, 101–104; and Ilsa Schuster, "Constraints and Opportunities in Political Participation: The Case of Zambian Women," *Genévè-Afrique*, 21, 2 (1983): 13–19. The women's brigade staged half-nude demonstrations at Lusaka airport to protest the arrival of the Colonial Secretary, Mr. MacLeod. Mrs. B. C. Kankasa, "Report of the Development of the Status of Women" (Delivered at the First General Conference of the Women's Brigade, Lusaka, September 27–29, 1974.

35. Wipper, "Riot and Rebellion," pp. 33–34.

36. Johnson, "Grass Roots Organizing," pp. 143–146.

37. Margarita Dobert, "Liberation and the Women of Guinea," *African Report*, 15, 7 (1970): 26–28; and Cyprian Ekwensi, *Jagua Nana* (New York: Fawcett Premier, 1961).

38. Stephanie Urdang, *Fighting Two Colonialisms: Women in Guinea-Bissau* (New York: Monthly Review, 1979); Stephanie Urdang, "The Last Transition? Women and Development in Mozambique," *Review of African Political Economy*, Nos. 27/28 (1984): 8–32; Sonia Kruks and Ben Wisner, "The State, the Party and the Female Peasantry in Mozambique," *Journal of Southern African Studies*, 11, 1 (October 1984): 113–115; and Organization of Angolan Women (OMA), *Angolan Women Building the Future* (London: Zed, 1984), p. 30.

39. Nyaradzo Makamure, "The Women's Movement in Zimbabwe," *Journal of African Marxists*, 6 (October 1984): 74–87; and Seidman, "Women in Zimbabwe," p. 426.

40. Walker, *Women and Resistance*, pp. 26–32, 37–40.

41. O'Barr, "Women in Politics," p. 152; and Urdang, "Women and Development," p. 16.

42. David Hirschmann, *Women, Planning and Policy in Malawi* (U.N., ECA, ATRCW/82/27, 1984), pp. 9–11, 19–21; Schuster, "Constraints and Opportunities," p. 19; and Robertson, *Sharing*, p. 16.

43. Urdang, *Fighting Two Colonialisms*; Urdang, "Women and Development in Mozambique," pp. 13–14; and Kruks and Wisner, "The Female Peasantry in Mozambique," pp. 121–122.

44. OMA, *Angolan Women Building the Future*, p. 30.

45. Seidman, "Women in Zimbabwe," p. 430. Also see, Makamure, "Women's Movement in Zimbabwe," pp. 76–80.

46. Sue Ellen M. Charlton, *Women in Third World Development* (Boulder: Westview, 1984), pp. 155–159; World Bank, *World Development Report 1981* (Washington, D.C., 1981), pp. 46–47; and Claire Robertson, "Women's Education and Class Formation in Africa, 1950–1980," in Claire Robertson and Iris Berger, eds., *Women and Class in Africa* (New York: Holmes and Meier, 1986).

47. Beverly Lindsay, "Issues Confronting Professional African Women: Illustrations from Kenya," in Beverly Lindsay, ed., *Comparative Perspectives of Third World Women: the Impact of Race, Sex and Class* (New York: Praeger, 1980) p. 83; Mbilinyi, "Changing Position," p. 178; and Eleanor Fapohunda, "Male and Female Career Ladders in Nigerian Academia," Women in International Development, Working Paper No. 17 (Lansing: Michigan State University, 1983), p. 1.

48. Afonja, "Changing Modes," pp. 311–312; and Enid Schildkrout, "Dependence and Autonomy: The Economic Activities of Secluded Hausa Women in Kano, Nigeria," in Bay, *Women and Work*, pp. 63–65.

49. Zenebeworke Tadesse, "Studies on Rural Women in Africa: An Overview," in *Rural Development and Women in Africa* (Geneva: International Labor Office, 1984), pp. 65–71; and Robertson, *Sharing*, Chap. 3.

50. Eleanor R. Fapohunda, "The Child-Care Dilemma of Working Mothers in African Cities: The Case of Lagos, Nigeria," in Bay, *Women and Work*, p. 284.

51. *The Weekly Review,* Sept. 21, 1984, p. 10.

52. Kikopa, "Law and Status," p. 6.

53. *The Times of Zambia,* July 19, 1982.

54. Urdang, "Women and Development," p. 15.

55. Seidman, "Women in Zimbabwe," p. 420; Kruks and Wisner, "The Female Peasantry in Mozambique," pp. 117–118, 121; and Rayah Feldman, "Women's Groups and Women's Subordination: An Analysis of Policies Towards Rural Women in Kenya," *Review of African Political Economy,* Nos. 27/28 (1983): 76–82.

56. Schuster, "Constraints," p. 24.

57. Susie Jacobs, "Women and Land Resettlement in Zimbabwe," *Review of African Political Economy,* Nos. 27/28 (February 1984), 33–42; and Seidman, "Women in Zimbabwe," p. 432.

58. Ophelia Mascarenhas and Marjorie Mbilinyi, *Women in Tanzania: An Analytical Bibliography,* (Uppsala: Scandanavian Institute of African Studies, 1983), p. 23.

59. Ilsa G. Schuster, *New Women of Lusaka* (Palo Alto: Mayfield, 1979), p. 157; and Monica Munachonga, "The Conjugal Power Relationship: An Urban Case Study in Zambia," an unpublished summary of field research findings for Ph.D., University of Sussex (1983), p. 2.

60. Confidential personal communication, Nigeria, June 1984.

61. Schuster, *New Women,* 107–108; Mascarenhas and Mbilinyi, *Women in Tanzania,* pp. 22, 31–32.

62. *Angolan Women,* pp. 43–44.

63. Mascarenhas and Mbilinyi, *Women in Tanzania,* pp. 18–19.

64. Filomina Chioma Steady, "African Women, Industrialization and Another Development: A Global Perspective," *Development Dialogue,* 1, 2, (1982): 57–59.

65. Jacobs, "Women and Land Resettlement," p. 41.

66. Zenebeworke Tadesse, "The Impact of Land Reform on Women: The Case of Ethiopia," in Lourdes Beneria, ed., *Women and Development: the Sexual Division of Labor in Rural Societies* (New York: Praeger, 1982), pp. 205, 214; Kruks and Wisner, "The Female Peasantry in Mozambique," p. 122; Fama Hane Ba *et al.,* "The Impact of Territorial Administrative Reform on the Situation of Women in Senegal," in *Rural Development and Women in Africa,* p. 112; and Kikopa, "Law and Status," p. 51.

67. J.A. Hellen, "Legislation and Landscape: Some Aspects of Agrarian Reform and Agricultural Adjustment" in Phil O'Keefe and Ben Wiser, eds., *Land Use and Development* (London: International African Institute, 1977), pp. 55–73.

68. For a fuller discussion of this point see Boserup, *Women's Role in Economic Development*; and Barbara Rogers, *The Domestication of Women: Discrimination in Developing Societies* (London: Tavistock, 1980).

69. Staudt, "Women's Politics," pp. 10–11.

70. For an example of this in Sierra Leone see Franklyn Lisk and Yvette Stevens, "Government Policy and Women's Work in Sierra Leone," in Christine Oppong, ed., *Sex Roles, Population and Development in West Africa* (London: Zed Press, 1986), pp. 311, 322, 327.

71. Robertson, "Introduction" in *Sharing.* See also Barbara Lewis, "The Limitations of Group Activity among Entrepreneurs: The Market Women of Abidjan, Ivory Coast," in Hafkin and Bay, *Women in Africa.*

72. Audrey Wipper, "African Women, Fashion, and Scapegoating," *Canadian Journal of African Studies,* 6, 2 (1972): 338-339, 346-347.

73. Bukh, *Women in Ghana,* p. 93; Staudt, "Women's Politics," p. 15; and Robertson, *Sharing,* p. 241.

74. *The Times of Zambia,* Oct. 28, 1982; and Schuster, "Constraints," pp. 28-30.

75. Kathleen Staudt, "Administrative Resources, Political Patrons, and Redressing Sex Inequities: A Case from Western Kenya," *The Journal of Developing Areas,* 12, 4, (July 1978): 403.

76. Obbo, *African Women,* pp. 123, 128, 131-132, 136.

77. Janet MacGaffey, "Women in the Second Economy in Zaire," in S. Stichter and J. Parpart, *Patriarchy and Class: African Women in the Home and the Workforce* (Boulder, Colorado: Westview Press, forthcoming).

78. Janet M. Bujra, "Production, Property, Prostitution: 'Sexual Politics' in Atu," *Cahiers d'Études Africaines* 65, 17 (1977): 13-41.

79. Kenneth Little, "Voluntary Associations and Social Mobility among West African Women," *Canadian Journal of African Studies,* 6, 2 (1972): 276-277, 280.

80. Obbo, *African Women,* pp. 39-52; and Schuster, *New Women.*

81. Agnes A. Aidoo, "Workers and Women: The Neglected Majority in the Lagos Plan of Action," (Paper presented at the Dalhousie University Conference on the Lagos Plan of Action and the Final Act of Lagos and Africa's Future International Relations: Projections and Implications for Policy Makers, Halifax, Nova Scotia, Nov. 2-4, 1984).

82. *Lagos Plan of Action for the Economic Development of Africa 1980-2000* (Geneva: ILLS for the Organization of African Unity, 1981) Chap. 12.

83. Aidoo, "Workers and Women," pp. 6-14.

84. Bolanle Awe, "Women in the Lagos Plan of Action: A Neglected Majority? A Brief Review," (Paper presented at Dalhousie Conference on the Lagos Plan, Nov. 2-4, 1984); and ATRCW Update (Addis Ababa: UNECA, 084-153, June 1984).

85. *Angolan Women,* pp. 131, 139.

86. See articles and briefings in *Review of African Political Economy,* Nos. 27/28 (1984).

87. Briefing, "Women in Nigeria," *Review of African Political Economy,* Nos. 27/28 (1984): 138; also see *The Weekly Review,* Sept. 21, 1984.

88. Mascarenhas and Mbilinyi, *Women in Tanzania,* pp. 31, 65; Kruks and Wisner, "The Female Peasantry in Mozambique," pp. 115-118, 125; and Seidman, "Women in Zimbabwe," p. 427.

89. Barbara Brown, "The Development of a Women's Movement: Class and Gender in Botswana," (Paper presented at the Canadian Association of African Studies Meeting, Montreal, May 15-17, 1985).

PART FOUR

The Changing State in Africa: Government and International Perspectives

10

African States and the Politics of Inclusive Coalitions

Donald Rothchild and Michael W. Foley

In this chapter we seek to examine the problem of political effectiveness, reviewing common mechanisms for channeling state-society relations, including, most notably, prominent forms of "elite consensus" systems.[1] In particular, we ask how state elites, irrespective of the regime types they have adopted, can augment their capacity for governance, putting themselves in a better position to achieve their policy objectives through reorganized governmental coalitions. Although most past regimes in independent Africa have brought some combinations of class and ethnic interests together into positions of political power at the center, they have often tended to underrepresent one interest group or another, at a great potential cost in terms of civil tension or strife. In light of this situation, we view the political incorporation of all major social interests as a "rule of the game" which offers the prospect of enhanced state influence and even the possibility of strengthened legitimacy. By co-opting leading class and ethnic representatives into the ruling elite, it is possible to reduce the scale and intensity of their demands and to maintain the political system (albeit at a possible cost in terms of economic efficiency).

In probing the potentialities of broadened coalition formation, we start by analyzing Africa's experience with "elite consensus" systems. We then look at current political recruitment policies under the two types of regime which have emerged during the first 25 years of independence: the hegemonial exchange and bureaucratic centralist patterns. These regime types represent variations in elite responses to the problems of the "soft state" in Africa; and extensive, but different, experiences with representative governmental coalitions have occurred under both. At this point it will be possible to examine coalition patterns with respect to their implications for heightened or reduced intergroup conflict. Under the best of circumstances, where incorporation of major social groups proceeds according to the rough guideline of the proportionality principle (*Proporz*), regime stability and capacity for effective governance will likely be strengthened. However, the

:ailure to include nationality groups or peasant interests in the ruling coalition, as well as the skewed resource allocation policies this might lead to, seems likely to produce increased conflict among interests and between these interest groups and the state. In our concluding section we discuss the nature of emergent class interests and the implications of this emergence for currently operating hegemonial exchange and bureaucratic centralist-type systems.

In brief, we foresee hegemonial exchange systems, where they do occur, being replaced over time by a more complex system of state-society relations in which both ethnoregional and functional groupings are incorporated, albeit in diverse ways, in "concertated" processes of decision making. Such a system, to which the bureaucratic centralist state is perhaps better adapted, would allow the state to exercise somewhat greater influence, in certain sectors, over private associations and interests than is the case at present. It would use these private agencies and groups to extend its administrative capacity, allowing them a degree of autonomy while integrating them into the state network. This process would simultaneously incorporate while disengaging, for the state would continue to be able to intrude only minimally on the autonomy of these various quasi-private and private interests.

The State and the Social Environment

State softness is attributable not only to such factors as resource scarcity and limited regulatory and coercive capacity, but also to social incoherence, i.e., the lack of recurrent patterns of political exchange and reciprocity in the relations among social forces. To be sure, diversity of class, ethnic and regional interests makes competition and conflict among groups and leaders virtually inescapable; however, the destructive effects of these struggles can be reduced if the patterns of interaction among these contending elements can be regularized and if the state can play an effective mediatory role, helping set out the terms of relationship among competing interests. This establishment of an organizing framework under soft state conditions is no easy matter. As Claude Ake notes, the "nonautonomization" of the African state results to some extent from the effects of the contradictions between forms of capital—contradictions arising from cultural pluralism and con-tradictions taking place within the dominant class—and this "in turn accentuates them, rendering them particularly difficult to mediate."[2] The African state is sometimes unable to restrain and bound intercommunity relations and, consequently, proves unequal to the task of channeling group conflicts along "constructive" lines. At times, informal practices, conventions, customs and understandings have emerged within the elite and have provided the basis for stable relations; at other times, however, conherent relations have failed to develop, with disastrous consequences for the well-being of the political community. In Chad and in Amin's Uganda, for example, a breakdown of the state involved *both* the collapse of rules regulating societal interaction and the inability of central institutions to carry out their policies and programs.

Since coherent societal relations in Africa often entail the emergence of a fully responsive state (i.e., one which not only directs interest group demands into legitimate channels but also implements policies and programs to meet the reasonable claims put forward by these groups), it is necessary to start by examining the politically mobilized categorical groups and their political demands. After that, we will look at the way different regimes have responded to these claims.

Political identities are mobilized and their demands directed at the state by the spokespeople for group interests. Depending upon the particular situation, these intermediaries can appeal variously to class, ethnicity or a combination of these identities. "Class and ethnicity, as well as regionalism or religion are," as Nelson Kasfir observes, "organising principles of social action that may act alone, may reinforce, or may work against each other, depending on the social situation."[3] An essential task of the intermediary is to gauge his constituency appeal correctly in terms of salient politically mobilizable identities in order to build the necessary support base for political action. Clearly, such identities differ in terms of attributes and behavior. While the ethnic group is a culturally based social organization, socioeconomic classes are distinguishable among themselves in terms of their relationships to the productive process. Yet class and ethnicity are in fact fluid and overlapping identities and, when organized by group leaders for social action, they share common organizational features. Thus, modern African inter- mediaries, whether representing class or ethnic interests, have acted rather similarly for the most part in the way they forge unity behind their leadership to secure political power, status and economic resources. In brief, if the categorical groups rest upon different organizational principles and make different claims upon their members, up to the present they have nonetheless tended to organize similarly to assert their interests to those in positions of power at the political center.

Normally, the African one- or no-party state is an inclusive mechanism of control, one which encloses and contains group struggles in order to manage them. By setting parameters on legitimate political action, the state seeks to establish the terms under which interest group competition and conflict occur and to regulate the procedures by which group claims may be directed toward public officials. But the soft state's ability to control the actions of social forces in its midst is strictly limited in practice—by the limited resources at its disposal, by the overextended nature of its institutions, by the existence of parallel market activities, and by what Ake describes as the "overpoliticisation of life" in many African societies.[4] Not only do interest groups place a premium upon securing political power, but they see political solutions to virtually all their problems. "Unable to deliver the goods," Ake notes, "successive Nigerian regimes have turned to political solutions; manipulating cultural and primordial loyalties to divert attention from the real issues: 'struggling' against enemies of progress who are found too ubiquitously and, most importantly, resorting to repression in the vain hope that this will prevent the people's frustrations from causing trouble for them."[5]

The soft state clearly is limited in its ability to cope with the over-politicization of social life. State elites can act defensively and seek to increase the repressive capacity of the state, but, as Ake asserts, this may prove a vain hope where the state's abilities to coerce are already strictly circumscribed. State elites can also attempt to deflect some claims through programs of decentralizing political power, reducing expectations by encouraging officials to rely on local resources for their developmental activities. In addition, they can try to encapsulate conflict within a system of control, making it possible for political exchange and reciprocity to take place within a framework of unitary government. However, the success of such a political exchange process is likely to depend, in part at least, on the application of a rule of inclusiveness—that is, spokespeople for all major interests must be included in the key decision-making institutions.

The possibilities of achieving such inclusiveness in an effective state system are related in part to the nature of group demands. National governmental coalitions, which bring together strong personalities who hold diverse ideologies and have different domestic and international commitments, are unlikely to survive intense disagreements over issues of territory, identity or group status. Stability over time clearly requires a degree of moderation in the pattern of demands made upon the state. In this regard, the African picture is mixed. Despite the already mentioned tendency to overpoliticize social life, the intensity and range of demands actually vary quite considerably in different time-place contexts. Surveys administered or processed by one of these authors in Kenya, Zambia and Ghana show demands in the peripheries of these countries which, for the time being at least, appear to be reasonable and attainable.[6] Contrary to popularly held assumptions on "the revolution of rising expectations," the claims put forward by peoples in the relatively disadvantaged subregions tended to be modest in scope, especially when compared with those advanced by their counterparts in the more advantaged areas. Those villagers who did communicate their dissatisfactions to party and government officials tended to urge minimal objectives: marketing facilities, clinics, primary schools, roads, adult literacy classes and community and homecraft centers. In a number of established political systems, then, the rural small-holder majority were generally reticent in their demands, but were not unlike privileged subregional or urban and large-farmer class interests in their emphasis upon improved state distributions. Because they were focused upon the tangible dimension, such group demands lent themselves to informal political exchanges among spokespersons for state and for ethnic and class interests.

In Africa as elsewhere, however, not all group actors· will be mobilized around distributive issues. Inevitably, those issues with a symbolic dimension in a pluralistic society—group status, identity or territory—are likely to become the basis for more inelastic or nonnegotiable communal claims, setting the stage for intense conflicts of a political nature. Societies established on a vertically stratified basis (contemporary South Africa; or Algeria, Zanzibar, Rwanda or Burundi around the time of independence), which rank group members differently in terms of power, status and wealth, invariably rely upon the control exercised by state organs to preserve public order and stability. In time, conflicts among competing groups are likely to become intense, leading the relatively disadvantaged either to submit helplessly to overpowering force or to react vigorously, even violently. The more the relatively disadvantaged are able to accumulate resources, the less they will be inclined to accept a state-enforced situation of inequality, and their demands for a significant restructuring of political power and economic opportunities will increase accordingly.[7] Failure of the state to respond to or repress these demands seems certain to have a conflict-producing effect: the demands of the less advantaged will escalate, bringing about a sharp but inconclusive reaction from those in power. As in the cases of Northern Ireland or South Africa, such intractable conflicts may endure over an extended time period.

Nonnegotiable demands are also in evidence in horizontally stratified African societies, i.e., those societies whose ethnoregional units parallel one another but none of whose elements make a claim to moral ascendancy over the others. In the bitter separatist conflicts involving claims to independent statehood of Biafra, Eritrea, and the Southern Sudan, the demands of the geocultural entity to political autonomy and sovereignty collided head on with the state's claims to respect for its legitimate authority and right to exercise control. A negotiated solution, involving such compromise arrangements as devolution, regional autonomy or federalism, was precluded by the weakness of social linkages, the lack of faith in legal guarantees and the uncompromising nature of the claims made by both state and ethnoregional elites. Again, in these worst-case situations, nonnegotiable demands contributed substantially to intense and destructive conflict, widening the cleavages between group leaders and sharpening a perception of menacing intentions on the part of adversaries. Clearly, the decision on the part of an ethnoregional elite to take matters into its own hands and to attempt to secede from the internationally recognized state is a desperate act born mainly of essentialist perceptions involving the survival of the collectivity. However, it may also involve instrumental calculations as well—an assessment of economic advantage, the desire for enhanced decision-making authority, or an estimation of the central state's fragility and inability to coerce compliance in the periphery. Not surprisingly, the state reacts forcefully to this assault upon its integrity—and to the risks of further separatist actions if it fails to respond adequately to the challenge—and a protracted struggle involving armed units ensues. In these instances, the nonnegotiable demands lead to a costly encounter with implications for the international community as a whole.

The potential here for inelastic, even nonnegotiable demands can alert the African statesman to a broader problem: namely, how the soft state can organize itself to make group claims more manageable. The state's softness places limitations upon the easiest and most direct choice of purchasing support by means of enhanced distributions. Instead, *it must*

expend *political capital in one way or another to promote cooperative behavior.*
We therefore turn in the next section to one such option—the augmentation
of state authority through a widely encompassing process of coalition
formation. As W. Arthur Lewis puts it: "The democratic problem in a
plural society is to create political institutions which give all the various
groups the opportunity to participate in decision-making, since only thus
can they feel that they are full members of a nation, respected by their
more numerous brethren, and owing equal respect to the national bond
which holds them together."[8] Only the grand coalition, then, and not merely
the minimum winning coalition which necessarily leaves some elements out
of the ruling elite, will be sufficient to overcome adversarial politics.

The grand coalition, described by Arend Lijphart as "not so much any
particular arrangement as the participation by the leaders of all significant
segments in governing a plural society," has in fact been used widely in
contemporary Africa.[9] In a situation where state functions have expanded
noticeably and state control over public resources is readily apparent, the
grand coalition, for all its costs in terms of decisive policymaking, seems a
logical alternative to an otherwise intense competition for the control of
state institutions. An inclusive governmental coalition may have a stabilizing
effect, for interest group intermediaries will be assured of a capacity to
protect the interests of their supporters from the inside. This is not to
suggest that all cabinet or executive appointments will be of equal weight
or that the people selected will have equal leadership potential, but only
that an ability to participate in the decision-making process identifies
intermediaries and their constituents with the political system. However,
the political exchange outcomes promoted by these broadly incorporative
grand coalitions have, thus far, worked more effectively to further ethnic
than class interests. As we shall see below, the proportionality guideline
has frequently assured the recruitment of ethnic strongmen into the central
cabinet on a roughly representative basis, but these ethnic intermediaries
are in practice allies of the dominant class if not also members of it. The
expansion of the state occurring under their hegemonic class rule has largely
benefited the members of the middle class who have been recruited to fill
both the Africanized and the newly created positions. In that sense, it is
possible to speak of an "antagonistic cooperation" occurring in many
contemporary African polities.[10] A dominant political class of state elites,
ethnoregional strongmen and bourgeois interests generally acts in concert
with middle class and petty bourgeois interests; the rural small-holders and
the working class are largely left out of the decision-making process. Because
such an unrepresentative governmental coalition limits participation to certain
classes and ethnic interests, it will have to be rearranged over time to
achieve full representativeness and *thus* political stability.

Elite Consensus: Formal Arrangements

In order for us to examine the operative nature of the elite alliance as
it exists in many African countries, it is necessary to look at the cooperation

that takes place within the dominant political class between the state and the representatives of the main ethnic groups. The co-optation of key ethnoregional strongmen into the cabinet and party national executive committee is especially critical to regime survival in Africa insofar as the organization of competitive groupings to secure public resources often takes an ethnic form.[11] Because inclusion of a group intermediary in the political institutions at the center frequently satisfies a strong popular desire for an effective voice, it is necessary for us to examine Africa's experiences with elite-consensual systems, focusing first on the use of formal rules to ensure representativeness and then on informal practices utilized to this end.

In an effort to reduce the likelihood of antagonistic conflict, various African countries have introduced formal rules to promote cabinet power-ersharing. In Mauritius, for example, the adoption of a "best loser" system ensures the representation of ethnic minority interests on a partially proportional basis in parliament. While most members of parliament are chosen in multimember constituencies on a simple plurality basis, the basic law also provides for the selection of the eight most successful losing candidates from those communities deemed to be underrepresented in parliament. The effect is to reserve parliamentary seats for otherwise under-represented communal interests, thereby making possible the formation of a political coalition which includes representatives of the various communities.

In Nigeria an intricate set of state and party constitutional rules was put into effect at the time of the return to civilian rule in 1979 which sought to ensure the proportional representation of ethnoregional interests. Even during the previous military regime it had been possible to speak of the government as being "very adept at maintaining an 'unofficial' ethnic balance in its ministerial and parastatal appointments."[12] Under both the 1979 Federal Constitution and the Constitution of the National Party of Nigeria (the ruling party), however, such inclusive practices were formally sanctioned by law. The Constitution of the Federal Republic of Nigeria (1979), expressly seeking to incorporate major ethnic interests into the decision-making apparatus, stresses that the country's "federal character" must be taken into account when making federal appointments. Article 14(3) is quite explicit:

> The composition of the Government of the Federation or any of its agencies and the conduct of its affairs shall be carried out in such manner as to reflect the federal character of Nigeria and the need to promote national unity . . . thereby ensuring that there shall be no predominance of persons from a few States or from a few ethnic or other sectional groups in that government or in any of its agencies.

A government reflecting Nigeria's ethnic diversity would, it was assumed, "command national loyalty" (Art. 14(3)). But if this provision left any doubts as to the constitution framers' determination to secure representativeness in public agencies and in the government itself, subsequent articles require adherence to the notion of "federal character." Thus, Article 135(3) states that appointment of ministers at the federal level should be in conformity with Article 14(3) and declares: "in giving effect to the provisions aforesaid the President shall appoint at least one Minister from each State, who shall be an indigene of such State." The constitution applies the principles of representativeness to state governments as well. Thus, Article 14(4) provides that the composition of state governments and local councils should "recognize the diversity of the peoples within [their] area of authority" and Article 173(2) makes it mandatory that state governors take Article 14(4) into account when appointing commissioners (ministers) at the state level.

In spirit and in practice, then, the 1979 Constitution deliberately sought to build ethnic coalitions, emphasizing the need to cope with social diversity through political inclusiveness. And even though this constitution was set aside following the military coup of December 31, 1983, the informal practice of coalition formation remained a regular feature of the Nigerian scene. The new Supreme Military Council, while consisting predominantly of northerners, nonetheless included both Yoruba and Ibo members; moreover, the 18-member Federal Executive Council contained a member from every state except Bendel, and that state was compensated by the selection of a person from this subregion as the head of the civil service.[13] Political change by no means involved a repudiation of the principle of inclusiveness.

During the period of the Shehu Shagari administration (1979–1983), the attempt to promote cooperation through inclusion was not limited to the 1979 Federal Nigerian Constitution but was carried over into the ruling party's constitutional rules and policies as well. Shagari's National Party of Nigeria (NPN), which won electoral support in the south as well as in his own north, sought to reduce ethnic and sectional tensions within the party (and the country) through specific measures to ensure the participation of all major interests in the affairs of state. Accordingly, the NPN sought to distribute offices at the central and state levels among its membership according to a "zoning" principle, which it described in the party constitution "as a Convention in recognition of the need for adequate geographical spread."[14] Although the NPN constitution gives few details about the nature of the rotation scheme for public offices, it does refer to spreading public positions among four zones: the ten northern states, the four Yoruba states, the two Ibo states and the minority states of Bendel, Rivers and Cross Rivers.[15] For Shagari, the zoning principle was "a necessary instrument," a "source of strength" in an ethnically pluralistic society.[16] And southern leaders of the NPN did in fact perceive the zoning principle as something of a guarantee of their participation in party and state-related activities. Thus, the governor of the Rivers State, Melford Okilo, praised the NPN as the only party which had instituted a zoning policy, and Chief Adisa Akinloye, the party's national chairman, described zoning as a fundamental party principle which contributed significantly to the party's acceptance throughout the country.[17] Southerners were able to appeal to the zoning principle in their struggle to retain the presidency of the Senate in 1983 and in their successful effort to hold on to the position of party national secretary at the NPN national convention that year, a success that contributed to a perception of the zoning principle as a source of fairness. If zoning was criticized by some as introducing an element of arbitrary and capricious behavior in the selection process,[18] it nonetheless helped the NPN to reflect the federal character of Nigeria, thereby contributing not unsubstantially to the party's electoral successes. Not surprisingly, in light of this success, there was talk under the Buhari regime of reintroducing the zoning principle in high government positions in a future basic law.

Elite Consensus: Informal Arrangements

Formal legal provisions intended to produce representative coalitions have displayed limited success at best. Where provisions of the law do encourage the coalition process, as in Mauritius and Nigeria (1979–1983), the resulting coalition is largely explained by the collaboration of opposing elites in putting the rules regulating their encounters into effect. While imposed power-sharing formulas have crumbled at the first serious confrontation, mutually agreed upon rules have proved more likely to survive, albeit as informal understandings rather than as constitutional limitations. Thus, the Buhari coup in Nigeria in 1983 terminated the constitution as a body of formal rules, but not the use of the principle of the country's federal character in the recruitment of ethnoregional notables into the federal cabinet.

At this stage, then, it is the informal practices of coalition formation that are decisive in the African states' abilities to contain conflict under difficult circumstances. To be sure, intense ethnic and sectional conflicts have surfaced and jarred the peace on various occasions in Rwanda, Burundi, Zanzibar, Zaire, Ethiopia, Nigeria, Zimbabwe, Angola and elsewhere. But these are worst-case confrontations and should not obscure the general achievements that have occurred in political networking and coalition building, even under conditions of grave subregional inequality and economic scarcity. If the politics of inclusiveness sometimes gives rise to political payoffs and backscratching within the dominant political elite, thereby complicating the process of increasing aggregate productiveness, it nonetheless has the positive effect of promoting interethnic cooperation.

Despite regime differences, African ruling elites have in fact responded rather similarly to the overriding need to include ethnoregional intermediaries in the ruling coalition. Such grand alliances are not the relatively static coalitions of Western European party politics, but represent shifting elite alignments which often reflect the changing patterns of patron-client relations in both the local and national political arenas. This impelling need to build broad-based coalitions is largely explained by the political necessities of governance under soft state conditions. Not only must African leaders accommodate ethnoregional strongmen to compensate for their lack of regulatory capacity, but they also must incorporate them into the elite cartel to prevent the formation of a counter-coalition.[19] The ruling coalition's ability to work out accepted norms of reciprocity among its members represents a critical factor in state stability, primarily because of the fluid, face-to-face nature of the encounters among state and interest group leaders.

Africa's experience with informal norms of ethnic incorporation in an elite cartel is so widespread that a few examples, drawn from a range of social systems and ideological preferences, will suffice to indicate just how extensive this type of cooperative behavior is. As might be anticipated, state elites in such non-Marxist countries as Nigeria, Kenya and Cameroon commonly make use of a rough proportional guideline when selecting cabinets, although ascribing different degrees of legitimacy to such accommodations. Less recognized, however, is the fact that their Marxist (Angola) and populist socialist (Tanzania, Guinea under Sékou Touré) counterparts also engage, albeit most reluctantly, in similar practices. Proportional inclusion, then, is quite prevalent—a conventional political response to the difficult environment in which these regimes operate.

As already noted regarding Nigeria, the non-Marxist states have been most adept at maintaining an unofficial ethnic balance in ministerial appointments. In Ghana Flight-Lieutenant Jerry Rawlings' Ewe-led regime has shown considerable sensitivity to ethnic feelings in making appointments to the Provisional National Defense Council (PNDC) and the cabinet. In addition to Rawlings (an Ewe himself), the PNDC, as of July 1984, included two Akans, two Gas, and two northerners; moreover, the twenty-nine-member cabinet was composed of seven northerners, seven Fante, three Gas, and twelve Akan members.[20] In making his high-level appointments, Rawlings has clearly gone out of his way to placate the northerners and, to a lesser extent, the Akans. If the Akans' perception of the government as Ewe-dominated is somewhat accurate with respect to military and police appointments, this seems somewhat wide of the mark in terms of the ordinary administrative apparatuses of the state.

In a number of French-speaking West African states—e.g., in Togo, Cameroon and Ivory Coast—civilian and military regimes have also promoted political stability through a process of "ethnic arithmetic." Togo's President Gnassingbe Eyadema has remained in power for nearly two decades now, a survival explained in part by his skill in balancing subregional appointments to the cabinet and to the politburo and central committee of the one legitimate political party, the Rally of the People of Togo. Eyadema, a northerner himself, has selected southerners for high military and ministerial posts (including that of the Minister of Interior and Information) and, as of 1980, had a nine-member politburo consisting of four northerners, four southerners and one person from the center.[21] To be sure, the army continues to play a pivotal role in preserving stability; however, the president's proficiency in balancing ethnic and subregional claims when making key appointments to state positions contributes substantially to this end.

Another leader who has shown himself to be keenly alert to the need for a regional balance in cabinet appointments is Ivory Coast President Félix Houphouêt-Boigny. Intent upon mollifying the resentment of Baoulé dominance and building a consensus for his rule, Houphouët-Boigny has been careful to co-opt powerful modernist and traditional leaders into his governing coalition.[22] The result has been the emergence of broadly understood political rules which involve an implicit recognition, but not a public display, of ethnic politics.[23] All major ethnic interests are represented in the central cabinet—and on a basis roughly proportional to their position in the National Assembly. Playing a key role by dominating, and if necessary mediating between, the different elements making up the cabinet coalition, Houphouët-Boigny has been able to establish a political structure which ensures his political survival despite growing ethnic, class and generational tensions in the 1980s. His formula for governance, which provides for the incorporation of ethnic and modernist interest group "patrons" within what Aristide Zolberg long ago described as "a one-party coalition, a heterogeneous monolith," has contributed to political stability at a time of rapid socio-economic change.[24] But whether such a "hegemonial exchange" formula can succeed in overcoming the tensions that seem likely to follow the Houphouët-Boigny period seems problematical.[25]

In the case of Cameroon, ethnic balancing has been a feature of the heavy-handed and authoritarian Ahmadou Ahidjo administration and its more pragmatic successor, the Paul Biya administration. Placing a strong emphasis on the requirements of national unity, Ahidjo, a northern Muslim from Garoua, acted to preserve an ethnic and linguistic "equilibrium" in his high-level political appointments. In particular, he selected Biya, a Catholic from the south-central subregion, to be his prime minister, and maintained a rough balance among the main sectional interests in his ministerial, parastatal and bureaucratic appointments. Upon Ahidjo's retirement from the presidency in 1982, Biya declared himself firmly committed to the principle of balanced representation. Contending at his swearing-in ceremony that the principle of "equilibrium" was no longer adequate for the needs of national unity, he stated that "[t]he time has come in our development to re-assess and re-orientate in order to consolidate and render irreversible our national unity."[26] What he promised was a new emphasis upon proportional recruitment policies to move the republic toward the goal of national integration. Implementing his pledge on the inclusion of ethnic, linguistic and sectional interests, Biya appointed Bello Bouga Maigari, a northerner, as prime minister, thus upholding the north-south balance at the top; this act also assured that another northern Muslim would succeed to the presidency in due course. While retaining the northern Muslim hold on key ministerial and party positions, the president also acted to secure the position of southerners, including the minority of English speakers from the western part of the country. Old-line Anglophone politicians, such as Tandeng Muna and Emmanuel Tabi Egbe, were kept on as National Assembly president and roving ambassador, respectively, and Muna's protégé, John Acha, was appointed secretary-general in the prime minister's office. Although these and other Anglophone ministers were dismissed by some of their younger constituents as "ineffectual anglophone peers," their inclusion nonetheless represented continuity in the practices of hegemonial exchange politics in the country.[27] The transition from the Ahidjo to the Biya presidency was not destined to be a smooth one, however. In 1983 a deepening quarrel between the two led to a growing north-south schism and, ultimately, to an attempted coup against the Biya regime in April 1984. Biya reacted strongly, crushing the coup, executing the main plotters (most of whom were northerners) and reshuffling northerners in his cabinet and the presidential guard.[28] Yet despite these forceful actions against what he perceived as a threat to his survival as president, Biya nonetheless took special pains to preserve a geographical balance in his high-level appointments and in his insistence that people from the south as well as the north were implicated in the coup attempt.

Various forms of ethnic coalition formation were also evident in Eastern and South-Central African politics as well. Although real power is exercised in Burundi by President Jean-Baptiste Bagaza, a Tutsi, and his army colleagues, reconciliation between ethnic rivals is in the air: Hutu are now estimated to comprise one-third of the membership of the National Assembly, and they are being incorporated gradually into the military services.[29] In the Sudan, the change in 1985 from President Gaafar Nimeiry's regime to that of President Abdel Rahman Siwar el-Dahab strengthened the tendency toward ethnoregional coalition formation. During the Nimeiry period southern regional interests were articulated at the center by political representations made by the various civilian and military presidents or acting presidents of the High Executive Council. In addition, during the 1980s the southern region was represented in the cabinet by the vice-president, Abel Alier, and then by Joseph Lagu, the former Anya-Nya leader, who served in the same post. However, it does seem fair to conclude about the Nimeiry period, as does Dunstan Wai, that "the Southern Region [was] neither proportionally nor adequately represented at the national level."[30] Then, in 1985, in something of an effort to overcome these southern grievances, President Siwar el-Dahab, after extensive negotiations with various interest groups, appointed a transitional civilian cabinet which included three southerners (among them Samuel Aru Bol, the deputy prime minister).[31] In addition, two southerners were appointed to the Military Council, the more powerful of the two decision-making bodies. Clearly, the incorporation of southern notables in the decision-making process was viewed as an important element in the broader initiative to end the spreading rebellion in the south.

While emphatically denying the validity of ethnic balancing in making high cabinet and party appointments,[32] Zambia's President Kenneth Kaunda has in fact shown himself to be quite pragmatic in his adherence to rough proportional guidelines. Kaunda regards the ethnoregional intermediary as an unpleasant reality, but a fact of life that must be accommodated in practice even if repudiated in principle. Thus, despite Kaunda's rejection of the Chuula Commission's recommendation for equal provincial representation in the United National Independence Party's Central Committee, various observers have commented on the presence of what amounts to regional spokespeople in this committee.[33] And in cabinet appointments,

Kaunda has taken great pains to represent all major ethnoregional groups and to maintain a rough balance between the Bemba from the north and the Lozi from the south.[34] Clearly, the 1972 move toward a legally recognized one-party system had little impact on the president's use of the proportionality principle when making cabinet appointments. The allocation of ministerial posts to Bemba speakers remained steady in the years that followed, despite the defection of some Bemba MPs from UNIP in 1971. From time to time the size of the cabinet has been increased, but with the notable effect of making it more inclusive of all ethnoregional interests. Kaunda had used the enlarged cabinet, William Tordoff notes, to "extend his patronage network and . . . to accommodate new claimants—the disgruntled Luapula and North-western Provinces, for example, from mid-1969."[35] The tendency, then, was toward fuller incorporation, emphasizing the possibilities for interethnic exchange and cooperation within the single-party framework.

Much like Kaunda in his outlook on ethnic balancing, Uganda's former president, A. Milton Obote, disapproved in principle of clientelist politics while in practice incorporating some ethnoregional intermediaries in his ruling coalition. This was a political position born of necessity—the softness of the Uganda state, the diversity of his society, the need both to overcome Buganda separatism and to steer his country to independence. Obote demonstrated his masterly abilities as an ethnic bargainer early in his career when, in September 1961, he negotiated an improbable coalition alliance between his nationalist, northern-based Uganda People's Congress (UPC) and Kabaka Yekka (KY), a neotraditionalist Baganda movement. In exchange for KY support for independence and new elections, Obote agreed to back Buganda's claim to federal status and its demand for indirect Lukiiko elections to the National Assembly.[36] Following the elections and the achievement of the country's independence, the UPC continued its formal alliance with KY; however, with important defections of KY members of parliament in succeeding years, the UPC gained a commanding majority in the legislature and was able to dispense with its erstwhile "ally." From that point foward, Obote appeared grudgingly to engage in informal political exchange practices with spokespersons from Buganda and other parts of the country. Though there were repeated allegations of Langi dominance in the cabinet and army, Obote, after his resumption of power following the fall of Idi Amin, did include several Baganda and Basoga in his cabinet. Yet these men were relatively unknown and hardly able to represent the opinions of their constituents.[37] Moreover, important elements, such as Yoweri Museveni and his Ankole-based National Resistance Army, remained outside the ruling coalition, revealing a failure to play the politics of inclusiveness, which contributed to the July 1985 downfall of Obote's second regime. It is significant that Museveni, as the new head of state in 1986, moved swiftly after coming to power to appoint a more broad-based government, including prominent Baganda, Acholi and Langi representatives. If continued after the interim period, this effort to incorporate could be interpreted as a recognition on the part of the new regime that the price of political stability must involve a partial accommodation of important ethnoregional and other interests in society.

Further to the east, Kenya's leaders have shown greater skill in maintaining political stability through the use of an elite cartel of rulers. Although Kenyatta governed largely through his bureaucracy, making effective use of the provincial apparatus in the hinterland areas, he nonetheless took care to include all major ethnoregional intermediaries in the cabinet at the political center (with the notable exception of Oginga Odinga and his colleagues, Luo as well as non-Luo, who bolted from the ruling Kenya African National Union (KANU) to form a rival party). What emerged under Kenyatta's aegis was a one-party coalition of ethnoregional notables who engaged in a process of political exchange within a one-party framework on issues of recruitment, fiscal allocations and power sharing. The system in the Kenyatta years was described as "highly plural, with bargaining and competition occurring among Cabinet members acting on behalf of supporting groups and between the ministries themselves."[38] Such elite reciprocity within a single-party framework was facilitated by the looseness of KANU control over affairs at the branch level; nevertheless, the willingness of Mzee (the Old Man) to work a hegemonial exchange system represents an act of political statesmanship which furthered interelite cooperation.

Kenyatta's successor, Daniel arap Moi, continued the grand coalitional practices of his predecessor during his first years in office. The Standard, praising Moi in 1978 for preserving the network of exchanges from past times, noted that he had "maintained the same 'balance of representation' at the Ministerial level hammered out by his predecessor."[39] This assessment proved a little hasty, however. As Moi consolidated his power, working closely through his own set of protégés, he altered the old practice of forging an alliance at the central level with representative ethnoregional strongmen from important areas. By 1983 the influence of the Kalenjin and other minority spokesmen in the cabinet had been strengthened—and at the expense of many of the older notables such as Oginga Odinga (Luo), Charles Njonjo (Kikuyu), and Masinde Muliro and Jean Marie Seroney from the Rift Valley.[40] Moi's moves to strengthen party discipline and to weaken the former Kenyatta alliance did not amount to an abandonment of coercive exchange politics as such, but only to a shifting of the bases of power within the system. Thus, Moi maintained a geographical balance within his 1983 cabinet even while reducing the Kikuyu proportion and bringing in his own team to replace the old influentials of the Kenyatta years. If anything, the new cabinet was more inclusive of minority ethnic interests than before, showing a determination on Moi's part to continue a top-down process of reciprocity among ethnic-based elites, even if the manner of selecting these elites had changed in significant ways.

The use of the proportional principle when recruiting elites for cabinet posts is by no means an exclusive feature of reformist or conservative regimes. Radical socialist and Marxist states also resort to the principle of ethnic balancing, even while disclaiming such practices. Commenting on former President Sékou Touré's method of "overcoming tribal stress upon the political system" by including opposition leaders within the government and party structure, Martin Kilson notes that "the first independence cabinet in Guinea contained several leaders of the Fulani tribe that had opposed the PDG—whose main support came from the coastal Malinke—and leaders of other tribal or ethnic groups were also included in this single-party government."[41] In subsequent years statistics show that Touré continued to be adept at practicing "ethnic arithmetic" in the distribution of key political and administrative positions. Thus, between 1958 and 1967 the president's own ethnic group, the Malinke, was only slightly overrepresented, holding 37 percent of the key posts while constituting 34 percent of the total population. Moreover, the Soussou were represented in numbers almost exactly proportional to their population and the Foulah were only slightly underrepresented. Only the Forest People, with 18 percent of the total population and 8 percent of the key posts, were significantly shortchanged.[42] Although committed in principle to the struggle against ethnic particularism (most notably in 1957, when he abolished the institution of chieftaincy), Touré was not above practicing the policy of inclusion when he deemed it essential to furthering his larger objectives.[43]

Similarly, in populist socialist Tanzania, President Julius Nyerere has been anything but unmindful of the need to incorporate ethnic interests to promote more harmonious relations. Thus, a former high official, commenting on Nyerere appointments of Zanzibaris as prime minister and vice-president in a 1984 reshuffle of personnel, described this action, which brought about an increased Zanzibari role in public affairs, as a "deliberate policy" on Nyerere's part.[44] Others assumed that Zanzibari opinion would interpret the new appointments most positively. A correspondent commented on the significance of Salim Ahmed Salim's appointment to the premiership as follows:

> More important, he is a Zanzibari who has strong support on the mainland. If, as it appears likely, Nyerere is grooming him to take over the presidency in a year's time, Salim's Zanzibari and Islamic background will be a major plus factor. A Zanzibari-born President on the mainland is likely to quell the groundswell of resentment against the union government. Anti-unionists will have little ground for claims that the mainland is trying to swallow up the islands.[45]

In addition, Marxist-oriented state elites in such countries as Angola, despite their strong preferences for central control and their all too apparent "disdain" for ethnic identity politics,[46] have found themselves with little choice but to mediate informally between different social interests. Like most of the reformist and conservative countries around them, the Angolan state is "soft" and lacks the capacity to implement its policies throughout the territory nominally under its control. Thus, while Angola's President José Eduardo dos Santos expresses his commitment to Marxist-Leninist principles and seeks to establish effective central regulatory authority, he must, for the time being at least, mediate differences within his ruling Popular Movement for the Liberation of Angola (MPLA) based on ideology (leftist versus pragmatic), personalities, race (whites and *mestiços* versus blacks), religion (church affiliated versus nonchurch affiliated), and ethnic identity (Kimbundu, Kikongo, Kongo, Cabindans and so forth). Showing great sensitivity in practice for ethnic identifications, dos Santos has ensured a good deal of representativeness in the recruitment of members of his Political Bureau. As in 1979, the Political Bureau included four Mbundu, two *mestiços*, three Bakongo and two Cabindans—all of the country's major ethnic peoples with the exception of the Ovimbundu, who are the main support base for Jonas Savimbi's National Union for the Total Independence of Angola (UNITA).[47] Clearly, MPLA, which views itself as a pan-ethnic party, would co-opt Ovimbundu into the Political Bureau once the South African connection with UNITA was decisively ended. The Kongo people to the north who were once staunch supporters of Holden Roberto's Front for the Liberation of Angola (FNLA) have been increasingly well-represented in ministries and parastatals, as have some Ovimbundu who are not members of the UNITA movement.[48]

Clearly, as Africa's broad experiences with ethnic coalition formation indicate, many African state elites, non-Marxist and Marxist alike, co-opt ethnoregional leaders on a roughly proportional basis to promote interelite cooperation and to reduce political instability. The grand coalition, then, is an important means of increasing the political (but not economic) effectiveness of soft states in the short term, largely irrespective of the ideology of the dominant political elite. But is there any chance that these highly informal and personalistic practices will give way to more formal procedures of incorporation in the years ahead? Certainly recent Belgian experience gives some cause for hope in this regard. "For many years," writes Arend Lijphart, "an informal norm had existed by which cabinets were formed with approximately equal numbers of ministers representing the Flemish majority and the French-speaking minority. One of the constitutional amendments adopted in 1970 made this into a formal rule."[49] As the coalition process becomes recurrent and predictable, such laws are then a reflection, in part at least, of cooperative relationships in ethnically pluralistic societies.

Patterns of Regime Response to State Softness

Thus far we have noted the widespread tendency of African state elites to build governmental coalitions, regardless of ideological orientation, to advance their objectives under conditions of scarcity and weak institutions. We now find it useful to comment very briefly on the two patterns of regime type—*hegemonial exchange* and *bureaucratic centralist*—as responses to the presence of partially autonomous group actors in a soft state environment. After that, we will explore strains on African coalitions and then turn to emerging trends that we see unfolding.

Although many middle African states are outwardly hierarchical in form, often emphasizing some variant of the one- or no-party system of governance, they differ among themselves with respect to a number of variables: subsystem autonomy, responsiveness to interest group claims, the degree of central disciplinary capacity, the extent of popular participation, the nature of ideological commitments, the values on civil liberties and pan-Africanism and the linkages they maintain with first and second world powers. But from the standpoint of this inquiry on coalition formation, nothing distinguishes the thrust and spirit of what may be called a hegemonial exchange approach more from its bureaucratic centralist counterpart than the preparedness of the dominant elite in a hegemonial exchange context to enter into political exchange relationships with local ethnic or class interests (or for that matter, with international actors such as the IMF or multinational companies). Whereas the pragmatic political leaders of a hegemonial exchange regime accept the need to bargain with ethnoregional and modernist group notables in a soft state context, the leaders of a bureaucratic centralist regime tend to pull back in principle from such exchange relationships, and they practice ethnic balancing with evident misgivings. Since political exchanges are regarded as bestowing some legitimacy upon the ethnic group and its intermediaries, these more ideologically inclined bureaucratic centralist elites are reluctant to do anything which might be interpreted as conceding ethnic representatives an acknowledged role in the political process.

The Hegemonial Exchange Regime Pattern

Unable to control and unwilling to accept the limitations of a formal consociational model, ruling elites in a hegemonial exchange situation are ready to negotiate as necessary with the representatives of various local interests in order to accumulate power at the political center. While bargaining is not a preferred course of action, it is nonetheless justified on the grounds that it integrates diverse economic and social interests under conditions of economic scarcity and fragile institutions. Hegemonial exchange emphasizes the informal and the personalistic in the relationship between state and ethnic (as well as modernist) interest group elites. In brief, it can be characterized as a form of state-facilitated coordination in which partially autonomous central and subregional actors engage in quiet and informal exchanges on the basis of commonly known and accepted norms, rules and understandings.[50]

Because hegemonial exchange involves informal and personalistic ties, the negotiations between state and ethnoregional leaders tend to be continuous at each level. Not only must ethnic (and class) intermediaries negotiate with various personal, factional, clan and subgroup interests to consolidate their constituency base, but these spokespeople must also represent their diverse clients at the political center, either in dyadic exchanges with state officials or as members of an elite coalition in cabinet or high party activities. In acting as an intermediary, the group representative at the top plays a dual role: both as a member of the dominant political class and as an ethnic intermediary. Thus, Ghana's Justice D. F. Annan is perceived by some members of the bar as speaking for professional interests in government while also being perceived as a Ga spokesman on the PNDC.

Certainly a range of interconnecting clientelist relations is present between the local and the system-wide levels. As René Lemarchand observes, "clientelism can lead to a pyramiding of client-patron ties, and, through the recruitment of new brokers, to an expansion of local or regional reciprocities on a more inclusive scale."[51] It is precisely these reciprocities, which normally take place within the framework of an African one- or no-party system, that act to promote cooperative behavior in a situation of weak state regulatory capacity. Whether the group intermediary can remain a legitimate spokesperson becomes increasingly problematic, especially in light of society's disengagement from the state, but in many countries a machine-like clientelist system still remains in place. The politics of proportionality and pork barrel may have costs in terms of institutional effectiveness and economic productiveness. Commenting on the impact of the "federal character" guideline in Nigeria's Second Republic experience, one reviewer observed that "the consequent preoccupation with sectional equality undermined the effective functioning of key institutions—and, since it has been an essentially elite affair, has meant a 'de-emphasis on the other forms of equality which directly involve the majority of the population.' "[52] But if proportionality may have had an adverse impact on institutional effectiveness, it may nonetheless have made interethnic conflict more manageable under soft state circumstances.

What, then, characterizes the hegemonial exchange regime's approach to the ethnic or class-based interest group? Because the hegemonial exchange state neither structures nor sanctions these partially autonomous interests, it views itself as having little choice but to enter into political relations with them. As a consequence, the hegemonial exchange state frequently opts for the easiest course under the circumstances: it co-opts the various ethnic and modernist interest group spokespersons into an elite coalition at the top of the system. Such a state utilizes its superior access to public resources to induce interest group representatives to participate in the decision-making process; it incorporates to reduce alienation and opposition. And provided these patron/intermediaries can retain their clients' support, the central state leader will be inclined to shape his or her reality in terms of an ongoing political exchange relationship with these powerful social forces. In taking the course of least resistance, the hegemonial exchange state leader at the center, conscious of the limited military and regulatory capacity at his or her disposal, organizes interelite reciprocity in such a way as to promote political harmony. However, the course of least resistance, which entails minimally satisfying all key actors, may contribute to a top heavy social structure little conducive to economic growth.

The Bureaucratic Centralist Regime Pattern

As noted in the discussion on the political process in Tanzania, Guinea and Angola above, the bureaucratic centralist regime co-opts ethnic and modernist group leaders into the ruling coalition, but, in the case of the ethnic intermediary, reluctantly and with evident disdain for the interests that person represents. The bureaucratic centralist regime emphasizes party consolidation and control over all elements in society, using government to implement the policies set by its party national executive. In fact, government dominance over the policy formation and implementation processes has become apparent to many recent observers. Thus, Dean E. McHenry, Jr. comments on the growth of bureaucratic power in Tanzania during the 1970s as follows: "The most salient characteristic of Tanzania as it has evolved in the first decade and a half since independence is the growing predominance of government. Rival bodies have been reduced in power, absorbed, or suppressed."[53] Chama cha Mapinduzi, the sole political party, continues to set broad lines of policy, but government grows as a consequence of its control over the policy implementation functions. Hence the bureaucratic centralist regime's response to the soft state conditions it finds itself in is somewhat different from that of the hegemonial exchange regime. Rather than adapt passively to the "reality" of clientelist politics, it seeks to structure group participation and to channel group demands along predetermined lines. If the bureaucratic centralist regime finds it politically expedient to co-opt ethnic representatives into the cabinet or administration on a roughly balanced basis, this is an informal adjustment on its part to social reality, and is likely to persist only for a temporary time.

Unlike the hegemonial exchange political system, then, the bureaucratic centralist state is less inclined to play a mediatory role between the social forces in its country. Since the partially autonomous ethnic group is not considered a necessary or desirable element of the society the regime wishes to construct, the bureaucratic centralist government tends not to accept the need for any long-term political exchange relations with such interests. The very fact of negotiations is perceived as according a degree of legitimacy to antagonistic interests and their spokespeople; hence the bureaucratic centralist elite, more ideologically oriented and uncompromising than its hegemonial exchange counterpart, frequently plays down reciprocity with ethnic intermediaries, preferring instead to consolidate regime control through administrative agencies and party branches. This inclination on the part of bureaucratic centralist regimes to rule out the accommodation of ethnic-based interests can prove counterproductive. Experience has shown the reconciliation of factional and ethnoregional interests to be difficult in Ethiopia, Angola and Mozambique—partly because of external interference in domestic disputes and partly because of the unwillingness of state elites to negotiate with opposition elements. We will deal with the implications of this unpreparedness to bargain and to incorporate separatist elements later, but for now it suffices to note the bureaucratic centralist regime's greater tendency toward inflexibility than its hegemonial exchange counterpart and its inclination to draw a clearer line between those included and those excluded from the political process occurring within the state system. If the bureaucratic centralist regime may increase its capacity to mobilize public support and to control social forces, its approach may also involve some cost in its ability to manage interethnic tensions in an environment of economic scarcity and weak institutions.

Strains in African Coalitional Practices

If it is fair to describe African regimes as making considerable efforts to promote national integration by co-opting prominent ethnic and modernist elites into the ruling coalitions, it also seems necessary to complete this picture by noting that acute conflicts have sometimes arisen over their failure to establish balanced cabinets and party executives. We regard such conflicts as largely reflecting domestic and international pressures in an environment of scarcity. Internal competition over public resources and political and administrative appointments can be intense, especially since the government plays such a critical role in determining which resources will be available to ethnoregional and other elites. For a group leader to be left out of the inner circle of decisionmakers is to be ineffective in championing the claims of his or her constituents. And externally, powerful states and multinational companies, concerned with retaining their ability to gain access to public officials, press for the appointment of sympathetic ministers and administrators—who are anything but likely to voice the sentiments of the less-advantaged classes on policy issues. The overall effect of these domestic and international pressures is sometimes to skew high-level appointments, making the cabinet and bureaucracy more reflective of certain ethnic and class interests than of others. Because an imbalance in appointments can create political strains among leaders and the interests they represent, a comprehensive picture of the coalition process requires that attention be paid to these sources of tension.

In terms of our models of hegemonial exchange and bureaucratic centralism, we see different exclusion and inclusion practices occurring in Middle Africa during the postindependence years. In the case of the hegemonial exchange regimes, the softness of the state has facilitated patron-client ties at various levels of the political system, promoting the establishment of a governmental coalition of ethnoregional and other elites at the top, most of whom, as indicated above, are members of the dominant political class. In certain time-place situations such a structure of relationships proved remarkably stable (e.g., Kenyatta's Kenya or Houphouêt-Boigny's Ivory Coast, in the 1960s and early 1970s). However, where this cartel of notables denied entry to an important and broadly accepted ethnic spokesperson or did not distribute resources among subregions and groups on a roughly proportional basis, the strains upon this highly personalized regime, with its complex networks of face-to-face relationships, became noticeable. The excluded party or parties, denied full participation in matters of state, had no reason to resist attacking the norms of a hegemonial exchange relationship at its weakest point: the legitimacy of an informal system of political exchange and reciprocity within the parameters of a one- or no-party system. Clearly, only the strong state can afford to exclude a major power figure from the policymaking process. In a soft state context it leads frequently to attacks on the moral integrity of the system as a whole. In Ghana, for example, in 1969 a member of parliament went so far as to question President Kofi Busia's commitment to sectional equality on the grounds that the chief executive had failed to appoint someone from his section of the country when making ministerial appointments. "[O]ne Region out of the nine Regions," he pointed out, "is totally out of the Government and I feel that the ninth Region which is not represented in the Government has been reduced to the status of a dependent territory."[54] In this MP's view, exclusion from the cabinet was tantamount to a situation of internal dependency; it violated a political "right" to a significant part of the country.

In the Ghanaian instance mentioned above the ethnoregional claim to the inclusion of the group remained a negotiable matter, but this has not always been the case. Thus, on certain occasions in the Sudan, Nigeria, Zaire, Zimbabwe, Uganda and Kenya, a failure to include prominent interests has contributed substantially to political tensions and even disorder and violence. Two examples of inadequate incorporations contributing to political instability will suffice.

First, the fact that the south was noticeably underrepresented in the Sudanese cabinet from 1978 to 1983 led to considerable southern misunderstanding and ill will. Southern Sudanese, a very heterogeneous grouping of Dinka and non-Dinka peoples, generally felt themselves to be excluded from critical decisions affecting their interests (e.g., the oil pipeline, the location of the refinery, development projects, administrative decentralization, university recruitment in Juba, and so forth). As a consequence, many reacted angrily and subsequently gave their support to the various guerrilla movements which sprang up in their area.

Second, the anarchy which previously held Uganda in its grip reflected, in part, Milton Obote's inability to give sufficient assurances to the southern Bantu (especially the Baganda and the peoples of western Ankole) that they would not be victimized by the militarily and politically dominant northern Nilotic peoples (themselves divided in the army between Langi and Acholi). Not only did Baganda informants speak forcefully and bitterly to one of these authors on a 1980 visit to the country about the deposing of the Kabaka and the central government's control over provincial affairs in the 1960s, but they also contended that the "Moshi Spirit" of equitable cabinet representation was being violated by northern favoritism.[55] After he reassumed power in December 1980, Obote's inability to stop the grave civil liberties violations occurring in much of Uganda (according to Amnesty International an estimated 300,000 people disappeared or were murdered during the second Obote regime) and his apparent unwillingness to enter into equitable political relations with prominent southern spokespersons helped to fuel the rebellion that ultimately contributed to the July 1985 military coup. Interestingly, the new interim government set up by President Yoweri Museveni after assuming power in January 1986 reflects his pledge to install a broad-based regime. The initial nineteen-member cabinet includes five members of the Democratic party (including a well-known Baganda leader, Paul Ssemogerere, as Minister of Internal Affairs), three members of former President Milton Obote's Uganda People's Congress, one from the Conservative Party, and one from the Uganda Patriotic Movement. In brief, the failure to include the spokespersons of important ethnoregional units within the ruling coalition of a hegemonial exchange regime denies them important channels for the communication of collective claims (Zimbabwe may be another case in point).[56] Because linkages in such a regime are typically informal and personal, exclusion of an intermediary has grave consequences. The ethnic patron/intermediary and his or her clients feel left out and therefore fundamentally disadvantaged in the allocation of scarce public resources. The resulting political instability, then, represents a failure in elite linkages. It can be dealt with, as has been the case in Ivory Coast, by prudently reinstating an expelled member of the elite cartel when deemed convenient. Thus, a political "machine" built upon personal connections rather than institutional imperatives has greater flexibility than its bureaucratic centralist counterpart.

The exclusion of an ethnoregional intermediary by certain bureaucratic centralist regimes is necessarily a serious matter. In countries such as Ethiopia and Angola the state leader attempts to cope with a hostile environment—economic scarcity, international dependency, separatist claims, weak institutions, external interventions—by striving to consolidate authority in the hands of the party and bureaucracy. As already noted, the institutions of state may incorporate subnational representatives within these state institutions, but always on the terms set by the dominant state-party elite. The thrust is toward centralized state power; hence, the resulting relationships among bureaucratic centralist leaders are less those of political exchange and reciprocity among powerful personalities at various levels than those of committed party members from various parts of the country carrying out their public functions as state-party officials. Frequently the result is inflexibility of interelite relationships, for some partially autonomous ethnoregional leaders come to feel largely excluded from affairs of state. In certain of these situations the demands that the central authorities make for conformity to their purposes are staunchly resisted by leaders in the periphery, who call alternatively for their inclusion in the ruling coalition (UNITA in Angola) or for separate statehood (Eritrean, Tigrean and Oromo nationalists in Ethiopia).

For its part, the MPLA government in Angola rules out any suggestions on including Jonas Savimbi's UNITA in the ruling coalition at the center. In something of a nonnegotiating stance, President José Eduardo dos Santos has categorically rejected the idea of a "coalition government" with UNITA, insisting that "this question will not be discussed at any negotiating table."[57] Describing UNITA as a South African "puppet band," the MPLA leadership dismisses the possibility of forging moral linkages with these elements it regards as traitors. The consequence is a heightening of the level of conflict between these political actors. By failing to represent the Ovimbundu (UNITA's main support base) on the MPLA Political Bureau and by underrepresenting them on the Central Committee, the regime in Luanda is virtually excluding the spokespersons of the country's largest group, representing over one-third of the country's population.[58] This exclusion gives rise to a grievance which lends some basis in Ovimbundu eyes to Savimbi's appeal for support.

Somewhat similarly, the unwillingness of Lt. Col. Mengistu Haile Mariam's regime to consider negotiations with various leftist and nationality movements in Ethiopia after the Revolution created an inflexible political situation that led to the ruthless repression of his ideological adversaries and an ongoing civil war with the nationality movements. The Dergue quickly moved to suppress all but one of the original political movements that had participated in the joint civilian front of 1977 and capped its triumph over these opponents by subsequently proclaiming a formal communist state. By building and operating a highly centralized state-party organization, it managed to crush its ideological opponents; however, with a weak institutional base, it was unable to extend this control to the separatist movements in the country's periphery. Thus, the soft Ethiopian state found itself caught up in an unending military struggle, which further sapped its capacity and weakened its ability to cope with pressing development problems. Efforts at a political solution to the Eritrean secessionist challenge proved ineffective, as both Aman Andom and Atnafu Abate, two members of the Dergue who appear to have seriously considered a negotiated settlement of the conflict, paid for their conciliatory attitudes with their lives.

In brief, then, the efforts of the ideologically oriented bureaucratic centralist regimes to consolidate power in central state institutions were rewarded by the suppression of most opposition groups. However, the bureaucratic centralist regimes' unwillingness to co-opt powerful ethnoregional strongmen or to negotiate on the issue of regional autonomy made them more susceptible than the hegemonial exchange regimes to subnational rebellions. Hence, the bureaucratic centralist leadership's determination to control and suppress dissent under soft state circumstances proved somewhat counterproductive, contributing not insubstantially to the civil wars that plagued their countries in the postindependence period.[59]

In our concluding section we focus on the failure of various regimes to include modernist interest groups, and most particularly the peasantry, in the political process. Unless African regimes can act to incorporate such interests into decision-making activities, we see additional strains arising which, in the long term, will have adverse effects on their political stability and task achievement.

Emerging Patterns of Accommodation

We have noted the weaknesses of the strategy of exclusion of ethnoregional interests characteristic of the bureaucratic centralist regime. But hegemonial exchange regimes increasingly face challenges with which they, too, are ill-equipped to deal. Founded on tacit, sometimes institutionalized, elite consensus, hegemonial exchange regimes foster inclusive policies and coalitions designed to mend ethnic and regional rents in the political fabric of countries only just beginning to acquire political identities. And as long as popular interests can be channeled in this way, as long as popular demands can be seen as regional demands or ethnic rights to be satisfied via simple mechanisms of redistribution and reapportionment, inclusion in the hegemonial exchange style may well succeed. But cleavages which cannot be interpreted in these terms are spreading in Africa today, calling into question both regional unities and ethnic identities, and demanding new strategies of accommodation and coalition building.

The most obvious sign of such realignment is the urban-rural split, a division that now encompasses not only the old colonial centers and the hinterland, but also new and old townships and the periphery within most of modern Africa. The urban decay so amply documented elsewhere in this volume is only in part a reversal of previous patterns of growth; to some extent, it can be seen as a reflection of urban growth and the pressures arising from it. The informal economy is both an urban and rural phenomenon and is intertwined in patterns of trade now international in scope. As such, it unites people in commercial and other functional ties across not only recognizably artificial state boundaries, but also regional and ethnic boundaries as well. Urban expansion also tends to pit town against countryside. Moreover, regional differences often become recognized as differences in degree of urban organization and opportunity, as their centers of population variously acquire the benefits of modernity and their political elites become the source of the political capital necessary to articulate regional demands effectively.

A related, and troubling, cleavage in modern Africa is that between a broad "urban coalition" and the scattered agricultural interests of the countryside. As Robert Bates has argued, a "cheap food" coalition of urban workers, industrialists and processing concerns (often parastatals) has formed in many African countries to force down the price of food and industrial crops and to open doors to cheap imports.[60] Bureaucrats, themselves urban consumers and the employers of urban consumers, not only share these interests, but they have also secured important resources for the state by siphoning off agricultural surpluses through marketing boards and parastatals. Pricing policy as well as government investment in agriculture have been affected—with disastrous results.

As Bates points out, such policies have only been mitigated in states where agricultural interests were relatively well represented within the founding coalitions, as in Ivory Coast and Kenya. Elsewhere, as in Ghana, where agricultural interests were systematically excluded by the "youngmen" of the Nkrumah regime, patterns of underrepresentation have grown, forcing demand making into local, subregional and ethnic channels ill-suited for acquiring the concessions required by a whole sector of a national economy.[61] Yet, as the agricultural economy of Africa declines, as the countryside ceases to produce foreign exchange earnings necessary to purchase imported foodstuffs, urban interests themselves have been affected. The coalitional realignments necessary to reverse the process, however, scarcely fit the traditional elite consensus model. They must, of necessity, be class and sector-based, just as the coalitions that created this situation were based on distinctly economic criteria and found little resonance in the ethnic divisions which elsewhere were so apparent in political life.

The agricultural economy also provides the basis for another change in the coalitional context of contemporary politics. For the drive to increase agricultural production, however crippled by adverse government policies, has served at times to soften ethnic barriers and create new class divisions in the African countryside. Bonnie Campbell, for instance, has recently argued that the success of intensive cotton production in the northern and central savannah of the Ivory Coast, entailing a demand for foreign capital, increased labor requirements and growing pressure on the land, has led to a rapid process of class differentiation whose political implications can only at this point be guessed.[62] Taisier Ali and Jay O'Brien, in analyzing the cotton industry in the Sudan, point to a series of contradictory possibilities. The economic power of the pump owners in the developing irrigation districts of the Sudan was quickly translated into political power. These agricultural capitalists, however, fell from grace in 1968 as a result of the union of tenant farmers and agricultural laborers, who displayed a militancy that was unthinkable prior to the industrialization of agriculture. Finally, as the labor market in the Sudan has expanded, occupational categories that were at one time ethnically defined are now relatively open markets; ethnic strangers mingle together in field and factory, and with this mixing comes increased class consciousness.[63]

Despite the economic disengagement documented elsewhere in this volume, and even *because* of the economic crisis that has prompted such "delinkage" from the state, the modernization of agriculture has continued and even accelerated in recent years. The Tanzanian state's response to the peasantry's withdrawal from the market in the wake of the *ujamaa* program of the 1970s was a turn to large-scale, state and multinational corporation-run farming schemes. New dependencies and new class fractions were politically the most significant outcome.[64] Elsewhere in Africa both the state and the multinational corporations have moved into areas of agricultural production where large-scale farming is feasible or large revenues could be realized from processing.[65] Not only has this created powerful new interests in agriculture (contradictorily, state farms have sometimes been notoriously inefficient, a drain on a system otherwise dedicated to draining agriculture), but it has also created the possibility of new class-based conflicts and alliances, as Campbell, Ali and O'Brien suggest.

The resulting social forces, however fragmented, are not amenable to control, by and large, in the old ways. Hegemonial exchange systems, in fact, are likely to find themselves increasingly pressed for political options, for the new forces in African society cannot easily be co-opted into existing ethnic blocs. The power of trades unions, urban consumers, industrial chambers and other constituent interests in the urban coalition stood as an exception to the rule of a political process governed by and large by distributive efforts in a context of ethnic rivalry. If the skewed benefits won by the urban coalition were geographically based, this geography cut across ethnoregional bounds and had the potential to universalize discrimination along functional as well as ethnic lines. The appearance of important functional cleavages in African society, in short, is not new, but increasingly it demands new political forms and expressions.

What forms are likely to emerge? An important distinction must be made at this point concerning the *kinds of issues* likely to be addressed by different sorts of groupings. On the one hand, there are issues which can be treated in redistributive terms; we might say they concern ethnically divisible goods. Here we have in mind goods such as representation, health-care facilities, educational opportunities and investments, transportation and communication, and targeted development funds. In all these cases ethnoregional claims can be put forward and defended for fairer distribution of the largesse of the state. Such claims are subject to the sort of bargaining described above. As we saw earlier, too, such bargaining, whether openly encouraged or officially disdained, tends to become institutionalized in systems of what Lehmbruch and Schmitter have come to call "concertation," organized efforts at concerted decision making where interested parties are explicitly included in a bargaining process and often in implementation as well.[66]

Other types of claims are either not redistributive in nature or imply distribution along class or functional lines. Claims concerning tax policy, monetary policy, credit lines, subsidies, some sorts of investment, health insurance, disability benefits and other social welfare measures, as well as state-wide budget allocations for the various economic or social sectors, all deal with (at least at the outset) universally or functionally divisible goods. Here, too, bargaining takes place and political power is brought to bear. But in such instances, functional groupings—trade associations, unions, farmers' organizations, associations of health care, education or other professionals—or political parties aggregating these interests are likely to dominate the debate. And in these cases, as well, concertation is possible. Indeed, as Schmitter argues, where functional groupings take on corporative features—hierarchical organization, monopoly of representation, centralized decision making—institutionalized, "concerted" policymaking may emerge as the most likely political form.[67] To what extent do we see this happening in Africa?

We have already examined patterns of ethnic and ethnoregional accommodation, with their wide extension in contemporary Africa. Equally obvious and no less important, as we have seen, is the persistent tendency of policymakers to favor urban interests over rural ones, in apparent response to a powerful coalition of urban and bureaucratic constituents. Up to the present regime in Ghana, for instance, rural interests have scarcely been represented in any cabinet.[68] Yet representation is not tantamount to incorporation,[69] and although it is clear that the underrepresented rural majority had no effective voice in decisions affecting their lives, it is not certain that urban functional groups were effectively incorporated—incorporated, that is, in a recognized and consistent manner—into a concerted decision-making process. Though General I.K. Acheampong attempted early in his reign to co-opt "key organized horizontal and ethnic groupings" in a military-bureaucratic state, challenges to his authority were quickly met with a reversion to tight military control.[70] The recent offer by Flight-Lieutenant Jerry Rawlings to organize a body of "fishermen, farmers and researchers" under the auspices of the Ministry of Agriculture to advise on policy matters may point in the direction of some form of concerted arrangement, but it still seems premature to draw any conclusions on this.[71] Whether, beyond such arrangements, the interests represented will take on specifically "corporatist" features is likewise unclear.

These distinctions are important for assessing the current situation and for understanding the strategies policymakers are likely to adopt in response to it. Concerted structures have displayed some capacity to channel ethnic and ethnoregional conflict along predetermined lines. Will they also be able to manage the class, sectoral and professional competition that modernization brings in its wake? The answer would seem to be a mixed one, just as the policymaking and policy implementation strategies adopted by African states are likely to be mixed. In this respect, a great deal depends on the nature of the issues advanced. Representation in high governmental and party positions, for instance, has great symbolic value among ethnic groups. Some functional interests may also value the public impact of representation in posts at the political center—especially if such groups represent large popular constituencies. In other cases, however, they may find their interests better served by participating in low-profile advisory bodies, economic and social councils, and ad hoc committees at the ministerial and subministerial levels. Alongside the informal bargaining that is a feature of every polity, we are likely to see, as in the Ghanaian case noted above, increasing pressure for the inclusion of interested parties in the decision-making process.

However, insofar as specific goals must be met from general allocations, functional demands are likely to be cross-cut by demands of an ethnoregional cast: The Minister of Agriculture may have the mandate of important farmers' organizations and sections of the old urban coalition for a new credit policy, for instance. Nevertheless, regional allocations may continue to be skewed in response to pressures from regionally based groups. In such a setting central decisions regarding, for example, tax policy, extension of credit to agriculture or social welfare benefits are likely to be made increasingly with the participation of functional groups, but with constant adjustments designed to accommodate older forms of interest representation. Considering these complexities, functional groups may very well take on a "corporatist" structure to increase internal coherence and political power. They may become the singular representatives of a functional category—

defined by class, economic sector or profession—with centralized decision-making powers over their respective constituents.[72] Groups like the Kenya Cooperative Creameries, whose power was carried over from the period of white domination, display such features and demonstrate the very substantial political power they give organized interests.

On the other hand, decisions regarding the regional distribution of goods, civil service recruitment, educational policy, and participation generally in the polity are likely to continue to be influenced by ethnically organized groupings.[73] The patterns of disengagement documented elsewhere in this volume will only serve to strengthen such structures. Though these structures are likely to conflict with those designed to meet more functionally specific demands, there is no reason to think the one will supplant the other in the near future. Ethnic claims continue to have an impact in even so functionally differentiated a polity as the United States. Thus, we are likely to see the continuing, more or less rapid, development of hybrid systems of interest representation and decision making, mixing in various proportions functional and nonfunctional interest groups, some open-textured, some more corporately organized, but all exerting considerable pressure for effective inclusion in governmental decision making through structures of concertation. These structures may include various patterns of ethnically mixed cabinets and ministries described earlier and the advisory bodies and economic and social councils familiar in contemporary industrial democracies.[74]

Though these developments, finally, are perfectly compatible with the practices of elite-consensus politics examined earlier and with patterns of patron-client relations usually associated with the hegemonial exchange model, it appears to us that bureaucratic centralist states will find it easier to accommodate the emerging social forces of middle Africa than will their counterparts. The reasons are both ideological and structural. Ideologically, as we have seen, the bureaucratic centralist state spurns ethnic accommodation, seeing elite claims as particularistic intrusions on processes of decision making that should otherwise respond to universalistic criteria. Structurally, too, the bureaucratic centralist state has adopted patterns of organization designed to serve specific functional goals, rather than to accommodate the conflicting demands of groups defined by ascriptive criteria. "Political interference" in decision making in this context is thus much more likely to be channeled through the familiar forms of more or less organized consultation with affected groups, so much the better if these groups be functionally defined and singular representatives of their constituents.

But no bureaucratic centralist regime, as we have seen, escapes the imperatives of some ethnic accommodation. If most find themselves in a position analagous to that of contemporary Nicaragua—weak in resources, struggling with a crippled economy, attempting to impose order in a situation of ethnic division and internal and external challenges to authority—the model both Nicaragua and contemporary bureaucratic centralist regimes in Africa may find themselves looking at in times to come is that of Mexico, where a single-party, heavily bureaucratized system has effectively channeled both regional rivalries and rapidly expanding functional groups into centralized decision-making processes, largely behind closed doors, and well-oiled by corruption and public displays of governmental generosity. This "model" has its own flaws, as no one today would deny, and, in contrast to much of Africa, ethnic divisions in Mexico have always taken second place to profound regional and class differences. Nonetheless, it suggests a way in which the demands for representation unleashed by independence—initially ethnically organized, then increasingly based on functional claims on the system—might be met by states weak in resources and authority but already experienced in strategies of accommodation and choice. Other, more democratic, forms of political organization are imaginable, but given the present patterns, the persistent scarcity of resources and the disintegrating effects of such scarcity, African governments are likely to continue to attempt to accommodate popular demands through explicit or tacit inclusion of a variety of social forces and through the relatively "cheap" and socially efficient forms of concertation described here.

Notes

1. For an earlier article on state effectiveness, see Donald Rothchild and Michael Foley, "The Implications of Scarcity for Governance in Africa," *International Political Science Review*, 4, 3 (1983): 311–326.

2. Claude Ake, "The Future of the State in Africa," *International Political Science Review*, 6, 1 (1985): 112.

3. Nelson Kasfir, "Relating Class to State in Africa," *Journal of Commonwealth and Comparative Politics*, 21, 3 (November 1983): 6.

4. Claude Ake, Presidential Address to the Nigerian Political Science Association, as quoted in *West Africa*, May 25, 1981, p. 1163.

5. Ibid.

6. Donald Rothchild, "Collective Demands for Improved Distributions," in Donald Rothchild and Victor A. Olorunsola, eds., *State Versus Ethnic Claims: African Policy Dilemmas* (Boulder: Westview, 1983), pp. 176–184.

7. Sammy Smooha, "Control of Minorities in Israel and Northern Ireland," *Comparative Studies in Society and History*, 22, 2 (April 1980): 278.

8. W. Arthur Lewis, "Beyond African Dictatorship," *Encounter*, 25, 2 (August 1965): 9; and idem. *Politics in West Africa* (London: Allen and Unwin, 1965), pp. 74–84.

9. Arend Lijphart, *Democracy in Plural Societies* (New Haven: Yale University Press, 1977), p. 31.

10. On the concept of "antagonistic cooperation" see Barrington Moore, Jr., *The Social Origins of Dictatorship and Democracy* (Boston: Beacon Press, 1966), p. 196.

11. Robert H. Bates, "Modernization, Ethnic Competition, and the Rationality of Politics in Contemporary Africa," in Rothchild and Olorunsola, *State Versus Ethnic Claims*, p. 164.

12. Richard A. Joseph, "Ethnicity and Prebendal Politics in Nigeria: A Theoretical Outline," (Paper presented at the American Political Science Association, Denver, September 2–5, 1982), p. 9.

13. Daniel G. Matthews, "Nigeria 1985: An Interim Report," *CSIS Africa Notes*, No. 24 (February 29, 1984): 3–4; and Larry Diamond, "Nigeria: The Coup and the Future," *Africa Report*, 29, 2 (March-April 1984): 13–14.

14. Article 21 of the Constitution of the National Party of Nigeria. Reprinted in Chuba Okadigbo, *The Mission of the NPN* (Enugu: Ejike R. Nwankwo Associates, 1981), Appendix 1.

15. Enukora Joe Okoli, "The NPN's Zoning Dilemma," *West Africa*, November 22, 1982, p. 3003.

16. *West Africa*, December 12, 1983, p. 2908.

17. *West Africa* (London), October 18, 1982, p. 2747, and January 31, 1983, p. 254. Also see Dr. Kingsley Mbadiwe's statement on zoning as an instrument of unity in *Daily Times*, June 17, 1982, p. 5.

18. *Daily Times* (Lagos), November 28, 1978, p. 3, and December 5, 1983, p. 13.

19. Norman Frolich, "The Instability of Minimum Winning Coalitions," *American Political Science Review*, 69, 3 (September 1975): 946.

20. Confidential interview, Accra, January 1985.

21. Victor Ndovi, "Eyadema's Rule in Togo," *West Africa*, October 27, 1980, p. 2104.

22. Robert A. Mortimer, "Ivory Coast: Succession and Recession," *Africa Report*, 28, 1 (January-February 1983): 5, 7; and Alex Rondo, "The Team Spirit in Ivory Coast," *West Africa*, April 21, 1980, pp. 685–687.

23. Mortimer, "Ivory Coast," pp. 5, 7.

24. Aristide R. Zolberg, "Politics in the Ivory Coast: 2," *West Africa*, August 6, 1960, p. 883. Also see his book, *One-Party Government in the Ivory Coast* (Princeton: Princeton University Press, 1964), pp. 234, 283.

25. On this see Richard E. Stryker, "A Local Perspective on Developmental Strategy in the Ivory Coast," in Michael F. Lofchie, ed., *The State of the Nations* (Berkeley: University of California Press, 1971), p. 134.

26. David Achidi, "Cameroon: Biya Calls for National Unity," *West Africa*, January 30, 1984, p. 246.

27. P.S. Engers, "Anglophone Cameroon: Drifting With the Rudderless Ship," *West Africa*, August 13, 1984, p. 1617.

28. According to the Armed Forces Minister, the great majority of the plotters hailed from the northern part of the country. See *West Africa*, April 23, 1984, p. 865.

29. *The Weekly Review* (Nairobi), January 6, 1984, p. 21.

30. Dunstan M. Wai, "Geoethnicity and the Margin of Autonomy in the Sudan," in Rothchild and Olorunsola, *State Versus Ethnic Claims*, p. 320.

31. To promote a lasting settlement with Col. John Garang and his Sudan People's Liberation Army, the new government was also urged to include a reserved seat for Garang's spokesman in the interim cabinet. *Manchester Guardian Weekly*, 132, 17 (April 28, 1985): 10.

32. For evidence of Kaunda's refusal to legitimate clientelistic politics and ethnic representations in Zambia see Donald Rothchild, "State-Ethnic Relations in Middle Africa," in Gwendolen M. Carter and Patrick O'Meara, eds., *African Independence: The First 25 Years* (Bloomington: Indiana University Press, 1985), p. 77.

33. *Times of Zambia* (Ndola), October 24, 1970, p. 6; and *Zambia Daily Mail* (Lusaka), October 7, 1970, p. 1.

34. On this point see Richard Hall, *The High Price of Principles* (New York: Africana, 1969), p. 195.

35. William Tordoff, "Introduction," in William Tordoff, ed., *Administration in Zambia* (Manchester: Manchester University Press, 1980), p. 15.

36. Donald Rothchild and Michael Rogin, "Uganda," in Gwendolen M. Carter, ed., *National Unity and Regionalism in Eight African States* (Ithaca: Cornell University Press, 1966), p. 359; also see Nelson Kasfir, *The Shrinking Political Arena* (Berkeley: University of California Press, 1976), pp. 125–126.

37. Colin Legum, ed., *Africa Contemporary Record 1981–82* (New York: Africana, 1981), pp. B299, B303.

38. Robert H. Jackson, "Planning, Politics, and Administration," in Goran Hyden, Robert Jackson and John Okumu, eds., *Development Administration: The Kenyan Experience* (Nairobi: Oxford University Press, 1970), p. 178. Also see Robert H. Jackson and Carl G. Rosberg, *Personal Rule in Black Africa* (Berkeley: University of California Press, 1982), p. 150.

39. *The Standard* (Nairobi), October 12, 1978, p. 4.

40. Victoria Brittain, "Five Months That Took Kenya to the Brink," *Manchester Guardian Weekly*, 127, 6 (April 8, 1982): 7. Also see Vincent B. Khapoya, "Kenya Under Moi: Continuity or Change?" *Africa Today*, 27, 1 (1980): 22–23.

41. Martin L. Kilson, "Authoritarian and Single-Party Tendencies in African Politics," *World Politics*, 15, 2 (January 1963): 275.

42. Ladipo Adamolekun, *Sékou Touré's Guinea* (London: Methuen, 1976), pp. 126–132.

43. By 1976, as Sékou Touré launched his attack on the Foulahs (and spoke of a "Foulah Plot"), the policy of ethnic accommodation appeared to have come to an end.

44. Confidential interview, Berkeley, California, April 15, 1985.

45. Anver Versi, "Tanzania: Time for a Change," *New African* (London), 202 (July 1984): 12.

46. John A. Marcum, "Angola: A Quarter Century of War," *CSIS Africa Notes*, No. 37 (December 21, 1984): 3.

47. Ibid.

48. I am indebted to Gerald J. Bender for a number of these points.

49. Arend Lijphart, *Conflict and Coexistence in Belgium* (Berkeley: Institute of International Studies, 1981), p. 5.

50. For a more extended discussion of the characteristics and dynamics of a hegemonial exchange model see Rothchild, "State-Ethnic Relations."

51. René Lemarchand, "Political Clientelism and Ethnicity in Tropical Africa: Competing Solidarities in Nation-Building," *American Political Science Review*, 64, 1 (March 1972): 76. (Italics in text.) Also see Richard A. Joseph, "Class, State, and Prebendal Politics in Nigeria," *Journal of Commonwealth and Comparative Politics*, 21, 3 (November 1983): 28.

52. K.W., "The Nigerian Milieu," *West Africa* (April 1, 1985): 625–627. [Quote from Ladipo Adamolekun, *The Fall of the Second Republic* (Ibadan: Spectrum Books, 1985).]

53. Dean E. McHenry, Jr., *Tanzania's Ujamaa Villages* (Berkeley: Institute of International Studies, 1979), p. 85.

54. Republic of Ghana, Parliamentary Debates, *Official Report* I, 6 (November 27, 1969): 101. (Statement by C.K. Nayo).

55. Committee One, *Uganda Since the War* (Nairobi: Stellascope, 1979), p. 3.

56. Nick Davies, "Matabeleland Turned into a Killing Ground," *Manchester Guardian Weekly*, 128, 11 (March 13, 1983): 8.

57. *West Africa*, January 7, 1985, p. 39.

58. Marcum, "Angola: A Quarter Century of War," p. 3.

59. On this see Ekkart Zimmerman, "Macro-Comparative Research on Political Protest," in Ted Robert Gurr, ed., *Handbook of Political Conflict* (New York: Free Press, 1980), p. 210.

60. Robert H. Bates, *Markets and States in Tropical Africa: The Political Basis of Agricultural Politics* (Berkeley: University of California Press, 1981).

61. On the localization of demand making in Ghana see Naomi Chazan, *An Anatomy of Ghanaian Politics: Managing Political Recession, 1969-1982* (Boulder: Westview, 1983), pp. 60-70.

62. Bonnie K. Campbell, "Inside the Miracle: Cotton in the Ivory Coast," in Jonathan Barker, ed., *The Politics of Agriculture in Tropical Africa* (Beverly Hills: Sage, 1984), pp. 143-171.

63. Taisier Ali and Jay O'Brien, "Labor, Community, and Protest in Sudanese Agriculture," in Barker, *Politics of Agriculture,* pp. 205-238.

64. Andrew Coulson, "Agricultural Policies in Mainland Tanzania, 1946-76," in Judith Heyer, Pepe Roberts and Gavin Williams, eds., *Rural Development in Tropical Africa* (London: Macmillan, 1981), pp. 81-82. Coulson, however, emphasizes only the increased dependency of bureaucrats on international development agencies.

65. Some sense of the importance of this process can be gleaned from a survey of the articles collected in Barker, *Politics of Agriculture;* and Heyer, Roberts and Williams, *Rural Development in Tropical Africa.*

66. The term is Schmitter's. See Gerhard Lehmbruch, "Introduction: Neo-Corporatism in Comparative Perspective," and Philippe C. Schmitter, "Reflections on Where the Theory of Neo-Corporatism Has Gone and Where the Praxis of Neo-Corporatism May Be Going," both in Gerhard Lehmbruch and Philippe C. Schmitter, eds., *Patterns of Corporatist Policy-Making* (Beverly Hills: Sage, 1982), esp. pp. 260-264.

67. Schmitter, "Reflections," p. 264.

68. Emmanuel Gyimah-Boadi, "The State and Agricultural Development: The Political Basis of Agricultural Policies in Ghana," (Ph.D. diss., University of California, Davis, 1985), Chap. 2.

69. We owe this important distinction to Rufus P. Browning, Dale Rogers Marshall and David H. Tabb, *Protest Is Not Enough: The Struggle of Blacks and Hispanics for Equality in Urban Politics* (Berkeley: University of California Press, 1984), pp. 24-27.

70. Naomi Chazan, *Anatomy of Ghanaian Politics,* p. 70. See also Donald Rothchild, "Military Regime Performance: An Appraisal of the Ghana Experience, 1972-1978," *Comparative Politics,* 12, 4 (July 1980): 459-479.

71. *Ghana News* 14, 3 (March 1985).

72. Schmitter, "Reflections," p. 246.

73. On this, see Donald Rothchild, "Middle Africa: Hegemonial Exchange and Resource Allocation," in Alexander J. Groth and Larry L. Wade, eds., *Comparative Resource Allocation* (Beverly Hills: Sage, 1984): pp. 151-180.

74. See Lijphart, *Democracy in Plural Societies.*

11

Three Levels of State Reordering: The Structural Aspects

Kwame A. Ninsin

Introduction

Despite the numerous political changes which have occurred on the African continent since the 1960s, Africa still remains firmly within the capitalist-dominated world economy. This situation has very important implications for the behavior of the state. Therefore, it has to be taken into account in any discussion of the state. In particular, it must be understood that changes in the world economy impinge adversely on the economies of African countries and the effectiveness of the state in dealing with this problem. Further, the state has consequently become deeply involved in economic management and production as well as the distribution of goods and services, in repeated efforts to overcome its own weakness as well as that of the economy. In short, the African state has become a big capitalist.[1] This raises the question of the nature of its relations with international capital (which is the dominant factor in the global economy) and local (or national) capital and social classes. This chapter is an attempt to explicate aspects of this problematique and how the state responds to the challenges arising out of it.

I shall argue in the following pages that state reordering is a peremptory process imposed by the state's own inability to promote economic growth and manage the efficient distribution of social wealth, and that this is the result of constraining factors arising from the global economy and its crisis. Severe political and social repercussions are attributable to this weakness. The process dates back to the period of independence, when the accession to formal political sovereignty was not matched by the development of a strong and independent capacity to transform the national economy from a state of backwardness.

It is remarkable that the factors which enforce state reordering have persisted in spite of the state's collaboration since independence with foreign financial, banking and commercial interests within the framework of the colonial economic and political linkages. Equally remarkable is the fact that the goals of such collaborative efforts have always been to elaborate on, extend and rationalize areas of cooperation between local and international capital in the expectation that such cooperation will promote internal resource control and ownership by members of the national bourgeoisie. In recent times this policy has taken the specific form of "Africanization," or "indigenization," of the national economy. Despite this record of collaboration with international capital, the result has been almost the same across the continent: disastrous. Every country on the continent has been experiencing a succession of economic crises, and each new round has generated political repercussions whereby the state reorganizes its political relations.

The State and Political Coalitions

Even though both functionalists and Marxist theorists recognize the state as essentially an organization of legitimate coercive force, there is no consensus regarding its relations with the various clusters of class groups over which it asserts legal authority. While functionalists emphasize the state's neutrality, Marxists underscore the opposite. The history of the state in Africa, from its colonial foundations, would seem to confirm the view that the state is not a neutral, impartial force—a kind of benevolent Leviathan.[2] There is ample evidence to show that the state systematically organized the relations of production and distribution within the colonies, on the one hand, and the external economic relations between individual colonies and their respective metropoles, on the other. This role was most glaring in the determination of investment priorities in agriculture and mining, as well as in the organization and distribution of labor among these sectors.[3]

The state did not carry out its functions randomly, but rather in a structured manner determined by the relative powers of the configuration of class forces within any given country. Thus, before independence, economic and other interests of the leading indigenous classes were effectively subordinated to those of foreign investors and traders, particularly from the metropole. By independence the dynamics of the nationalist politics had crystallized new social forces at the level of state politics, including workers in both the private and public sectors, such as the civil bureaucracy. There were also clusters of agro-based classes. The state now had to deal, in one way or another, with various fractions of the incipient national bourgeoisie, the working classes and other social classes spanning the urban-rural circuit. Thus, by independence the colonial state had been transformed into the foci of all the major conflicting interests operating in the former colonies. Meanwhile, the state's relations with the metropole and consequently with the world economy not only remained essentially the same, but more especially were strengthened as various national capitals became transnationalized.[4]

The conduct of the state at any particular time was therefore not highly structured. The state itself came to reflect the structured social relations that it organized in the specific manner determined by the positions of the various class groups within the social economy and was reinforced by international capitalist interests. In other words, the conduct of the state has always been conditioned by the social structure. The direction and content of state policies, therefore, do in a way reflect the interests of such social groups in relation to their relative positions within the existing configuration of class groupings.

However, in all societies it is the hegemonic classes that directly exercise this organized social power expressed in the state. This does not mean that the functionaries of state power, including those of the government, ought to be, or are necessarily, members of the hegemonic classes. While they are not, or need not be, the political class (regime) of any society and the state salariat at any single historical moment are guided in their conduct by the same ideological principles that determine the conduct of the hegemonic classes and indeed the entire social structures.[5]

The distinction between regime and hegemonic class(es) helps to address two significant issues in political inquiry—namely, the relationship between political regimes and hegemonic classes, and the problem of instability vis-à-vis the unity or otherwise of the hegemonic classes. It is my view that regime and hegemonic or ruling classes are not coterminous. There is nonetheless a categorical relationship of dependence of regimes on the latter. This relationship is guided by the need to employ state power to organize the economy and society as a whole in order to enhance the material interests of the hegemonic classes. Regimes are therefore impelled to respond to such interests and to prevent their being jeopardized. Failure or inability to respond effectively to such interests, especially when they are clearly in danger, may lead to a change of government without the character of the state being altered. Regime change implies the emergence of a new coalition and the decline of the old.

Coalition building may occur either mainly within the ruling classes or between fractions of the ruling classes and others outside it. Whether a coalition will be intra- or inter-class is determined by the political and economic exigencies of the given society. As will be argued below, the rise and fall of coalitions and, therefore, of regimes are specific responses to internal economic vicissitudes determined largely by the nature and crisis of the global economic system.

The Economic and Political Crises

Since independence not one African country has succeeded in transforming its economy into a self-sustaining and viable system. It is true that some—and they are very few indeed—have at times given the impression of success (e.g., Ivory Coast and Kenya,[6] especially in the 1960s and early 1970s). But since the late 1970s the overall economic performance on the continent has been, on the average, dismal.[7]

This catastrophic performance was compounded by two equally severe problems—namely, rapidly deteriorating terms of trade and a growing external debt. According to the 1982 *Annual Report* of the International Monetary Fund, the terms of trade of African countries, which were already bad during the 1978-1980 period, became worse during the 1981-1982 period. As the purchasing power of their exports declined, African governments felt compelled to borrow more from nonconcessionary sources at a time when nominal and real interest rates on the international money market had started to reach exceedingly high levels.

The cumulative effective of these unfavorable developments has been the debt crisis.[8] Thus, while in 1974 the total external debt of sub-Saharan African countries was about $14.8 billion, by 1983 the figure had jumped to $870 billion. Most African countries therefore had to commit a greater percentage of their earnings to debt repayments. In 1983 the debt service ratio for Sudan was 15%; for Togo about 80%; for Uganda and Guinea about 40%; and for Ivory Coast between 40% and 50%. This problem was further exacerbated by the appreciation of the US dollar. In effect, the state since independence has had to make attempts to cope with the problem of promoting capitalist accumulation; its growing incapacity in this con-nection, however, has forced the problem to reach crisis proportions.

As the abysmal failure of African economies attained crisis dimensions, two major responses became clear. One is the growing intervention of the state in economic management and production. As Ake points out: "All African countries, even the most obviously capitalist, such as Nigeria, Zaire, Ivory Coast and Senegal, have very large public sectors which are getting larger in every case."[9] In effect, the state in every single African country has come to assume the role of a big capitalist. In this regard it has either acted in opposition to local and foreign capital, as was the case in Ghana from 1960 to 1965 and has been the case in Tanzania since 1967, or it has intervened to support local capital in active collaboration with foreign capital (as in Nigeria, Ivory Coast, Senegal and Kenya). But on the whole, the intention has been to reverse economic decline and stimulate growth.

In both instances, however, the state has come to command considerable social wealth. Moreover, this advantage has reinforced the colonial tradition that control of state power presents significant possibilities for shaping or reshaping economic policies. It is in this sense that the control of political power becomes crucial for the leading class forces in African countries.[10] The result has often been fierce intra-class struggles for control of state power. These struggles have been the principal underlying factor in the constant change of regimes—mainly through coups d'état.

As pointed out above, such changes do not alter the essence and functions of the state. Rather, they imply the composition or formation of new coalitions and their crystallization at the level of state power—the second major response. Accordingly, while the state may be functioning to promote the interests of the whole hegemonic class in the long run, it acts immediately to promote economic and other interests of the fractions within this class which, with the coming into power of the new regime, have moved into a position of relative political strength vis-à-vis other fractions. In this regard, then, state policies relate in specific ways to such new coalitions, at any particular time, and then generally to the social formation as a whole.

The economic crisis therefore has serious political repercussions. It fosters political instability and undermines the already fragile political institutions of the state. Ultimately it exacerbates their ineffectiveness, and thereby gives rise to a political crisis: the state's growing inability to legitimize itself as an effective social force for implementing definite social programs of both economic and political value to its members.

Similarly, the responses are mutually related: The economic affects the political, and vice versa. In this connection we have identified only two responses so far: namely, growing state involvement in the economy as a capitalist, and crystallization of new coalitions which lead to changes in government as shifts in economic policy become necessary. These two responses imply a redefinition of the state's position vis-à-vis foreign and national capital, and they immediately generate a third response—namely, a redefinition of the relationship between the state and the nonhegemonic classes. The outcome of this redefinition is, in fact, determined by the interests of the hegemonic classes as a whole—in brief, of capital in general.

Reordering

These three interrelated levels of response constitute what I term "state reordering." The term is used here to refer to the constant within its environment (i.e., the global economy and the national economy). These power blocs are foreign investors (or foreign capital), the national hegemonic classes (or national capital) and the lower classes. The source of all three levels of state reordering is the accumulation crisis that confronts and undermines the legitimacy of the state.

Independence: Crises and Response

The independence struggle was waged around an economic agenda: land, trade, credit, industrial and other economic policy grievances. Victory for the nationalist movement was therefore an opportunity for the victorious coalition within the nationalist front to implement an economic program that would respond to most, if not all, of their economic grievances. Basically, it implied the promotion of a policy of capitalist accumulation whether the regime that was in power was conservative or progressive—that is, whether it was committed to a policy of "gradualism" such as that which has characterized state policy in the Ivory Coast or to one of "structural transformation" such as that which prevailed in Ghana under the Convention People's Party (CPP).[11]

Whatever the differences, the new regimes implemented such economic programs within definite policy boundaries that had been informally agreed upon during the period of constitutional negotiations for the peaceful transfer of political power to the nationalist leaders. Invariably this meant that those regimes were to formulate and implement economic policies under the institutionalized vigilance of the former colonial power and allied international financial institutions;[12] because the politico-economic institutional framework of free enterprise (the implementation of which alone makes the new nations still attractive markets for foreign capital) had to be safeguarded. In every conceivable case the state played a central role in attracting foreign capital and creating the requisite internal political and legal conditions to enhance the interest of capital.[13]

For the benefit of the national capitalist elements, the state intervened to facilitate access specifically to industrial and commercial capital (in the form of loans and equity shares) as well as to the commodity market in general. These interventions took the specific form of restructuring commercial, financial and other institutions inherited from the colonial power and bringing them under direct state control and/or regulation. In both Tanzania[14] and Ghana the state also set out openly to secure a direct partnership with private foreign capital, whereas in Kenya, Ivory Coast, Senegal and Nigeria the state intervened to promote a partnership between private indigenous capitalists and their foreign counterparts. Invariably, however, it was the independence coalition that benefited from such policies. As Zolberg explains in the case of Ivory Coast, "This coalition could be maintained only by enhancing the legitimacy of its [the country's] leader . . . and by distributing tangible benefits to key components, including the emerging bourgeoisie and the ethnic groups."[15] This is what Nyongo calls the "pact of domination."[16] As he explains, the constitution of this pact is determined by the need for capital accumulation felt by the hegemonial classes. The state, in such conditions, becomes the instrument as well as a source of economic power for the indigenous bourgeoisie.

By the late 1960s the postcolonial hegemonial pacts had come under severe strain. In most of the countries with gradualist regimes as well as those with structural transformation regimes, economic policy had not succeeded in promoting capital accumulation for the rising local bourgeoisies. The legitimacy of regimes and the credibility of the capitalist model of development were plunged into serious crisis, necessitating regime turnover. The exceptions could be counted on one's finger tips: Kenya, Senegal, Ivory Coast and possibly the Gambia. All of these countries had escaped the horrific effects of the global economic crisis, largely as a result of the advantages conferred upon them by direct foreign involvement in the management of their economies.[17] The coups of that era, which were really the first of the tidal waves to come, were therefore a response to the economic and political crises. They were aimed at finding new economic and political formulas to meet the crises. Thus, in Ghana, for example, successive regimes in the 1966–1979 period pursued policies devoted to the promotion of foreign investments as well as the development of indigenous private and state capital.[18] The emphasis in investment policy shifted from merely promoting foreign investment to ensuring mutual advantages for both local and international capitalists. Even in Kenya where the regime had attained a relatively higher level of stability, state power was employed to promote the accumulation needs of the national bourgeoisie in collaboration with foreign capital.[19]

Across the continent the specific policies formulated for realizing such mutual advantages differed from country to country, but the political goals remained the same: legitimacy and stability. The differences in emphasis were dictated by the balance of class forces in any given country during the decisive period and what the hegemonic classes therefore defined as their immediate needs. In Nigeria, for example, the 1966 coup paved the way for expanding the formal boundaries of the entrepreneurial class to include a select few from the lower classes. As some provisions of Nigeria's indigenization law emphasized it had become necessary to recognize the economic rights of some groups from the lower classes also to become "capitalists" in the face of the growing opposition from labor and other sections of the lower classes. In Ghana, on the other hand, the 1966 coup meant the restoration of the leading capitalists within the bourgeoisie. Accordingly, public policy served the interests of that group until the 1970s. By then the glaring inability of both the National Liberation Council (NLC) and Progress Party (PP) regimes to deal with the economic crisis facing the nation had provoked the same level of confrontation between the lower classes and the two regimes as was the case in Nigeria. The Supreme Military Council (SMC) regime's policies, especially the Investment Policy Decree and related laws attempted,[20] as its Nigerian counterpart had done,[21] to incorporate the lower classes into a new coalition through a policy of democratizing capital. This policy created the appropriate framework for political stability until 1979, when the new consensus which had developed out of the existing coalition broke down under the weight of the contradictions of that very same policy.[22] In contrast, in Kenya, where the lower classes have usually been brought firmly under state control through various forms of repression, the restructuring of the state's relationship with international capital since the latter half of the 1960s has favored both foreign investors and the politically most powerful members of the indigenous capitalist class.[23] The independence coalition has remained fairly stable here, as it has in Senegal and Ivory Coast.

"Hegemonic Vacancy"

Despite their clamorous efforts to implement more effective economic policies, African governments have been unable to generate and sustain an appreciable level of economic growth. Particularly since the 1970s, most, if not all, African economies have suffered a catastrophic decline.[24] This is, indeed, a sad comment on what has become a chronic situation of incapacity of the state to implement the capitalist programs to which it has committed itself over the years. This weakness has also affected its ability to meet the growing needs of the vast majority of its people, especially the lower classes, for improvement in their living conditions—that is, for material and spiritual security. In contrast, the ability to manage the production of wealth and distribute it so as to achieve a positive political effect is the hallmark of the state in advanced capitalist societies.[25] One must therefore agree with the view that in African countries "the hegemony of capital over labor is hard to come by. . . . The capitalists . . . rule, but they . . . rule in a situation of 'hegemonic vacancy.'"[26] In other words, the inability of the state to provide or ensure a certain level of material and spiritual well-being for the bulk of its people is a function of the weakness of the national bourgeoisie. This correlation is important because it enables us to understand the implications of the crises of the state as accumulation and legitimacy crises for the entire social formation. In particular, it also makes sense out of the arguments in the essays of Callaghy, Lemarchand and MacGaffey in this volume that both the state and the national bourgeoisie are not merely inefficient, but are also predators fleecing both the peasantry and the nation as a whole.

This is a kind of generalized weakness which also expresses itself as an ideological and political weakness. In this regard, it is the inability to practice a definite ideology and to institutionalize definite state political organizations, processes and practices that would confer credibility on the state's apparatus of government and thereby enable it to implement successfully the capitalist ideology and model of development. Insofar as the state is therefore bereft of any significant economic capacity, it also lacks the moral authority to demand obedience to its laws as well as loyalty and support. The outcome of this hegemonic vacancy is the widespread use of political violence against the people.

These political and economic crises account largely for the emergence of the process of marginalization, which has, in turn, produced the unusual phenomenon of a large informal economy. According to Lemarchand, the parallel economy may be viewed as a response to the economic and social vulnerabilities arising from the declining capabilities of the state and the predatoriness of its local representatives.[27]

Growing state intervention in the economy has substantially increased the size of the market economy as a whole. Theoretically, this should be a sufficient index of the growth in the power of the state over its environment and therefore, logically, of its successful incorporation of peripheral social groups into the national political and economic orders. Empirically, however, the failure of the state to promote economic growth as well as to improve the living conditions of its citizens has weakened its integrative capability and retarded (but not negated) this incorporation process. As stated above, it has given considerable impetus to the expansion of the informal economy, a phenomenon which some would prefer to describe as indicative of disengagement from the state.[28] The growing importance of the informal sector and various forms of primordial associations, and the rising tempo of state activity in economic restructuring and decentralization are both responses to this crisis. The first is the periphery's reaction to the deepening process of marginalization, as one economic crisis succeeds another, while .the second is the center's attempt to reintegrate the periphery. In reality, the latter is a strategy to retain the periphery within the ambit of the state to ensure its continued subordination and exploitation.

I consider the growth of the informal economy primarily an outcome of the state's act of delinking certain social strata from its legal and moral responsibilities as its economic capacity continues to decline. I therefore define "delinking" as a mechanism by which the state gradually abandons its legal and moral obligations toward the weaker sections of society as a result of its own growing incapacity to discharge them effectively. In the process masses of people in this category become increasingly proletarianized (if they have not been already), or unemployed and even more impoverished. But I would insist that this process does not disengage the delinked strata from the state. Rather, insofar as the so-called informal economy is not exclusive of the formal sector, which is governed by capitalist laws of accumulation, the actors in the informal economy do participate, even if indirectly at times, in the formal economy. They are therefore subject to the laws of the formal sector. As marginalized persons (women, the unemployed, school leavers, peasant farmers, petty traders and indeed the whole "nation" of the marginalized), they have to contend daily with the rapacious accumulation laws of the free market merely to survive. MacGaffey's contribution to this volume illustrates this point graphically, even though she denies it to the extent of asserting that capital accumulation is possible independently of state policies and action or inaction.[29]

The heart of the matter is that the lower classes involved in the informal economy are effectively exploited by people in positions of undisputed political and economic advantage. Persons in this latter category are constantly manipulating the strategic political and economic structures that they control in order to ensure extraordinary benefits for themselves. The informal economy is therefore no more than an extension of the formal economy. This situation can be attributed to the latter's inefficiencies for purposes of accumulation by the national bourgeoisie and the uncertainties which are the trademark of any accumulation project. This last point affirms the view that the national bourgeoisie and highly placed administrators in both the public and private sectors are active participants in the informal sector of the economy. However, for them the informal sector is a source of super profits and not a survival response. The state has an interest in the persistence and growth of the informal economy, precisely because it serves the accumulation needs of its social base—the leading social classes and its key political and administrative cadres—for whom the formal sector does not provide adequate security.

Africa's Second Collapse

I have already provided some data on the African continent's crisis. The specific manifestations of this pervasive crisis are staggering indeed—namely, widespread famine arising from the collapse of most African countries, chronic shortages of essential consumer goods, the general decadence of the manufacturing and export sectors, and a crippling debt burden. These are a grim, but unqualified, testimony to the continent's second collapse in the face of the towering technological, scientific and economic achievements, as well as the extraordinary economic, political and military might, of the West. Accordingly, Africa seems to be literally tottering as it becomes more deeply entangled in a new vortex of subjugation by the West—a new colonialism which finds its greatest advantage in the nominal independence of the countries of the continent.

The response of regimes to the current crisis has followed the classical colonial pattern whereby the majority of the continent's ruling groups, sooner or later, volunteered alliance with the colonizers, exhibiting total disregard for the interests of their subjects as well as their own political survival. Today the new alliance is being forged by a better organized and more socially conscious group that is represented by a legally constituted national institution called government and operating under the general superintendence of the modern state. In addition, the representatives of Western capital are no longer trading firms. They are transnational financial institutions—the IMF and the World Bank—that are exercising effective sovereignty over states and governments on behalf of Western capital.

The specific form of this new reordering is the so-called adjustment of Africa's economies which is occurring under the close direction of these two powerful agencies of Western capital. Thus, currently, as many as 18 African countries south of the Sahara are implementing this IMF–World Bank structural adjustment program, which includes the removal of subsidies from a wide range of commodities and services. As the critique of the Berg Report by the OAU, ECA, and the ADB emphasizes,[30] this new offensive on the continent is aimed at restoring it to its colonial role as producer and exporter of raw agricultural and mineral products.

In the context of this response three main patterns are currently discernible: (a) attempts to strengthen the capitalist base of state and society; (b) a return to constitutionalism or (where this has failed) to the "strong regime" of military dictatorship; and (c) decentralization of the state apparatus. I shall comment briefly on the first two.

To begin with, strengthening the capitalist base of state and society has taken the form of elaborate incentives to the private sector. But contrary to the earlier bias in state intervention which emphasized joint ventures, the current practice seems to shift the emphasis to big local capitalists. These are persons who succeeded under the previous indigenization policies and can now stand on their feet, more of less, as exporters of agricultural commodities or as manufacturers. The emphasis on the export sector therefore dovetails with the interest of this powerful fraction of the national bourgeoisie.

There is a corresponding emphasis on small food and cash crop producers. Three reasons may be adduced for this renewed interest in the peasant economy. First, it is partly a strategy to boost local grain production in order to reduce the gaping grain deficit. The second and quite remarkable reason is political: the need to maintain a stable and content peasant population in order to ensure political stability.[31] The third reason stems from the urgent need to sustain the export capability of African countries by stepping up their cash crop production so that a larger number of exports will generate enough foreign exchange to service their foreign debt.[32]

Turning to the second pattern, current economic policies have also produced very significant changes on the political level. The return to liberal democratic politics (i.e., to constitutional rule as was the case in Ghana and Nigeria in 1979) has marked a return to the democratic elitist politics of the period immediately following independence. This corresponds with the emphasis being placed on the big local capitalists in economic policies. Since electoral politics in liberal democracies is essentially coalition politics, the small farmer has become a necessary ally of the big capitalists. Kenya is a classic case where district level notables, chiefs and the sizeable population of prosperous farmers have been mobilized to serve as intermediaries between the national hegemonic bloc and the peasantry.[33] Ivory Coast and Senegal are two other classic examples. These three cases have a long history dating back to the period of independence. Nonetheless, they still serve as models from which foreign economic and political advisers draw parallel lessons in recommending a peasant-based, agricultural modernization program throughout Sub-Saharan Africa. This model, as the Berg Report emphasizes, is the only feasible basis for economic growth in Sub-Saharan Africa. And it may also be added that it is seen as the basis for lasting stability.

Conspicuously absent from the new coalitions are: the large middle group of small importers and traders, the strata engaged in the informal economy and lastly, the salariat in both the public and private sectors. Some of these groups, depending on their potential political clout, are being catered to within the clientelist structure generally associated with liberal democratic politics in some African countries. For example, the small entrepreneurs in both the formal sectors of the economy are, or seem to be, thriving under the free market regime which is being zealously implemented under the direction of the IMF and the World Bank. They are beneficiaries of the trickle-down effect of the so-called economic prosperity which the free trade economy seems to promise. Even under military regimes such as those in Ghana and Nigeria in 1985, this new coalition is quite evident and is constantly being stressed as the solution to the political and economic crises.

On the other hand, members of the salariat, especially those in the public sector, are being asked to increase productivity as a condition for obtaining needed improvements in their living standards. Large numbers are being retrenched in both the public and private sectors. In Nigeria and Liberia they are also the target of salary cuts, ranging from 15 to 5 percent downward of the salary structure in Nigeria. The essential point, however, is that an important component of the ideology of capitalist development (namely, government is not a philanthropist) is being ruthlessly implemented.

Two reasons for what appears to be an uncompromising emphasis on classical monetarist solutions to the crisis are: (a) the diluted form of capitalist development which combined "business" with philanthropy failed and almost undermined the credibility of the capitalist model as an efficient development option, and (b) foreign capitalist interests are deeply interested in the success of the capitalist model of development, especially in key African countries. What amounts to the suppression of workers' rights is therefore being presented as the only credible foundation for social progress. Hence, it is being actively promoted by international financial, banking and governmental interests.

Where electoral politics can be implemented as an alternative to the strongman regimes of military government, as was recently achieved in Liberia, the prospects for consolidating the existing neocolonial economic arrangements become brighter, for electoral coalitions are regarded as more effective mechanisms for containing the political impact of the lower classes. But what all this really seems to be doing is to give a new emphasis to the state's incapacity for dealing with the crisis of accumulation and legitimacy. It is evidence of almost complete capitulation to the dictates of foreign financial and banking interests led by the IMF and the World Bank. Indeed, the current economic adjustment programs being implemented across the continent with the insistence of these multilateral agencies are the most compelling manifestation of the incapacity of the state.

Conclusion: The Atavistic Response

In this essay, I have tried to show how the state in Africa has been reacting to its crisis of legitimacy and accumulation. The crisis emanates from the state's own history, the fragility of the economy which it manages and the weakness of the various class forces whose interests it has been trying to reconcile, uphold or suppress. All of these can be traced back to the colonial period.

This colonial background offers the clue to both the past and current crises and responses. Colonialism was essentially a response to the political and economic crises of Europe, as Hobson and Lenin have explained. That period was one of intense competition among European states, within Europe as well as Africa and Asia. The carving up of the African continent was followed by a skewed pattern of investment and development which emphasized the primacy of exploiting the agricultural and mining sectors for export.

The current thrust of economic adjustment programs suggests that African countries have come full circle. Since independence successive regimes in almost every African country have tried various models of development from the repertoire of capitalist development strategies but none of them has worked. On the contrary, they have all exacerbated the economic and political crises of the state. From the mid-1970s these crises have been coinciding with the intensification of the crisis of the world economy. And now, as before, this global crisis is manifesting itself in severe competition among the leading capitalist nations. This time, however, the competition is between various transnational corporations. But as usual, it is taking place inside Western countries, as well as in Africa, Asia and Latin America.

The emphasis in development ideology today also has a parallel in the colonial period. Currently, there is a visible return in economic development policy to the private sector, as was the case during the colonial period. Because of the growth of a powerful local capitalist class from independence, a return to the private sector means promotion of the interests of this group. It also means forging definite and concrete class alliances behind the indigenous political elite that is in direct control of state power. Furthermore, considerable attention is being given to the agricultural and mining sectors because the commodities from these industries allow the continent to enjoy an advantage on the international commodities market. Correspondingly, a great effort is being made to rehabilitate the transport sector, in order to facilitate the export of such commodities, which is actually another way of perpetuating the continent's dependence on a handful of primary export commodities and on loans from the developed countries.

The other side of this atavistic response to the current crises is the almost total triumph of neoclassical economic theories which, among others, deemphasize the role of the state in economic development (i.e., as a capitalist), promoting instead the liberalization of both internal and external trade as well as the credit system for the benefit of the private sector. Accordingly, not only has a massive privatization movement emerged in the economies of most African countries, but existing import-export regimes are also being rapidly deregulated. Whatever the justification for these policies may be, the fact is that in a situation where the export sector and local manufacturing are extremely weak, the import sector invariably becomes dominant and a channel for dumping merchandise from the advanced capitalist countries, as well as for syphoning off the meager surplus available for implementing development programs. The market of a weak and open economy, as exists in African countries, is therefore a potent and important channel for perpetuating underdevelopment and hence the weakness of the state.

The return to neoclassical economic-development models has had a significant impact on the formation of classes and class alliances. First, the emphasis on agriculture, mining and trade has revived the old colonial "pact"—namely, the alliance between cash crop producers and the business interests (both foreign and local) which are located in mining, commerce, timber and, to some extent, manufacturing. Essentially, this is an alliance between the peasantry and big capitalists. The only exception is that today the big men in business, the state bureaucracy, the military, the police and banking are busy drifting into agriculture. Here they hope to secure their accumulated capital against the hyper-inflationary pressures of our time and to increase it through the lucrative trade in food and cash crops. The ranks of the peasantry are therefore swelling with this new influx, such that the urban-based bourgeoisie will soon be able to count on the support of an agrarian bourgeoisie core which also has a strong interest in the urban economy.

Second, the expansion of the informal economy is both a solvent of and cement for the social structure. In the first sense, it facilitates accumulation by a new stratum of entrepreneurs, that emerges from the lower rungs of the social ladder to take advantage of the easy profits available in the informal economy. This stratum assumes the role of intermediary between producers of food crops and suppliers of scarce merchandise and the final consumers. As the case of Zaire shows,[34] some of the intermediaries in the distribution of local food and cash crops do become illegal exporters. In any event, they accumulate a considerable profit at the expense of the state and peasant producers. This is a widespread development on the continent. Even though the peasant food and cash crop producers as well as small retailers of various kinds of scarce merchandise who participate in this informal economy also make a greater profit than usual, the size of their profit is nonetheless only relative; in absolute terms it is small. In short, they are, in fact, fleeced by the middlemen. This explains the struggles that have been waged by peasant cash and food crop producers against middlemen throughout Sub-Saharan Africa since colonial times.

People in strategic political, economic and administrative positions are, in most instances, the foremost beneficiaries of the informal economy. They manipulate the distribution or allocation of scarce goods to create artificial shortages and thereby gain excess value for themselves.[35] They are thus able to enhance the illegal incomes they generate for themselves. On the whole, then, the biggest losers are those caught in between the price squeeze—the masses of small people who are mostly the unemployed, peddlers or retailers, salary and wage earners, and peasant food and cash crop producers. Since the expansion of the informal economy is being accompanied by the growth of hyper-inflation, what appears to be increased income to these strata is in fact valueless income. In most cases, the real wage is actually a significant number of percentage points below its level a mere decade ago. In effect, the rich are getting richer, and very few indeed are scrambling up from the lower classes and moving any closer to the bourgeoisie; rather the poor are getting poorer.

Politically, this equals the consolidation (even if temporarily) of the rule of the bourgeoisie. It is realized through the creative coalition of expedience which certain fraction(s) from its ranks are able to forge with the peasantry through the stratum of big and influential farmers. This is the key not only to the stability enjoyed by the bourgeoisies in Kenya, Ivory Coast and Senegal, but in Ghana today, as well, there is a strong likelihood that this would be achieved if the present government's economic policies would succeed in restoring self-confidence and strength to the bourgeoisie.[36]

To understand this atavism in the emerging political economy of Africa one requires a critical knowledge of the function of debt in the current

global political economy and the role of the national bourgeoisies. Undoubtedly, the staggering *debt burden* is not a new phenomenon. It has
especially become a rather potent weapon for perpetuating the subordination
of Third World countries within the current global economic order. However,
the ruling classes in these countries, due to material and political considerations, are committed to a policy of maintaining the linkages that assure
them further borrowing rights, even if this means merely being able to
repay a fraction of the old debt and to import a few consumer items for
themselves.[37] Multilateral financial institutions and donor nation-governments
find this disposition beneficial and are exploiting it to their advantage. They
are actively encouraging collaboration in pursuing policies and programs
that perpetuate and, in fact, exacerbate the debt crisis, but do so mainly
within safe limits. This leads logically to the further weakening of the state,
for the ruling classes remain at the behest of international capital. The
crises of the state are therefore a function of the current global political
economy. Accordingly, the responses to these crises are bound to remain
within the parameters described by the functional prerequisites of the global
system. And as long as the state persists in this framework, it is unlikely
that lasting solutions to the crises will be found. In that event, the state
will simply gyrate in a fruitless search for survival and effectiveness.

Notes

1. This phenomenon is common to Third World countries where the public
sector has been identified as the leading sector in economic development. See United
Nations Economic and Social Council, *The Role of the Public Sector in Promoting
the Economic Development of Developing Countries.* Report of the Secretary-General,
E/5690 and E/4690. Add. 1., New York (1975).

2. The Marxist and neo-Marxist views of the state and their adversaries were
recently locked in an open controversy on this subject. See *Review of African
Political Economy* 5 (January–April 1976).

3. For very representative examples see, Richard D. Wolff, *The Economics of
Colonialism: Britain & Kenya, 1870–1930* (New Haven: Yale University Press, 1974);
R.M.A. Van Zwanenberg, *Colonial Capitalism and Labour in Kenya 1919–1939*
(Kampala: E. African Literature Bureau, 1975); and A.T. Nzula et al., *Forced Labour
in Colonial Africa*, Robin Cohen, ed. (London: Zed, 1979).

4. This development, especially following World War II, is succinctly analyzed
by Dan Nabudare, *The Political Economy of Imperialism* (London: Zed, 1978), Chap.
17.

5. For a discussion of some of these points see the Poulantzas-Miliband debate,
reproduced in Robin Blackburn, ed., *Ideology in Social Science* (Glasgow: Fontana/
Collins, 1972).

6. The suggestion that the Kenyan and Ivorian models of development are
successful has been subjected to biting criticism in certain circles. See, for instance,
A. Amin, *Neo-Colonialism in West Africa* (Harmondsworth: Penguin, 1973); Raphie
Kaplinsky, "Capitalist Accumulation in the Periphery: Kenya," in Martin Fransman,
ed., *Industry and Accumulation in Africa* (London: Heinemann, 1982), pp. 193–221.

7. Data is taken from G.K. Helleiner, "The IMF and Africa in the 1980s," *Africa
Development*, 8, 3 (1983): 44–45.

8. Data comes from Thomas M. Callaghy, "Africa's Debt Crisis," *Journal of International Affairs*, 38, 1 (Summer 1984): 62.

9. Claude Ake, "The Congruence of Political Economies and Ideologies in Africa," in Peter C.W. Gutkind, and Immanuel Wallerstein, eds., *The Political Economy of Contemporary Africa* (London: Sage, 1976), p. 208.

10. Compare with Ake, "Congruence of Political Economies," where he states that "the control of the machinery of the state is the key to wealth."

11. Such categorizations are discussed by Elliot J. Berg, "Structural Transformation versus Gradualism: Recent Economic Development in Ghana and the Ivory Coast," in Philip Foster and Aristide R. Zolberg, eds., *Ghana and The Ivory Coast: Perspectives on Modernization* (Chicago: University of Chicago Press, 1971), pp. 187–230.

12. Kenya is the most fascinating example of an independent African country which enjoyed such vigilant supervision. Colin Leys discusses this in his *Underdevelopment in Kenya: The Political Economy of Neo-Colonialism* (London: Heinemann, 1976). On Uganda see Mahmood Mamdani, *Politics and Class Formation in Uganda* (London: Heinemann, 1977), Chap. 8.

13. The policies of the Convention People's Party Government from 1951 to 1959 illustrate this clearly. The intellectual foundations of those policies will be found in Sir W. Arthur Lewis, *Report on Industrialisation and the Gold Coast* (Accra: Government Printer, 1953).

14. In this case refer to Issa G. Shivji, *Class Struggles in Tanzania* (Dar es Salaam: Tanzania Publishing House, 1975); A. Coulson, *Tanzania: A Political Economy* (London: Clarendon, 1982); and W. E. Clark, *Socialist Development and Public Investments in Tanzania, 1964–1973* (Toronto: University of Toronto Press, 1978).

15. Aristide R. Zolberg, "Political Development in the Ivory Coast Since Independence," in Foster and Zolberg, *Ghana and the Ivory Coast*, p. 13.

16. Peter Anyang Nyongo, "State and Society in Africa," *Africa Development*, 8, 3 (1983): 75–90.

17. Reginald H. Green, "Reflections on Economic Strategy, Structure and Necessity: Ghana and The Ivory Coast, 1957–67," in Foster and Zolberg, *Ghana and the Ivory Coast*, p. 242. But even in such instances there was the usual shift in policy, made in response to a conjuncture of international and national imperatives. See, for example, Colin Leys' discussion of this shift in his "Accumulation, Class Formation and Dependency: Kenya" in Fransman, *Industry and Accumulation in Africa*, p. 186, where he views the "'class project' of international capital" of the mid-1950s to mid-1960s, and the "class project of the indigenous bourgeoisie" of the mid-1960s to the present as constituting two distinct phases.

18. See, for instance, The Ghanaian Enterprises Decree, 1968 (NLCD 323), and the Ghanaian Business (Promotion) Act, 1970.

19. Apart from Leys, *Underdevelopment in Kenya*, also see Kaplinsky, "Capitalist Accumulation."

20. Especially the Ghanaian Enterprises Development Decree, 1975 (NRCD 330).

21. The Nigerian Enterprises Promotion Decree, 1972, which came into effect in 1974.

22. For a discussion of these contradictions see Kwame Ninsin, *Political Struggles in Ghana, 1966–1981* (Accra: Tornado Publications, forthcoming), Chap. 5.

23. N. Swainson, *The Development of Corporate Capitalism in Kenya, 1918–1977* (London: Heinemann, 1980), Chap. 5–6.

24. See data in the section "The Economic and Political Crises" above.

25. This capacity also enables the state to grant tactical concessions to the working class—a practice that has given rise to the welfare state. For a discussion

of this see James O'Connor, "The Expanding Role of the State," in R.C. Edwards, et al., eds. *The Capitalist System, A Radical Analysis of American Society* (London: Prentice-Hall, 1972), pp. 193–201.

26. Nyongo, "State and Society," p. 11.

27. René Lemarchand, "The State, the Parallel Economy and the Changing Structure of Patronage Systems," in this volume.

28. This point has been most forcefully made in Naomi Chazan, *Anatomy of Ghanaian Politics: Managing Political Recession, 1969–1982* (Boulder: Westview, 1983).

29. Janet MacGaffey, "Economic Disengagement in Zaire," in this volume.

30. For a summary of the official African reaction to the Berg Report, see *Africa Development* 7, 3 (1982): 109–138.

31. This point has been argued forcefully by colonial anthropologists, such as Buell, and its efficacy was acclaimed by colonial officials such as Lord Lugard. For an analysis of this view see Kwame Ninsin, "Chieftaincy, Land Tenure and Political Stability in Colonial Ghana," Mimeo (Legon, University of Ghana, Department of Political Science, 1985).

32. International Monetary Fund, *World Economic Outlook* (1985).

33. In the words of Leys, "The middle and poor peasantry thus constituted a typical 'supporting' class for the bloc of classes in power, a class kept 'underdetermined' through the ideology of tribalism, in particular." "Accumulation, Class Formation," p. 192, note 40.

34. MacGaffey, "Economic Disengagement in Zaire."

35. Ibid. See also Kwame Ninsin, "The Root of Corruption: A Dissenting View," *Journal of Management Studies* (Legon) 3rd series, 1 (March 1984).

36. In this regard the present Ghanaian government has been pursuing not only a policy of subsidizing peasant food and cash crop producers through price incentives, but also a policy of reorganizing such producers into a cooperative movement under its own wings.

37. Albert Fishlow, "The Debt Crisis: Round Two Ahead?" in Richard Feinberg and V. Kallab, eds., *Adjustment Crisis in the Third World* (New Brunswick: Transaction Books, 1984), p. 50.

12

Redrawing the Map of Africa?

John Ravenhill

This chapter will focus primarily on the state as defined in the traditional international relations sense, that is, as a territorial entity.[1] Rather than attempting an impossible reconciliation, the existing definitional confusion will be exploited by ranging across a number of the dimensions of divergent interpretations of the state. By having an impact on one dimension, external factors will inevitably affect others. For instance, an incursion across the boundaries of a state (in the juridical sense)[2] will certainly have an impact on the state apparatus,[3] both in terms of its ability to administer the territory nominally under its control and on its distribution of expenditure; it may also lead directly or indirectly to a change of government.

One of the strengths of writings in the Marxist tradition is to remind us of the limited utility of approaches that perceive the state as an abstract entity divorced from its historical context.[4] A general theory of the state is thus impossible. Most writers in this tradition have emphasized the necessity of perceiving the state as a social relationship—arguing emphatically that state institutions *qua* institutions cannot exercise power. State power reflects the changing balance of social forces, which in turn are shaped in part by the state through its forms of representation, its internal structure and its forms of intervention.[5] Rather surprisingly, most Marxist theorists of the state have tended to neglect the international context in which states operate. Theda Skocpol, however, in her *States and Social Revolution*, attempted to reintroduce the international dimension, drawing on the writings of Otto Hintze. In her words, the state is "Janus-faced, with an intrinsically dual anchorage in class-divided socio-economic structures and an international system of states."[6]

Much of the writing on political economy of the state in Africa has gone to the other extreme, however. The predominance of crude dependency and world systems approaches in the study of Africa's international economic relations has led to the international system being accorded an overdeterministic role at the expense of internal factors. One of the more encouraging trends in the analysis of African politics in recent years has been the reassertion of the importance of domestic socioeconomic structures, of opportunities for indigenous capital accumulation, etc., while reexamining more carefully the international context in which such factors operate.[7] Yet, despite this more sophisticated analysis of domestic structures, there has been relatively little attention paid to the manner in which changes in the international system present new challenges and opportunities for the African states. Dependency and world systems analyses have tended toward an overly static perspective by overemphasizing the continuities in the international system. Again, Skocpol's work provides a useful contrast, pointing to how changes in the structure of the international system affect the autonomy available to states. In doing so, she reintroduces central issues in the classical study of international relations: the systemic balance of power, how peripheral states may be affected by the presence of wars in the system, etc.

This emphasis on how the evolution of the international system has changed the opportunities available to states will be taken up in the African context in this paper. The focus is on how the map of Africa is being redrawn by evolving security and economic conditions. The major part of the work examines how changes in the *de facto* boundaries of Africa have been produced by territorial expansionism and by armed dissident movements; the last part briefly reviews the prospects for a voluntary reordering of African states through regional integration in response to the continent's contemporary economic crisis.

African Boundaries

One hundred years after the completion of the Congress of Berlin is a particularly appropriate time to reexamine the "boundary" issue in African politics. The boundaries bestowed by the colonial powers on Africa have simultaneously been significant assets and liabilities. On the positive side, as Jackson and Rosberg have argued, internationally acknowledged (if not always respected) boundaries have given African states much-needed legitimacy. To the extent that the present international system of states does, in fact, place a greater emphasis than its predecessors on preserving its constituent components as defined by internationally recognized boundaries, African states are much more secure than states of equivalent relative weakness have ever been before in the international system. On the other hand, there are equally significant negative aspects of Africa's boundaries. The arbitrary division of the continent by the European powers, with little or no respect for preexisting social and political groupings or even, sometimes, for "natural" geographical features, has immensely complicated the tasks of nation and state building faced by African governments. There is also a marked discrepancy between the *de jure* sovereignty accorded to African states through the recognition of their international boundaries and the empirical permeability of these boundaries. Africa's boundaries have seldom interfered with the migration of people—only in a few instances are there markers, let alone barriers to denote the existence of international borders;

African states, given their economic and political weaknesses, are particularly open to the influence of transnational forces.

Given the "empirical" weakness of African states (in the Weberian sense) and the problems of governing multiethnic populations, the preservation of inherited boundaries (with only a few marginal changes brought about not so much through armed conflict as through negotiation and international treaties) has often been noted as one of the most remarkable achievements of African international relations since independence. This has been succinctly summarized by Jackson and Rosberg:

> In spite of the weakness of their national governments, none of the Black African states have been destroyed or even significantly changed. No country has disintegrated into smaller jurisdictions or been absorbed into a larger one against the wishes of its legitimate government and as a result of violence or the threat of violence. No territories or people—or even a segment of them— have been taken over by another country. No African state has been divided as a result of internal warfare. In other words, the serious empirical weaknesses and vulnerabilities of some African states have not led to enforced jurisdictional change.[8]

Many scholars attribute the credit for boundary "maintenance" to the emergence of an African state system and its institutionalization in the Organization of African Unity (OAU). Article III of the OAU Charter provides that member states "solemnly affirm and declare their adherence to the following principles: 1) the sovereign equality of all member states; 2) non-interference in the internal affairs of States; 3) respect for the sovereignty and territorial integrity of each State and for its inalienable right to independent existence." Respect for inherited boundaries is the logical consequence of a desire to avoid the inevitable opening of a Pandora's box of irredentist and separatist claims, which would accompany the application of the right to self-determination to the populations of states that have already received their independence. In concluding his review of three failed attempts at separatism, Crawford Young predicted that "whatever else may lie ahead, 'respect for the sovereignty and territorial integrity of each State' appears one of the safer political forecasts."[9]

Young's prediction notwithstanding, I suggest that we can expect to see less respect for Article III of the OAU Charter in the future as a result of growing interstate conflict in Africa. Although over the past twenty years the African state system has generally been successful in preserving boundaries, this may well be attributable in large part to a fortuitous conjunction of national and international circumstances which has increasingly disappeared. In recent years we have witnessed the growth of intra-African territorial aggrandizement, which has changed the *de facto* boundaries of African states. Elsewhere, similar *de facto* changes have resulted from the success of various anti-government forces, including secessionist movements. Whether *de facto* changes in boundaries and international jurisdictions will be translated into *de jure* changes is more problematic. Recent trends away from respecting the sovereignty of African states, however, can be expected to continue and, indeed, intensify.

African governments' commitment to inherited frontiers has never been as unqualified and determinate as some writers suggest. And respect for the sovereignty of neighboring countries has been noticeably absent in African international politics. Four African countries—Morocco, Somalia, Ghana and Togo—initially claimed exemption from the OAU principle of upholding existing boundaries.[10] The norm of upholding the territorial integrity of other countries has always been subordinated to realpolitik and foreign policy advantage. As is so often the case in international politics, principles are seldom decisive when political or material interests are perceived to be at stake. Kautilyan calculations frequently have led governments to support separatist movements in neighboring countries; as Daddieh and Shaw point out, support for these movements has involved various ideological, material and moral considerations—often producing coalitions of strange bedfellows.[11]

Before the establishment of the OAU, for example, the Casablanca Group supported Morocco's claims to sovereignty over Mauritania. Ghana was willing to give its support for the Moroccan claim and for the Arab stance against Israel in return for the group's endorsement of its position on the Congo. The Brazzaville Group and subsequent Monrovia Group were equivocal on the need to maintain the territorial integrity of the former Belgian Congo—in part because of the hostility of the Brazzaville government toward the regime in Leopoldville. Subsequently, four African countries took the dramatic step of recognizing Biafra, even though the prospects for the cause from the outset were dim. While no African country has given diplomatic recognition to Eritrea, several have been willing to supply arms to the secessionist forces. Similar support for separatist and irredentist movements has been given in Somalia and Sudan.

None of these conflicts has resulted in *de jure* change in the jurisdictions of African states. The failure of early challenges, as Zartman notes, reinforced the norm of territorial integrity.[12] Supporters of separatist and irredentist movements remained in a comparatively small minority within the OAU. Yet, if the western Sahara and Chad cases are indicative, the minority of dissidents is growing in number. A number of factors can be expected to increase the potential for conflict: a greater incidence of boundary disputes as the locations of the continent's natural resources become better mapped, the attraction of external conflict to populist regimes desperately seeking a means of diverting public attention from domestic economic problems, and several long-standing conflicts over territorial boundaries, e.g., Burkina-Mali and Libya-Niger, remain unresolved. Meanwhile, although constitutional engineering has at least temporarily reduced the saliency of some ethnic and regional conflicts, as Rothchild and Foley demonstrate in their contribution to this volume,[13] many ethnic and regional tensions remain ripe for exploitation and can be reactivated by domestic and foreign politicians alike when the moment seems propitious.

The success of the African state system in maintaining inherited boundaries over the last twenty years was facilitated by a fortuitous combination of circumstances: a relatively equal distribution of capabilities among African states (or, more accurately, the inability of countries to project their power beyond their borders in the years immediately following independence); a general lack of interest in territorial aggrandizement (with the exception of countries with an indigenous state tradition or with a culturally homogeneous ethnic community with irredentist claims on their neighbors);[14] and relatively few opportunities to engage in such behavior, coupled with a widespread respect for the norms of behavior developed by the OAU. Meanwhile, neither states interested in pursuing intra-African adventurism nor secessionist movements have been able to attract significant support from external powers. However, there have been significant changes in a number of these dimensions in recent years, greatly increasing the prospects that there will be a *de facto* redrawing of the map of Africa.

Growth in Interstate Inequalities in Africa

One of the most obvious changes in the African state system over the last fifteen years has been the growing relevance of interstate inequalities. This is particularly important in determining the ability of some African states to project their power beyond their borders.

Although African states were not born equal, their relative inequalities appeared unimportant: for all countries the most relevant contrast appeared to be not with their neighbors but between the magnitude of their problems and the meagerness of the resources available to tackle them. Per capita incomes in most countries were remarkably similar at independence, as were their economic structures. Inherited military forces were universally small and poorly equipped.

Subsequently, there have been rather dramatic changes in the economic structures of some countries, a factor partially obscured by the worsening economic crisis faced by the region as a whole and by the continuing relative equality in per capita income. Even on this last indicator, however, the ratio of richest to poorest is now over 50:1 (in excess of $4000 per capita in Gabon in contrast to $80 per capita in Chad, according to World Bank estimates). While both economists and political scientists continue to focus on per capita incomes, the more relevant figure in examining interstate inequalities is often the aggregate size of the economy, since this factor determines the potential for economic diversification and the like.[15] Here the disparities within Africa are even more marked, ranging from Nigeria with a Gross Domestic Product (GDP) of nearly $72 billion in 1982 to Guinea Bissau whose GDP in that year totaled only $213 million (a ratio of more than 330:1).

Economic divergence has been translated into marked disparities in the capacity of African states to project their power. Oil wealth in particular has enabled some countries to sustain large armies and acquire more sophisticated weaponry (which links with an extra-continental factor discussed in more detail below, the greater willingness of countries to supply more sophisticated weaponry to Africa). Others have been able to exploit their geopolitical positions to acquire sophisticated weaponry from the super-powers. Although most African countries participated in a continent-wide arms race in the late 1970s (which slowed down, it appears, primarily as a result of the onset of the economic crisis after 1979), a marked increase in the inequality of capabilities throughout the continent was the outcome. Whereas it used to be argued that African armies were only capable of undertaking internal policing duties, this is clearly no longer the case. Tanzania's toppling of Idi Amin in 1979 demonstrates that one of Africa's more poorly equipped armies from one of its poorest countries had the organizational and logistical capabilities to invade a neighboring country, to defeat its (admittedly ragged) army, to occupy its capital and to install a friendly regime. This was achieved without any significant external assistance, albeit at tremendous cost to the local economy. Other evidence of increased African military capabilities is to be found in Morocco's role in the Shaba debacle, Guinea's interventions in support of the governments of Liberia and Sierra Leone, and Nigeria's peace-keeping operations in Chad (although the Nigerian forces could hardly be said to have distinguished themselves before the provisional government that they were supposed to be protecting requested them to leave).

Opportunities to Exercise Power

Growing disparities in capabilities become important when there are obvious opportunities to project power. There are a number of factors here which may increasingly tempt African countries to intervene beyond their existing borders. There has already been growing political disintegration in many countries as a result of economic crisis. There is little reason to presume that this factor will become significantly more favorable in the foreseeable future; indeed, it may well be expected to get worse. Disintegration in a neighboring state may offer the opportunity to revive old irredentist claims, to support secessionist movements, or to make a new grab for valuable resources. Those states in which disintegration has been most marked—Chad, Uganda and, at times, Zaire—are also those which have experienced external military intervention. Disentangling cause and effect in these cases is impossible; all that can be said is that external intervention has played a significant role in the vicious disintegrative spiral which these countries have experienced.

Another facet of the economic crisis is an increase in the attractiveness of promoting conflict with neighbors as a means of diverting attention from domestic difficulties. This might be expected to be particularly attractive to the populist regimes of Africa, although, as the Falklands War vividly reminded us, external adventurism has appealed to a variety of governments facing domestic difficulties. Other economic factors are also pertinent here. Growing shortages of land may encourage regimes to attempt a stricter supervision of their boundaries and curtail traditional nomadic grazing patterns (a problem which has long exacerbated tensions between Ethiopia and Somalia). Meanwhile, the more complete exploration of the continent's mineral resources will open up new boundary disputes, e.g., over offshore oil fields, and again may encourage preemptive territorial grabs.

In the Southern African region economic crisis has facilitated South Africa's destabilization actions against neighboring countries, most notably Mozambique. As South Africa's *cordon sanitaire* has progressively disappeared, it has been more inclined to intervene across state boundaries—a phenomenon which is unlikely to diminish so long as the liberation struggle intensifies.[16] Mozambique's signature on the Nkomati Accord is testimony to the effectiveness of externally inspired economic sabotage at a time of economic crisis.

Growing External Intervention

With the establishment of the Organization of African Unity, external powers generally were ready to acquiesce in the formula of "try the OAU first," in order to find African solutions to African problems. There have always been exceptions, of course. France continued to view francophone Africa as part of its sphere of influence and did not hesitate to intervene when it perceived that this was in its interests. The Congo marked the first trial of strength of the superpowers on the continent and, as such, led to significant extra-continental intervention, albeit primarily in the name of the United Nations. For the most part, however, the years up until the mid-1970s saw relatively little superpower interest and activities in Africa. Africa was fortunate in gaining its independence at a time when Cold War tensions were climaxing; in subsequent years the more relaxed relationship between the superpowers was reflected in a reduction of their competition for clients in the Third World. Nonalignment became acceptable to the superpowers. In a more relaxed international environment there appeared to be little need for bases on African soil; the number of foreign troops on the continent declined quite dramatically.

For the United States, Africa has traditionally been the least strategically important of all the continents. Although priorities and styles changed with various administrations, all kept a relatively low profile on the continent until the mid-1970s.[17] While the Soviet Union flirted with a number of self-styled African socialist regimes in the 1960s, its experience proved to be less than encouraging. Particularly important at this time was its general lack of capability to support operations on any scale south of the Sahara. Britain effectively withdrew from the continent during the 1960s, its parting military intervention being the suppression of the East African military mutinies in early 1964. Only France retained both a substantial military capability on the continent and the desire to intervene in support of its clients.

External military involvement in Africa—both direct and indirect through the supply of arms—has increased dramatically over the last dozen years. France may be a partial exception to this trend. Although Paris continues to play a significant role in its former colonies in West Africa, as seen in the dethroning of Emperor Bokassa, the French military presence has been reduced somewhat from the high levels of a decade ago. In contrast, superpower military interest and involvement in Africa has changed dramatically in the last dozen years. Probably the single most important factor here has been the Soviet Union's increasing capability to project its power into Africa either directly or with the assistance of not-always-compliant proxies, such as Cuba. Soviet support for the MPLA in Angola, Somalia and subsequently the Derg in Ethiopia ushered in a new era of superpower rivalry on the continent.

Growing Soviet influence in Africa has been viewed as a threat to U.S. interests, particularly in light of its negative effect on the perceptions of U.S. allies regarding U.S. capacity and determination to provide them with the necessary support to withstand internal and external challenges. Whether appropriate or not, the Iran analogy has become a powerful guiding force behind U.S. policy. The U.S. response, already visible in the late Carter years (with the refusal to recognize the MPLA and U.S. logistical support for the Shaba II forces), but even more pronounced under Reagan, has been to intervene more actively in Africa in support of "friendly" countries without necessarily paying attention to the prevailing African consensus as enunciated by the OAU. Coupled with the desire to resist the influence of the Soviet Union and its perceived proxies, such as Libya, has been a new scramble for bases as global superpower competition has intensified. Where these two factors have been combined, notably in Morocco, the Reagan administration, despite Congressional resistance, has been willing to give economic and military assistance, enabling Morocco to continue its occupation of the Western Sahara in defiance of OAU resolutions, and has blocked moves in the United Nations to condemn Morocco.

The Moroccan case illustrates another important change in the relations between African states and their external supporters. In the 1960s there appeared to be an informal consensus among suppliers on the undesirability of selling sophisticated weaponry to Africa. These reservations have increasingly disappeared. This has resulted not only from the growing rivalry of the superpowers but also from two other factors: the growing competition among suppliers following the emergence of new producers, such as Brazil and Israel, and the growing importance of arms sales to Western economies facing balance-of-payments problems. The latter, for instance, was surely a major factor in the *volte-face* of the Mitterand administration on the desirability of increasing French arms sales. Competition among suppliers enables potential purchasers to demand state-of-the-art weaponry; management of the market by the Big Four weapons producers is becoming increasingly difficult. While few African states can themselves afford to purchase the more sophisticated weapons, this has not always prevented their acquisition. Rather, a new dependence has arisen on external actors, such as Saudi Arabia, that have been willing to bankroll arms purchases.

In this era of intensified global competition, then, the superpowers appear willing to support their clients in Africa, even where their activities conflict with the norms of the African state system. Superpower intervention in the form of arms supplies has helped promote growing interstate inequalities. Another important dimension of superpower involvement, especially Soviet/Cuban support for the Derg and for the MPLA, has been the supplying of military advisers, thereby enhancing the effectiveness of recipients' armed forces. Secessionist and other antigovernment forces have also benefited from superpower competition on the continent. Material and military aid has been provided to antigovernment forces, as one superpower attempts to undermine the security of the other's client. One of the best examples of this has been the growing U.S. support for the UNITA forces in Angola, certain to be increased following the success in 1985 of the Reagan administration's efforts to repeal the Clark Amendment.

Heightened tension within and between states has in turn opened the way for other external powers to either increase their existing role on the continent or regain a foothold. Despite the relative decline in its capabilities, France's influence on the continent has been reinforced by the needs of not only its traditional clients among francophone countries but also their neighbors for protection against the perceived Libyan threat. France's success in bringing 37 African countries together in Kinshasa for the ninth Franco-African Summit, at a time when the OAU was unable to hold its annual summit for want of a quorum, was a humiliating illustration of the continent's new external dependencies.[18] Meanwhile, that Israel, ejected from the continent on a wave of oil power, has been welcomed back again is testimony to the anxiety of West African states over the antics of Colonel Kaddafi as well as their disappointment with their receipts of OAPEC aid.

Weakening Support for the OAU

Maintenance of inherited boundaries and respect for the sovereignty of neighbors were achieved in large part because of the high esteem in which the OAU was held by its member states. There are a number of reasons for postulating that this is changing.

First, there is the disappearance of the "inheritance elite," the first generation of postindependence leaders whose names are associated with the founding of the Organization. With the retirement of Julius Nyerere, of the original founding fathers only Bourguiba, Hassan, and Houphouêt-Boigny survive (Malawi and Zambia received their independence the year after the OAU's establishment, so Banda and Kaunda might also be included in the list). On an *a priori* basis it is impossible to predict how significant an impact the passing of Africa's elder statesmen will have on the organization. Personalities should become less important as an organization is increasingly institutionalized. But since the OAU was never intended to be more than an intergovernmental organization, the influence of heads of government and state has always remained crucial. In this context, the founding fathers have enjoyed significant stature; no other individuals have emerged with comparable influence. And, as yet, there is little consensus within the OAU which allows comparable stature to be afforded countries by virtue of their relative economic and/or political strength—although Nigeria may have come close to this at times. One of the problems currently besetting the OAU is the absence of figures who can assume a leadership role.

Probably the most important factor weakening support for the OAU has been its own inability to resolve crises during the last decade. Here, cause and effect become intertwined in what at times has threatened to become a vicious downward spiral. There is a danger here, however, of circular reasoning: the OAU is just as easily reified as the state. Zartman has reminded us that "there is no OAU; there are only members, and their interests come first."[19] If the OAU has been ineffective, then this is primarily a repercussion of the divergence of interests among member states and their lack of unity on the norms of the African system. Certainly, there has been, in Zartman's words, a "sharpening ideological confrontation"[20] within the organization in recent years which has inevitably reduced the prospects of reaching consensus on contentious territorial issues. What has been most noticeable in the last decade is that the OAU has been far more evenly divided on matters of vital importance than in the past. Whereas only four African states recognized Biafra, the Organization split 22 to 22 on the recognition of the MPLA until member states became aware of the intervention of South African forces in support of UNITA; similar dissention has characterized African opinion on the Western Sahara and Chad issues.

The OAU's cumbersome procedures have contributed to its ineffectiveness. It has never been successful in conflict resolution when powerful external interests have been involved. Greater external intervention, *ipso facto*, will reduce the prospects for successful OAU mediation. This has been most noticeable, for instance, in the Ethiopia-Somalia conflict. The Organization has also been markedly unsuccessful in the last decade in resolving conflicts primarily involving African actors, for instance, the two Shaba affairs, where attempts to raise a peace-keeping force failed. The one instance where peace-keeping forces were provided—in Chad in 1981–1982—did little to inspire confidence: there were lengthy delays before the promised troops actually arrived, and their mandate was unclear. As a result they were unable to enforce a ceasefire and largely stood back while the warring parties imposed their own resolution through force; member states failed to make their financial contributions, so consequently the OAU is still attempting to resolve the financial problems arising from the expedition.

As a result of the increasing difficulties in reaching agreement on key issues in the OAU within a reasonable period of time, African countries have increasingly taken to external intervention outside OAU auspices, either unilaterally or with African or external allies. Such intervention does not necessarily breach commitments to respect sovereignty or territorial integrity, since it may come at the request of the recognized government, as, for instance, in the case of the Shaba excursions. However, there are instances where breaches of fundamental OAU norms have occurred, and there seems to be an increasing acquiescence among member states in these breaches. This derives in part from the growing importance of ideological divisions: member states wish or feel obliged to support their friends on the continent regardless of whether their actions have breached the norms of the African state system. A second factor is a tendency long-established within the OAU of a willingness to accept the status quo—especially if the alternative appears likely to prolong conflict and ultimately to threaten member states' own interests, a tendency reinforced by a bandwagon effect which sees member states anxious to be backing a winner.

These changes in the politico-economic environment have fostered the growth of conflict on the continent. This in turn may lead to a *de facto* redrawing of the map in Africa from two sources: territorial aggrandizement on the part of states with superior military capabilities, and the *de facto* secession of regions which are able to resist the forces of governments that enjoy nominal *de jure* sovereignty.

A New Age of Territorial Aggrandizement?

There are two principal examples of territorial aggrandizement in contemporary Africa: Morocco's occupation of the Western Sahara, and Libya's annexation of the Aouzou Strip of Chad.

The Western Saharan dispute raises particularly interesting political and jurisprudential questions. Morocco's claim to the territory rests on its assertion that it exercised sovereignty over the land in the period prior to its incorporation as a Spanish colony. When the case was referred at Morocco's request to the International Court of Justice for an advisory opinion in 1975, the decision handed down by the Court rejected Morocco's claims. The Court ruled that while there was evidence that legal ties of allegiance had existed between the sultan and some of the nomadic peoples of the area prior to Spanish rule, the evidence did not support the view that Morocco had exercised "effective and exclusive State activity in Western Sahara." Morocco's claim to sovereignty over the territory was therefore denied. Similarly, while acknowledging that there were certain legal ties between some nomadic groups in the territory and what it termed the "Mauritanian entity" (there being no recognizable precolonial Mauritanian state), the Court rejected Mauritania's claim to sovereignty over the southern part of the territory.[21]

Subsequent developments are well known: the partition of the territory between Morocco and Mauritania with Spanish complicity; the proclamation of the Sahrawi Arab Democratic Republic (SADR) by the Algerian-backed Frente Popular para la Liberacion de Saguia el-Hamra y Rio de Oro (Polisario Front); Polisario attacks on Mauritanian forces, which caused Mauritania to renounce its claim on the western Sahara and subsequently to back the admission of the SADR to the OAU; Morocco's "Green March," which led to its occupation of the territory; the subsequent building of a defensive wall over 600 kilometers in length, to exclude Polisario fighters from Moroccan-controlled territory; and the eventual admission of the SADR as the fifty-first OAU member state. In the interim the issue prevented the

OAU from holding its nineteenth summit and at one time appeared to threaten the Organization's very existence.

In Chad, where French colonial authority was tenuous at best, state disintegration occurred early and has been complete. It has also been accompanied by sustained external intervention. On assuming power, Colonel Kadaffi revived Libya's claims to the Aouzou Strip, annexed to Libya by an agreement between Mussolini and the Vichy regime. Rapprochement between Chadian President Tombalbaye and Kaddafi provided Libya with access to the Strip in 1972, an occupation subsequently contested by the Malloum regime which overthrew Tombalbaye in 1975. As Chad disintegrated into a group of feuding fiefdoms in the 1970s, Libya was able to extend its influence by being the most forceful and most generous of the external actors. Support for one of the warring factions, FROLINAT, under the leadership of Goukouni Oueddei, although not always consistent, eventually assured that Libya would inevitably play a major role in determining Chad's future. FROLINAT forces, backed by Libyan tanks in defiance of OAU resolutions, swept the rival forces of Habre from the capital in December 1980. Although the pronounced merger of Chad and Libya proved as short-lived as Kaddafi's other paper unions, and the withdrawal of Libyan troops from the capital enabled Habre to reestablish his government, Libya until recently remained in control of not only the Aouzou Strip but substantial portions of northern Chad.

Libyan and Moroccan behavior demonstrate not only a readiness to employ force in pursuit of national goals, but also a new capability to project force beyond territorial boundaries and to sustain the occupation of seized territory for indefinite periods. These cases illustrate the interrelated nature of the factors discussed earlier: growth in interstate inequalities, the acquisition of sophisticated weaponry, the importance of external support, and the impotence of the OAU.

The ability of Libya and Morocco to sustain their occupation of seized territory is a new feature of African international relations. The increased capability of these countries' armed forces in large part reflects the relative size of the economies of these North African states: according to the World Bank's *World Development Report 1985*, Morocco had a GDP in 1983 of $13.3 billion, while that of Libya exceeded $31.3 billion. Nigeria alone of the states of Sub-Saharan Africa had a larger GDP than Libya; only two other black African state—Ivory Coast and Cameroon—had GDP's that were more than half the size of that of Morocco. Even if Tanzania had wished to sustain its military role in Uganda, it was clear that it lacked the financial resources to do so. Imperial ambitions in the era of modern warfare impose a severe strain on any economy: the Western Saharan occupation, which has led to an increase in the size of the Moroccan army from 85,000 to over 150,000, is estimated to be costing Morocco between $2 and $3 million a day.[22]

External support—both in the form of arms sales and in the unwillingness of external sponsors to upset their allies by condemning their acts of aggression—has been important in both cases. Libyan expansionism has been underwritten by its oil wealth. Despite its obvious reservations about the erratic militant Islam of Colonel Kaddafi, the Soviet desire for increased influence in the Mediterranean has enabled him to acquire sophisticated weaponry in quantities which most commentators suggest are far in excess of any conceivable Libyan needs. East European advisers reportedly have played a significant role in directing the Libyan army of occupation in Chad. But the Soviet Union and its allies are not alone in providing weaponry to sustain Libyan adventurism; France, despite its proclaimed opposition to Libyan activities, continued to make substantial arms sales to the Kaddafi regime throughout most of the period.

Morocco, similarly, would not have been able to continue its activities in the Western Sahara without extensive external support. Particularly important here has been the role of the United States. Morocco's attractiveness as a long-established "friend" (its role in the Shaba incidents being particularly appreciated) and as a bulwark against Libyan expansionism was reinforced by King Hassan's offer to grant transit facilities at Moroccan air bases for U.S. troops en route to the Persian Gulf and access to Moroccan ports for the Sixth Fleet. Hassan has subsequently been richly rewarded. Although the Carter administration attempted to exert pressure on Morocco to at least make the pretense of complying with OAU resolutions, the Reagan administration has publicly voiced no criticism, despite Congressional prodding, of Moroccan expansionism. In November 1982, for instance, the U.S. was one of 15 countries to vote against a resolution in the U.N. General Assembly which reaffirmed the "inalienable right of the people of Western Sahara to self-determination and independence," and which called for direct negotiations between Morocco and the Polisario Front to establish a ceasefire and hold a referendum.[23]

Other Western countries have also been willing to indulge Moroccan expansionism in order to preserve their interests in the country. Although the socialist parties in both France and Spain while in opposition had supported the Polisario Front, their concern for the export market provided by Morocco outweighed ideological considerations once they achieved power. Morocco is the third largest African market for French exports and the fourth largest for Spanish. Spain was also anxious to retain Moroccan friendship in order to avoid controversy over its enclaves on the Moroccan coast, Ceuta and Melilla, while negotiating its entry into the EEC.

Arms sales and military assistance have been particularly important to the success of the Moroccan campaign. Construction of the defensive perimeter would have been far less effective without the provision of sophisticated Western listening devices and mines. U.S. forces have not only engaged in joint training activities with their Moroccan counterparts, but the United States has also provided IMET assistance to train elite Moroccan units in order to enable them to pursue Polisario guerrillas beyond the defensive perimeter. The U.S. has sold antipersonnel cluster bombs to King Hassan, permitted Italian aircraft manufacturers to sell U.S.-designed helicopters, manufactured under license, to Morocco and recently supplied sophisticated tanks. France has also been active in arms sales and maintains a team of more than 200 military advisers in Morocco.[24] The cost of the arms purchases (Hassan announced in early 1985 that over $1 billion would be spent on arms acquisitions in the following five years), and of maintaining the Moroccan army of occupation has increased Morocco's dependence on assistance from sympathetic Arab states, particularly Saudi Arabia.[25]

These conflicts also illustrate the impotence of the OAU in the face of aggression by its member states in defiance of both the Organization's norms and resolutions. Although, as discussed below, the resolutions adopted on the Western Saharan and Chad issues have been surprisingly mild in avoiding direct condemnation of Moroccan and Libyan actions, neither of the expansionist regimes has paid any heed to the Organization's calls for, respectively, ceasefire in the Western Sahara and withdrawal of foreign troops from Chad.

One of the most interesting products of these disputes, certainly one which few observers predicted, was the emergence of Africa's first alliance of imperialist states, the "Arabo-African Union" between Libya and Morocco. This unlikely union for once was not one of the bizarre initiatives of the Libyan colonel, who apparently was taken by surprise by the proposal from his long-time foe, King Hassan. The Union was the formalization of a process begun when Kaddafi was invited to visit Morocco in June 1983. At that time an unpublished agreement was reached whereby Kaddafi would refrain from supplying arms to the Polisario Front in return for Morocco's abstention from interference with Libyan activities in Chad. Available evidence suggests that the agreement on noninterference has held to date, even if the Union itself has had little substance. Although Polisario representatives claim that Libya continues to provide financial support to the Front, it appears that the flow of arms has ceased. Meanwhile, Hassan has been quoted as arguing that Kaddafi's designs on Chad have a historical justification in the "blood ties between northern Chad and southern Libya."[26]

Hassan's reference to blood ties reproduces one of the arguments used by Morocco before the International Court in its claim for the Western Sahara. In both the Western Saharan and Chad cases, claims based on historical grounds are reinforced by very real material factors: in Chad, the possibility of uranium deposits; in the Western Sahara, rich phosphate deposits—alone a powerful motivation for Moroccan control—are supplemented, if Morocco's recent announcements prove correct, by one of Africa's largest iron ore deposits as well as significant oil reserves. A prediction of the outcome of either conflict is hazardous.

Armed Struggle Within: Africa's Civil Wars

A second source of change in the *de facto* jurisdiction of African states has been the success enjoyed by various dissident movements in removing large areas of territory from the control of the central government. Armed struggle may be seen as the ultimate form of disengagement from the state. As Lemarchand notes in his contribution in chapter 6 of this volume, breakdown of the state has in some cases been reflected not only in the decay of economy and infrastructure but also in the "inability of the state to provide a minimum of security." Agents of the state themselves have often become the primary source of insecurity insofar as they take to plunder and extortion as a means of supplementing their irregular salaries.

Dissident movements are heterogeneous in their origins, ideologies, objectives and sources of support. Economic crisis and state disintegration have encouraged the revival of secessionist movements such as the Anya Nya in the southern Sudan. Other dissident movements appear to be concerned primarily with securing a voice in the central government, rather than in secession, for instance, the National Resistance Army of Yoweri Museveni in Uganda and UNITA in Angola. The division between movements on the basis of these objectives is far from clear-cut: failure to secure a power-sharing role may turn ambitions toward full secession, while professed secessionist movements may be tempted by offers of a political coalition. Yet another form of dissident movement, typically one under significant external control, appears to have few positive goals but aims primarily at sabotage of the central government. The best example in this category is the Mozambique Resistance Movement, a creation of the Rhodesian intelligence service in 1976, which was revived as the Mozambique National Resistance (MNR) in 1980 by South Africa in order to destabilize the regime of Samora Machel.[27]

The fragility of the contemporary African state has been exposed by these movements, some relatively small in numbers and poorly equipped. Although armies in many African states were expanded rapidly in the 1970s, even the resources of a well-disciplined force would be severely stretched policing the large expanse of territory over which African governments nominally exercise control. For most African armies, however, discipline is sorely lacking; central government soldiers themselves frequently alienate the populace through their extortionary activities or their heavy-handed methods where dissident movements are operating. Guerrilla movements have been able to tie down large numbers of regular soldiers for indefinite periods, Eritrea being an excellent example, and create their own fiefdoms. At the present time large tracts of Angola, Mozambique, Uganda, Sudan, Ethiopia and Chad are effectively outside the control of the nominally sovereign central government. It is difficult to see what characteristics these countries have in common that would distinguish them from other African states not currently subject to armed dissident movements. In all cases ethnic and regional sympathies have been mobilized by the dissidents.

The activities of armed dissident movements have had a number of serious negative effects on African states. Where dissident movements are operating, regular economic activities become impossible and/or the central government is unable to extract any surplus from these regions. At best the population retreats into subsistence activities; frequently, large numbers flee from the areas of fighting and become refugees. Angola has the third largest population in Africa being fed by international relief agencies (after Ethiopia and Sudan), primarily because of the civil war rather than drought. Foreigners are often targeted by dissident movements in their efforts to halt international aid and investment activities. This has frequently had the desired effect: the activities of the Sudan People's Liberation Army led Chevron to halt oil exploration, while the French company CCI was forced to suspend work on the construction of the Jonglei Canal.

Dissident groups have also been particularly effective in disrupting vital transportation routes. Railways are easy targets for determined guerrillas: the Benguela railroad and the line from Umtali to Beira have been frequent victims. Oil pipelines (again the Umtali-Beira route has been disrupted) and power lines have also been prime targets. Besides imposing costs on the central government through damage to infrastructure and through preventing cash crop and mining activities in areas subject to their interference, the activities of dissident movements inevitably cause additional funds to be diverted to defence expenditures. With most African states already facing severe economic crisis, the costs imposed on states by dissident movements add further momentum to the downward spiral of disintegration.

Minimal funding and arms appear necessary to wage an effective guerrilla struggle. As has been the case in Eritrea, many of the arms used by the insurgents are captured from government forces—and where state disintegration has gone furthest, dissident movements have often been reinforced by defections by soldiers from the central government's army. However, the upsurge in the effectiveness of dissident movements in recent years has often been accompanied by an increase in external support. Two factors discussed above again are important here: the erosion of South Africa's security buffer, and growing superpower rivalry on the continent. South Africa has been the main benefactor of the UNITA and MNR forces. Although the superpowers have generally avoided being perceived as intervening directly to undermine sovereign African governments, the Reagan administration successfully sought repeal of the Clark Amendment in order to provide aid to UNITA forces as a way of pressuring the Angolan government into concessions on the Namibia issue and in a rather perverse attempt to induce it to expel Cuban troops assisting government personnel in their struggle against UNITA and South African forces.[28]

From *De Facto* to *De Jure* Reordering?

Over the last decade the disparity between Africa's *de jure* and *de facto* boundaries has increased markedly, resulting from both territorial expansionism on the part of some states and the activities of armed dissident movements in others. In this section the prospects of *de jure* boundaries being adjusted to recognize these new realities is considered.

Crawford Young presents a very effective argument on the limited prospects of success of separatist movements.[29] Attempts to justify separatist movements in ethnic terms, he asserts, will inevitably be regarded as illegitimate within Africa (besides, in most cases, being self-defeating in that the inhabitants of territories claimed by separatists usually are themselves divided by clan, ethnic and/or religious cleavages). Ultimately, in order to succeed, separatist movements have to gain the recognition of the international community. Even if one discounted Young's argument that external powers are constrained by the norms of the African state system (given the increasing divisions within it), separatist movements face formidable difficulties in attracting external support. By definition, separatist movements are attempting to create a smaller entity than that which previously existed. Where existing countries are regarded as having significant geopolitical importance, it is rational for external powers to attempt to maintain their influence with the larger entity, rather than throw their support to a smaller state whose future is uncertain.

In the Biafran case, for example, it was entirely rational for external powers to support the federal government, given the potential influence that a united Nigeria could exert on the continent. Only those countries—France, Portugal, South Africa—that perceived the emergence of a united Nigeria as a threat to their interests in the region were tempted to back the Biafran cause. Similarly, in the Eritrean case, Ethiopia is so important in geopolitical terms that both superpowers have courted the Addis Ababa government, rather than support the separatist cause. U.S. reticence in supporting Somalia may be perceived as stemming largely from its hope that the strategically more important Ethiopia has not been irretrievably lost to the opposite camp. An exception to this generalization might occur where the separatist territory has substantial mineral resources. Again, there would have to be significant divisions between African states if the external intervention was to be regarded as anything other than a neocolonialist ploy. While the original Katangan secession was regarded as illegitimate on these grounds, a replay of it at the current time, given the new divisions between African states, might not elicit the same response from either African or extra-continental actors.

Young also reminds us that there has been only one successful case, Bangladesh, in the postwar period of a separatist movement establishing a recognized state where secession was opposed by the existing central government. Two factors appear to have been particularly important in this case: the fact that the territory of Pakistan was divided in two with a hostile neighbor between the two halves, and the support received by the separatists from a contiguous territory.

There are only a few African states whose territories are divided in a way which even partially resembles the Bangladesh situation: Angola (the Cabinda enclave) and Equatorial Guinea are the most important. Such territorial divisions, then, are unlikely to be of great significance in the African context. The second factor, the support from contiguous territory, through the medium of the Indian army, was particularly important to the outcome of the Bangladesh case. In contrast, in the Biafran case, the refusal of the Cameroon government to allow the Biafran forces to be supplied through its territory was a major handicap to the insurgents. Support from a contiguous state is more likely to be forthcoming when that state does not have movements of its own which can be activated in retaliation—a rare phenomenon in Africa. Sudan's fluctuating position on permitting its territory to be used to supply Eritrean separatists has been determined in large part by the prospects of Ethiopian retaliation through support for the southern Sudanese secessionists.

Taking all of these factors together, it would be a highly unlikely conjunction of circumstances which would produce a reordering of boundaries in Africa through the success of a separatist movement. Dissident movements may attract external assistance as a means of destabilizing the incumbent regime: to gain support for secession is an entirely different matter. Where the state breaks down to the extent that full-scale civil war occurs—as, for example, in Chad and Uganda—dissident movements may well attract external support and eventual recognition as the legitimate government. Again, however, no adjustment in the territory under the nominal control of the state would occur.

The instances of territorial expansionism offer a greater likelihood of a realignment of de jure boundaries to match new empirical realities. A number of suggestions can be made on the basis of the Moroccan and Libyan cases. First, unlike separatist movements, expansionary states already enjoy international recognition. They are members of the community of nations and, like all participants, exploit the resources that the community makes available, while at the same time attempting to minimize the constraints that other actions attempt to place on state behavior. Secondly, external powers are not faced with such a "hard choice" situation as is the case with separatist movements: supporting expansionary powers is logical when their activities can be expected to make them even more significant actors on the local scene. Thirdly, the reaction of the African community, if recent events are indicative, may well be more ambivalent than it would be toward a separatist movement—especially if the expansionary power is able to announce the establishment of some form of "union" with the subjected territory. In both the Moroccan and Libyan cases, the OAU has appeared impotent to enforce its norm of respect for inherited boundaries. Indeed, it has raised few objections to the occupations: although the Polisario Front has made Moroccan withdrawal from the Western Sahara a prerequisite for the holding of a referendum, the OAU itself has not adopted this position. Similarly, Libya largely escaped denunciation for its occupation of northern Chad.

Particularly interesting from the perspective of this chapter is the sympathy given by a significant minority of OAU members to the Moroccan position. At the Council of Ministers meeting held in Addis Ababa in February 1976 (after the advisory judgment of the International Court had been handed down and the Tripartite Agreement on partition had been signed between Spain, Morocco and Mauritania, but immediately before Spain completed its withdrawal from the territory), 17 member states reportedly favored recognition of the Polisario Front, 9 were opposed, and 21 abstained.[30] These figures indicate a substantial sympathy among members for the claims of Morocco and Mauritania. In 1977–1978 four attempts to schedule a special OAU summit on the issue failed because of the divisiveness of the issue. Even after Mauritania withdrew from what it proclaimed as an "unjust war" in the territory in 1979, there was still substantial support for the Moroccan position: seven members (Morocco, Senegal, Ivory Coast, Zaire, Gabon, Cameroon and Guinea) were reported to be ready to withdraw from the OAU had the SADR been admitted to the Freetown Summit in July 1980.

Even though the intransigence of the Moroccan position cost it support within the Organization, subsequent OAU proposals can be perceived as lending a surprising degree of legitimacy to Moroccan behavior. Although the Committee of "Wisemen" appointed to investigate the issue proposed a ceasefire, neither it nor the OAU in its resolutions demanded Moroccan withdrawal during this period. And the question which was to be posed in the proposed referendum again lent legitimacy to the Moroccan position: voters were to be asked to choose between independence and integration with Morocco (implying that the Western Sahara was not perceived as already having gained independence).

Support for the Moroccan position is all the more surprising given the dangerous precedent that it sets, for Morocco's argument was that boundaries should be based not on colonial frontiers but on precolonial ties. This, of course, is the very justification for irredentism that the OAU has long sought to avoid. Subsequent Moroccan behavior substituted a might-makes-right principle for respect for OAU norms. Even as late as 1982, however, by which time Morocco had partitioned the territory through the construction of its first defensive perimeter, 19 members of the OAU were prepared to risk the breakdown of the Organization rather than accept the decision of the Secretary-General to admit the SADR to membership.[31] As with other African conflicts, member states of the Organization had various motives in supporting the Moroccan position. For some it was a matter of loyalty to old friends (and, to some extent, reciprocity for past assistance, as in the case of Zaire, which was the only state to join Morocco in walking out of the OAU when the SADR was finally admitted at the Organization's twentieth summit). For others, possibly Somalia, Morocco's irredentist justification for its claim to the Western Sahara may have had appeal. Still others may well have supported Morocco simply as an apparent means of thwarting one dimension of Colonel Kaddafi's aspirations. Whatever the motive, OAU members were willing to sacrifice the norms of the African state system in their pursuit of their perceived interests.

Although Morocco may have lost the recognition battle, it has not as yet lost the war. In the meantime, by admitting the SADR as a full member state (rather than recognizing the Polisario Front as a "liberation" movement) *and* simultaneously insisting on a referendum of self-determination, the

OAU has opened a new Pandora's box. Admission of the SADR to the OAU has made it less likely that Moroccan control of the Western Sahara will be legitimized through a change in the *de jure* boundaries. The desire of the majority of OAU states to see the conflict ended should not be underestimated, however. A scenario whereby a sham referendum is held in Moroccan-controlled territory producing a vote in favor of "union," a vote which is subsequently accepted by a significant number of OAU members, may yet materialize.

A similar equivocation has characterized OAU behavior on the Chad issue. Apparently grateful for the temporary peace brought to the war-torn country, the OAU in 1981 was willing to recognize the regime of Goukouni, despite its having been imposed by Libyan troops at a time when the OAU had planned to send its own peace-keeping force to the country. If it had not been for Kaddafi's precipitate announcement of union between Libya and Chad and Goukouni's ineptness as head of state, Libya may have succeeded in obtaining recognition of its claim to the Aouzou Strip.

As Vincent reminds us, the contemporary international system is still characterized by a Hobbesian conception of international morality. There is a tendency to accept *faits accomplis* as "creative of values regardless of previous conceptions of right."[32] Over the years, for example, opposition to Indonesia's territorial expansionism through its occupation of East Timor and West Irian has all but ceased. A similar resignation toward *faits accomplis* has been visible at times in OAU policies on the Western Saharan and Chad issues. Morocco is currently pursuing a favorite imperial tactic adopted by Indonesia in West Irian—settlement of occupied territory with migrants from the metropole. When both the United Nations and the Organization of African Unity are powerless to enforce *de jure* boundaries, the empirical reality of occupation tends to outweigh any legal niceties.

Beyond the State in Africa: Toward Regional Reordering?

If imposed reordering of *de facto* boundaries appears to be on the increase, what are the prospects for a voluntary reordering through regional integration or other forms of union? Here there has always been a marked disparity between Africa's pronounced faith in regional solutions and the willingness of governments to give up any of their sovereign powers.

Africa has experienced more "paper" unions than any other region in the world. There seems little reason to believe, given the continuing emotive power of Pan-Arabism and Pan-Africanism, that there will be fewer of them in the future. The bizarre Arabo-African union is the latest manifestation. Such unions have been ephemeral and lacking in substance; again, there is no reason to believe that this will change. The one possible exception to this is the gradual absorption of Gambia by Senegal, a repercussion of the extreme vulnerability of the Gambian state.

Africa's economic crisis has left its states even more vulnerable than before to external influences. The impact of the international political economy on state reordering in Africa is beyond the scope of this paper and therefore will not be examined here, except insofar as the economic crisis has led to a new interest in moving beyond the state in Africa.

Africa's official response to economic crisis has emphasized the need for a new path, a turning away from unequal exchange with industrialized countries toward a more self-reliant strategy.[33] This, it is proposed, will ultimately be achieved through the construction of an African Common Market. The Lagos Plan of Action's plea for collective self-reliance appears to have achieved as much symbolic importance as a rallying cry in contemporary African affairs as did Pan-Africanism in the 1960s. It appears equally devoid of real content.[34] Although there are currently more economic integration schemes in existence on paper in Africa than at any time in the past, many have not moved far beyond the initial stage of collecting the signatures of potential members. A positive outcome, however rational from an economic point of view, is highly unlikely given the record of African integrative schemes.[35] Successful economic integration imposes strains on economies which are difficult to manage at the best of times; integrative activities are often early casualties in periods of crisis, inasmuch as countries inevitably give highest priority to short-term national needs. Prospects for successful regional economic cooperation are diminished even further by the insistence of the ECA/OAU on following the long-discredited model of establishing free trade areas, a form of integration which maximizes short-term costs while providing minimal short-term benefits.[36]

The effects of regional economic schemes on state reordering will be marginal at best. Like the OAU, all such schemes are intergovernmental, rather than supranational, in design (although should any succeed in their goal of establishing a working common market, some governmental powers would inevitably have to be given up to a supranational authority). If anything, the regional economic schemes recommended by the OAU and ECA are likely to increase conflict between countries within the regions as frustrations mount due to the unequal distribution of gains from integration. Some might argue that this helps to create a sense of national identity; for example, Nigerians are brought closer together when their government acts to expel "foreigners" who have allegedly been exploiting the freedom of movement provisions of ECOWAS. To see this, however, as the solution to Africa's problems of nation building is to misunderstand the nature of cultural pluralism; as Crawford Young has reminded us, there are many levels of identity, depending on the context.[37] To perceive oneself as "Nigerian" vis-à-vis "Ghanaians" does not preclude the adoption of a sub-Nigerian identity when the struggle for resources at the state level is between indigenous groups.

Conclusions: Armed Conflict and the State in Africa

One hundred years after the Congress of Berlin, African states remain as vulnerable to external intervention as they were at the time of European conquest. The forms that such intervention takes may have changed, but the permeability of boundaries persists.

Despite the empirical weakness of African states and the strength of centrifugal tendencies to which they are subject, the norms adopted in the formative years of the African state system have so far sustained even the weakest of states as independent juridical entities. They have not prevented individual regimes from being toppled by external intervention, however; nor has the formal priority given to noninterference in external affairs of other states been translated into meaningful constraints on state behavior. Those parts of Article III of the OAU Charter which pledge respect for the sovereignty of member states and noninterference in their internal affairs have long been ignored by states attempting to gain advantage over neighboring governments. As early as 1965, for instance, an OAU summit nearly failed to materialize because of the host state's interference in the internal affairs of its neighbors. A more recent phenomenon is the growth of military intervention across boundaries by African states. Some excursions have been intended to prop up existing regimes, for example, the Shaba interventions. Others, however, have made such attempts and achieved the opposite, the most notable example being the 1979 overthrow of Amin by Tanzanian forces (after Uganda had itself invaded Tanzania in the previous year). Less successful was the raid on Benin in 1977. Meanwhile, the toppling of Bokassa's Central African Empire demonstrated that France still had no qualms about ignoring the norms of the African state system whenever it sees fit.

This paper has suggested that the capacity of the African state system to sustain inherited boundaries was the product of a fortuitous conjunction of circumstances. In the last decade these have changed to such a degree that *de facto*, if not yet *de jure*, external reordering of African boundaries has begun to take place. A major reason for this has been the growth in interstate inequalities and the quest by some states for regional hegemony. By no means do all African states have either the capability or the inclination to undertake external interventionism. Many still lack the capability of projecting their military power to their own boundaries, let alone beyond them. Yet the success of the Tanzanian army in toppling the Amin regime demonstrates that even the poorer states can, in favorable circumstances, intervene beyond their boundaries. Power, in the African context as elsewhere, is situationally specific and cannot be considered outside the relationship in which it is exercised.

Africa's economic crisis multiplies the opportunities for intervention. These range from the revival of separatist and irredentist claims at a time of state disintegration to the enhanced effectiveness of economic sabotage as waged, for example, by the South African government on its neighbors, to the ability of external agencies to determine the shape of policies, administration and even regimes through the dictation of economic policies from Western capitals.

Crises have played a decisive role in shaping the path along which states develop.[38] In particular, war has long been regarded as one of the most important factors which determined the shape of the European state system.[39] The necessity of finding the means to finance warfare was a principal factor in forcing states to improve their extractive capabilities; demands from governments for money also sometimes had a decisive impact on the course of state development by sparking revolts and even revolutions. Advantages were gained from spin-offs from the technological development of weaponry. Wars helped to develop a national consciousness. And defeat in war occasionally produced the necessary dislocation to foster social revolution.

Few of these "benefits" will accrue to Africa if external conflict becomes more prevalent. Armaments are imported; the costs of modern weaponry are so prohibitive that its import for most African states cannot conceivably be financed from domestic resources, but instead increases their dependence on the suppliers of foreign military assistance or on countries willing to subsidize such purchases. Mass mobilization is seldom feasible or relevant to modern battles, the Iranian example notwithstanding. Battles themselves are rarely decisive; the advent of guerrilla warfare has made the cost of defending the spoils of victory a very heavy one. African states which have engaged in military adventures more often appear to have been weakened, rather than strengthened, by the experience (for instance, Tanzania and Morocco).

Although the payoffs may be doubtful, the increased opportunity to project power and the possibility it offers to divert attention from desperate domestic situations is likely to tempt more states into military adventurism. Elsewhere, continuing economic crisis provides an ideal environment for the growth of armed dissident movements. Disparities between *de facto* and *de jure* boundaries can be expected to increase as growing conflict serves primarily to exacerbate the trend toward state disintegration.

Notes

I am grateful to participants at the Hebrew University workshop on the Reordering of the State in Africa, particularly Donald Rothchild and Crawford Young, for their comments on an earlier draft of this paper; to Liz Kirby for research assistance; and to the Hebrew University and the University of Sydney for travel funds that enabled me to participate in the workshop.

1. Harold D. Lasswell and Abraham Kaplan, *Power and Society* (New Haven: Yale University Press, 1950), p. 181.

2. Robert H. Jackson and Carl G. Rosberg, "Why Africa's Weak States Persist: The Empirical and the Juridical in Statehood," *World Politics*, 35, 1 (1983): 1–21.

3. Ralph Miliband, for instance, refers to the state as being made up of the government, the administration, the military and the police, the judicial branch, subcentral government and parliamentary assemblies. *The State in Capitalist Society* (London: Quadrant, 1970), p. 50.

4. Nicos Poulantzas, *Political Power and Social Classes* (London: New Left Books, 1973).

5. Bob Jessop, *The Capitalist State* (New York: New York University Press, 1982), p. 221.

6. Theda Skocpol, *States and Social Revolutions* (Cambridge: Cambridge University Press, 1978), p. 32.

7. For example, Gavin Kitching, *Class and Economic Change in Kenya* (New Haven: Yale University Press, 1980).

8. Jackson and Rosberg, "Why Africa's Weak States Persist," p. 1.

9. Crawford Young, "Comparative Claims to Political Sovereignty: Biafra, Katanga, Eritrea," in Donald Rothchild and Victor A. Olorunsola, eds., *State Versus Ethnic Claims: African Policy Dilemmas* (Boulder: Westview, 1983), p. 269.

10. Saadia Touval, *The Boundary Politics of Independent Africa* (Cambridge, Mass.: Harvard University Press, 1972).

11. Cyril Kofie Daddieh and Timothy M. Shaw, "The Political Economy of Decision-Making in African Foreign Policy: Recognition of Biafra and the Popular Movement for the Liberation of Angola (MPLA)," *International Political Science Review*, 5, 1 (1984): 21–46.

12. I. William Zartman, "Issues of African Diplomacy in the 1980s," *Orbis*, 25, 4 (Winter 1982): 1028.

13. Donald Rothchild and Michael Foley, "African States and the Politics of Inclusive Coalitions," in this volume.

14. Ravi L. Kapil, "On the Conflict Potential of Inherited Boundaries in Africa," *World Politics*, 18, 4 (July 1966): 671.

15. See, for example, the comments of Guillermo O'Donnell in *Modernization and Bureaucratic-Authoritarianism* (Berkeley: Institute of International Studies, University of California, 1973).

16. For an excellent examination of South Africa's destabilization activities see the essays in Thomas M. Callaghy, ed., *South Africa in Southern Africa: The Intensifying Vortex of Violence* (New York: Praeger, 1983).

17. For a brief discussion see Donald Rothchild and John Ravenhill, "From Carter to Reagan: The Global Perspective on Africa Becomes Ascendant," in Kenneth A. Oye, Robert J. Lieber and Donald Rothchild, eds., *Eagle Defiant* (Boston: Little Brown, 1983), pp. 337–340.

18. Olajide Aluko, "Alliances within the OAU," in Yassin El-Ayouty and I. William Zartman, eds., *The OAU After Twenty Years* (New York: Praeger, 1984), p. 67.

19. I. William Zartman, "The OAU in the African State System: Interaction and Evaluation," in El-Ayouty and Zartman, *OAU After Twenty Years*, p. 41.

20. Ibid., p. 22. On the increasing divergence of ideologies in Africa see Crawford Young, *Ideology and Development in Africa* (New Haven: Yale University Press, 1982).

21. Malcolm Shaw, "The Western Sahara Case," *The British Year Book of International Law 1978* (Oxford: Oxford University Press, 1979), pp. 119–154.

22. Richard B. Parker, "Appointment in Oujda," *Foreign Affairs*, 63, 5 (Summer 1985): 1101.

23. Tony Hodges, "The Western Sahara: A Conflict that Has Divided Africa," in Colin Legum, ed., *Africa Contemporary Record*, Vol. XV, 1982–1983 (London: Africana, 1984), pp. A61–A63.

24. Ibid., pp. A64–A67.

25. *Africa Research Bulletin*, Political Series 22, 3 (April 15, 1985): 7562. Parker estimates that Saudi support for Morocco peaked in 1981, when it may have amounted to $2 billion. Parker, "Appointment in Oujda," p. 1101.

26. *West Africa*, March 12, 1984, quoted in *Africa Research Bulletin*, March 1–31, 1984, p. 7175. See also Parker, "Appointment in Oujda."

27. Thomas M. Callaghy, "Apartheid and Socialism: South Africa's Relations with Angola and Mozambique" in idem, *South Africa in Southern Africa*, pp. 309–313.

28. Donald Rothchild and John Ravenhill, "Subordinating African Issues to Global Logic: Reagan Confronts Political Complexity," in K. Oye, R. Lieber, and D. Rothchild, *Eagle Resurgent? The Reagan Era in American Foreign Policy* (Boston: Little, Brown and Co., 1987), pp. 413–414.

29. Young, "Comparative Claims to Political Sovereignty."

30. John Damis, "The OAU and Western Sahara," in El-Ayouty and Zartman, *OAU After Twenty Years*, p. 274.

31. Ibid., p. 280. The 19 states were: Cameroon, the Central African Republic, Comoros, Djibouti, Equatorial Guinea, Gabon, Gambia, Guinea, Ivory Coast, Liberia, Mauritius, Morocco, Niger, Senegal, Somalia, Sudan, Tunisia, Upper Volta and Zaire. This action cannot be interpreted as suggesting that all of these states necessarily supported the Moroccan position. Some undoubtedly were upset by the unprecedented use of discretionary power by the OAU Secretary-General in admitting the SADR; others opposed the SADR because it was backed at that time by Libya.

32. R. J. Vincent, "Western Conceptions of a Universal Moral Order," *British Journal of International Studies*, 4 (1978): 27.

33. See the first six essays in John Ravenhill, ed., *Africa in Economic Crisis* (New York: Columbia University Press, 1986).

34. John Ravenhill, "Collective Self-Reliance or Collective Self-Delusion: Is the Lagos Plan a Viable Alternative?" in idem, *Africa in Economic Crisis*, Chap. five.

35. For a discussion of the reasons underlying the failure of Africa's integrative schemes, see John Ravenhill, "Regional Integration and Development in Africa: Lessons from the East African Community," *Journal of Commonwealth and Comparative Politics*, 17, 3 (November 1979): 227–246.

36. See John Ravenhill, "The OAU and Economic Cooperation: Irresolute Resolutions," in El-Ayouty and Zartman, *OAU After Twenty Years*, pp. 173–192.

37. Crawford Young, *The Politics of Cultural Pluralism* (Madison: University of Wisconsin Press, 1976).

38. Stephen D. Krasner, "Approaches to the State: Alternative Conceptions and Historical Dynamics," *Comparative Politics* (January 1984): 223–246.

39. See the contributions to Charles Tilly, ed., *The Formation of National States in Western Europe* (Princeton: Princeton University Press, 1975).

13

State of Crisis:
International Constraints,
Contradictions, and Capitalisms?

Timothy M. Shaw

In the current debate about the African condition it is surely axiomatic that the state of/in Africa cannot be taken out of its historical and contextual situation: it is inseparable from its inheritance, resources, environment and dialectics. The crisis in Africa is all too apparent,[1] as well as generalized.[2] Yet its incidence and coincidence are not monocausal, but rather a mixture of ecology, economy, polity, personality and opportunity.[3] While the character of the crisis is subject to variations, some of its correlates are common: the changing international division of labor and alternative responses of countries and classes to it. This paper seeks to identify some of the salient features of both the crisis and the response to it by situating them within the global political economy, with its many constraints and occasional opportunities. The connections are problematic and the analysis radical. We need to transcend not only established international relations and comparative politics[4] but also orthodox materialism in any description or explanation of contemporary *peripheral social formations*, their genesis, dynamics, directions and constellations.[5]

My basic argument is that these social formations remain under great pressure as the crisis continues. But they are moving inexorably in the direction of renewed yet partial liberalism at the level of politics and of capitalism at the level of economics, indicating a greater openness at both levels as inherited institutions decay. This direction is not so much a function of external forces, although the International Monetary Fund (IMF) and others serve to stimulate and legitimize such tendencies; rather, it is a function of internal conditions and contradictions, such as decline in goods production, needs satisfaction and living standards. The initial response in the early 1970s to the high cost of energy and industrial decline was to borrow more; however, this produced a second wave of shocks: rapid inflation and rural decay in the late 1970s. The third period of great

debate—the *Lagos Plan* versus the *Berg Report*[6]—witnessed a reconsideration
of past assumptions, particularly the widespread adoption of state capitalist
structures. In individual and incremental ways many regimes have moved
to dismantle the paraphernalia of state capitalism: deregulation, deparasta-
talization, desubsidization and devaluation. Such measures may have occurred
parallel with IMF conditionalities, but they have not always resulted in the
Fund's "seal of approval" or the extension of SDR credits; likewise, they
may have reflected the International Bank for Reconstruction and Development (IBRD) strictures without securing Bank special funding for structural
adjustments. Rather, such measures represent internal social forces responding
to a period of insufficient food, industrial and service production: the people
recognize the crisis to be structural, and not cyclical, even if leaders deny
it. Hence the position of particular peoples and products in the international
political economy is in a state of flux, even if from a global perspective
Africa's overall position seems to be ever more marginal.[7]

Africa's place in the new international division of labor is in general
highly peripheral, the most marginal of all the continents.[8] However, some
states and classes are less peripheral than others, a function of differentiated
links to international chains of production. First, a few "Third World"
states—Algeria, Ivory Coast, Kenya, Nigeria and Zimbabwe—are still important markets, producers and regional centers. Second, the bourgeoisie
everywhere, but especially in the Third World, plays a more important role
in decision making and distribution than nonbourgeois elements. And the
fraction that is dominant is also in flux, as always; the postcolonial bureaucratic
and military bourgeoisies may yet come to be replaced by comprador and
national elements with the postcrisis dispensation. Given the decline in
continental production, any gain by Third World states and bourgeois
interests is likely to be at the expense of the Fourth World and nonbourgeoisie;
hence, the new vulnerability of such countries and classes to drought:
famine rarely affects the rich. In any event, the constellation of forces—
inter- and intranational—is changing as the global economy emerges from
its decade of crisis.

While the social map of Africa is changing once more in the direction
of market forces, the economic map of the world is changing in the direction
of the Pacific Rim. Interimperial rivalries, new technologies and financial
innovations have facilitated the rise of Newly Industrializing Countries (NICs)
in East Asia: from Japan to South Korea, Taiwan and Singapore. Not that
the EEC and the United States, let alone select OPEC (Saudi Arabia), non-
OPEC (Mexico) or NICs elsewhere (Brazil), are quite moribund; but the
cutting edge of capital is around the North Pacific rather than the North
Atlantic, concentrating in a mixture of old and new industries, particularly
high-technology electronics. African entrepreneurs do not seem to have as
yet appreciated this shift of locus, still being preoccupied by old metropoles
or old industries. They need to move beyond Europe, North America and
Afro-Arab connections to relate to the NICs of the Pacific, however novel
or problematic such (South-South?) linkages may be. The new frontiers are
no longer around the Atlantic.

Clearly, the neocolonial connections of the independence era are largely vestigial: Metropolitan centers and producers no longer need most African markets and commodities either because of economic decline in the center (e.g. Great Britain) or the periphery (e.g., Uganda), or because of technological change (e.g., sisal) or foreign exchange arrears (e.g., Ghana). However, the replacement for neocolonialism has not yet become clear: revival of neo-colonial-type links between East Asia and other NICs (e.g., Brazil), on the one hand, and Africa's Third (not Fourth) World, on the other, in barter-style arrangements? Or self-reliance, both collective and national, as espoused by the *Lagos Plan of Action?*[9]

The State of Africa: New Inequalities and Intricacies

The African crisis has generated not only external interest and debate but also internal tensions and discussion. The experience of depression and drought has undermined the widespread postcolonial tendency toward state capitalism; nascent forces favoring degrees of "liberalization" have been reinforced, partially because of IMF and World Bank pressures and partially because of internal contradictions. Thus, the readiness of regimes to follow external IMF conditions is a function of pressure for foreign exchange, food, inputs and growth. The new respectability of the private sector has been reinforced and legitimized by the IMF; however, the latter has also identified a constituency for conditionality. The shift in domestic social forces, debates and policies has also undermined established foreign policy consensuses. For instance, the early Zambian division over Southern Africa and state control, reflected in the Mwanakatwe Commission,[10] is now a decade later generalizable in renewed disagreement over African foreign and development policies: neither Southern African nor economic nationalist stances are sacrosanct in the mid-1980s.[11]

The breakup of state capitalist policies and structures generates prospects for new movement and alignment reflecting postcrisis realities. The pos-sibilities of a revival of hitherto circumscribed comprador elements (i.e. local agents for external interests) should be treated with some caution, however, inasmuch as external countries and companies are hardly excited about marketing or manufacturing opportunities in Africa as a whole. In other words, African national bourgeoisies may now be ready to renegotiate with international capital, which is no longer especially interested in such reincorporation or "recompradorization" (i.e., it no longer is seeking to open up local opportunities). It is problematic to revive neocolonialism, based as it was on unequal import-export exchange, when the metropoles have lost interest, even if peripheries are once again up for grabs. If renewed comprador fractions are possible as one element of IMF conditionality, then established political economies may break down in one other important way: "repeas-antization" (i.e., a return to rural subsistence production) as well as recom-pradorization. Whereas revived external connections are feasible under freer market conditions, renewed rural production has been crucial as national

economies have declined. The retreat or return to basic agricultural production has become quite widespread as both a personal and a collective
survival strategy.[12]

From the mid-1970s onwards—earlier in Ghana, Tanzania, Uganda and
Zaire, later in Kenya, Nigeria and Zambia—the imperative of food led to
a remigration away from the cities. As commodity prices tumbled, national
economies lost both their structures and their *raisons d'être*: there was no
longer any rural surplus to be extracted through which to sustain them.
Further, they provided fewer and fewer services to their hinterlands.
Consequently, a form of "self-reliance" reappeared in rural regional areas
which was characteristic of precolonial and precapitalist eras: the rediscovery
of traditional technologies for shelter, cooking, storage, clothing, etc. When
combined with the "smuggling" of both primary commodities and manufactured goods across boundaries, local communities became quite autonomous. Rural credit institutions were created to facilitate such regional
economies. Thus, there is an apparent contradiction between renewed
permissiveness toward compradors (i.e., external orientation) and the exigencies of regionalization (i.e., internal emphasis). Together, these new social
forces challenge the established position of urban, state-centric bourgeois
fractions: the classic bureaucratic bourgeoisies with their military and political
accomplices. Self-determination and self-reliance at a local level may be
coming together in interesting ways in post-neocolonial Africa. For the mix
of collective breakdown in a series of classic neocolonial states—Ghana,
Mozambique, Tanzania, Uganda—with communal survival suggests a new
balance between centers and peripheries on the continent. When the *raison
d'être* of colonial cities has evaporated and communities survive on their
own wits, they not only become more self-sufficient, they may also become
more autonomous. This is because postcolonial states have lost not only
much of their rationale, but also their ability to intervene in the national
peripheries. Thus, the local community survives within its boundaries with
minimal national regulation and growing autonomy usually related to free-
wheeling informal sectors—black markets and smuggling—which are real
laissez faire, not World Bank, prescriptions. While the OAU establishment
may resist any recognition of such prevalent social relations, the reality of
Africa in crisis is quite different. Peoples and communities survive by seizing
self-reliance—not the national or regional kinds prescribed by the *Lagos
Plan*, but effective self-control and self-determination.[13] As David Knight
notes:

> [W]e are now in a post-colonial era and the status quo is inadequate, for
> many sub-state groups with distinctive, regionally focused identities also desire
> self-determination. The concept of self-determination has changed in the past
> and there are signs that reformulations are continuing to occur.[14]

The African post-neocolonial "revolution" may be neither apparent nor
attractive—inasmuch as it contains a mixture of foreign-exchange dealers
and tenacious peasant survivors—but it should be considered. Despite the

resistance of incumbent bureaucratic interests, their period may be passing with the decline of neocolonial linkages and logic.[15] And their demise has important implications for external connections: beyond assumptions of state capitalist foreign policies,[16] compradors seeking contracts and peasants seeking survival. Simultaneously, northern regimes are preoccupied by either private profit or collective security, except for occasional humanitarian crises such as those in Ethiopia and the Sahel.[17] In short, national interest is being redefined and recalculated in Africa as elsewhere: personalization and privatization, rather than development and security.

The redefinition of political economies—toward revived urban "embourgeoisement" and rural self-reliance, at least in the Fourth World—may reinforce established inequalities between as well as within states. Africa, as the least-developed continent, has the largest number of least developed, Fourth World countries. On the other hand, its Third World states are aspiring for regional dominance in a variety of ways.[18] While metropoles may now be disinterested in reconnecting with the Fourth World, they have never really withdrawn from the Third; despite austerity in Nigeria, inflation in Kenya or decline in Senegal, they hang on anticipating better times. The contrast between Third and Fourth Worlds is thus magnified and perpetuated. And regional centers became such not only for communications, finance, industry and security, but also for black market and smuggling activity. Kenya, for example, may have lost its status as the center of the East African Community, but it has never lost its position of *entrepôt*, formal and informal, for Uganda, Tanzania and parts of Rwanda and Zaire. Such collective self-reliance is not quite what the *Lagos Plan* was advocating, but it does reinforce established patterns of informal trade, in migrants as well as manufacturers. However, not all of these relations and contradictions have been recognized, let alone dealt with, in the political economy literature; regrettably, this includes radical African as well as Africanist analysts.[19] Thus, while there is always a danger of critical perspectives becoming the new orthodoxy, this has not yet happened on the continent, even if among foreign Africanists there is a prevailing mood of radical revisionism.

State of Political Economy: Conflicts and Coalitions

The emergence of new inequalities, forces and alliances, within as well as between states, poses major challenges for both analysis and praxis. Not that materialist *methodology* should be abandoned even if much of Marxist *theory* is outmoded. While neo-Marxist perspectives are imperative for advanced industrialized states, they are also becoming so for post-neocolonial African states. Old assumptions and contradictions are yielding to new ones: the revival of comprador and national fractions (i.e., subgroupings within a class), in contrast to bureaucratic and political bourgeois elements, and the resilience of peasant, rather than (de-) proletarianized, classes (because of the demise of the "modern" sector). In turn, these new forces generate possibilities for coalition as well as contradiction:[20] national bourgeoisies in alliance with big peasants in a nationalist state, and comprador bourgeoisies in alliance with cheap labor in a dependent political economy. With the abandonment of the tendency toward state capitalism, new forms of political economy may be expected to emerge, particularly post-neocolonial states. Thus far, few analysts have been prepared to transcend established assumptions and perspectives as well as to deal with new sets of contradiction and coalition no matter how elusive or unpalatable.

Thus, the current nationalist-materialist perspective is replete with contradictions and limitations. Despite its claims to historical, contextual, critical and comparative relevance, it is characteristically dominated by nationalist, not materialist, insights. There is a lack of recognition of changes in the post-Bretton Woods global economy and divergencies between African political economies. In short, the dynamic of dialectic is highly disregarded: neocolonial assumptions are pervasive and Africa's difficulties are treated as transitional, rather than structural. A pair of radical Nigerian essays in the recent *International Political Science Review* issue on "Pluralism and Federalism" is symptomatic.[21]

While both Claude Ake and Aaron Gana go beyond ethnicity and pluralism, their materialism is limited by their nationalism, even "Nigero-centrism." Despite their claim to materialist analysis, they deal mainly with Marxist theory or mythology; they fail to recognize fundamental and continuing shifts in African and global political economies. Gana, for example, could still claim in 1985 that

> like their colonial antecedents, the post-colonial economies of Africa remain organically tied to the economies of the former metropoles. . . . The postcolonial state in Africa is the state of the international bourgeoisie and continues to function in the interest of capitalist imperialism.[22]

Such an assertion is particularly remarkable insofar as a) interimperial rivalries and changes mean that only some metropoles are interested in certain "neocolonies," and b) national sensibilities constrain external influences. Likewise, Ake tends to espouse Marxist terminology while excluding materialist reality when he argues that "the state is essentially a capitalist phenomenon,"[23] but goes on to claim that:

> In Africa, there are few social formations that are capitalist enough or socialist enough to be identifiable as clearly boasting the state form of domination. The unique feature of the socioeconomic formations in postcolonial Africa is that the state, if we can properly talk of such an existence at all, has extremely limited autonomy.[24]

Ake proceeds to revive the dualist perspective, albeit in somewhat different guise: "In the social formations of Africa that are supposedly capitalist, the capitalist sector that dominates the economy is small and retains an enclave character."[25] He goes on to argue that one element in nonautonomization and nonaccumulation is the lack of ruling class discipline; paradoxically, it is "vulnerable despite its political authoritarianism,"[26] a rather Nigero-centric perspective—"War Against Indiscipline" being a distinctively Nigerian response to ubiquitous corruption—that does not account for, *inter alia,* Cameroon, Gabon, Ivory Coast, Kenya or Zimbabwe.

Ake's brief overview is more nuanced than that of Gana, who still espouses *dependencia* assumptions. But the latter has a finer sense of history than the former: "The specificity of the colonial state from 1880 to 1960 . . . derived from the particular contradictory social forces that it struggled to contain."[27] However, a lack of critical awareness of the changing character of contemporary capitalism—Pacific Rim and "hi-tech," rather than Europe and early industrialization—limits Gana's realism: "That the origins of the postcolonial state explain their present necessity is clear from a) the continuing pre-eminence of the metropolitan fraction of the ruling class in all the capitalist oriented formations of Africa, and b) the subordination of the 'national question' to imperialist interests."[28] Such dated orthodoxies not only confuse analysis—"the state in contemporary Africa is a state of imperialism because imperialist social relations of production have been domesticated and the state itself is the very pivot around which the system of imperialist domination rotates"[29]—they also divert policy and informed projection. Thus, Ake believes "[r]epression is such a prominent feature of social formations of Africa that there can now be no question of the people being the end of development: there is now no question of any meaningful pursuit of self-reliant strategy."[30] He also suggests that the future is in many ways the present; hence he dismisses any idea of liberal societies in Africa. He expects repressive "socialist revolutions" to produce eventually their own pressures, generating a "revolutionary resolution."[31] Yet somewhat "anarchic" regimes are neither ruthless nor responsive, extracting individual, rather than collective, responses. By contrast, Gana at least recognizes the new external ambivalence, asking "How much longer African ruling classes can maintain their grip on the postcolonial state in the face of the deepening crises of global capitalism?"[32] Like his apparent mentor, Ake, Gana posits a variety of revolutionary forces against state repression and containment. Neither, however, seems to appreciate the variety of divergencies both within and between African states in the 1980s, which are sufficient, I believe, to assert that "renewed liberalism," albeit of a limited variety, is feasible in post-neocolonial Africa.

The one conceptual area in which both of these Nigerian radicals offer suggestive comments, because they treat the reality of contemporary contradictions, is over distinctive inter- and intraclass relations: the limited salience of labor and effectiveness of local capital (Ake) and the injection of national fractions (Gana), all within a "triple alliance" framework.[33] They also point to the resilience of "primordial" or ethnic networks—erstwhile patron-client linkages which cut across and dilute class formations. Ake emphasizes nonaccumulative repression combined with access to the informal sector—state control is necessary but not sufficient for reproduction—while Gana sees national fractions as dependent yet competitive:

A situation has emerged throughout the length and breadth of the African continent in which the ruling class is far less passive about who governs and becomes engaged in bizarre factional struggles for hegemony through the control of the formal access to state power. This battle is all the more grim because government and state power have tended to become the means of accumulation for the African bourgeoisie.[34]

Thus, ethnicity and class must be juxtaposed for any realistic and sustained analysis and scenario.

However, to expect diverse political economies to generate homogeneous social relations—classic compradors in typical neocolonies—is quite unscientific and ahistoric; given changes in global as well as national and regional situations, divergencies and diversities will increase in the foreseeable future. And the division of labor postulated by Claude Ake which underlies some aspects of the triple alliance may be transcended: "the African bourgeoisie [is] to continue to concentrate on maintaining the political conditions of accumulation while leaving the production side to international capital."[35] If it is transcended, then the division may be between new compradors and old capitals using floating and informal exchange rates. In turn, producers of primary commodities will seek maximum real prices (i.e., hard currencies) for their crops, thereby further eroding the surplus extraction capacity of colonial cities. The social and spatial impacts of such trends are quite profound: affluent rural regions, especially those in border areas, versus decaying cities. Perhaps this is a reversal of previous urban-biased policies and realities characteristic of the neocolonial era?

State of Foreign Policy: Hegemony or Vulnerability?

The reconstruction of national political economies is likely to lead to redefinitions of foreign and development policies: the external expression of internal conditions and contradictions. With the demise of North-South dialogue over any New International Economic Order (NIEO), African foreign relations have become increasingly realistic: how to survive as both states and classes in the new international division of labor. Aside from formal, often still unresolved, battles with the IMF and IBRD, the reality of foreign relations has shifted in the direction of pragmatism. While this new modesty is, in part, a reflection of the passing of a first generation of more charismatic leaders, it is also a reflection of fatigue, maturation and reevaluation.[36] Moreover, the complexities of African international relations multiply as issues increase and resources decline. Thus, African foreign policy in the mid-1980s is concerned with national and fractional survival— most dramatically illustrated by the Sahel/Horn droughts and the siege of incumbent bureaucratic bourgeoisies. To be sure, some established concerns remain (e.g., African cohesion and liberation), but the preoccupations are no longer symbolic, diplomatic victories. Rather, in a world dominated by a revival of American nationalism as well as capitalism, they are immediate and tangible: foreign exchange, food aid, imported inputs and spare parts, and the cost of energy and money.[37] The neocolonial era of grand gestures is over; that of economic imperatives is dawning, as reflected in the July 1985 OAU economic summit and Addis Ababa declaration on debt and development.

In the present period, foreign policies vary in their coherence and competence.[38] Many African diplomats are now as senior as non-Africans and therefore have a sense of the limits, and utilities, of orthodox diplomacy. The fifty-odd members of the OAU have lost much of the anger and radicalism they expressed prior to independence, particularly before their return from exile. Now they concentrate on the opportunities of duty-free, foreign-exchange life-styles; only SWAPO and ANC, at times reinforced by Sankara of Burkina Fasso or Jerry Rawlings of Ghana, keep the old flame of idealism alive.

Much diplomacy has become, of course, economic in content, with prevalent debates on Africa's economic crisis, the Law of the Sea, development priorities, debt rescheduling and communications infrastructures. To be sure, diplomatic and strategic questions remain, but economic survival is the current imperative. This is reflected in the mid-1985 African economic summit,[39] in the late-1984 Lome III convention,[40] and in continuous negotiations over aid, finance and trade, whether collective or national. The agenda for Third World states may differ from that of the Fourth—foreign investment, rather than foreign assistance, and debts, rather than grants—but the quest for economic survival is ubiquitous. Yet here, too, divergence is apparent. Third World interests may tend to be focused in the direction of renegotiation on the basis of a new liberalization, whereas the Fourth World may be more inclined to accept disengagement as inevitable and probably desirable.

Meanwhile, foreign policy in Africa, as elsewhere, is becoming increasingly the articulation of the dominant bourgeois fraction. Thus, as national or military fractions become hegemonic, we may expect foreign policy to become more concerned with production or security. The new division of Africa is along structural, rather than ideological, lines—Third and Fourth Worlds and different dominant fractions, rather than "African socialists" and "Afrocommunists." Hence, new continental alliances may arise: more conservative versus less conservative regimes. Moreover, befitting a post-neocolonial period, policy is tending to become pragmatic as well as calculating, taking the form of protracted negotiation, rather than protracted struggle. And regimes appear to have fewer reservations or to be less embarrassed about strategic connections of their choosing, usually along the lines of superpower fissures. But the one preoccupation, compatible with the concentration on economic issues, is development policy: will it be more or less introverted? Agriculture and/or industry? National, regional and/or continental self-reliance?

State of Development Policy: Self-Reliance or Conditionality?

The great debate about Africa's development direction was rejoined at the end of the 1970s, after the shock waves of expensive petroleum and

industrial decline washed over the continent's fragile economies: the OAU/
ECA Monrovia Symposium symbolized not only Africa's plight but also its
resistance and creativity. In the 1970s there was a growing awareness among
Africa's leading thinkers that the problems were not merely cyclical and
short-term but structural and long-term; hence, the determination to turn
adversity to advantage, to transform enforced into determined self-reliance.[41]

If in Africa and the Third World the major motif of the 1960s was that
of growth and of the 1970s that of development—the "Basic Needs" decade
with its emphasis on personal habitat, health and education—then the 1980s
is being designated the decade of self-reliance, a natural successor to individual
needs now aggregated into *community* (or collective?) goals. Under the
intellectual-*cum*-political guidance of Adebayo Adedeji, the ECA forged a
new transnational consensus among Africa's leading scholars, thinkers,
planners and politicians. In a remarkable series of meetings and moves,
Adedeji and others orchestrated the intellectual and ideological reorientation
of the continent: from collective political demands to consensual economic
nationalism.[42] Despite reservations from certain countries and classes, the
Adedeji ginger group initiated a bandwagon effect resulting in the 1980 and
1985 economic summits and in the transformation of Africa's economic
direction and debate from tentative *Lagos Plan* to definitive "Addis Ababa
Declaration." The new keywords are self-reliance, self-sustainment and the
longer-term: an emphasis on agriculture, industry, finance, technology, gender
and regionalism. Fortuitously, then, Africa was well prepared, at least in
terms of policy, for two major challenges in the 1980s: one at the level of
policy and politics (the World Bank's Berg Report), and the other at the
level of *praxis* and economics (Ethiopian and Sahelian famines).

Characteristic of Africa's contradictions, its World Bank governors had
requested an emergency report on the continent's difficulties in late 1979,
the catalyst for the Berg Report. Simultaneously, the OAU/ECA system
was moving unsteadily, but ineluctably, toward the Lagos summit. The early
1980s were thus marked by a great debate between more outward-looking
and shorter-term proposals (Berg Report) and more inward-looking and
longer-term plans (*Lagos Plan*), which reflected different country and class
(let alone external and corporate) interests. The character of the intellectual
debate and the balance among internal forces have varied over time, between
the two African economic summits. At the level of summitry and sophistry,
the *Lagos Plan* has been supplemented by the ECA Report on the next
25 years, to 2008,[43] and the Addis Ababa Declaration and the Berg Report
by two successor documents, *Progress Report* and *Joint Program of Action*.[44]
At the level of policy and practice, after an initial divergence and riposte,
the ECA and IBRD perspectives began to converge, at least to a degree.
However, while the Bank claims to take ECA priorities into account and
vice versa, in reality the two sets of proposals remain dialectical in terms
of genesis, assumption, preference and projection: more outward looking
versus national and collective self-reliance, respectively.[45] And while the
global economy may have been revived somewhat, the prospects for most

African economies remain very limited. Nevertheless, the Bank does have its advocates in more conservative regimes, ministries and fractions; the ECA network is less prestigious, cautious and connected. The 1985 summit indicated continuing areas of dispute as well as agreement: debt moratorium versus rescheduling, food versus commodity production, and parastatals versus privatization.

Meanwhile, as donors continue to rush emergency aid to Ethiopia, Sudan and the Sahel, diverting attention from the longer- to the immediate-term, the pressures, social and structural, on Africa continue to impact. The overall resultant direction, irrespective of continental or national policy preferences, is toward the rural areas in terms of increased agricultural—especially food—production and revival or reapplication of traditional and appropriate technologies: habitat, clothing, soap, storage, etc. The high prices of Omo and Kibo may yet deter a return to such consumption in the rural regions, except those located on the borders of hard currency areas, where such consumer imperatives are attendant on the apparent revival of the post-neocolonial state—trade is being revived at a high cost so only a minority can consume from the restocked shelves—and therefore may ease pressures for self-reliance. Not that it is necessarily compatible with grander ECA schemes at national, regional, or even continental levels. Indeed, the reappearance of rural, regional autonomy may be seen to pose a threat to inherited national systems: an end to the logic of postcolonial capital cities and structures. Nevertheless, for Africa to survive in a new and ungiving international division of labor, some return to rural self-reliance may be crucial: not subsistence alone, but Basic Human Needs first along with compatible commercial or commodity activities as bases for subsequent accumulation for reindustrialization.

Thus, the conditionalities imposed by the IMF and the World Bank may not be incompatible with the interests of some indigenous bourgeois fractions: the rehabilitation of comprador and commercial bourgeois fractions as proposed in diverse post-1980 development "plans." On the other hand, the costs of such liberalization are high for other fractions and classes, particularly when they do not come with IMF facility funds. The exclusion in new corporatist arrangements of established bureaucratic, technocratic and political elites may yet result in a backlash, often depending on which way interventive military forces react—that is, whether more bourgeois officers or more proletarian NCOs are dominant. Moreover, the support networks which alternative self-reliant versus extroverted fractions can assemble may yet prove critical: will revived commercial networks be able literally to deliver enough goods to undermine recently established subregional communities?

Thus, the class struggle, anticipated by Ake, Gana and others, exacerbated by unemployment, depression and drought, is intensifying, albeit in distinctive and unanticipated ways; nonetheless, it may yet be contained by repression, rather than resolved by radicalization. And the alternative ECA and IBRD proposals will be espoused by different regimes and fractions at different times, insofar as the former suit the latter's purposes. In short, Africa will continue to be characterized by a variety of voices and drums, particularly by different social forces and national positions. The post-neocolonial state may be generic and ubiquitous but its structure and status are quite variegated.

Future States:
African Capitalism, Communism or Corporatism?

The future of Africa, is, then, unlikely to be straightforward, singular or decisive over the medium-term: the variety of external, internal and structural constraints is likely to lead to swings of fortunes and forces which deviate from both ECA and IBRD projections and proposals. The incidence of drought, windfalls and conflicts will be variable, and the vagaries of international politics will continue to impinge on particular regimes and classes.[46] Further, the timetable and process of Southern Africa's liberation remain problematic, with profound implications for the direction and rate of the rest of the continent's (under)development.[47] Yet a few longer-term forces are quite discernible and predictable: The new international division of labor, particularly the emergence of new technologies and NICs around the Pacific, will further intensify Africa's marginalization.

In this context, given the articulation of alternative bourgeois projections expressed in the *Lagos Plan* and Berg Report, a few plausible scenarios are identifiable. Revolution, pace Ake and others, is the least likely future—the formation and articulation of social forces is not sufficiently advanced. But repression is quite feasible: the physical and psychological containment of embryonic or anomic discontent by praetorian or military regimes (i.e., indirect or direct government by soldiers, be they sergeants or generals).

Aside from these polar opposites, the intermediate clusters of forces and factors can be encapsulated as African capitalism, corporatism or communism. Such distinctive political economies are characterized by different hegemonic fractions, class alliances and class contradictions. The latter, "Afrocommunism," the combination of progressive bureaucratic and technocratic fractions with proletarian and/or peasant interests (the size of Africa's peasantry and un/underemployed has, of course, been growing, while that of the proletariat has been decreasing as "industrial" production has declined), is decreasingly feasible in a competitive capitalist world economy. The cases of Angola, Algeria, Mozambique and Tanzania, among others, are illustrative of this trend back toward "market forces": only Benin, Burkina Faso and Ethiopia (and Libya?) remain true to socialist ideals, at least at the level of ideology.

The alternatives to repression, revolution and communism are capitalism and corporatism: two relatively "liberal" systems. The former is most likely to emerge in Third World states; the latter, in the Fourth World. The resilience of capitalism on the continent is a remarkable testimony to its ability for reformation and rejuvenation. In Egypt, Gabon, Ivory Coast, Kenya, Nigeria, Senegal and Zimbabwe comprador and national fractions have successfully resisted bureaucratic and aristocratic interests to redefine their external connections and internal correlates. Despite contradictions and austerity, they have reinforced import-substitution industrialization and attempted to revive agricultural production for both local food and foreign commodity needs. But the possibilities of further subcenters being established in a continent in crisis are limited: the new international division of labor is not sufficiently expansive.

Thus, the most familiar response in Africa, as elsewhere, is likely to be a distinctive, indigenous variant of corporatism: a continuation of mixed economies still dominated by bureaucratic and military fractions because other interest groups are weak and dependent—incorporated—yet neither capitalist nor socialist and hardly stable.[48] This type of constellation—the careful and calculating arrangement of major institutions and interests under centralist control—will tend to swing from bureaucratic to military dominance and from state to private control. Yet its primary characteristic—the exclusion of nonbourgeois interests—would remain intact no matter which fraction rules. Thus although revolutionary pressures could explode, without viable leadership they are unlikely to do so. Africa is ripe for repression, not revolution; hence the tendency for people to retreat to the rural areas to subsist, rather than be marginalized, if not eliminated, in the decaying cities. And, in turn, the character of national political economy defines foreign-policy orientation, at least in terms of relations, if not declarations. The corporatist response—an apparently "liberal" survival strategy by established post-neocolonial bourgeoisies despite its calculating and centralist tendencies—constitutes an ambiguous reaction to both the *Lagos Plan* and Berg Report, reflective of disparate national and comprador fractional interests, respectively.

As Africa's marginalization and inequality intensifies, its range of options contracts. Given the exponential character of many of the challenges facing the continent—environment, agriculture, population, peripheralization, etc.—an immediate response is imperative. Projections based on 1985 data are less promising than those based on 1980 or 1975 data. Thus, the African emergency is really one of long-term development rather than short-term drought, of economy rather than ecology.[49] Is the distinctive post-neocolonial African state, particularly its functionaries and analysts, at all prepared for such a challenge, given its genesis, character and orientation?

Notes

1. See the trio of World Bank reports which describe the crisis correctly but diagnose it controversially: *Accelerated Development in Sub-Saharan Africa: an Agenda for Action* (the infamous "Berg Report") (Washington, 1981); *Sub-Saharan Africa: Progress Report on Development Prospects and Programs* (Washington, 1983); and *Sustained Development in Sub-Saharan Africa: a Joint Program of Action* (Washington, 1984).

2. See John Holmes and Colin Leys, "The Western Hemisphere in the World Crisis," *Institute of Development Studies Bulletin*, 16, 2 (April 1985): 1–51.

3. See Timothy M. Shaw, "Toward a Political Economy of the African Crisis: Diplomacy, Debates and Dialectics," in Michael Glantz, ed., *Drought and Hunger in Africa: Denying Famine a Future* (Cambridge: Cambridge University Press, 1986), pp. 127–147.

4. See Joan Edelman Spero, *The Politics of International Economic Relations*, 3rd ed. (New York: St. Martins, 1985); David H. Blake and Robert S. Walters, *The Politics of Global Economic Relations*, 2nd ed. (Englewood Cliffs, N.J.: Prentice-Hall, 1983); Christopher Clapham, *Third World Politics: An Introduction* (Madison: University of Wisconsin Press, 1985); and Richard Hodder-Williams, *An Introduction to the Politics of Tropical Africa* (London: Allen and Unwin, 1984), respectively.

5. For one attempt to do this see Timothy M. Shaw *Towards a Political Economy for Africa: The Dialectics of Dependence* (London: Macmillan, 1985).

6. See OAU, *Lagos Plan of Action for the Economic Development of Africa, 1980–2000* (Geneva: International Institute for Labour Studies, 1981); and Robert S. Browne and Robert J. Cummings *The Lagos Plan of Action vs. the Berg Report: Contemporary Issues in African Economic Development* (Washington: Howard University, 1984).

7. See Adebayo Adedeji and Timothy M. Shaw, eds., *Economic Crisis in Africa: African Perspectives on Development Problems and Potentials* (Boulder: Rienner, 1985).

8. See John Ravenhill, ed., *Africa in Economic Crisis* (London: Macmillan, 1986).

9. See Timothy M. Shaw and Olajide Aluko, eds., *Africa Projected: From Recession to Renaissance by the Year 2000?* (London: Macmillan, 1985).

10. See Timothy M. Shaw "Dilemmas of Dependence and (Under)Development: Conflicts and Choices in Zambia's Present and Prospective Foreign Policy," *Africa Today*, 26, 4 (1979): 43–65.

11. See Ibrahim S.R. Msabaha and Timothy M. Shaw, eds., *Confrontation and Liberation in Southern Africa: Regional Directions after the Nkomati Accord* (Boulder: Westview, 1987); on the bellwether Zimbabwean case see Michael Schatzberg, ed., *Political Economy of Zimbabwe* (New York: Praeger, 1984), pp. 144–181.

12. See Naomi Chazan and Timothy M. Shaw, eds., *Coping With Africa's Food Crisis: Popular Strategies for Survival* (Boulder: Rienner, forthcoming).

13. See Timothy M. Shaw "Debates about Africa's Future: The Brandt, World Bank and Lagos Plan Blueprints," *Third World Quarterly*, 5, 2 (April 1983): 330–344.

14. David B. Knight, "Territory and People or People and Territory? Thoughts on Post-Colonial Self-Determination," *International Political Science Review*, 6, 2 (1985): 248–249.

15. Cf. Claude Ake, *A Political Economy of Africa* (London: Longman, 1981).

16. See Timothy M. Shaw and Olajide Aluko, eds., *The Political Economy of African Foreign Policy* (Aldershot: Gower, 1984).

17. Contrast, for instance, recent Canadian policy statements and Canadian interests: *The African Famine and Canada's Response: Recommendations; A Report by the Honourable David Macdonald, Canadian Emergency Coordinator/African Famine, November 1984 to March 1985* (Ottawa: CIDA, 1985); and *Competitiveness and Security: Directions for Canada's International Relations; Presented by the Right Honourable Joe Clark, Secretary of State for External Affairs* (Ottawa: External Affairs, 1985). For policy critiques of these "gaps" see Timothy M. Shaw "Africa's Development Crisis: Contradictions in the Ethiopian Famine," in Ian McAllister and David F. Luke, eds., *Canada and International Development: Perspectives on the Mid-1980s* (Typescript).

18. See Timothy M. Shaw, "Kenya and South Africa: 'Sub-Imperialist' States" *Orbis*, 21, 2 (Summer 1977): 375–394.

19. See Dennis L. Cohen and John Daniel, eds., *Political Economy of Africa: Selected Readings* (London: Longman, 1981).

20. On the Zambian case see Jane L. Parpart and Timothy M. Shaw, "Contradiction and Coalition: Class Fractions in Zambia, 1964–1984," *Africa Today*, 30, 3 (1983): 23–50; on the Nigerian case see Julius O. Ihonvbere and Timothy M. Shaw, "Petroleum Proletariat: Nigerian Oil Workers in Contextual and Comparative Perspective," a paper delivered at the Canadian Association of African Studies (Montreal, May 1985).

21. See Claude Ake, "The Future of the State in Africa," and Aaron T. Gana, "The State in Africa: Yesterday, Today and Tomorrow," *International Political Science Review*, 6, 1 (1985): 105–115.

22. Gana, "The State in Africa," pp. 119, 127.

23. Ake, "Future of the State," p. 106.

24. Ibid.

25. Ibid., p. 109.

26. Ibid., p. 113.

27. Gana, "The State in Africa," p. 118.

28. Ibid., p. 125.

29. Ibid., p. 127.

30. Ake, "Future of the State," p. 112.

31. Ibid., p. 114.

32. Gana, "The State in Africa," p. 129.

33. On this heuristic framework see Peter Evans, *Dependent Development: The Alliance of Multinational, State and Local Capital in Brazil* (Princeton: Princeton University Press, 1979), pp. 32–34, 50–54. Contrast Evan's "triple alliance" for Brazil with Teresa Turner's analogous "triangle" framework for Nigeria; "Nigeria: Imperialism, Oil Technology and the Comprador State," in Petter Nore and Terisa Turner, eds., *Oil and Class Struggle* (London: Zed, 1980), pp. 211–220.

34. Gana, "The State in Africa," p. 128.

35. Ake, "Future of the State," p. 112.

36. See Timothy M. Shaw and Naomi Chazan "The Limits of Leadership: Africa in Contemporary World Politics," *International Journal*, 37, 4 (Autumn 1982): 543–554.

37. See *President Nyerere's Address to the OAU Summit Meeting at Addis Ababa November 1984 when Accepting Chairmanship* (Dar es Salaam, 1984).

38. See the definitive collection by Baghat Korany and Ali E. Hillal Dessouki, eds., *The Foreign Policies of Arab States* (Boulder: Westview, 1985). For Sub-Saharan case studies see Jerker Carlsson, ed., *Recession in Africa* (Uppsala: Scandinavian Institute of African Studies, 1983).

39. For background materials for this second economic summit see ECA *Survey of Economic and Social Conditions in Africa 1983–84* (E/ECA/CM.11/16, April 1985); *The Establishment of an African Monetary Fund: Structure and Mechanism* (February 1985); and "Progress Report on the Implementation of the Lagos Plan of Action by the ECA Secretariat" (E/ECA/CM.11/74, April 1985). See also Timothy M. Shaw "Africa Prepares for Economic Summit" *West Africa*, 3533, 13 (May 1985): 948–949; and idem, "African Solutions Prepared in Addis," *Africa Now*, 50 (June 1985): 16.

40. See Robert Boardman, Timothy M. Shaw and Panayotis Soldatos, eds., *Europe, Africa and Lome III* (Washington: University Press of America, 1985; for Dalhousie African Studies Series).

41. See Timothy M. Shaw, ed., *Alternative Futures for Africa* (Boulder: Westview, 1982).

42. See Adebayo Adedeji, "The Monrovia Strategy and the Lagos Plan of Action: Five Years After," in Adedeji and Shaw, *Economic Crisis in Africa*, pp. 9–34.

43. See *ECA and African Developoment, 1983–2008: Preliminary Prospective Study* (Addis Ababa, April 1983).

44. See Timothy M. Shaw and David F. Luke, "The Lagos Plan of Action and Africa's Future Economic Relations," *Canadian Journal of Development Studies*, 6, 1 (1985): 173–178.

45. See Adebayo Adedeji, "The African Development Problematique: Demography, Drought and Desertification, Dependency, Disequilibrium, Debt and Destabilization," (Addis Ababa: Economic Commission for Africa, 1985).

46. See Timothy M. Shaw, "The Future of the Great Powers in Africa: Towards a Political Economy of Intervention," *Journal of Modern African Studies*, 21, 4 (December 1983): 555–586; and William J. Foltz and Henry S. Bienen, eds., *Arms and the African: Military Influences on Africa's International Relations* (New Haven: Yale University Press, 1985).

47. See Mafa Sejanamane and Timothy M. Shaw, "Continuing Crisis: Regional Coercion, Cooperation and Contradiction in Southern Africa," in Zbigniew Konczacki, Jane L. Parpart and Timothy M. Shaw, eds., *Economic History of Southern Africa*, Vol. I (London: Frank Cass, 1986).

48. See Timothy M. Shaw, "Beyond Neocolonialism: Varieties of Corporatism in Africa," *Journal of Modern African Studies*, 20, 2 (June 1982): 239–261.

49. Cf. *The African Famine and Canada's Response* and the notion of "environmental bankruptcy" in Anders Wiljkman and Lloyd Timberlake, *Natural Disasters: Acts of God or Acts of Man?* (London: International Institute for Environment and Development, 1984). For preliminary critiques of an overconcentration on ecology and science see Timothy M. Shaw, "Ethiopia: Beyond the Famine," *International Perspectives* (July/August 1985): 6–10; and idem. "Not by Relief Alone," *Policy Options*, 6, 6 (July 1985): 33–36.

PART FIVE

Conclusion

14

State and Society in Africa: Images and Challenges

Naomi Chazan

State and Society in Africa: The Issues

Twenty-five years of African independence have yielded results far different from those anticipated by the architects of the postcolonial era. By the mid-1980s the continent appeared to be at a veritable turning point. Economic performance, marked at best by anemic growth rates, had given way in many countries—through a combination of drought, external neglect and mismanagement—to pervasive poverty and debilitating famine. Multiple survival mechanisms surfaced, further calling into question the utility of conventional development strategies. The political climate of uncertainty signaled the breakdown of many existing arrangements and highlighted the fraying character of the relations between government agencies and civil society.[1] Political experimentation, already in evidence, became even more widespread. In many places the pervasive quality of the crisis of the early part of the present decade fostered an active quest for alternatives to old mythologies.

The International Workshop on the Reordering of the State in Africa, held at the Hebrew University, at which initial drafts of the papers in this volume were first presented, was convened to attempt to come to grips with the shifts currently taking place on the continent. The challenge presented to participants was interpretive in nature: to trace unfolding patterns of political and social organization and to assess their implications for the understanding of emerging power configurations. The agenda focused on the systematic analysis first of the dilemmas of the state in the postin-dependence period, then of the modes of societal responses, and finally of the trajectory of political realignments in various parts of the continent. Although the methods employed by contributors varied from the comparative-historical, philosophical and literary to the theoretical state-centric or micro case study, all made an effort to address these issues.

What vision of African politics emerges from these essays? How does this image differ from the conventional wisdom of the early years of independence? What are the areas of interpretive consensus? Where do analyses differ and why? And what are the implications of this altered view for empirical research, theoretical refinement and conceptual reconsideration? These concluding remarks seek to shed light on these questions and suggest directions for further study and reflection.

The political picture which derives from this discussion is in many respects as diverse as the events it seeks to capture. Nevertheless, there are indications that in many countries a real transformation is beginning to occur. As the postcolonial era is gradually drawing to a close and a new generation of leadership is coming to the fore, parts of Africa are entering a new phase in their political history. The disaggregation of inherited structures and institutions may be giving way to the reaggregation of concerns in innovative ways in redesigned arenas of sociopolitical and economic interaction. The diverse impulses guiding political currents in different countries suggest that existing analytical approaches—already stretched to their limits—may be ripe for more thorough review to better reflect the realities they seek to convey. As the field of political vision expands, so too must the conceptual tools and analytical schema needed to study the nuanced accommodations which are such an integral part of the contemporary African experience.

State and Society in Africa: Patterns and Trends

Political processes in Africa in recent years display a complex image of governmental enfeeblement, growing societal activity beyond the reach of the state and heterogeneous forms of political reordering. While the vision of major trends exhibits marked similarities, interpretations of these patterns differ drastically, and hence implications also vary substantially.

The Dilemmas of the State

State institutions in Africa have undergone a cycle of attempted consolidation, the entrenchment of hegemonic domination and, more recently, deterioration, if not disintegration. The postcolonial state in Africa in the early 1980s was undergoing a crisis of not insignificant proportions.

Several dimensions of this malaise emerge from the essays in this book. The first, and most readily apparent, feature of state structures at this juncture has been their extensiveness. The public sector, as John Ayoade demonstrates, has grown consistently during the past several decades. The overbloated administrative apparatus has been both costly and parasitic: it has avidly consumed scarce resources and proliferated unnecessarily. A second, related characteristic focuses on the patrimonial quality of state institutions. The close connection between state expansion and class formation is implicit in these writings; so is the correlation between social exclusivity and proximity to public goods. Selective representation of social groups in ruling cliques remains a prominent feature of African states, even if the precise composition of ruling coalitions, as Kwame Ninsin and Don

Rothchild and Michael Foley point out, varies over time. The elitist character of the social make-up of state agencies comes together, third, with a personal view of the public domain. In many instances the separation between the civic and private realms is ill-defined. As a result, state institutions have frequently been diverted for personal gain and decision-making patterns have assumed an idiosyncratic quality. Fourth, the absence of regularized channels of communication with social groups has nurtured authoritarian tendencies. The overconcentration and monopolization of power at the core is the most prominent by-product of the statist propensities exhibited almost universally by the first generation of African leaders.[2]

The combination of centralization, proliferation, personalization and social inequality has, all contributors concur, severely hampered the effectiveness of the state machinery in many parts of the continent. Certain tasks associated with public institutions—most notably the promotion of internal security, autonomy on the international front and the formulation of binding norms of behavior—have been fulfilled with lesser regularity in recent years. But most significantly, central government organs have failed in many of their economic roles: they have not used their revenue judiciously, they have distorted distribution systems, they have regulated production in ways that have reduced output, and they have formulated policies with many urban, gender and industrial biases, thereby further constraining economic prospects. Inefficiency, it appears from these chapters, has generated not only real problems of legitimation but also, somewhat ironically, a constriction of central government hegemony.[3]

Public structures emerge from these analyses as simultaneously more repressive and more detached, more coercive and more aloof, more oppressive and more feeble, more intrusive and yet hardly more influential. As Thomas Callaghy notes, the power of the state in many African countries is not unlimited; it is, however, unsupervised. Indeed, it may be that formal institutions, as John Ayoade suggests, constitute points of control without adequate power. They may be omnipresent, but they are hardly omnipotent. The beginning of the third decade of African independence coincided, in the minds of many of its observers, with the realization that the organization of the public domain, purportedly the key instrument for the promotion of the general welfare, was itself possibly the cause of the failure of many development efforts. And, as the economic situation worsened, the capacity of state agencies further diminished.

The pervasive syndrome of weak yet exploitive governmental structures has been explained in these pages in a variety of ways. One approach, best exemplified by Ayoade, Ninsin, Lemarchand, MacGaffey and, to some extent, by Callaghy, Parpart and Shaw, views state officials as predatory and the state as abusive. From this perspective the managerial class has monopolized resources for its own private use and purposefully prevented major portions of the population from gaining access to public resources. The constriction of the reach of government bodies in recent years is therefore not random; it is an outcome of the conscious abandonment by state bureaucrats of economic and moral responsibility for the welfare of their citizens.[4] This process, leading to the diminution of capacity and the loss of will, is seen concurrently as pernicious, inexorable and ongoing.

Even within this general approach there are quite distinct theoretical assumptions. Ninsin, Parpart and MacGaffey argue that the weak state is predatory precisely because of what they consider to be the malformation of national classes and the constant and deleterious influence of international capitalist forces. Ayoade and Lemarchand, extremely scathing in their observations on the exploitation of ruling groups in various parts of the continent, underscore more personal explanations for the phenomenon they seek to describe. Ayoade highlights the failure of leadership; Lemarchand, the prebendal structure of state patronage. Both tend to find the actions of individuals simultaneously perverted and highly destructive of the common fabric.

Callaghy's perspective differs qualitatively from those of the other contributors: he sees the current conjuncture as part of the ongoing historical process of state formation, capitalist penetration and capitalist expansion. In historical terms the evolution of political forms in contemporary Africa bears a marked resemblance to early modern phases of political change in Europe and Latin America. Callaghy asserts that the contemporary African experience is merely one stage in the long process of state consolidation and economic growth. He thus joins in the diagnoses proffered by many of the other participants, but diverges in his identification of the factors involved.

A second approach to the understanding of the crisis of the state stresses more institutional explanations. Rothchild and Foley, Young, Ravenhill and, to some extent, Olorunsola and Chazan prefer to examine current trends from a more institutional point of view. They see the state as an actor in its own right and favor a more functional concept of the state entity. The weakening of state structures is attributed in this approach to a costly, overbloated and highly inefficient apparatus that has systematically forfeited its capacity to govern. Corruption and individual abuses of office have compounded difficulties and yielded a palpable reduction in the scope and depth of government action during the past two decades. This perspective emphasizes weakness, as opposed to maliciousness, as the core reason for state diminution: a process that may therefore be both temporary and correctible.

Here, too, however, there is disagreement on the root causes for institutional incapacity. Rothchild and Foley imply that economic, social and external constraints have combined to limit options and reduce choices. Young prefers, through careful historical analysis, to stress the peculiar colonial structures inherited by African leaders at independence as the underlying reason for the hegemonic impulses which he so completely elaborates. Olorunsola also concentrates on the statist propensities of officials at the point of transition to independence, while highlighting poor preparation as well as motivational factors. Together, these authors do concur on the centrality of political variables in the explication of the dilemmas of the state in contemporary Africa.

A third, quite distinct approach is also evident in these writings. The Azarya and, to a lesser degree, Chazan essays, while cognizant of the oppressive character of formal structures in many places, nevertheless grasp the weakening of the state as a function of the detachment of social groups from involvement in central activities. Adopting a more avowedly society-centered vantage point, these authors suggest that the incapacity of the state is the end result of the disengagement of social forces from the public sphere. As government agencies have faltered, individuals and groups have devised alternative methods of sustaining themselves economically and pursuing their interests. The condition of the state has deteriorated because many of its constituents have relinquished it and found more conducive frameworks for social and economic interaction.

Thus, the chapters in this book represent a wide array of reasoned opinions for the weakness of governmental structures in Africa. They differ not only in the immediate explanations they offer for present difficulties, but also in their identification of the underlying causes for these processes. Nevertheless, these essays do share some common precepts. Despite their preferences for either sadistic (predatory), masochistic (institutional) or disenchanted (from a social viewpoint) accounts of ongoing events, all stress the primacy of political factors, are sensitive to historical and comparative trends, and are deeply rooted in the details of the African environment. They also converge on certain major themes in the analysis of the postcolonial state: the perception of the state as an actor in its own right, the notion of the state as fulfilling (or not realizing) certain functions, and the conceptualization of the state as a pact of domination.[5] Regardless of whether this autonomous, distinctive and functional idea of the state is indeed adequate to encompass the diversity of state forms and the variety of stateness evident on the continent, the perception of state shrinkage and contraction unites the chapters in this volume. As René Lemarchand so aptly puts it: "Just as the concept of the state has gained an unprecedented vogue among Africanists, its reality seems to have dissolved into a host of invertebrate species which for the most part defy categorization."[6]

If, indeed, the findings of these studies question the assumption of the socioeconomic and political centrality of the state (without, of course, dismissing its durability), then even the interpretive prowess displayed in these pages may be insufficient to embrace the complex processes at hand. The analysis of African states in terms of an ideal model, however divergent, leaves many questions unanswered: how, even in diminished circumstances, is the state organized? What exactly do state organs do at various levels? How have specific domestic relations changed? What are the external repercussions of these changes? What is the extent of the social isolation of state agencies? Are current presentations of the condition of formal institutions merely a temporary and unhappy phase? Or, conversely, are they part of a broader regressive cycle that has not yet reached its nadir?

How is it possible to capture process and change in the analysis of formal institutional networks? Is a reconceptualization of the idea of the state a precondition for such an endeavor? These and other queries, of an empirical as well as a theoretical and conceptual nature, emerge from these analyses; an accurate assessment of the implications of state enfeeblement in the early 1980s must await the answers they will provide.

Societal Activities

The whittling away of the preeminence of state institutions perforce redirects attention away from the central arena and to other, usually subnational, units of socioeconomic and political exchange. In the past, preoccupation with affairs at the state level led to a neglect of activities beyond the realm of the formal and the visible by not only political scientists and economists but also sociologists and historians. The extensiveness of the economic and institutional predicament of recent African history has reaffirmed what to many Africans is a truism: that much meaningful economic activity takes place in a complex web of social institutions hidden from the sight of national censors, data collectors and policymakers. These activities possess a political relevance of some import.

The most apparent and best-documented patterns of action relate to a variety of economic mechanisms of questionable legality or connection with state-controlled markets. Individuals have managed, in both rural and urban areas, to hone techniques to cope with reduced circumstances. More significantly, elaborate parallel economies, escape and communal self-preservation strategies have come to the fore, suggesting that at lower levels various entrepreneurial skills have been refined and relatively autonomous pockets of capitalism have begun to strike roots in the countryside.

The political dimensions of these multifaceted phenomena project an alternate vision of state-society relations. Many of these activities are antistate in essence: they are either quasi-legal or totally illegal; they consciously circumvent the state and ignore many of its precepts as well as its dictates. Others are nonstate in thrust: migration and even temporary economic withdrawal demonstrate the degree to which state channels and policies are ignored. And still other forms of societal action display direct resistance to and confrontation with existing national power structures and their incumbents.[7] Thus, state avoidance and state aversion have accompanied the appearance of niches of seemingly autonomous accumulation.[8]

The meaning imputed to these growing and diversified coping mechanisms documented so precisely at the local level differ, at times dramatically, throughout the pages of this volume. In the first place, the definition of the so-called informal sector varies. MacGaffey, Lemarchand, Ninsin and by implication Callaghy conceive of the parallel economy "as activities . . . supposedly controlled by the state but they either evade this control or involve illegal use of state position. By this definition the second economy is as much a political phenomenon as an economic one."[9] In this view, the nonformal is a corollary of the formal: it consists of the underside of the legal and the permissible, it is the shadow of the officially sanctioned economic network. In stark contrast, the definition implicit in Azarya, Chazan and perhaps Olorunsola is far more comprehensive: it refers to ongoing societal activities conducted by individuals and groups beyond the public domain. Although these actions may contain illicit elements, the crux of informal social behavior in this sense relates to that which is not ordinarily counted or recorded. The field of vision is defined not by the state but by society; not by governmental preference, but by associational interest. These contributors distinguish between the informal (illegal) and the nonformal (invisible). Thus, the treatment of survival strategies differs in this volume because the focus of analysis is not always precisely the same.

In these conditions it is hardly surprising that perceptions of the origins of seemingly separate socioeconomic mechanisms also diverge. Kwame Ninsin is most empathic in considering ". . . the growth of the informal economy primarily as an outcome of the state's act of delinking certain social strata from its legal and moral responsibilities as its economic capacity continues to decline."[10] He suggests that individuals are pushed into illegal actions by government policies. Decentralization and privatization, purportedly undertaken to free the markets and open access, are, in this perspective, merely more sophisticated methods of ensuring the continued domination of the ruling class. In Ninsin's opinion, "the informal economy is therefore no more than an extension of the formal economy."[11] MacGaffey and Lemarchand, while conceding that the state mediates the retreat from the official economy, nevertheless view the variety of coping techniques also as autonomous responses to official failures. "The second economy expanded in the 1970s because, as conditions worsened, people responded to the depradations of the political aristocracy and took advantage of the weakening of administration and control to organize an independent system of production and distribution outside state control."[12] The operation of nonformal activities is therefore both an extension of state actions and beyond its reach. Other contributors suggest that the pull of historical forces is even greater: Parpart discusses the continuity of patterns of production and association of women despite real shifts in their relative power positions; Azarya highlights the attractiveness of local institutions and practices in conditions of economic adversity. He also views the growth of the nonformal sector as an outcome of the inability of government institutions to absorb increased demands during the early years of independence. Both Azarya and Chazan see shifting societal involvement or detachment from the state as evidence of the ongoing importance of institutional options beyond those associated with the governmental apparatus.

Those in control of these social networks are consequently identified in different terms. Almost all the contributors concede that the second system is maintained and manipulated by persons who have had access to state resources and have used this position to establish themselves and enrich their cohorts. But Azarya, MacGaffey and Chazan also suggest that new sets of leaders with different interests have been involved in these processes. There is no consensus on the origins and allegiances of those benefiting from the unfolding patterns of social differentiation: in the view of some authors survival strategies solidify the position of state managers; in the view of others, independent processes of class formation are taking place around access to and control of material and not political resources.[13]

The manifestations of societal activity range, therefore, from the narrowly economic to include the more broadly cultural and symbolic. To be sure, the most detailed treatment is accorded to economic activities beyond the formal domain. Even in this sphere interpretations vary as emphasis is placed, alternately, on distributive versus productive and accumulative processes. New forms of economic relations may be accompanied by the construction or revival of relevant institutions and by the affirmation of allied normative precepts. Conversely, as Ninsin implies, the expansion of the informal economy may cement statewide processes of social stratification and intensify inequalities.

The divergent approaches to the analysis of burgeoning survival strategies extend to the assessment of the significance of these endeavors. On these issues, not unexpectedly, value judgements abound. Some essays evaluate extra-formal behavior as intrinsically negative, unproductive and pernicious. Others insist that these strategies have enabled survival and even growth in conditions of severe deterioration. By allowing for productive enterprise and by supplying outlets for entrepreneurial initiative they have contributed directly to production and the creation of new markets, thereby exposing real sources of development in the otherwise grim landscape of contemporary Africa.[14] By implication, therefore, societal economic impulses are either an indication of the rearrangement of political relations, a confirmation of existing social inequalities, further corroboration of elaborate modes of authoritarian rule, ambiguous and transitory epiphenomena not to be taken too seriously, or a reflection of the syncretic quality of economic and social life in many parts of the continent.[15] Whether these processes will yield greater inequality, disaffection, repression, fatalism or local self-reliance remains unclear.

Intense disagreement characterizes analyses of the unofficial economy contained in this book. Evaluations differ in large part because approaches to the state diverge: where state consolidation is intimately linked to capitalist penetration and social stratification, the emergence of the unofficial economy is seen as an aberration and perversion. Where state construction is tied to institutional fortification and social incorporation, other activities not only mirror the frailties of recent efforts, but also point to possible directions of state-society realignment. The first approach speaks of the state de-linking from society in order to serve the interests of state managers, enhance their access to rural areas, reduce competition and reinforce the hegemonic nature and predatory character of the postcolonial state. The second approach posits, in stark contrast, that the new economic proliferation is a result of societal disengagement from the state. The formulation of sophisticated economic and social techniques highlights the ingenuity of African producers and consumers, furnishing a vivid demonstration not only of the breakdown of state mechanisms but also of the resilience and flexibility of indigenous constructions of social and material life.[16] From this vantage point the nonformal sector may be the harbinger of the dissociation of states and markets, auguring a more fundamental kind of political rearrangement.

While ample evidence can be mustered to corroborate either of these conflicting interpretations (since the derivation and operation of social responses may vary from country to country), both approaches have certain commonalities. In the first place, they see current economic and social adjustments as intrinsically political occurrences. Social organization and group behavior relate directly to the location, bases and concentration of power; the delineation of power vectors is thus closely allied to the identification of foci of production and social interchange. Secondly, these analyses seek to uncover enduring social processes at the substate level. They delve into the intricacies of social structure, interest aggregation and normative precepts to extrapolate unfolding patterns of interaction. And, most emphatically, these essays attempt to come to terms with the relationship between modes of daily life and broader political trends. An underlying theme, therefore, unites these seemingly disparate views: there is consensus that societal actions are neither random nor incohesive, that the tracing of their shape and mutating forms is critical for understanding the dynamics of political configurations in specific countries.

Viewed from below, the state is seen as both a distributor of benefits and an intruder.[17] It is simultaneously an oppressor and an ally, a source of much needed goods as well as of uncertainty and interference. The various chapters included in this volume depict the behavior of local communities and specific groups as autonomous *and* interconnected, as disengaged but interactive. Precisely because the boundaries between the formal and the nonformal are difficult to determine, these essays concur on the centrality of straddling (to use Callaghy's terminology) as a cardinal feature of the sociopolitical scene in Africa today.[18]

The stress on many different kinds of transactions raises a host of questions to which answers are not readily available. There is much empirical information which is lacking: what are the actual frameworks of social organization? How are interests defined in these groups? What are the dominant patterns of decision making? What are the resources available to these groups (including land, labor and capital)? Who do they ally with to further their concerns? What symbols do they wield and how are these manipulated? What transactions are undertaken and with what results? On a different level there is a need to address a further set of issues: how is it possible to meaningfully disaggregate categories of social analysis, such as class and ethnicity, to better mirror the web-like structure of social exchanges? How can the flow of fluid processes be conceptualized and analyzed? More to the point, is it possible to avoid the dichotomous terminology and consequent theoretical bifurcation which has marred many analyses of state-society relations in recent years? Is the relationship between formal action and social response so neatly collapsed into a one-to-one relationship? Perhaps a more comprehensive outlook which incorporates shifts at various levels may be more fruitful? The conceptual difficulties raised by these studies are quite daunting: the thrust of analyses suggest that exceedingly blunt tools are in need of a great deal of refinement if political processes are to be traced with any degree of accuracy.

Political Reordering

The deterioration of formal institutional networks and the assertion of a variety of survival mechanisms together have implied adaptations in the form, if not the substance, of political relations. Certain ingredients in these adjustments are reiterated in most of the papers in this volume. On the economic plane, special attention is devoted to the significance of increasing capitalist impulses displayed at different levels of social organization in various parts of the continent. In one way or another, virtually all contributors point to the greater economic latitude as an important feature of Africa in the 1980s and highlight the rearrangement of market mechanisms.[19] Institutionally, emphasis is placed not only on the revamping of governmental structures, but also on the reconsideration of the forms and principles of linkages between specific social groups and government agencies. Rothchild and Foley, Young, and especially Ninsin, as well as other authors perhaps less explicitly, assess the various techniques of accommodating politicized associations within given settings. Another element of political reorientation addressed in these chapters therefore relates to methods and means, to changing patterns of political practice. Regime changes, with particular emphasis on liberalizing tendencies, are entertained. And all of the studies deal with external dimensions of political reordering, whether as a continuous influence on domestic events or, more radically, as Shaw and Ravenhill discuss, as a facet of the redefinition of political boundaries.

The exact admixture of these components, however, varies substantially from chapter to chapter and from country to country. Different emphases on each of these aspects suggest quite distinct political alignments and qualitatively separate outcomes. Some of these studies insist that even though the precise composition of coalitions is changing, the political pulse in Africa remains one of gyrations and growing inequality. Ninsin is most emphatic in his perception of unfolding political processes as part and parcel of an ongoing pattern of increased cleavage and tension generated by unbridled state domination evident since independence. This sentiment is echoed by Lemarchand, who discerns new manifestations of social division and inequity, and by Callaghy, who suggests that the predominance of the political level will persist, as in Europe in the past, until the more complete development of capitalism permits a shift in emphasis toward the economic.

Some of the authors view the progression of political occurrences at this juncture as reflective of a reduction in the position and the role of official organs. Rothchild and Foley highlight different types and rules of exchange between government personnel and ethnoregional factions as indicative of a more decentralized reorientation of political relations. Ravenhill does not dismiss some boundary adjustments in this process.

Other contributions suggest a trend away from highly centralized modes of rule, but are less precise about subsequent political directions. Timothy Shaw sees social formations as ". . . moving inexorably in the direction of renewed yet partial liberalism at the level of politics and capitalism at the level of economics, indiating a greater openness at both levels as inherited institutions decay."[20] In a not dissimilar vein, Crawford Young elegantly posits that: "The hegemonic impulses which we have suggested flow from the logic of the first construction of the colonial state seem impossible to sustain. Possibly out of the mood of anxiety and foreboding will emerge a formula for the decolonization of the state."[21] MacGaffey, Ayoade, Olorunsola, Azarya and Chazan also foresee varying combinations of state-societal relations resulting from the tensions intrinsic in conflicting currents in specific countries. They, too, envision a heterogeneity of political directions evolving in diverse parts of the continent. These trends will be determined by specific revisions in government policy and/or by the direction of socioeconomic processes. Regardless of the exact triggering mechanism, outcomes may vary according to local conditions and circumstances.

In very different ways, then, the interpretations in this collection converge in the estimation that the thrust of political movement is now different than in the past. More voices are presently heard on the African political scene; these are evocative of distinctive reations to changing conditions. "The growing importance of the informal sector and various forms of primordial associations and the rising tempo of state activity in economic restructuring and decentralization are both responses to this crisis."[22] While state resilience is not seriously questioned, state forms are being redefined. This reorientation is marked more by its internal diversity than by any firm path or direction.

The meaning associated with these shifts is not, however, shared. Some contributors view present patterns as a passing deviation from a rhythm of central consolidation. Others suggest, however hesitantly, that a different plateau has been reached: that henceforth power allocations and limitations will be more salient than power concentrations at the state level. Indeed, in this perspective, strife and conflict will proceed along qualitatively different lines; the focus of political attention has changed. In the overall historical scheme, the assessment of present vacillations varies from incidental to significant. Somewhat ironically, some authors grounded in the more pluralist tradition, generally associated with notions of continuity, tend to be those espousing most vociferously a more radical reading of contemporary trends: in their minds the uncontrolled statist experiments of the first 25 years of independence have been played out and can no longer be sustained. They argue, in essence, that "those who envisage only long-term stagnation and decline forget that it is out of the crises and struggles to which these inevitably lead that new social forces, capable of new solutions, are gradually emerging."[23] On the other hand, some authors of the materialist persuasion maintain that shifting emphases do not alter the broad strokes of historical patterns. They contend that no watershed has been reached, that no disjuncture is evident. Contemporary realities are perhaps more complex and contradictory, but with time they will reveal an ongoing picture of central domination. Attitudes toward the political vibrations of Africa in the mid-1980s therefore range from the gravely pessimistic or cynical, through the coldly realistic and skeptical, to the promising and optimistic.

Coming to terms with the changing trajectory of African politics exposes several glaring analytical difficulties. First, in the past, studies of African political occurrences employed unidirectional growth and decline models which, although based on quite divergent normative and theoretical presumptions, were nevertheless concerned with explaining the nature of conditions at any given time. In recent years these instruments have been mustered to account for the decline of postcolonial institutions and the deterioration of the economies of most African countries. They therefore emit an *ex post facto* aura: in many senses the scholarly endeavor has remained one step behind the events it seeks to explore. A conscious shift to the study of contemporary political process, on the order of that essayed in these papers, magnifies the poverty of dynamic concepts. How is it possible to go beyond historical evaluation to an understanding of the components of historical movements in the African context? What guidelines exist for delving into the fluid and the seemingly inchoate?

These questions point to a second area of analytical discomfort: that related to the identification of the components of dynamic processes. The vision of political reordering presented in this work rests on the relative weight accorded, alternatively, to structural, social, economic, institutional, normative, idiosyncratic and external variables. Implicit in these projections, therefore, is a cause and effect reasoning which, however sophisticated, may not be sufficient to encompass the multiple dimensions of process and change. Is a more interactive outlook needed? Isn't the political picture at any given historical moment the reflection of a unique conjuncture of forces? If so, how can their interplay be addressed and the extent of change measured? What criteria need be applied and how? Can the dynamics of relationships provide a more solid foundation for political study?

These are not idle ruminations. The exposition of trends and the identification of foci of policy concern rest not only on some understanding of the reasons for present circumstances, or on a preferred image of objectives, but also on a grasp of the forces at work in any given context. The essays in this book, in one way or another, seek to grapple with the implications of manifestations on the ground. They consequently assume that finding the causes for the dilemmas of the 1980s without expounding on their concrete ramifications provides an insufficient guide to the substance of available options and choices. Herein lies the crux of the connection between analysis and praxis, another, elementary, issue confronting participants and observers of the African scene.

What, then, is the unfolding vision of state-society relations in Africa on the eve of the second 25 years of independence? The interpretive offerings in these pages suggest that the center of political gravity is shifting. Viewed from above, institutional mechanisms have been undergoing a process of contraction and disaggregation. But from below, social and economic niches have been carved out and are beginning to interact and adhere in new ways. State structures are not the sole repositories of power in African countries; multiple loci of politics are emerging. From this perspective, political rhythms may lack cohesion; they are not, however, incoherent (hence the multiple change orientations apparent in these essays). As local arrangements come into play, political spaces are being reorganized and diverse links between government structures, specific social groups and resource bases are being devised. A more diffuse and variegated, but perhaps more viable, pattern of political realignment is slowly taking shape.

State and Society in Africa: The Challenges

A great deal of intellectual excitement permeates these pages. Out of the various efforts to come to terms with the meaning of political flows in contemporary Africa new insights have been gleaned and intriguing possibilities raised. However, a healthy dose of caution and reasoned sobriety also punctuates these analyses: a prudence which emanates not only from what is seen, but also from the realization that the capacity to see is severely limited. Many avenues of examination have been pursued in these chapters. Each contributes additional layers to the composite picture of political life on the continent; each provokes as it illuminates. A feeling of unease nevertheless remains. The paths of interpretation are frequently dissociated; full understanding is all too often obfuscated. Intellectual tools are masterfully employed and extended, but a sense of incompleteness prevails. Existing categories shed light on portions of the political landscape; however, they are only partially reflective of realities and hence only partially assist in the quest for greater comprehension. Conflicting interpretations raise more questions than any single approach can adequately accommodate. The new vision therefore presents new obligations at the same time as it assails old conventions. What are the implications of these shifting political perceptions for the study of politics in Africa?

Recent events in Africa as portrayed in this volume compel an expansion of the field of political vision. Seemingly apolitical activities carry broad political meaning; actions of state leaders may have less of a bearing than heretofore assumed. The refreshing return to political analyses should not be confined to a preoccupation with the state. Predetermined notions of political change have been a poor guide to unfolding processes, and the social agents active on the continent do not fall neatly into any one classificatory scheme. The impact of environment and context does not preclude choice and the exercise of political will; neither does preoccupation with economic matters foreclose consideration of the cultural and symbolic.

The continuous impact of external forces hardly prevents the assertion of different indigenous paths of development.[24] The apparent detachment of state and society, the lack of incorporation of many social groups into the polity, does not obviate careful treatment of modes of articulation—of the substance and directions of transactions and flows. Conceptual analysis must be combined with dynamic discourse and specific events placed in proper historical perspective. Above all, in order to understand the nature of states in Africa, it is vital to put the state in its proper context.

A fivefold challenge emerges from the undertaking. The first is empirical. The lacunae in existing knowledge of political mechanisms are primarily at the middle level: at the point of intersection of government agencies, external forces and social groups. Little is known about intermediate social organizations, their internal structure, their aims and their activities. The disaggregation of social categories is necessary to begin to grasp political movements. The types of relations between these actors as well as the subjects of their exchanges are not necessarily clear. The rules governing these interactions remain hazy, and the degree and nature of foreign and domestic linkages, obscure. Consequently, it has been difficult to trace shifting coalitions over time, to specify types of collaboration and conflict, or to identify changing patterns of differentiation, subordination and domination. The range of the factual vacuum is not inconsiderable. Case studies may be the critical foundation for addressing these questions.

The second challenge is analytical. The accent on understanding political alliances and rhythms cannot be directed merely to local concerns, national considerations or international interests. The key analytical task is to unravel the ways "in which people at different levels of social agency have mobilized and organized resources, allies, and ideas in a continuous effort to cope with changing circumstances."[25] In other words, the connections between the macro and the micro, between state and society, between autonomy and dependence, require much more careful probing. Because the African environment contains institutional alternatives to formal structures, the analysis of politics should revolve around the understanding and significance of their intertwining. In such a situation it is not inconceivable that competition may carry different meanings than in areas where the distinction between the private and the public is more clear-cut. Similarly, production, distribution and the values governing interrelationships require reexamination. Standard ways of isolating and classifying variables must be reassessed, and, more significantly, new ways of breaking down and reassembling issues need to be explored. Such a reinterpretation is grounded in an understanding of the multidimensionality of the organization of political spaces, and consequently may conceive of changing political linkages along channels other than the purely vertical. The analytical charge therefore underscores the fluctuations inherent in the attempt to place shifting ties, heterogeneous patterns of articulation, and their consequences at the center of political investigation.

The third challenge is theoretical. Much has been said in this reflective summary about the limitations of strictly causal reasoning in explaining political manifestations at any given point. The dynamic combinations of social confrontations over time furnish more compelling explications of particular conjunctures than unilinear cause and effect models. These are clearly both political and economic in character. The mapping out of convergences and sequences of a variety of factors holds more promise than separatist explanations in the ongoing quest for greater predictability. A more concerted emphasis on accounting for heterogeneity may further promote this cause. The theoretical task, however, cannot be accomplished without some reevaluation of assumptions and terms.

The fourth challenge, then, is conceptual. The chapters in this volume stress the importance of commencing any full study of politics in Africa with an understanding that official, social and economic fields do not always coincide. Since societal action goes beyond the formal institutional network, and since market interactions span the state nexus as well as state frontiers, intersecting and intertwining spheres of social existence do not necessarily overlap. Many concepts regularly used to capture aspects of the political realm leave out potions of this human behavioral mosaic. Two possibilities, strategically, have been suggested in these pages. One proposes the refinement or the reconceptualization of existing terms, such as the state, development, ethnicity, class and capitalism, to incorporate the various manifestations and meanings apparent in the African context.[26] The other advocates the formulation of new concepts that would encompass the networks of inter-action as opposed to the separate variables involved. In paradigmatic terms, the first approach suggests looking at the multiple connections between the separate variables of state and society; it propounds a mixing of available paradigms, a new eclecticism. The second method sees transactions themselves as the key, with the state, society and economy as products of distinctive kinds of conjoining. In order to come to terms with the relational nature of political occurrences, it may be necessary to shift to another paradigm entirely. Thus, although the former possibility sharpens the dialectical and the latter the dynamic, some conceptual review geared toward the intricate web of relations seems to be in order.[27]

The fifth and final challenge is programmatic. Much has been written in recent years on structural adjustment, policy reform, institutional change and normative reorientation. Many practical steps, such as freeing the markets, avoiding the state or rehabilitating governmental agencies, have been placed on the agenda.[28] The debate between those who wish to reduce the state and those who want to enhance its scope and functions without altering its size continues to rage. The answers, however, are not as simple as these discussions suggest. Technical improvements have little meaning unless power considerations are taken into account. The honing or aug-mentation of the instruments of control cannot be accomplished without affecting the organization of societal relations. Clearly, how problems are identified, dissected and interpreted has a direct bearing on what is done. The tracing of political configurations and their mutations is therefore a vital precondition for designing practical measures. Hence, the fine-tuning of action cannot be fully achieved and the subtleties of particular settings cannot be properly discerned until more is known and the task of intellectual review is expedited.

Many observers of the African political arena have expressed genuine frustration over their inability to pinpoint processes and explain their progression. As conditions in Africa have deteriorated, this malaise has mounted. What the contributions to this volume do highlight, if nothing else, is that many questions remain open and many arenas of analysis are yet to be explored. The message emanating from this interpretive endeavor is that in order to grasp the full meaning of state vagaries and state mutations, it is important to leave the state and its environs and to focus more squarely on power and politics in broader spaces, if only to come back to the state and its potentialities better equipped in the future. From this alternate vision new possibilities emerge, and these may permit greater options and more choice. Herein lies the challenge of African politics and African political studies in the years ahead.

Notes

1. These points are discussed in detail in Crawford Young, "The African Colonial State and its Political Legacy," in this volume.

2. This is explored here most extensively in Thomas M. Callaghy's contribution, "The State and the Development of Capitalism in Africa: Theoretical, Historical and Comparative Reflections," but is also alluded to in most of the essays.

3. Young, "The African Colonial State," discusses these problems in terms of the imperatives of hegemony, security, autonomy, legitimation and revenue.

4. This view is presented most forcefully by Kwame Ninsin, "Three Levels of State Reordering: The Structural Aspects."

5. For a critique see Otwin Marenin, "The Managerial State in Africa: A Conflict-Coalition Perspective," in Zaki Ergas, eds., *The African State in Transition* (London: Macmillan, forthcoming), pp. 3–6 of the manuscript.

6. René Lemarchand, "The State, the Parallel Economy and the Changing Structure of Patronage Systems," p. 1. Echoed by Victor Azarya, "Reordering State-Society Relations: Incorporation and Disengagement," in this volume.

7. Catharine Newbury, "Survival Strategies in Rural Zaire: Realities of Coping with Crisis," in Nzongola-Ntalaja, eds., *The Zaire Crisis: Myths and Realities* (Trenton: Third World Press, 1986), pp. 3–4.

8. Best demonstrated in this book by Janet MacGaffey, "Economic Disengagement and Class Formation in Zaire." See also Jane Parpart, "Women and the State in Africa," and Lemarchand, "The State, the Parallel Economy." The social, spatial and symbolic facets are discussed in Naomi Chazan, "Patterns of State-Society Incorporation and Disengagement in Africa."

9. MacGaffey, "Economic Disengagement," in this volume.

10. Ninsin, "Three Levels of State Reordering," in this volume.

11. Ibid., in this volume.

12. MacGaffey, "Economic Disengagement," in this volume.

13. Lemarchand, "The State, the Parallel Economy and Structure of Patronage Systems." For a more general discussion see Richard L. Sklar, "The Nature of Class Domination in Africa," *Journal of Modern African Studies*, 18, 4 (1979): 531–552.

14. Goran Hyden, "La Crise Africaine et la Paysannerie Non-Capturée," *Politique Africaine*, 18 (June 1985): 111.

15. These various possibilities are explored and demonstrated most meticulously in Victor Olorunsola, "The Withdrawal of the State: Adjustment in the Political Economy."

16. Jane I. Guyer, "Comparative Epilogue," in ibid., *Feeding African Cities: Studies in Regional Social History* (Manchester: University of Manchester Press, 1986), p. 27. Special thanks are due to Jane I. Guyer for her perceptive comments on an earlier draft of these conclusions.

17. John Ayoade, "States Without Citizens: An Emerging African Phenomenon," in this volume. Also see Sara Berry, *Fathers Work for their Sons: Accumulation, Mobility and Class Formation in an Extended Yoruba Community* (Berkeley: University of California Press, 1985), p. 194.

18. Callaghy, "The State and the Development of Capitalism." Also see Nelson Kasfir, "State, *Magendo* and Class Formation in Uganda," *Journal of Commonwealth and Comparative Politics*, 22, 3 (1984): 99 and elsewhere.

19. See Timothy Shaw, "State of Crisis: International Constraints, Contradictions and Capitalisms?"

20. Ibid.

21. Young, "The African Colonial State" p. 64.

22. Ninsin, "Three Levels of State Reordering." For a fuller treatment see Donald Rothchild and Michael Foley, "African States and the Politics of Inclusive Coalitions."

23. Colin Leys, "African Economic Development in Theory and Practice," *Daedalus*, 3 2 (1982): 121.

24. Richard Joseph, "The Crisis in African Governance and Development: Implications for the Social Sciences" (Discussion paper presented at Boston University, African Studies Center, Walter Rodney Seminar, December 1985).

25. Berry, *Fathers Work for their Sons*, p. 6.

26. This tactic is suggested by Young, "The African Colonial State." Also see John Ravenhill, "Redrawing the Map of Africa?"

27. Marenin, "The Managerial State in Africa," p. 28.

28. Richard Sandbrook, *The Politics of Africa's Economic Stagnation* (London: Cambridge University Press, 1985).

About the Contributors

John A.A. Ayoade is a reader in political science at the University of Ibadan, Nigeria. He taught at both Williams College and the University of Pennsylvania. He also conducted research at Boston University as a Fulbright scholar. He has published papers on federalism and comparative politics in *Publius, The Journal of Federalism, Plural Societies, African Studies Review,* and *Journal of Commonwealth and Comparative Politics.*

Victor Azarya is associate professor in the Department of Sociology and Social Anthropology at the Hebrew University of Jerusalem. He has recently held visiting professorships at the University of North Carolina and the University of Pennsylvania. His books include *Dominance and Change in North Cameroon; Aristocrats Facing Change: The Fulbe in Guinea, Nigeria and Cameroon; State Intervention in Economic Enterprise in Pre-Colonial Africa;* and *The Armenian Quarter of Jerusalem.*

Thomas M. Callaghy is associate professor of political science and research associate of the Research Institute on International Change at Columbia University. He is author of *The State-Society Struggle: Zaire in Comparative Perspective,* editor of *South Africa in Southern Africa: The Intensifying Vortex of Violence,* and coeditor of *Socialism in Sub-Saharan Africa: A New Assessment.*

Naomi Chazan, currently Matina S. Horner Radcliffe Distinguished Visiting Professor and visiting professor of government at Harvard University, teaches political science at the Hebrew University of Jerusalem, where she also heads the African studies department. Author of *An Anatomy of Ghanaian Politics: Managing Political Recession, 1969–1982* (Westview, 1983) and (with Deborah Pellow) *Ghana: Coping with Uncertainty* (Westview, 1986), she has also written numerous articles on comparative politics in Africa.

Michael W. Foley is assistant professor of political science at Texas A&M University and a specialist in political development and the politics of agrarian change. He has written on peasant mobilization in contemporary Mexico and on Marxist theory and is the coauthor, with Donald Rothchild, of two articles on political development in Africa.

René Lemarchand is a professor of political science at the University of Florida at Gainesville. His works include *Political Awakening in the Former Belgian Congo, Rwanda and Burundi* and *Selective Genocide in Burundi.* He is coauthor and editor of *African Kingships in Perspective* as well as *American Policies in Southern Africa: The Stakes and the Stance* and coeditor, with S. N. Eisenstadt, of *Political Clientelism, Patronage and Development.*

Janet MacGaffey, an anthropologist, has taught at Haverford, Bryn Mawr, and other colleges in the Philadelphia area. She has lived in Zaire and has visited there as a researcher and consultant. Her publications include articles in books and journals and a book, *Entrepreneurs and Parasites: The Struggle for Indigenous Capitalism in Zaire.*

Dan Muhwezi is a Ph.D. candidate at Iowa State University.

Kwame A. Ninsin is senior lecturer in the Department of Political Science at the University of Ghana, Legon, and has written extensively on Ghanaian politics, ideology, and agricultural policies.

Victor A. Olorunsola is dean of the College of Arts and Sciences at the University of Louisville. He is an editor and a contributor to *The Politics of Cultural Sub-Nationalism in Africa* and *State Versus Ethnic Claims: African Policy Dilemmas.* He has contributed chapters in many books, and he is the author of *Societal Reconstruction in Two African States* and *Soldiers and Power* as well as several articles in professional journals.

Jane L. Parpart is associate professor of history and associate director of the Centre for African Studies at Dalhousie University. She is the author of *Labor and Capital on the African Copperbelt* and *Patriarchy and Class: African Women in the Household and Workplace* (forthcoming), coedited with Dr. Sharon Stichter. She has authored several articles on women, labor, and human rights.

John Ravenhill is senior lecturer in international politics at the University of Sydney, Australia. He previously taught at the University of Virginia. He is the author of *Collective Clientelism* and editor of *Africa in Economic Crisis.*

Donald Rothchild is professor of political science at the University of California, Davis, and visiting fellow at the Center of International Studies at Princeton University. He has been a visiting faculty member at universities in Uganda, Kenya, Zambia, and Ghana. In recent years, he has written or edited the following books: *Racial Bargaining in Independent Kenya; Scarcity, Choice, and Public Policy in Middle Africa; Eagle Entangled; Eagle Defiant; Eagle Resurgent?* and *State Versus Ethnic Claims: African Policy Dilemmas* (Westview, 1982).

Timothy M. Shaw is professor of political science and director of the Centre for African Studies at Dalhousie University. He has been a visiting faculty member at Makerere, Zambia, and Ife universities. He is author of *Towards a Political Economy for Africa* and coeditor of *Southern Africa After the Nkomati Accord, Corporatism in Africa, Coping with Africa's Food Crisis,* and *Newly Industrialising Countries and the Political Economy of South-South Relations.*

Crawford Young is a professor of political science at the University of Wisconsin, Madison, where he has been associate dean of the graduate school, chairman of the department, and chairman of the African studies program. He has also been dean of the faculty of social science, national

University of Zaire (Lubumbashi), and visiting professor, Makerere University, Uganda. He is author of *Ideology and Development in Africa*, *The Politics of Cultural Pluralism* (winner of the Herskovits Award), and *Politics in the Congo* and coauthor of *Cooperatives and Development*, *Issues of Political Development*, and *The Rise and Decline of the Zairian State*.

Index

← BC

mL